DATE DUE

S.16			
DEC 12 1997			
MAY 10 1999			
APR 25 2016			
GAYLORD			PRINTED IN U.S.A.

CLARENDON LIBRARY OF LOGIC AND PHILOSOPHY
General Editor: L. Jonathan Cohen

WHAT IS EXISTENCE?

Also published in this series

The Probable and the Provable by L. Jonathan Cohen
The Scientific Image by Bas C. van Fraassen
Interests and Rights: The Case Against Animals by R. G. Frey
Ontological Economy by Dale Gottlieb
Relative Identity by Nicholas Griffin
Equality, Liberty, and Perfectionism by Vinit Haksar
Experiences: An Inquiry into some Ambiguities by J. M. Hinton
Knowledge by Keith Lehrer
Metaphysics and the Mind-Body Problem by Michael E. Levin
The Cement of the Universe: A Study of Causation by J. L. Mackie
Truth, Probability and Paradox by J. L. Mackie
The Nature of Necessity by Alvin Plantinga
Divine Commands and Moral Requirements by P. L. Quinn
Simplicity by Elliott Sober
The Coherence of Theism by Richard Swinburne
The Emergence of Norms by Edna Ullmann-Margalit
Ignorance: A Case for Scepticism by Peter Unger
Works and Worlds of Art by Nicholas Wolterstorff

WHAT IS EXISTENCE?

C. J. F. WILLIAMS

CLARENDON PRESS · OXFORD
1981

Oxford University Press, Walton Street, Oxford OX2 6DP

London Glasgow New York Toronto
Delhi Bombay Calcutta Madras Karachi
Kuala Lumpur Singapore Hong Kong Tokyo
Nairobi Dar es Salaam Cape Town
Melbourne Wellington

and associate companies in
Beirut Berlin Ibadan Mexico City

Published in the United States by
Oxford University Press, New York

© C. J. F. Williams 1981

All rights reserved. No part of this publication may be reproduced,
stored in a retrieval system, or transmitted, in any form or by any means,
electronic, mechanical, photocopying, recording, or otherwise, without
the prior permission of Oxford University Press

British Library Cataloguing in Publication Data

Williams, C. J. F.
  What is existence? — (Clarendon library of
logic and philosophy).
  1. Ontology
  I. Title
  111'.1   BD331   80-41967

ISBN 0-19-824429-0

Reproduced from copy supplied
printed and bound in Great Britain
by Billing and Sons Limited
Guildford, London, Oxford, Worcester

'Est ist ja Bejahung der Existenz nichts Anderes als Verneinung der Nullzahl.' Frege, *Die Grundlagen der Arithmetik*, section 53.

'I think an almost unbelievable amount of false philosophy has arisen through not realizing what "existence" means.' Russell, *Logic and Knowledge*, p. 234.

Preface

Why should philosophers interest themselves in the notion of existence? Someone who feels the need to answer this question regards himself as under attack. But from whom? Against whom does he need to defend himself for engaging in what might be called the philosophy of existence? Against those who claim that so much of what philosophers do is superficial and trivial? Surely it is natural for us to regard the idea of being or existence as something deep and important. Religious people have talked of God as the ground of our being: St. Paul, preaching to the Athenians, says that 'in him we live and move and are'. Theologians who complain of an arid and unreal manner of presenting Christian doctrine call for a more existential understanding of religious truth. Or is it that the philosopher of existence needs to defend himself against a charge of remaining on the periphery of philosophical activity? Surely existence must be recognized as one of the central, if not the central, topic of philosophy. Nor does the philosopher whose subject is existence need to answer the charge of talking only in technical jargon. Existence, as the topic of a book or an article, is not likely to deter the plain man as would 'referential opacity' or 'illocutionary acts'—not, at least, for the same reasons. The philosopher who promises to talk about existence begins at least by talking with the vulgar. 'Exist' is not some invention of Newspeak.

The philosopher whose topic is being or existence finds himself in good company—or at least in company. Philosophers of the Analytic School have not stopped discussing the themes introduced by W. V. Quine's paper 'On What There Is'. Followers of Sartre and Heidegger adhere to a doctrine which states that existence precedes essence, and regard this, perhaps, as the principal reason for calling themselves Existentialists. These are our contemporaries. But we can go backwards in the history of philosophy and at every stage find great thinkers who have had things to say about existence and being. Kant regarded existence as a 'category', that is to say, as one of the innate concepts essential to all human thinking. Hume made one of the corner-stones of his philosophy the distinction between matters of fact and existence, on the one hand, and mere relations of ideas, on the other. Berkeley's slogan for expressing his fundamental thesis was 'To be is to be perceived'. Descartes held that all human knowledge must be founded on a proposition that asserts existence: 'I am thinking, therefore I am'. Aquinas taught that one of the first attributes of God was his simplicity, i.e. his lack of complexity: in God there is no distinction between essence and existence. Metaphysics, which is thought to be the central core of philosophy, takes its name from a book of Aristotle's whose professed subject was 'being *qua* being'. Aristotle's answer to the question 'What is there?' is 'Primarily, substance'; but the word we translate 'substance' is '*ousia*', which is a verbal noun from the Greek equivalent of the verb 'be'. '*Ousia*' is also one of Plato's favourite names for his Forms, which alone, he believed, fully *are*. Plato's interest in being obviously stems from his fifth-century predecessor Parmenides, whose principal philosophical work is devoted to the elaboration of the view that what is is, and in no way is not. Earlier still the author of the book of Exodus represents God as revealing his name to Moses in the mysterious sentence 'I am that I am'. If the children of Israel question Moses about his mission, the answer is to be 'Thus shalt thou say unto the children of Israel, I AM hath sent me unto you'.

With the author of the book of Exodus we have left the company of those who, like ourselves, philosophize in an Indo-European language. And the sense of the Hebrew words traditionally rendered 'I am that I am' is too controversial for much philosophical weight to be placed on it. The Indo-European languages in which all the other philosophers from Parmenides to Sartre have written have a verb represented in English by 'be', which some of the time at least does the same work as is done by 'exist'. Everything that can be called philosophy of existence that was written by the Greek philosophers of antiquity was expressed with the help of *'einai'*, the Greek equivalent of 'be'; and it is impossible to reach any clear understanding of their doctrines without examining how they used this word, and how its synonyms in other languages are used. It has been suggested that the concept of being is something that has no significance outside an Indo-European culture, that the problem of being is a little local difficulty.[1] I shall make some attempt to assess the strength of this claim. The spirit of the claim, if not the letter, is one with which I sympathize. Philosophies of Being or Existence, of the kind I have been alluding to, are paradigms of what Wittgenstein called men's bewitchment by language. Almost everything that has been said by philosophers about existence is the result of their treating 'is' or 'exist' as a predicate of objects. The very belief, which I appealed to earlier, that the idea of existence is something deep and important, that existence is the central topic of philosophy, rests on this assumption. Since I hold that the assumption is false, the theme of this book will be metaphysical only in the sense that it attempts to destroy the foundations of an enormous amount of metaphysics. Those who pick it up expecting metaphysics will, no doubt, soon put it down, having found only logic and philosophy of language. But if they wish to prove themselves entitled to the metaphysical doctrines they cherish, they must show where the logical claims of the book are wrong, where the arguments in the philosophy of language which it contains are fallacious. It is with philosophy of language as Aristotle said it was with philosophy in general: if it is to be established that it is not necessary to engage in philosophy of language, it is necessary to engage in philosophy of language—*ei mē philosophēteon, philosophēteon.*

My main task, therefore, will be to explore the reasons which led Kant to maintain that being is not a real predicate, to show how more recent philosophers and logicians, notably Frege, have given a clear sense to this Kantian thesis, and to defend the thesis against recent objections. Quine, more recently still, has

[1] See A. C. Graham, '"Being" in Linguistics and Philosophy', in *Foundations of Language*, 1, 1965, 223-31, reprinted in J. W. M. Verhaar (ed.), *The Verb 'Be' and its Synonyms*, Philosophical and Grammatical Studies, in the Supplementary Series of *Foundations of Language*, 1967 onwards; Part 5.

maintained that 'existence is what the existential quantifier expresses'. It is my hope that I shall clarify this thesis too, and show in what sense it is true, though detaching it from certain well-known Quinian corollaries about 'ontological commitment'.

In the course of these proceedings a good deal of use will be made of the logical symbolism which originates from Łukasiewicz, and which has become generally known as the Polish notation. A friend, irritated by my use of this notation in preference to the more widely used Russellian symbolism, demanded 'Don't you want to communicate?' I hope that certain parts of my argument, particularly what I say in Chapter III, section 3, will show that my reasons for using this symbolism are not merely aesthetic. The guiding principle of the Polish notation is that it consistently writes functors to the left of their arguments. It thus has a single unambiguous method of expressing distinctions of scope. These distinctions, whose importance for logic was perhaps Frege's greatest discovery, are above all what has to be grasped for a clear understanding of existence. The problems of existence are, whatever Existentialists may say, problems whose solutions are provided by logic. The explanation of the meaning of 'exist' and 'be' is not even a matter of semantics: it is a matter of syntax. This is the claim made in this book. And since so much will turn on questions of syntax, it is reasonable to use a symbolism which, more economically and consistently than any other I know, displays the syntactical distinctions that are essential in this matter. Those who do not know, but are willing to learn, how the Polish notation works may be helped by a table of equivalences on page xix. Those who are not willing to spend the five minutes or so required to learn these symbols are unlikely to have time to read the rest of the book.

It must be confessed, however, that a further reason for my using this notation is piety towards the memory of Arthur Prior. Prior used the notation in almost all his writings, and did more than anyone else to popularize its use west of the Oder–Neisse line. So many of the ideas in this book come from Prior, that it would seem discourteous to develop what is so often his teaching in a logical symbolism other than the one he used. I should like to think that in continuing his practice I was in a small way honouring his memory.

PREFACE

As will become apparent, I owe a similar debt to Peter Geach for having prompted much of my thinking on this topic. Where he has prompted me to disagree with him, I must be prepared for counter-arguments. Where I believe myself to agree with him, but turn out to have misunderstood him, I look to be corrected. I recall the stimulating effect of reading his early article 'Subject and Predicate' while I was still an undergraduate, and learning then that it was possible to find anticipations of Frege in Aquinas.

I wrote the first draft of this book while teaching at the University of Notre Dame in the spring semester of 1977. My thanks therefore are due above all to the Philosophy Department at Notre Dame for not only inviting me to visit them but allowing me during the five months I was with them to talk about nothing except existence. (As Parmenides would say, what else is there to talk about?) I am grateful to the colleagues, graduates, and undergraduates who attended my classes and discussed much of the material which has developed into this book. University facilities were kindly made available for typing and making copies for circulation of draft chapters, and in this way I was able to receive comments on and criticism of my ideas, not only from those who attended my classes, but colleagues and friends in America, at home, and even in Austrialia. Parts of the book have been usefully discussed at meetings at Notre Dame, the University of Virginia, and King's College, London. I should like to express particular thanks for comments and criticism to the following: R. G. Swinburne, J. L. Mackie, James Garson, Fred Freddoso, Alvin Plantinga, Stephan Körner, Malcolm Millar, Aaron Sloman, John Lyons, Jonathan Cohen, John Mayberry, Barry Miller, Anthony Kenny, and Simon Orde. Bristol University enabled further parts of the book to be typed after I returned to England, and the British Academy, to whom I am extremely grateful, made a grant to cover the expenses of typing a final draft and making the Index. My thanks are also due to Peggy Gullidge for producing this typescript, and to Simon Orde for compiling the index.

I wish to dedicate the book to my mother, but for whom I should not have existed (see Chapter IV), let alone written a book.

C.J.F.W

Midsomer Norton, Candlemas, mcmlxxxi

Contents

Polish Logical Symbols   xix

I. Existence and Being   1
    1. *The question 'What is existence?' to give way to the question 'What does "exist" mean?'*   1
    2. *Comparison of the verb 'exist' with the verb 'be'*   2
    3. *The variety of senses of 'be' and its synonyms*   3
    4. *The copulative sense of 'be'*   4
    5. *The alleged 'identity' sense of the verb 'be'*   10
    6. *Is 'be' purely equivocal or analogical?*   12

II. 'Existence is not a Predicate'   17
    1. *The Ontological Argument depends on taking existence as a predicate*   17
    2. *Hume's view that we have no distinct idea of existence*   18
    3. *Hume identifies thinking of* x *and thinking of* x *as existent*   21
    4. *Kant's view that 'exist' is a 'merely logical' predicate*   23
    5. *Kant's explanation of 'being' in terms of 'positing'*   26
    6. *'The real contains no more than the possible'*   32
    7. *Plato's Beard*   37

III. Frege's Doctrine of Existence   42
    1. *Frege's account of statements of number*   42
    2. *Geach's criterion for predicables and Prior's criterion for predicates*   44

CONTENTS

    3. The philosophical significance of logical notations   49
    4. The relevance of Prior's criterion to Frege's doctrine   53
    5. Statements of number and statements of existence   54
    6. The difference between existing and being instantiated   55
    7. Predication and 'being wrapped round'   60
    8. Extension of the meaning of 'second-level predicable'   64
    9. Can '— exist' ever function as a first-level predicate?   69
  10. An explanation of the illusion that 'Aristides exists', etc., make sense   73

IV. Embedded Existential Propositions   81
    1. Propositions in which singular existential propositions are apparently embedded   81
    2. How to relieve President Ford's ignorance of David Pears's existence   85
    3. Examples where the embedded proposition is formed by attaching '— exists' to a definite description   87
    4. Preliminary analysis of 'President Ford does not know that David Pears exists'   91
    5. Restriction of the sort of predicables required for the range of ϕ in this analysis   94
    6. Difficulties involving opacity   97
    7. Indeterminacy in claims about a's knowledge of b's existence   99
    8. Analysis of 'I might not have existed'   101
    9. General form of analyses of propositions apparently involving embedded singular existential propositions   105

V. Tensed Existential Propositions   108
    1. Tensed existential propositions as involving embedded existential propositions   108
    2. 'Arkle no longer exists' and Plato's Beard   108
    3. The Tensed or Qualified Version of Plato's Beard   109
    4. Intentional exceptions to the rule   111

CONTENTS

5. *Causal exceptions to the rule*   114
6. *Is 'Arkle no longer exists' entangled in the Unqualified Version of Plato's Beard as well?*   117
7. *Attempts by Miller and Plantinga to avoid the qualified version of the paradox*   123
8. *A similar attempt by Prior*   129
9. *Aristotelian accounts of coming into existence and ceasing to exist*   134
10. *Analysis of 'Arkle no longer exists'*   139
11. *Generalization of the analysis and solution of the Qualified Version of Plato's Beard*   141
12. No longer existing *a property, and a temporal property, of individuals*   145

VI. Quantification, Reference, and Ontological Commitment   153
1. *Quantification of non-individual variables*   153
2. *Reference and the variables of quantification*   154
3. *'Quantifying over' and 'ontological commitment'*   161
4. *'Nouns might better have been named pro-pronouns'*   165
5. *Quine's inadequate view of proper names explains his confusion of reference with quantification*   168

VII. Ontology called in Question   172
1. *'Ontological' has different senses corresponding to the different senses of 'be'*   172
2. *The vacuity theory of* actualité   173
3. *Actual and possible worlds, fact and value, ontology and epistemology*   175
4. *The connection between this use of 'ontological' and the copula*   177
5. *Ontology and what there is*   178
6. *Ontology as the use of Ockham's Razor*   182
7. *Aristotle's 'ousia': substance and existence*   184
8. *Strawson on the 'ontological-categorial' and the 'logico-grammatical'*   185

VIII. Objectual, Substitutional, and Prioresque Quantification   189
1. *Quine's two ways of defining the quantifier*   189

CONTENTS

2. The two main differences between objectual and substitutional quantification — 193
3. The 'Prioresque' interpretation of quantification — 198
4. Prioresque quantification and Tarskian truth theory — 203
5. Are the quantifiers equivocal? The relation between the objectual and the substitutional interpretation — 206
6. The relation between the objectual and the Prioresque interpretation. No special objectualist sense of the quantifier — 210
7. Objectualists misled by too much attention to ordinary language — 212
8. The philosophy of 'exist' and the philosophy of 'some' — 214
9. Objectualists' hankering after a first-level concept of existence — 215

IX. Intentional Inexistence and Referential Opacity — 218
1. Opacity and intentionality — 218
2. Three examples of intentionality — 218
3. Distinctions of scope sufficient to explain these examples — 221
4. Proper names occurring in intentional contexts similarly explained — 227
5. 'Quasi-relations' or 'one-sided relations' an illusion — 230
6. Intentionality and existence — 235
7. Referential opacity and quantification — 236

X. Fictional Characters and Possible Worlds — 242
1. Substitional quantification and fictional names — 242
2. 'Most characters listed in the Classical Dictionary existed'. — 243
3. The reference of fictional names — 244
4. Fiction and pretending — 248
5. Pretending and proper names — 251
6. Stories and fictional worlds — 255
7. Negative existential propositions containing fictional proper names — 258

8. Existence in possible worlds	261
9. Fictional characters and possible thalers	263
10. Existence of possible words	268
11. Realism about possible worlds and '— exist' as a first-level predicable	272

XI. Existence, Validity, and Instantiation   277

1. The relation between the existential and the unversal quantifier	277
2. The relation between quantification and the notion of valid inference	278
3. Quantified propositions with simple matrices, to which no inference corresponds	284
4. Existential propositions with indefinable predicables	288
5. Confirmation of this view from Kahn's study of the uses of 'einai'	290
6. Validity, variables, instantiation, and existence	293
7. The existential sense of 'be' not definable in terms of 'exist' or 'There is', but in terms of instantiation	294
8. Purpose of this chapter	298

XII. Being and Existence   300

1. The use of 'There is' in feature-placing propositions	300
2. 'There is' as a verbalizer: connection with the copula	302
3. Feature-placing statements not internally negatable	308
4. The transition from mass-nouns to count-nouns	310
5. Locative phrases as adverbial and as predicative	315
6. 'Dividing the reference', locative phrases, and the ambiguity of 'be'	317
7. Location and existence	318
8. Summary of the argument of this chapter	321
9. Syntax, semantics, and formal concepts	324

Appendix A: Kahn's Survey of the Uses of 'Einai'   327

Appendix B: Kant's Criticisms of the Ontological
    Argument   333
Bibliography of Works Cited in this Book   345
List of Formulae and Expressions given labels in the text 351
Index   355

Polish Logical Symbols

The following equivalences with Russellian and other formulae may help to explain the notation, invented originally by Jan Łukasiewicz and made more familiar by the writings of A. N. Prior, which is extensively used in this book.

Polish	Russellian	English
Np	$\sim p$	Not-p
Apq	$p \vee q$	Either p or q
Kpq	$p \cdot q$ (p & q)	Both p and q
Cpq	$p \supset q$ ($p \rightarrow q$)	If p then q
Epq	$p \equiv q$ ($p \leftrightarrow q$)	p if, and only if, q
Mp	$\Diamond p$	Possibly, p
Lp	$\Box p$	Necessarily, p
$\Sigma x \phi x$	$(\exists x)(\phi x)$	For some x, ϕx
$\Pi x \phi x$	$(x)(\phi x)$	For every x, ϕx
Ixy	$x = y$	x is the same as y

Prioresque

Pp		It has been the case that p
Hp		It has always been the case that p
Pnp		It was the case n time-units ago that p
$E!x$		x exists

I
Existence and Being

1. *The question 'What is existence?' to give way to the question 'What does "exist" mean?'*

The question 'What is existence?' is like the question 'What is truth?'. Both have the appearance of being about a property. In this way each seems to resemble questions like 'What is smoothness?' or 'What is jealousy?'. But it is always safer to ask what it is to ascribe a property to something than to ask, starkly, what the property is itself: better to seek to discover what people are about when they say that someone is jealous or that something is smooth than to hunt the abstract entities 'jealousy' or 'smoothness'. Indeed the question 'What is jealousy?' just *is* the question 'What is it to call a person jealous?', or perhaps 'What is it to be, or to feel, jealous?'. So the only sensible way to tackle the question 'What is truth?'[1] is to investigate what might be meant by calling something true, by saying, for instance, that what Percy says is true. And the only sensible way to tackle the question 'What is existence?' is to investigate what might be meant by saying that certain things, e.g. tame tigers, exist.

All this is true despite the fact that neither truth nor existence is a property. 'What Percy says is true' calls for a different logical analysis from that required by 'Your lawn is smooth'; and 'Bored children quarrel' is not a good model for understanding 'Tame tigers exist'. But if we do not move from the abstract nouns 'truth' and 'existence' to the adjective 'true'

---

[1] Pilate need not be supposed to have been interested in sensible ways of answering the question. He may indeed have been jesting precisely at the use that had been made of the abstract word 'truth'. Christ had in fact been talking, not about truth, but about *the* truth (John 18: 37; cf. 14: 6).

and the verb 'exist', we shall never get started. Once that move has been made there will still be a long way to go, so we had better make the first move quickly.

2. *Comparison of the verb 'exist' with the verb 'be'*

To say 'Tame tigers exist' is to say no more than would be said by 'There are tame tigers'. In some languages, Latin for example, the word translated as 'are' can replace the word translated as 'exist' without any other change in the containing sentence: *'Sunt tigres mansueti'* has the same meeting as *'Existunt tigres mansueti'*. But making a simple substitution of this sort in English produces 'Tame tigers are', which is offensive to English ears. Certain rules of English sentence formation dictate that the verb 'be', when it is used to express an existential judgement, should be placed in front of the words which are its grammatical subject. Furthermore, having been placed there, idiom requires that it should be preceded by 'There' to avoid the unpleasantness, for speakers of English, of a verb standing at the beginning of an indicative sentence.[2] These two features of the sentence 'There are tame tigers', the inversion of the normal order of noun and verb and the prefixing of 'There' to the sentence as a whole, might be thought to remove the temptation to construe 'There are tame tigers' as parallel to 'Bored children quarrel', a temptation that is strong in the case of 'Tame tigers exist'. But more is needed if we are to be immune from temptation. Certainly the superficial grammar of 'There are tame tigers' may sound a warning note, but these features by themselves are not sufficient to force us to distinguish at a deeper level the forms involved. The features can occur in other sentences where their presence seems purely optional and dispensable. 'There dwelt in Transylvania a holy man' is only superficially distinguishable from 'A holy man dwelt in Transylvania' and 'There came down the road a boy with a limp' from 'A boy with a limp came down the road'. To anticipate by using some technical vocabulary we have yet to introduce, there seems no reason to deny that '— dwelt in Transylvania' or '— came down the road' can, like ' — quarrel', be a genuine

---

[2] Cf. Charles H. Kahn, *The Verb 'Be' in Ancient Greek*, Dordrecht: D. Reidel, 1973, pp. 31ff. This work is Part 6 of *The Verb 'Be' and its Synonyms*, ed. J. W. M. Verhaar, in the Supplementary Series of *Foundations of Language*.

predicate of individuals. Is there then sufficient reason to deny that '— are' in 'There are tame tigers' can also be regarded as a predicate of individuals? Certainly the fact that 'There are tame tigers' cannot be replaced idiomatically by 'Tame tigers are', as 'There came down the road a boy with a limp' can be by 'A boy with a limp came down the road', seems an insufficient reason.

German and French idioms, which most frequently use *'Es gibt'* and *'Il y a'* in place of 'There is', seem to show a stronger awareness than English of the difference between existential propositions and propositions ascribing properties to objects. Nevertheless even these languages have forms *'Es ist'* and *'Il est'*, which make use of equivalents of the verb 'be', as English uses 'be' in 'There is' and 'There are', and one would have to look further afield to find languages where there was no possibility of construing an existential judgement as predicating *being* of an object or objects in the same way as *dwelling in Transylvania* or *coming down the road* can be predicated of an object or objects. Latin, as we have seen, has the simple unadorned use of *'est'* and *'sunt'* as a possible substitution for the verbs *'existit'* and *'existunt'*. Classical Greek, which lacks any word obviously equivalent to 'exist', is forced to use parts of *'einai'*, its synonym for 'be', much more widely than the languages we have mentioned, for the expression of existential judgements. Thereby hangs a philosophical story of epic dimensions, a Great Chain of Philosophies of Being.

3. *The variety of senses of 'be' and its synonyms*

The subject we are to investigate is existence, and, as I have argued, the way to discuss the topic is to examine how we use sentences containing the verb 'exist'. I have further maintained that in many Indo-European languages the same work that is done by 'exist' and its synonyms is done, and in much the same way, by 'be' and its synonyms. It might therefore have been thought reasonable to entitle this study 'What is Being?' instead of 'What is Existence?'. To have done so, however, would have been to cast the net too wide. For the verb 'be' and its synonyms have a range of uses which coincides at some points with, but at others goes far outside and beyond, the range of uses of the verb 'exist'. The examination of the uses of 'be' and its synonyms has been undertaken by students of linguistics, and their findings[3] are of great interest to philosophers. There is, of course, nothing new in such an examination. Plato and Aristotle were concerned to distinguish different senses of *'einai'*, the Greek equivalent of 'be'. But it cannot be pretended that the ancient philosophers, or their medieval successors, or the post-Renaissance philosophers who touched on the same subject, provided a clear picture. It is my own view that such a picture was totally impossible until Frege produced his conception of a second-level predicate; but even that allows us to get a precise specification only of one use of the verb 'be'—what has sometimes been called 'the quantifier use'. Other uses remain sources of considerable philosophical and linguistic difficulty.

4. *The copulative sense of 'be'*

Most important amongst the uses which have to be distinguished from the existential, or quantifier, use is the use of 'be' as copula. Aristotle's way of distinguishing these uses was to label the existential use 'being *haplōs*' and the copulative use 'being something'. 'Being *haplōs*' might be rendered 'being without qualification' or 'being *tout court*': 'being something' explains itself. For examples Aristotle might have used 'Tame tigers are' and 'Tame tigers are lazy'. 'Tame tigers are' uses 'are' without qualification, i.e. *haplōs*: he might have said 'Tame tigers are —period'. 'Tame tigers are lazy' obviously uses 'be' in the sense of 'being something': 'Tame tigers are something—namely, lazy'. The medieval Aristotelians used *'simpliciter'* to render '*haplōs*' and talked of 'being *secundum quid*' instead of 'being something'.

The difference between 'being *haplōs*' and 'being something' might be thought to be simply an instance of the difference between intransitive and transitive verbs. 'His hand moved' and 'His hand moved the pen' seem analogous to 'Tame tigers are' and 'Tame tigers are lazy'. But transitive verbs like 'moved' in 'His hand moved the pen' are not the same as copulative verbs like 'are' in 'Tame tigers are lazy'. How then are copulative verbs to be distinguished from non-copulative ones? In highly

---

[3] See the multi-volume work, *The Verb 'Be' and its Synonyms*, ed. J. W. M. Verhaar.

inflected languages like Latin and Greek it is easy to give a rule for this. In English 'James killed a soldier' is not superficially different from 'James was a soldier': both are of the form 'Proper name—verb—indefinite article—common noun'. In Latin, however, the first is rendered '*Jacobus occidit militem*', whereas the second comes out as '*Jacobus erat miles*'. The common noun in the first example is in a different case, namely the accusative, from that of the proper name: in the second example it is in the same case, the nominative. But although English does not have distinct nominative and accusative forms for nouns (as opposed to pronouns like 'we' and 'us'), it does have ways, shared also by Latin, of distinguishing copulative from non-copulative verbs. 'James killed a soldier' can be transformed into the passive 'A soldier was killed by James', but there is no parallel transformation for 'James was a soldier'. Subordinating 'James killed a soldier' to the causative operator 'His father made' requires us to transform 'killed' into the infinitive 'kill': 'His father made James kill a solider'. The result of subordinating 'James was a soldier' to the same operator is, or at least can be, 'His father made James a soldier', where the verb 'be' has been, as the transformational grammarians say, zeroed.

It is possible in this way to give a clear specification by syntactic methods of the copulative use of 'be' It is much more difficult to give a semantic account of this use of the verb. Certain considerations point to the view that copulative uses of 'be' make no semantic contribution whatsoever to the sentences in which they occur. It is arguable that sentences containing 'be' in this sense can always be replaced by sentences that do not.

This may perhaps be appreciated by recalling a transformation in the opposite direction which used to have wide currency. At one time students of elementary logic were regularly set the exercise of 'putting propositions into logical form'. The only logical forms that were recognized in this tradition were those in which substitution instances of the schema '*S* is a *P*' were preceded by one or other of the following expressions: 'Every', 'No', 'Some' or 'Not every'. Since the expressions substituted for '*S*' and '*P*' had to be interchangeable for the purposes of syllogistic inference, only nouns or noun-phrases were permitted, as indeed the formula 'S is a P' demands if it is rigorously applied. Thus 'Every husband snores' would not be in logical form, but would have to be altered to 'Every husband is a snorer'. Only thus could the predicate term of this proposition appear without modification as the subject term of, for example, 'No snorer is a pleasant bedfellow', as would be required if we were to obtain, for example, a syllogism in *Celarent*.

The possibility of translating verbs like 'snores' by phrases such as 'is a snorer' suggests the possibility of translation in the opposite direction. This latter possibility was recognized by Greek philosophers. Aristotle in the first book of the *Physics* mentions philosophers who were worried by the possibility of multiple predication: the fact that many different things can be predicated of one object (the possibility of S's being a Q and an R as well as a P) seemed to give rise to the danger of things being one and many at the same time. 'Some', he says, 'like Lycophron, did away with the word "is"; others sought to remodel the language, and replace "That man is pale", "That man is walking", by "That man pales", "That man walks", for fear that by inserting "is" they would render the one many.'[4] These thinkers took the contrary view to those who regarded 'S is a P' as a necessary part of any formula representing the true logical form of a proposition. The view of Lycophron and his friends seems to be that the essential structure of any proposition is represented rather by the formula 'N V's', where N represents a noun, or name of something, and V a verb. This is the view expressed by Plato in the *Sophist*.[5] Aristotle in the *De Interpretatione*[6] seems to agree with Plato in adhering to the 'N V's' school, but by the time he wrote the *Prior Analytics*[7] he seems to have transferred his allegiance to the 'S is a P' school. Professor Geach has represented this event as the original sin of logic.[8]

How would it work out in practice if we adopted as a rule for 'putting propositions into logical form' the inverse of the

---

[4] *Aristotle's Physics*, translated with notes by W. Charlton, 1970, 185ᵇ27-31.
[5] In *Platonis Opera*, 1, ed. J. Burnet, 1953, 261C-262E.
[6] In *Categories and De Interpretatione*, Eng. tr. with notes by J. L. Ackrill, 1963.
[7] *Aristotle's Prior and Posterior Analytics*, ed. W. D. Ross, 1949.
[8] 'A History of the Corruptions of Logic', in P. T. Geach, *Logic Matters*, 1972, pp. 44 ff.

rule imposed on students of traditional 'Aristotelian' logic? We should now be obliged to substitute for every sentence, or part of a sentence, which exhibited the form 'S is a P', a corresponding expression of the form 'N V's'. Thus, 'James is a soldier' might be replaced by 'James soldiers' and '— tame tiger is a big eater' by '— tame tiger eats copiously'. In some cases we should have to invent verb forms corresponding to the noun or adjective forms which appeared in the original 'S is a P' string. Thus 'mammalize' might have to be invented to produce a canonical rendering of 'Every rodent is a mammal'. Some suffix like '—ize' might regularly be employed to convert nouns and adjectives into verbs. Should we not then say that the copulative use of the verb 'be' was the same as that assigned to this suffix, that the function of 'be' as copula simply was to convert nouns and adjectives into verbs?[9]

Light may perhaps be shed on the consequences of this suggestion if we consider languages which appear to do without, at least in some instances, a copulative use of the verb 'be' or its synonym. In Greek and Latin it is possible to omit the copula and express a complete proposition by juxtaposing a name and a general term. '*Justus Dominus*' is a quite adequate rendering of 'The Lord is righteous'; to insert '*est*' is possible but not necessary. It is also a rendering of the Hebrew '*Tsaddiq Jahweh*', but here the insertion of a copulative verb between '*Tsaddiq*' and '*Jahweh*' is not only unnecessary but impossible. Perhaps Lycophron had met languages like Hebrew that 'did away with the word "is"', in the sense that they had no verb to represent 'is' in 'That man is pale'. It seems then that there are languages which cannot, or need not, employ copulas to produce a complete sentence out of the elements *S* and *P*.[10]

[9] Cf. G. Frege, 'On Concept and Object', *Translations from the Philosophical Writings of Gottlob Frege*, edd. Peter Geach and Max Black, 1952, pp. 43 f.: 'In this sense [the German word *ist*] can sometimes be replaced by the mere personal suffix: cf. *dies Blatt ist grün* and *dies Blatt grünt*'.

[10] Hobbes appears to have known *a priori* of the possibliity of such languages: 'And as we use the Verbe *Is*; so the Latines use their Verbe *Est*, and the Greeks their Ἐστι through all its Declinations. Whether all other Nationals of the world have in their severall languages a word that answereth to it, or not, I cannot tell; but I am sure that they have not need of it: For the placing of two names in order may serve to signifie their Consequence, if it were the custome, (for Custome is it, that give words their force,) as well as the words *Is*, or *Bee*, or *Are*, and the like.' (*Leviathan*, p. 372, original pagination). I am grateful to Mr Michael Bradley for drawing my attention to this passage.

It should be noted that in Latin and Greek at least the so-called nominal sentence, '*Justus Dominus*', for instance, which omits the copula, can occur only when the verb omitted is in present indicative. Russian, indeed, has a copula which is found only in tenses other than the present and in moods other than the indicative. In these languages, and many others, the normal way of expressing differences of tense and mood is by inflexion of the verb. If one needed to say that the Lord will be just, or express the hope that the Lord would be just, one would have to say '*Justus erit Dominus*' or '*Justus sit Dominus*'.[11] A total exclusion of the copula is thus impossible in Latin. But it is not difficult to imagine a modification of Latin in which tense and mood distinctions are expressed by operators standing outside sentences, most naturally at their beginning. Arthur Prior[12] outlined a modification of English in which 'The Lord will be just', for example, would be replaced by 'It will be the case that the Lord is just', and 'The Lord was just', with no respect for the rules for sequence of tenses, by 'It was the case that the Lord is just'. Similarly Anthony Kenny[13] proposed a system in which '*Fiat p*' ('would that *p*') produced the same result as is in some languages obtained by putting the main verb of the sentence for which *p* stands into the subjunctive or optative. In these systems the primary[14] operand on which tense and modal operators operate is always in the present indicative, and thus the only occurrence of the copula would be in this form. In our supposed modification of Latin it could always be omitted.

The possibility of omitting the copula is some indication of its lack of importance from the logical point of view. So is the fact that in some languages it has a much wider use than in English. Spanish has two verbs which perform the function of the copula, but, more interestingly, Basque, which also has two verbs to perform this function, has the further requirement that they perform it in every sentence; they are the only verbs which have a finite form. One supposes that affirmative sentences

[11] '*Dominus vobiscum*', however, is normally taken to be the expression not of an assertion but of a prayer: 'The Lord be with you'.
[12] *Past, Present and Future*, 1967, pp. 14 ff.
[13] *Analysis*, 26, No. 3.
[14] I say 'primary' because of the possibility of iteration of tense operators. For this point about the primary operand, see below, Ch. VII, pp. 173 ff.

in Basque are constructed rather as negative sentences are in contemporary standard English: we do not in general say 'N V's not', but 'N does not V'. There are dialects of English where the form 'N do V', for the affirmative 'N V's', is as regular as 'N does not V'; and in the majority of our tenses, including the continuous present (e.g. 'Charles is laughing'), we insert 'is' 'will', 'has', or the like, between N and some part of the verb V.

So there is a tendency in a wide variety of languages to substitute for the simple 'N V's' form a more complex form which involves inserting an auxiliary verb between N and V. We may symbolize this form by the formula NaV. Can it be said that sentences exemplifying the formula 'S is P' also exemplify this formula NaV? There is no difficulty in allowing that anything which exemplifies S will also exemplify N: these are simply alternative symbols for indicating names. A sentence like 'Charles is laughing', where the verb-phrase is in the continuous present tense, has already been envisaged as an exemplification of the NaV formula, so 'is' can easily be regarded as an appropriate substituion for a. What about sentences like 'Charles is cunning', which certainly exemplify the 'S is P' form? Do they also exemplify NaV? 'Laughing' exemplifies V, because it is a non-finite form of the verb 'laugh'. 'Cunning' would not qualify on this score. There are certainly differences between them: 'Alice saw Charles laugh' is a transform of 'Charles is laughing', but there is no parallel transform of 'Charles is cunning'. Whether or not 'cunning' exemplifies V depends on how much of the grammar of words like 'laughing' the symbol V is intended to capture. What does seem clear is that the 'is' in 'Charles is cunning' is not being used differently from the 'is' in 'Charles is laughing'. In the latter the 'is' was of no logical interest, being a merely superficial feature of English grammar, to which nothing corresponds, for example, in the French translation of 'Charles is laughing', namely, '*Charles rit*'. If 'Charles is cunning' differs from 'Charles is laughing' it is because of the difference between 'cunning' and 'laughing', not because of any difference between the two occurrences of 'is'. We may conclude that 'is' in 'is cunning', and in phrases of the 'S is P' form generally, is a purely superficial linguistic element of no special interest to logicians, an operator which forms a verb out of an adjective or out of a noun with the indefinite article.

As I remarked earlier, this account of the function of the verb 'be' as copula is given in purely syntactic terms. Normally, a syntactic account of the meaning of a word—its assignment to a particular category, the specification of the ways in which it can combine with other words to form coherent strings of discourse—is insufficient to provide a full understanding of the word's meaning. More needs to be done, and this further explanation is often called the 'semantic' account. Where, however, the sole function of a word is to convert an element of one category into one of another (as 'is', we maintain, has the effect of converting an adjective like 'cunning' into a verb-phrase, 'is cunning', which is of the same category as 'snores') it is hard to see what more is needed for the understanding of the word. The function of the copula, we may say, is simply to act as a verbalizer. The syntactic account, in this case, *is* a semantic account.

5. *The alleged 'identity' sense of the verb 'be'*

Can a semantic account be provided of other alleged uses of 'be'? Let us begin with the supposed 'identity' use. It has become a philosophical commonplace to distinguish such a use from both the copulative and the existential use. Thus Russell is a well-known passage said that it was 'a disgrace to the human race' that it had chosen to employ the same word 'is' for two such entirely different ideas as predication and identity.[15] Frege had earlier drawn a sharp distinction between 'is' when it functions as the mere copula, which he thought entirely lacking in logical significance, and the 'is' which means 'is no other than' and which in his view signifies a function of two arguments.[16] And to trace the history of this distinction very much further back, Plato's *Sophist* has been interpreted as an attempt to solve certain philosophical problems by distinguishing a sense of *'esti'* in which it expresses participation by a particular in a form from the sense in which it expresses the contradictory of the relation of difference.[17] Nevertheless, it may well be doubted whether there is any real justification for distinguishing a special identity use of 'is' from the more general copulative

[15] Bertrand Russell, *Introduction to Mathematical Philosophy*, 1919, p. 172.
[16] Frege, *Philosophical Writings,* p. 44.
[17] See J. L. Ackrill, 'Plato and the Copula: *Sophist* 251-259', in *Plato: A Collection of Critical Essays*, ed. G. Vlastos, 1972, 1. 212-14.

use. In a monogamous society 'Hecuba is Priam's wife' is interpretable as a statement of identity; but in a polygamous society it is no more an identity-statement than 'Hector is Priam's son'. It seems intolerable, in any case, to suppose that the word 'is' has two different meanings in 'She is his wife' and 'He is his son'. The difference is imported from the context, or the social institutions which speakers and hearers take for granted.[18]

The reasoning just given can perhaps be filled out in the following way. In a sentence like 'Hecuba is Priam's wife', uttered in a monogamous society, the phrase following 'is' is what Russell would call a definite description. This is more obviously the case in a sentence like 'Charles is the King of France'. The expressions 'Priam's wife' and 'the King of France' could be paraphrased by 'sole wife of Priam' and 'sole King of France', respectively, and 'is' prefixed to either of these phrases would clearly be the copula. Its function would be that which we have described above, of turning a noun or an adjective or, in this case, a noun phrase into a verb phrase. 'Charles is sole King of France' stands to 'Charles is the King of France' as 'My father owns this shop' stands to 'My father is the owner of this shop'. 'Is' has the effect of turning 'the King of France' into a predicative expression in the same way as substituting 'owns' for 'the owner of' turns 'the owner of' into a predicative expression. But it is the definite article[19] which secures uniqueness, as does the word 'sole'. There is no need to postulate a special sense of the word 'is' in order to do this, nor in order to explain the distinction between 'Priam is the father of Hector' and 'Hector is a son of Priam'. The former implies that no one else begot Hector, whilst the latter leaves open the possibility that other sons were begotten by Priam (a possibility which, we are given to understand, was only too well actualized). But this distinction between what the two propositions imply is explained, perhaps, by the presence in one case of the definite and in the other of the indefinite article. Or, more likely, since the same distinction would hold if both articles were omitted or the definite article used each time, it is explained by the meaning of 'father' and 'son', respectively. But either way there

---

[18] I have borrowed this argument from Professor Kahn (*The Verb 'Be'*, Ch. VIII, n. 33; see also his more general remarks in n. 1 to the same chapter).

[19] In most cases; 'the son of' seems to be an exception.

is no call to attribute the distinction to a supposed difference between a 'copula' and and 'identity' sense of 'is'.

Most sentences which would be said to express statements of identity have definite descriptions following 'is' or whatever other form of the verb 'be' is appropriate in the context. Sentences like 'China is Cathay' or 'Octavian was Augustus' can be explained as elliptical for 'China is the country otherwise referred to as "Cathay"' and 'Octavian was the man later known as "Augustus"'.[20] Sentences like 'Hector's father was Priam' are not to be dealt with in this way; they are not concerned to tell us what Hector's father was called. Octavian might not have been Augustus if the Senate had not decreed that he should be so called; but Hector's father would still have been Priam, even if Priam's parents had decided to call him 'Agamemnon'. 'Hector's father was Priam' seems to be a mere stylistic variant of 'Priam was Hector's father'. The feeling that 'Priam' is here complement of the verb 'be', and 'Hector's father' subject, is an illusion of surface grammar.[21] Identity-propositions can always be represented as having a definite description as their second term. We have, therefore, no need to postulate a separate sense of the verb 'be', over and above its use as copula, to account for its appearance in sentences which are used to state identity.

6. *Is 'be' purely equivocal or analogical?*

The existential use, the copulative use, and the identity use represent the three senses of 'be' that have normally been distinguished in modern logic. Other uses have been attributed to *'einai'*, the Greek equivalent of 'be', and interesting subdivisions of these uses have been noticed.[22] Once the case for a separate identity use has been dropped, however, the only uses which seem totally distinct are the existential and the copulative use. What is the relation between these two?

There are different ways in which words can be said to be equivocal, i.e. to have different senses. 'Date' can be used to name a fruit grown on a palm tree, but it can also be used in

---

[20] For further remarks on this topic, see below, Ch. IX, pp. 227 ff., and Ch. XI, pp. 287 f.

[21] Though not, it seems, of Polish grammar: See P. T. Geach, *Reference and Generality*, 1962, § 36.

[22] See Appendix A for further discussion.

a phrase such as 'the date of the new President's inauguration'. That the same sound and the same written symbol are used in these two totally unconnected ways is the merest linguistic accident. Here we have a case of *pure equivocation*. But that 'date' should be used of a particular day of the month and also of someone's girl-friend is not a matter of accident. No doubt one's 'date' was originally the person with whom one 'made a date', i.e. with whom one arranged to meet on a particular date. What we have here is not pure equivocation, but what the medieval philosophers called 'analogy': if a word is used in one sense and also in another, which, while not the same, is not entirely different either, it is said to be used *analogically*.

Is the twofold sense of the verb 'be', as copula and as verb of existence, a case of pure equivocation or a case of analogy? One philosopher who took the former option was John Stuart Mill. His remarks bear extensive quotation:

> It is important that there should be no indistinctness in our conception of the nature and office of the copula; for confused notions respecting it are among the causes which have spread mysticism over the field of logic, and perverted its speculations into logomachies.
> It is apt to be supposed that the copula is something more than a mere sign of predication; that it also signifies existence. In the proposition, Socrates is just, it may seem to be implied not only that the quality *just* can be affirmed of Socrates, but moreover that Socrates *is*, that is to say, exists. This, however, only shows that there is an ambiguity in the word *is*; a word which not only performs the function of the copula in affirmations, but has also a meaning of its own, in virtue of which it may itself be made the predicate of a proposition. That the employment of it as a copula does not necessarily include the affirmation of existence, appears from such a proposition as this: A centaur is a fiction of the poets; where it cannot possibly be implied that a centaur exists, since the proposition itself expressly asserts that the thing has no real existence.
> Many volumes might be filled with the frivolous speculations concerning the nature of Being (Τὸ ὄν, Οὐσία, Ens, Entitas, Essentia, and the like) which have arisen from overlooking this double meaning of the word *to be*; from supposing that when it signifies to exist, and when it signifies to *be* some specified thing, as to *be* a man, to *be* Socrates, to *be* seen or spoken of, to *be* a phantom, even to *be* a nonentity, it must still, at bottom, answer to the same idea; and that a meaning must be found for it which shall suit all these cases. The fog which rose from this narrow spot diffused itself at an early period over the whole surface of metaphysics. Yet it becomes us not to triumph over the great intellects of Plato and Aristotle because we are now able to preserve ourselves from many errors into which they, perhaps inevitably, fell. The fire-teazer of a

modern steam-engine produces by his exertions far greater effects than Milo of Crotona could, but he is not therefore a stronger man. The Greeks seldom knew any language but their own. This rendered it far more difficult for them than it is for us, to acquire a readiness in detecting ambiguities. One of the advantages of having accurately studied a plurality of languages, especially of those languages which eminent thinkers have used as the vehicle of their thoughts, is the practical lesson we learn respecting the ambiguities of words, by finding that the same word in one language corresponds, on different occasions, to different words in another. When not thus exercised, even the strongest understandings find it difficult to believe that things which have a common name have not, in some respect or other, a common nature; and often expend much labour very unprofitably (as was frequently done by the two philosophers just mentioned) in vain attempts to discover in what this common nature consists. But, the habit once formed, intellects much inferior are capable of detecting even ambiguities which are common to many languages: and it is surprising that the one now under consideration, though it exists in the modern languages as well as in the ancient, should have been overlooked by almost all authors. The quantity of futile speculation which has been caused by a misapprehension of the nature of the copula was hinted at by Hobbes; but Mr. James Mill (*Analysis of the Human Mind*, i. 126 et seq.) was, I believe, the first who distinctly characterized the ambiguity, and pointed out how many errors in the received systems of philosophy it has had to answer for.[23]

Mills's view that the two things that are meant by the verb 'be', in its copulative and in its existential sense respectively, do not have 'in some respect or other a common nature' amounts to holding that this verb is purely or accidentally equivocal. This is hard to accept. Purely equivocal uses of words, like 'date', are usually specific to a single language. But the use of synonyms of 'be' as copula and as equivalent, in some contexts, of 'exist' is common at least to many Indo-European languages. Mill's remark about 'ambiguities that are common to many languages' shows that he was aware of this. The question whether what we have here is an analogical or an equivocal use of language cannot be decided without some attempt to survey the empirical data provided by students of linguistics.

Mill's view that 'be', as copula and verb of existence, is purely equivocal, would find strong support if the use of the same word to perform both these roles was a purely Indo-European phenomenon. A brief survey of the linguistic evidence, therefore, will indicate whether or not this is the case.

[23] John Stuart Mill, *A System of Logic*, Bk. I, Ch. IV, § 1, 85-7.

IS 'BE' PURELY EQUIVOCAL OR ANALOGICAL? 15

Hebrew, as we have seen, does not have a verb which can function as copula, but it does make use of a word which occupies the same position as a copula in Indo-European languages and performs the role of linking a name with a predicative expression. The word in question is, however, a pronoun rather than a verb. The Hebrew sentences that contain this word in this use resemble, in fact, pidgin-English sentences like 'Mr Jones he mighty fat man', where 'he' replaces 'is'. Another Semitic language, Arabic, uses the same pronoun in the same way, and one Chinese equivalent of the copula is also reckoned to be in origin a pronoun. Arabic, however, unlike Hebrew, has a verb, '*kana*', which, like '*einai*' in Greek, can function either as the verb of existence or as the copula. And Chinese, which uses a completely different word from any which has a copulative use to translate 'There is' or 'There are' in English, nevertheless has a word which is used as copula with locative phrases (i.e. to translate 'is' in contexts like 'is in Canton' or 'is on the table'), and which also translates 'is' in the sense of 'is alive'.[24] This latter sense of 'is', to which Professor Geach has drawn attention, citing the biblical 'Joseph is not and Simeon is not',[25] corresponds to one of the uses of 'exist'. 'Joseph is not' is equivalent to 'Joseph no longer exists'. It has accordingly been regarded as an existential use of 'is'.[26] But it has important differences from the use of 'is' in 'there is', the use more commonly indicated by the label 'existential', and it will be an important task of this book to bring these differences to the fore.[27] In a number of other languages, as widely separated as Japanese, the Indian language Telugu, and the African language Twi, the word which serves as 'locative copula', i.e. to translate 'is' in phrases like 'is in Illinois', 'is in the garden', has a further existential use in translating 'There is' or 'There are'. It is in this area, if anywhere, that we shall eventually find a link between the copulative and the existential uses of 'be'.[28]

[24] See below, Ch. XII, pp. 319 f.
[25] P. T. Geach, *God and the Soul*, 1969, p. 55. Geach quotes the remark (Gen. 42: 36) as it is translated in the Authorized Version. The Hebrew original, literally translated, reads: 'Joseph, nothing of him; Simeon, nothing of him'.
[26] See Kahn, *The Verb 'Be'*, pp. 240-5. Kahn labels this 'The Vital Use', because it is here that the Aristotelian '*vita viventibus est esse*' is appropriate. See below, Appendix A, p. 330.   [27] See below, particularly Ch. V.
[28] See below, Ch. XII, § 7. The information about languages other than Hebrew given in this paragraph is drawn from Verhaar, *The Verb 'Be' and its Synonyms*.

So it does not seem possible to say that the equivocal use of 'be', as verb of existence and as copula, is a purely Indo-European phenomenon, although Indo-European languages seem to provide the most striking and uniform instances of it. It is accordingly difficult to follow Mill in regarding this two-fold use as a case of pure equivocation rather than analogy. The Aristotelian and medieval doctrine of the 'Analogy of Being' still has some mileage in it. But linguists who have concerned themselves with the uses of synonyms of 'be' and the relations between the various uses have not always been sensitive to the issues that have worried philosphers in this area. In particular they have classified certain uses as 'existential' on unsatisfactorily subjective grounds, either because the use of a synonym of 'be' had an 'existential feel', or because a paraphrase was available which made use of the English word 'exist'. The problems that have exercised logicians and philosophers are a long way removed from the phenomena which fix the attention of linguists, such as the distinctive copulas that are appropriate to animate and inanimate subjects. The philosophical problems centre around the well-known adage 'Existence is not a predicate'. It is to this that we must now turn our attention. The significance of the adage has to be set out in stages. It will be as well to examine first certain classical statements of the position. When these statements have been looked at, and their inadequacies recognized, we shall be in a position to look at the discoveries made by modern logicians, beginning with Frege, which alone provide us with clear criteria for distinguishing 'existential' from other uses of 'be' and its synonyms. Armed with these criteria we shall be able in the final chapter to return to the topic of the 'Analogy of Being' and give what we hope will be an explanatory account of the meaning of 'be' in all its main uses. Although the greater part of the book will be concerned with the logic of the word 'exist', we shall thus attempt to justify the claim to have continued the work of philosophers who in every century have concerned themselves with the Parmenidean topic of *being*.

II
'Existence is not a Predicate'

1. *The Ontological Argument depends on taking existence as a predicate*

In modern philosophy interest in existential propositions has stemmed in the main from disputes about the validity of a particular argument, or group of arguments, for the existence of God. Because of the crucial role which the concept of *existence* or *being* plays in this argument it has been called the Ontological Argument.[1] Since Kant the main challenge to its soundness has come from those who, with Kant, deny that existence, or being, is a 'real predicate'. What they mean by this, and what the relevance of it is to the Ontological Argument, can be discovered only by a close examination of their discussions. Undoubtedly the *locus classicus* for the thesis that existence is not a real predicate is Kant's attempted refutation of the Ontological Argument in the *Critique of Pure Reason*. Kant in this passage is the forerunner of Frege: the doctrine that being is not a real predicate is an anticipation of the doctrine that '— exist' is never a first-level predicate. One of the main purposes of this book is to expound and defend this latter doctrine, and it seems appropriate to preface the exposition of Frege's claims by examining those of Kant, which remain familiar to a wider circle than Frege's, even among the ranks of professional philosophers. Before turning to Kant it is necessary to set out the bare bones of the argument itself, and convenient to look briefly at Hume's discussion of existence, which is itself anticipatory of Kant's. Finally, after examining Kant's

---

[1] The word 'ontology', with its derivatives, was coined from the participial stem '*onto-*' of '*einai*', the Greek equivalent of 'be'. See below, Ch. VII. The introduction of the word '*Ontologia*' into philosophical usage is due to Goclenius (see C. Lejewski 'Ontology and Logic' in *Philosophy of Logic*, ed. S. Körner, 1976, p.1).

arguments, we shall turn to a still older argument which Quine has made familiar by the name of 'Plato's Beard'.

Anselm and Descartes are the most famous exponents of the Ontological Argument, though neither of them gave the argument that title. The popularity of the title seems to be due to Kant. Anselm's argument is subtle and complicated, and the fallacies involved in it take a great deal of unravelling. Nevertheless, the most important of these is the same one that Descartes perpetrates more blatantly, so it saves effort if the version of the argument we examine is that of Descartes. Descartes maintains that the idea of God involves the notion of a being who possesses every perfection. Existence, he thinks, is a perfection—an attribute which it is better to possess than to lack. (Anselm's premiss, that to exist in reality is greater than merely to be thought of, amounts to the same thing.) To deny that God exists is therefore like denying that a triangle has three interior angles. To exist is part of what it is to be God, just as having three interior angles is part of what it is to be a triangle. Against this numberless philosophers, before and after Kant, have argued that existence is not a perfection. A perfection is an attribute, something which can be possessed or lacked, and something whose possession or lack is asserted by affirming or denying a predicate of a subject. But '— exist', it is held, is not a predicate, or not a 'real' predicate.

2. *Hume's view that we have no distinct idea of existence*

Hume, who is no logician, does not talk in terms of subjects and predicates, real or otherwise. He talks of ideas. But his remarks on the idea of existence have relevance to the question whether 'exist' is a predicate. He starts from the claim that 'there is no impression nor idea of any kind of which we have any consciousness or memory, that is not conceived as existent'.[2] Hume is notoriously confused and confusing about the relation between ideas and their objects. What we should expect him to be saying is that whenever we think of anything, say a daffodil or a corkscrew, we think of *it* as existing. Every idea of an x is the idea of an existent x; and this he does in fact go on to say two paragraphs further on. But what he actually says here is that every impression and idea is *itself*

[2] *A Treatise of Human Nature*, ed. L. A. Selby-Bigge, 1951, p. 66.

conceived as existent. If therefore there is a distinct impression from which the idea of existence is derived, it must be one which is conjoined with, and inseparable from, every perception that we have. It is inconceivable that I should have an impression or an idea that does not exist. But Hume believes that there are no two perceptions which cannot be conceived as separate. The only conclusion left for him to draw is that the idea of existence 'is the very same with the idea of what we conceive to be existent'. He presumably means that any idea, say of a corkscrew, is also an idea of existence.

Note, however, that he has passed from talking of the idea itself as existent to the idea as being *of* an existent object. Hume is unclear about this distinction. Since he is later to maintain that ideas and impressions are all that there is, it is not very important to him. But, however he comes by it, he is certainly committed to the view that 'whatever we conceive we conceive to be existent'. 'To reflect on any thing simply and to reflect on it as existent, are nothing different from each other.' Existence, then, is seen as a universal property. But because universal, it is no property at all. Existence could only be distinct from corkscrew-hood if we could conceive of a corkscrew as non-existent. And the same with daffodility. Since it is not a distinct idea, 'that idea, when conjoined with the idea of any object, *makes no addition to it*' (The italicized words antiticipate Kant). 'Any idea we please to form is the idea of a being; and the idea of a being is any idea we please to form.'

It has been pointed out[3] that Hume's remarks here contradict a doctrine which he several times put forward elsewhere. It is a cardinal point with Hume that all matters of fact are contingent. For 'matter of fact' he is often willing to substitute 'matter of existence'.[4] And his principal argument to support this doctrine is that, take any object you like, you can always conceive its non-existence. The fact that Queen Elizabeth II has a daughter is contingent, a mere matter of fact, because it is quite conceivable that there should have been no daughter born to her, that there should have been no such person as Princess Anne. But what is this but to conceive the Queen's daughter as non-existent?

[3] Cf. J. Passmore, *Hume's Intentions*, 1952, pp. 26 f., 97 f.
[4] *A Treatise on Human Nature*, p. 458.

Can we defend Hume by drawing a distinction between thinking of *x* as non-existent and entertaining the thought that *x* does not exist? It might be that some person always thinks of Cicero as having grey hair but has never entertained the thought *that Cicero had grey hair*. If this distinction works, perhaps Hume can be represented as saying that no one can think of an object as non-existent, although it is possible in the case of every object to entertain the thought *that it does not exist*.

Whatever the merits of the distinction it is not open to Hume to draw it. The distinction depends on a contrast between what we think and what we think of, between thinking that *x* exists and thinking of *x* as existent. But Hume explicitly identifies these, and identifies both with simply thinking of *x*. 'When I think of God, when I think of him as existent, and when I believe him to be existent, my idea of him neither encreases nor diminishes.'[5] Believing that *p*, which in this context is the same as judging that *p*, is, of course, different from entertaining the thought that *p*, but only because there is more to the former than the latter. If there is no difference in my idea when I believe or judge that *x* exists and when I think of *x* as existing, *a fortiori* there is no difference in my idea when I entertain the thought that *x* exists and when I think of *x* as existing.

Few passages in the *Treatise* throw as much light on the logical foundations, or lack of them, for Hume's philosophy as the footnote on pages 96–97. He disputes the doctrine, which he attributes to the Schoolmen, but which surely derives from Plato and Aristotle,[6] 'that in every judgement, which we form, we unite two different ideas; since in that proposition, *God is*, or indeed any other, which regards existence, the idea of existence is no distinct idea, which we unite with that of the object, and which is capable of forming a compound idea by the union'. This shows quite clearly that Hume makes no difference between thinking of God as existent and entertaining the 'proposition, *God is*', since both are identified with having the idea of God. It also shows where Hume's error lies; and again the objection against Hume arises from consideration of negative existential propositions. The objection raised earlier was that

[5] Ibid., p. 94.
[6] Cf. *Theaetetus* 201–2, *Sophist* 261–2, *De Interpretatione*, Ch. 4.

there is an inconsistency between Hume's claim that whatever we conceive is conceived as existent and his claim that whatever can be conceived can be conceived as non-existent. The objection now to be raised is that Hume's account of affirmative existential propositions leaves no room for negative existential propositions. Suppose we entertain the proposition that there are things which are mortal, that mortal things exist. According to Hume, this is nothing more than to have the idea of something mortal. What then is the negation of this thought? Presumably, having the idea of something immortal, which, by the same token, is no different from entertaining the proposition that immortal things exist. But this is not the negation of the proposition that mortal things exist; it is quite compatible with it. The true negation of the proposition 'There are things which are mortal', namely, 'There are no things which are mortal', is quite distinct from the proposition 'There are things which are not mortal', i.e. 'Immortal things exist'. The distinction follows from the fact that negation can be applied to either of the terms of the proposition 'Mortals exist', with different results. But for Hume there is no distinction between the terms; the proposition is identified with a single idea, and thus admits of negation in one way only. The thought that an object does not exist, so far from being always possible, as Hume elsewhere maintains, is, by the reasoning of this footnote, never possible.[7] The fact that his doctrine here is incompatible with his claim that this thought is always possible proves him inconsistent, but does not show either doctrine taken by itself to be wrong. But the fact that it entails its never being possible to make a denial of existence constitutes a *reductio ad absurdum* of the doctrine.

3. *Hume identifies thinking of* x *and thinking of* x *as existent*

Hume's claim that 'the idea of existence is nothing different from the idea of any object' must be rejected. Nevertheless, some of the points he makes about the idea of existence are valid. Entertaining the proposition that God exists *is* something different from merely thinking of God, but thinking of God as existent may not be. For Hume, having an idea or thinking

---

[7] For a discussion of Hume's positive attempt to explain the idea of non-existence, see below, Ch. XII, pp. 318 ff.

of an object is contemplating a picture in the mind's eye. Thinking of *x* and thinking of *x* as *y* will thus be different, in that the sort of picture whose contemplation can constitute thinking of *x* will not necessarily constitute thinking of *x* as *y*. There are pictures, mental and otherwise, of Mr Heath which are not pictures of Mr Heath conducting an orchestra. Thinking of Mr Heath as conducting an orchestra is thus something more than thinking of Mr Heath *tout court*. A picture has to satisfy more conditions if it is to count as a picture of Mr Heath conducting an orchestra than if it is to count simply as a picture of Mr Heath. But it is difficult to see what conditions a picture would have to satisfy to be a picture of Mr Heath as existent which were not already satisfied by a picture of Mr Heath *tout court*. What is true of pictures is true of Hume's ideas. Both are like descriptions. The description of someone as a politician is less specific than the description of someone as a politican conducting an orchestra; but the description of someone as a politician existing (as opposed to an existing politician, about which we shall have more to say later[8]) is hardly intelligible.

It may be objected that there are other ideas which are not different in this respect from the idea of existence. There are no conditions which a picture would have to satisfy to be a picture of Mr Heath as male, or as human, which are not already satisfied by a picture of Mr Heath *tout court*.[9] Generalizing, for any *x*, nothing can be a picture of *x* which is not already a picture of *x* as *y*, provided *y* stands for some essential property of *x*. All that the above argument seems to show is that existence is one of the essential properties of Mr Heath. But there is a difference. Granted that masculinity and humanity may be regarded as essential properties of Mr Heath, they are not essential properties of everything. A picture has to satisfy more conditions if it is to be a picture of a male British sovereign than it would have to satisfy to be a picture of a British sovereign *tout court*; and a picture has to satisfy more conditions if it is to be a picture of a nursing mother who is human than if it is to be a picture of a nursing mother *tout court*. Masculinity and humanity may be essential properties

---

[8] See below, Ch. V, p. 146, n. 36.
[9] Caricatures present special difficulties. It would be interesting to see what a cartoonist could produce in response to the request for a picture of Mr Heath as non-existent.

of Mr Heath; but masculinity is not an essential property of British sovereigns, nor is humanity of nursing mothers. Keeping to this terminology we may say that existence is an essential property of everything—which arouses the suspicion that it is not really a property (of any sort) of anything.

Hume's doctrine that we have no distinct idea of existence is untenable; but there is truth in it in so far as it recognizes the difference between existence and redness or corkscrew-hood or masculinity or maternity, or any of the other items which fit more readily into Hume's theory of ideas.

Being red or a corkscrew or masculine or a mother are things that can be predicated of objects. Hume's 'idea' seems very often to be the psychological correlate of the logical notion of 'predicate'. This argument which he advances for the view that we have no separate idea of existence is very like one of the arguments Kant uses to show that existence is not a 'real', but only a 'logical', predicate. To this argument we may now turn.

4. *Kant's view that 'exist' is a 'merely logical' predicate*

Kant attempts to illustrate the distinction between a 'real' and a 'logical' predicate by saying that a subject which is predicated of itself would count as a 'merely logical' predicate. People who say 'Boys will be boys' no doubt wish to emphasize the possession by young male human beings of some properties not included in the definition of 'boy'; but on the face of it the sentence predicates its subject of itself. If it is not meant as a tautology, it is its tautological appearance which makes us choose it as a pithy expression of our meaning. But not every sentence containing 'boy' has this appearance of tautology. Just as 'male' may not add anything to the idea of Mr Heath in the sentence 'Mr Heath is male', but can add something to the idea of the Belgian sovereign in the sentence 'The Belgian sovereign is male', so 'boys' may not be a 'real' predicate in 'Boys will be boys', but is capable of adding something in other contexts: 'The scholars of Eton are boys', for instance. Nothing tautological about this: Eton may go coeducational any day now. 'Boys' in this latter proposition is what Kant would describe as a predicate 'which is added to the concept of the subject and enlarges it'. The difference between 'boys' and 'exists', however, is that the latter is not a real predicate in any context. Kant does not seem properly aware of this difference.

The difference in question is one which has importance in the philosophy of logic.[10] The word 'predicate', as it is normally used, is ambiguous between a role that a particular word or phrase is playing in a particular proposition—'boys' is the predicate of the proposition 'Hilary and Vivian are boys'—and a syntactic category to which expressions belong in virtue of their ability to play this role. It was to remove this ambiguity that Geach proposed to recycle the word 'predicable' (a term of art of traditional logic now fallen into desuetude) to signify membership of the syntactic category, reserving 'predicate' for signifying actual performance of the predicative role.[11] The distinction is important, because an expression which is capable of playing a predicative role, and is thus a predicable, may occur in a given proposition without actually playing the role. Thus in 'No scholars of Girton are boys' the word 'boys' is not being predicated of anything or anyone, although in 'Hilary and Vivian are boys' it is so predicated.

As well as using the description 'real' to make the contrast with 'merely logical' predicates, Kant talks of a 'determining predicate'. A determining predicate is one which, in Mill's terms, enlarges the connotation of a word. Thus the connotation of 'vixen' is larger than that of 'fox' because it includes the added determination 'female', and the connotation of 'square' is larger than that of 'rectangle' because it includes the added determination 'equilateral'. In 'This fox is female', 'female' is used as a determining predicate, but in 'This square is equilateral' 'equilateral' is not so used. But, as we have seen, words like 'boys' or 'female' or 'equilateral' can be used as determining predicates in some propositions although in other propositions they are, in Kant's terminology, 'merely logical' predicates. This, however, is a distinction between predicates, not predicables. It is a distinction between the roles that expressions actually play in particular propositions. What is significant about 'exist' is that it can never play the role of determining predicate in any proposition. Whereas 'boys' and 'female' are 'equilateral'

---

[10] An importance not always sufficiently appreciated: see Geach's review of Strawson's *Subject and Predicate* in *The Times Literary Supplement*, 28 February 1975.

[11] Geach, *Reference and Generality*, § 18.

are all determining *predicables*, 'exist' is a merely logical *predicable*. The distinction Kant needs is one between syntactic categories, not between actual roles. We may perhaps see some faint recognition of this point in Kant's remark that 'being' is not 'a concept which *could* be added to the concept of a thing'.[12]

'Exist', then, is not a determining predicable. But neither, it may be objected, are 'self-identical' and 'either square or not square' and many others. Non-determining predicables are those predicables which can be regarded as signifying properties essential to everything. The fact that an expression is not a determining predicable does not show that it is not a predicable at all. It is misleading for Kant to deny that 'exist' is a real predicable, just because it is not a determining predicable.

We remarked earlier, in discussing Hume, that where an expression, if it stands for anything, stands for a property which is essential to everything, it looks suspiciously like an expression which does not stand for any real property at all. Doubts have indeed been raised about the claim that self-identity is a universal property,[13] although it is a candidate for this role which has been much favoured by logicians. But it is more difficult to dismiss the claim of tautological expressions like 'either square or not square' or 'weighs more than a ton if it weighs more than a ton' to be truly predicable of everything. Such expressions are, however, essentially compound: they owe their tautological character to the truth-functions which occur in them, which yield predicables only when compounded with simpler predicables like '— is square' or '— weighs more than a ton'. It is difficult to imagine how a simple predicable could be capable of being truly predicated of everything.[14] If existence is to count as a property essential to everything, it seems necessary to suppose that '— exist', like '— weighs more than a ton if it weighs more than a ton', is a complex predicable. What then are the simpler components out of which it is compounded? If no such components can be found, we are left with a difficulty. The notion of a simple predicable which signi-

---

[12] *Critique of Pure Reason*, Eng. tr. by N. Kemp Smith, 1963, B 626 (my italics).

[13] See L. Wittgenstein, *Tractatus Logico-Philosophicus*, tr. D. F. Pears and B. F. McGuinness, 5.534, and see below, Ch. III, p. 77, n. 34.

[14] This claim is argued for at somewhat greater length in Ch. XI, below, pp. 284 ff.

fies something essential to everything is a very dubious one. Are there many such predicables? If so how do we learn the differences between them?

Kant's reasons for classifying '— exist' as a merely logical, i.e. a non-determining, predicable would require supplementation along the lines we have been suggesting. By themselves they fail to be conclusive.

5. *Kant's explanation of 'being' in terms of 'positing'*

Kant has, however, a more positive account of being, which is worth examining. It is couched in terms of 'positing'. Positing is what is done in affirmations of existence. 'Being', he says, 'is merely the positing of a thing or of certain determinations [as existing] in themselves.'[15] This seems to present 'the positing of a thing' and 'the positing of certain determinations in themselves' as alternative descriptions of a single procedure. Positing certain determinations in themselves is contrasted with positing a predicate (which is the same as 'certain determinations') *in its relation* to the subject'. To say 'Some Persian philosopher is a specialist in logic' posits the determination 'specialist in logic' in relation to some Persian philosopher: 'Some Persian philosopher is (or exists)' posits the determination 'Persian philosopher' in itself; or, alternatively, posits a thing.

It is commonly objected against Kant, as against Leibniz, that the only form of proposition he considered was the subject-predicate form.[16] If by subject-predicate propositions we understand only singular propositions, i.e. propositions in which a predicate is attached to a proper name, this objection cannot be sustained. Kant of course assumes that propositions like 'A triangle has three angles' should be given a subject-predicate analysis: he makes this assumption in the passage we are considering. But his analysis of these propositions, as far as it is explicit, assimilates them to the type of proposition which the quantified formulae of modern logic aim to represent. Only so can we make sense of the pervasive appearance of the word 'posit' in this discussion. So far from considering only subject-predicate propositions, in the sense of singular proposititions,

---
[15] B 626. Kemp Smith places a comma after the word 'determinations', but there is no justification for this in the German; nor is there anything in the German corresponding to the words 'as existing'.

[16] Cf. S. Körner, *Kant*, 1955, pp. 22 ff.

to the exclusion of existential propositions, it could be maintained that Kant (following Leibniz) considered only existential propositions and their denials and neglected genuine subject-predicate propositions altogether.

Some support for this view can be found from Russell's account of Leibniz's 'division of propositions into two classes'.[17] This is odd, when one considers that it was Russell, in this book, who first popularized the belief that Leibniz's errors were the result of his failure to consider any form of proposition other than the subject-predicate form. Russell tells us (ibid.) that 'contingent propositions, in Leibniz's system, are, speaking generally, such as assert actual existence'. The proviso 'speaking generally' is inserted to allow 'God exists' to be excepted from the general rule that all existential propositions are contingent. Leibniz makes no exceptions from the converse rule, that all contingent propositions are existential, strange though this may seem to us: 'so long as we do not assert actual existence, we are still in the realm of eternal truths' (ibid., p. 27); but 'as for the eternal truths, we must observe that at bottom they are all conditional' (ibid., p. 26). This applies as much to propositions about individuals *sub ratione possibilitatis* as to propositions about species, in virtue of the doctrine that all predicates other than existence must be included in the notion of the subject. Again, in virtue of the identity of indiscernibles, to assert something of a given subject is to assert it of whatever possesses the predicates which together make up the subject. Either, therefore, a proposition is existential, of the form $\Sigma x \phi x$, 'There is something which ϕ's', or it is universal and hypothetical, of the form $\Pi x C \phi x \psi x$, 'Whatever ϕ's, ψ's', which is, of course, the negation of the existential form $\Sigma x K \phi x N \psi x$, 'There is something which both ϕ's and does not ψ'. Russell maintains that Leibniz's distinction between necessary and contingent propositions corresponds 'to what is perhaps the most important classification of which propositions are capable' (ibid., p. 25), i.e. the classification into those which are existential and those which are not. But we might just as well have described the classification as separating affirmative existential propositions from negative ones,

[17] Bertrand Russell, *A Critical Exposition of the Philosophy of Leibniz*, p. 25; cf. the whole argument of pp. 8-30.

to which universally quantified propositions are equivalent. Non-existential propositions, including genuine subject-predicate ones, are ignored by Leibniz as completely as they are excluded by Quine from his 'canonical notation'.

This neglect of subject-predicate propositions, which I believe can be found in Kant as well as in Leibniz, is probably a consequence of the disrepute into which the Aristotelian doctrine of substance fell in the seventeenth century. Professor Anscombe complains that 'in modern times words like "man" which signify substances have been interpreted as signifying a complex of qualities'.[18] Hence Locke's despair of saying anything more about a substance divested of all its qualities than that it is 'a something, I know not what'. Leibniz in his criticism of this passage of Locke's *Essay* identifies a substance with the sum of its predicates, and ridicules Locke's surprise that nothing appears to remain when all the predicates of a substance have been taken away.[19] This takes for granted that there is no important distinction between substantial predicates like 'man' or 'dog' and accidental predicates like 'white' or 'barks'. Similarly modern logicians have attempted to reduce as many propositions as possible to the form 'There is an x such that

---

[18] G. E. M. Anscombe and P. T. Geach, *Three Philosophers*, p. 10. We may exemplify this by Kant's equation (see above, p. 26) of 'the positing of a thing' and 'the positing of certain determinations'. Professor Anscombe wishes to absolve Aristotle from any suspicion of having made this identification or of falling into a notorious trap which she believes stems from it. 'Because Aristotle distinguishes between substance and quality, those who take a predicate like 'man' to signify a complex of properties readily suppose him to be distinguishing between the being of a thing and the being of any attributes that it has. They then take the thing itself to have no attributes. It would be almost incredible, if it had not happened, to suppose that anyone could think it an argument to say: the ultimate subject of predication must be something without predicates; or that anyone who supposed this was Aristotle's view could do anything but reject it with contempt.' (ibid., p. 11.) Whether or not contempt is the appropriate attitude here, Professor Anscombe has clearly done an important service to the philosophy of substance by showing the absurdity of this famous paradox. It is less clear that she is correct in discharging Aristotle from any responsibility for the view. Speaking, not of substance, but of matter, and of matter precisely as 'the ultimate subject of predication' and for this reason considered as a candidate for the role of substance, he says: 'I call matter that which in itself is neither something nor so big nor anything else of the things by which being is determined. *For* it is something of which each of these is predicated.' (*Metaphysics* Z, 1029^a 20-22). I italicize 'For' to emphasize that Aristotle does seem to regard this as an argument: just what Professor Anscombe says 'would be incredible, if it had not happened'.

[19] *Nouveaux Essais*, in *Die Philosophischen Schriften*, 1960, pp. 201 f.

x is a dog and x is white and x barks'.[20] The view that substances are just complexes of qualities or predicates and the view that all propositions are at bottom assertions or denials of existence (positing or rejecting) are both symptoms of a mistake about the concept of identity. In an existentially quantified proposition with a conjunctive matrix, like the example just given, the repetition of the variable presupposes, e.g. that what is a dog is the same as what is white and as what barks. But the same what? Clearly, the same dog. 'What is a dog is the same white as what barks' is nonsense. It is substantival predicates which carry criteria of identity. Similarly it is the subject term in subject-predicate propositions which identifies what the proposition is about. Neglect of logical subjects and neglect of substantival predicates go together and are characteristic of philosophers of the seventeenth and eighteenth centuries. The existential interpretation of subject-predicate propositions is thus in harmony with other features of the systems of Leibniz and Kant, and there is much in their writings which betrays the unconscious assumption that this interpretation is correct.

Some disquiet may be felt at this point by a reader who bears in mind the aim of my argument in this chapter: the exposition of Kantian and other arguments for the thesis that existence is not a predicate. This thesis, when it is finally stated in the Fregean form which I set out in the next chapter, requires precisely that a sharp distinction be made between general, quantificationally expressible propositions, like 'Blue roses exist', and singular, genuinely subject-predicate propositions, like 'The Mediterranean is blue'. The importance of this distinction is a consequence of, or at least closely bound up with, the thesis that existence is not a predicate. It is my hope that this connection will be made clear at a later stage in the book. Is it not, therefore, question-begging to use this distinction, to take it for granted, in developing Kant's arguments for existence not being a predicate? If I interpret 'Blue roses exist' as equivalent to 'There is an x, such that x is a rose and x is blue', have I not already assumed what Kant is setting out to prove?

Against this charge I would defend myself as follows: Frege,

[20] Cf. Anscombe and Geach, *Three Philosophers*, p. 34.

I believe, and intend shortly to argue, gave a clear sense to the doctrine that Kant obscurely expressed (and then obscurely defended) in the sentence '*Being* is not a real predicate'. Frege's account of the concept of existence is the correct one. It uncovers the grammatical rules according to which existential propositions are actually used, and *were* actually used by Kant. Kant did not, in the way Frege did, know how the word 'exist' is used; but he did know, as we all do, how to use it. And in discussing it he of course used it and allied expressions, 'posit', 'actual', 'object', 'given', etc., whose use can only be fully understood in the light of what Frege and his successors have said. Since what they have said is, I maintain, right, Kant's use of the expressions can only be made sense of with its help. To proceed in this way is not anachronistic—it is the only way to make sense of what philosophers have said about existence, because it is the only way to make sense of existence. An appreciation of the importance of Frege's work may, however, be heightened by experience of the difficulties that beset philosophers such as Kant, and to a lesser extent Hume, in their stumbling search for the light which Frege eventually found.

If I am right in attributing to Kant the view that all propositions are either affirmatively or negatively existential, we can see how he might come to the view that existence is not a predicate (real or otherwise). To say that such and such a thing—a black swan for example,—exists is to posit the thing in question, to posit a black swan. To say that all swans are white, on the other hand, is to reject—the opposite of positing —swans that are not white. All assertion, on this view, is positing or rejecting, and the existential content of what is asserted has been moved to the act of positing or rejecting itself. Predicates (determinations) are what I posit: what I posit is a *black swan*, or blackness in relation to swanhood. That a black swan *exists* is already given in my positing; it has no need to reappear in what is posited.

We are now better able to understand the things Kant has to say about 'is' in the famous paragraph which begins: '*Being* is obviously not a real predicate'. This paragraph requires detailed examination.[21] He argues, in a way that we might well

---

[21] The paragraph in question is on B 626 f. Those readers who have little taste

KANT'S EXPLANATION... 31

regard as fallacious in the light of what was said in Chapter I about the copulative and existential senses of 'be', that, since 'is' in 'God is omnipotent' is not a predicate, it is not a predicate in 'God is' either. But for Kant there is no equivocation, since he believes that both occurrences of 'is' signalize 'positing'. To say 'God is omnipotent' is 'to posit the predicate *in its relation* to the subject'. To say 'God is' is 'to posit the subject in itself with all its predicates'. In the light of what we have said about positing, these interpretations appear tantamount to equating 'God is omnipotent' with 'There is an x such that both x is God and x is omnipotent' and 'God is' with 'There is an x such that x is God'. Kant's description of the first as 'positing the predicate *in its relation* to the subject' might well prompt the question 'What relation?'. A possible answer is 'The relation expressed by "There is an x such that both x is — and x is —"' or, symbolically, by $\Sigma x K$— x—x.' Given this interpretation of 'God is omnipotent', and subject-predicate propositions generally, it is clear that 'is' is not a predicate. A predicate is something which can fill the second blank in the formula 'There is an x such that both x is — and x is —'. In 'God is omnipotent' it is 'omnipotent', not 'is', which fills this blank.[22] In Kant's equivalent of 'God is' there is no such blank, because the filling of the first blank by the subject expression is sufficient to yield a complete proposition.

Kant elaborates on the description 'posit the subject in itself with all its predicates' by adding 'and indeed posit it as being an object that stands in relation to my concept'. Again we might ask 'What relation?', but perhaps we are told in the next sentence, 'The content of both must be one and the same'.

for, or have already had enough, exegesis may wish to skip the next few pages, and turn to § 7, on 'Plato's Beard'.

[22] If 'God is omnipotent' is thought of as having the same form as 'A triangle has three angles', positing the predicate *in its relation* to the subject might be thought of as asserting 'If anything is God, it is omnipotent'. Since this proposition is of the form $\Pi x C \phi x \psi x$ ($= N\Sigma x K \phi x N \psi x$), asserting it is not, strictly speaking, a case of 'positing' anything, but rather of 'rejecting'. But Kant (see below, Appendix B, pp. 334–7) thought of this proposition as conditionally asserting 'the existence of the predicate', perhaps as asserting something of the form $C\Sigma x \phi x \Sigma y \psi y$, although propositions of this form are at most entailed by, not equivalent to, propositions of the form $\Pi x C \phi x \psi x$. This may have led him to speak of it as 'positing the predicate *in its relation* to the subject'. If so, the relation in question would not be that expressed by $\Sigma x K$—x—x, as argued in the text, but that expressed by $\Pi x C$—x—x or perhaps $C\Sigma x$—$x \Sigma y$—y.

This suggests that the relation is that of correspondence: if my concept is the concept of a ϕ, the object itself must be a ϕ.[23] However, the whole enterprise is unhelpful. 'God is' is interpreted as 'There is an object corresponding to my concept of a God', which, apart from the gratuitous appropriation of the concept of a God to myself, says no more than 'There is a God'. The phrase 'an object corresponding to the concept of a ϕ' is a mere pleonasm for 'a ϕ'. Which is, in a sense, what Kant goes on to say, when he concludes that 'the real contains no more than the possible'.

Kant talks not only of 'positing [the subject] as an object', but of 'thinking its [the concept's] object (through the expression 'it is') as given absolutely'. This seems to mean that when I say 'It (the object of the concept) is' I mean that the object of the concept, say, *a letter from Simon*, is given absolutely. But this again is mere pleonasm. To say 'The object of the concept *a letter from Simon* is given absolutely' is simply to produce a blown-up version of 'A letter from Simon is given absolutely'. As for 'is given', it presumably gets its sense from '*Es gibt*' ('It gives') which is the regular German equivalent of 'There is': 'absolutely' is mere Kantian bluster.

6. *'The real contains no more than the possible'*

Next, and most famously, 'A hundred real thalers do not contain the least coin more than a hundred possible thalers'.[24] Kant immediately interprets this apophthegm: 'the latter signify the the concept, and the former the object and the positing of the

---

[23] I have argued elsewhere, in the last chapter of my book *What is Truth?*, (1976), that propositions of the form '*x* corresponds with *y*' are often to be analysed with the help of an existential quantifier binding two occurrences of a propositional or predicative variable. Thus 'The way you described him corresponds to the way I found him' comes out as 'For some ϕ, both you described him as being ϕ and I found him ϕ'. If my concept corresponds to the object, this is because, for some ϕ, both my concept is the concept of a ϕ and the object is ϕ. 'What Percy says corresponds to the facts' is analysable as 'For some p, both Percy says just that p and p'. Even correspondence as a perceptible phenomenon can be analysed in this way: 'This piece of paper with a corner torn off corresponds exactly with the fragment found in the murder victim's hand' can be paraphrased 'For some ϕ, part of boundary-line of this piece of paper is ϕ and part of the boundary line of the fragment found in the murder victim's hand is ϕ', where ϕ ranges over precise specifications of the shape of a line.

[24] The word 'coin' is a frill added by Kemp Smith. The English 'do not contain the least coin more' represents '*enthalten nicht das mindeste mehr*'.

object in itself'.²⁵ When he says that 'a hundred possible thalers' signifies 'the concept', he presumably means that we use this expression to talk about a hundred thalers existing in somebody's mind, or somebody's thought of a hundred thalers. This allows us to understand the apophthegm as saying that a hundred real thalers cannot contain the least bit more than what someone thinks of when he thinks of a hundred thalers. And this makes some sense. But Kant complicates matters by saying that 'a hundred real thalers' signifies, not only 'the object', i.e. a hundred thalers, but 'the positing of the object in itself'. Positing an object in itself, as we have seen, is asserting or judging that so and so is *tout court*, i.e. exists; so what we have here, on this interpretation, is the judgement, tacit or openly expressed, that a hundred thalers exist,²⁶ sc. in my bank account. The comparison now is not between a hundred thalers and what I think of when I think of a hundred thalers, but between judging that there are a hundred thalers, sc. in my bank account, and what I think of when I think of a hundred thalers. On this interpretation, what he is saying is that what I judge there are, when I judge that there are a hundred thalers in my bank account, must correspond exactly with what I think of when I entertain the thought of a hundred thalers in my bank account. And this too makes sense, because if what I judge to exist were not the same as what I originally thought of, the description of that thought could not have been correct. These two interpretations allow us to express Kant's thesis in general terms as follows: (i) If I am thinking of ϕs, any ϕs there may be must be just ϕs, neither more nor less, if they are to qualify as the correct specification of what I am thinking *of*; (ii) If I am entertaining the thought of ϕs, what I judge to exist, if I judge it to be the case that there are ϕs, must be precisely ϕs, neither more nor less, if what I judge to exist is indeed what I am thinking of. As Kant says, 'should the former (the real thalers) contain more than the latter (the possible thalers), my concept would not, in that case, express the whole object, and would not therefore be an adequate concept of it.'

But Kant's exposition of this thesis is calculated to confuse

---

[25] I amend Kemp Smith's translation, which omits anything corresponding to the German '*an sich selbst*' at this point.

[26] Cf. below, Appendix B, pp. 333 ff., where I discuss Kant's assimilation of 'things' and 'their existence' in an earlier passage.

almost anyone who tries to understand it. The more he says about it the worse it gets. If it can be said without undue anachronism, his thought in the few sentences that follow constitutes an almost Hegelian dialectic. Thesis: the real contains no more than the merely possible. Antithesis: but there is more in my financial resources when there are a hundred real thalers than when there is merely the concept of them (i.e. their possibility).[27] Antithesis: for the object, as it actually exists, is not analytically contained in my concept, but is added to my concept (which is a determination of my state) synthetically. Thesis: and yet the conceived hundred thalers are not themselves in the least increased through thus acquiring existence outside my concept.[28] The key to finding a synthesis is, I think, the recognition that by 'a hundred possible thalers', or 'the concept of them', or 'their possibility', Kant is referring to someone's thought of a hundred thalers—cf. the parenthetical gloss on 'my concept', '(which is a determination of my state)'. The remark 'the object, as it actually exists, is added to my concept synthetically', taken literally, is nonsense, since it is judgements which are analytic or synthetic, and objects cannot be 'contained' in or added to judgements or concepts. However, what Kant means to say is that there is no contradiction in saying that someone has thought of a ϕ, but there are no ϕs. The proposition that someone has thought of a ϕ and there *are* ϕs is accordingly synthetic. Similarly, if I am merely thinking of a hundred thalers in my bank account ('merely' signifying that the hundred thalers are not actually there), there is less in my account than there would be if the hundred thalers were really there (the adverb 'really' is less misleading than the adjective 'real'). And yet, if I think of a hundred thalers and there are a hundred thalers there, what really exists is precisely what I am thinking of, no more.

It would be possible to interpret Kant in an over-literal manner and expound his comments as the wildest nonsense. He talks about 'the concept' and 'the object' and seems to link the concept with the grammatical subject and the object with

[27] Kemp Smith's translation fails to bring out the repetition of the same word '*mehr*', in the antithesis, as was found in the thesis. The German reads: *Aber in meinem Vermögenzustande ist mehr bei hundert wirklichen Talern, als bei dem blossen Begriffe derselben (d.i. ihrer Möglichkeit).*

[28] The arrangement: thesis, antithesis, antithesis, thesis, is chiastic.

the grammatical predicate of an existential proposition: 'God' in 'God is' signifies the concept (possibility), 'is' the object (actuality). There is then a daunting prospect of finding that the addition of the object to the concept both does and does not add something to it: 'if I think a thing, nothing in the slightest is added to it (*kommt hinzu*) if I add (*hinzusetze*) "This thing is". Otherwise', he continues, 'it would not be exactly the same thing that exists, but something more. . . .' *What* exists must be the same as *what* I think, but its existence must be something more than my thinking it, since the judgement that it exists is synthetic; i.e., the predicate, though unreal, adds something to the subject.

This ungenerous manner of interpreting Kant can, I think, be avoided if we note two sources of confusion in his exposition. One is that his talk of 'possible' thalers or 'the concept' of thalers, i.e. thalers existing in someone's mind, is systematically misleading. The word 'possible' shares this systematically misleading character with a host of adjectives and adjectival phrases: 'imaginary', 'fictitious', 'intentional', 'existing in the mind', 'existing only on the conceptual level'. I shall have a good deal to say about this variety of systematic ambiguity in the chapter 'Fictional Characters and Possible Worlds' (Ch. X, § 9). Suffice it to say now that darkness comes over us as soon as we think of the contrast between possible (or imaginary) thalers and real thalers as analogous to the contrast between Prussian thalers and Austrian thalers. Anselm too had been misled by such an analogy when he contrasted something than which no greater could be conceived *existing only in the understanding* with something than which no greater could be conceived *existing in reality as well as in the understanding*. Existing in reality and existing in the understanding are no more two ways of existing than real leather and artificial leather are two sorts of leather. When Kant talks of possible thalers he must be understood as talking about *someone thinking* of thalers, or *someone thinking that* there are thalers somewhere. As long as we understand him this way we shall avoid one of the traps his style of language prepares for us.

The other trap, the other source of confusion, lies in Kant's use of pronouns and relative clauses. He says, 'if I think a thing, nothing in the slightest is added to *it* if I add "This thing is"'. If this were not so, he adds, 'it would not be exactly the same thing *that exists*'. I have expressed Kant's thesis as the thesis that *what* exists must be the same as *what* I think. Now the use of pronouns and relative clauses and the language of identity is constantly liable to mislead people into thinking that we are dealing with *objects*.[29] It is felt, however obscurely, that every use of a 'what-clause' involves commitment to some sort of 'entity'. But these confusions can be to some extent dispelled by substituting for these ordinary language expressions the logician's apparatus of quantifiers and variables belonging to appropriate syntactic categories. 'What I think of is the same as (corresponds to) what exists' looks like 'What I put into the bottle is the same as what I take out'. But the latter is represented by 'For some x, both I put x into the bottle and I take x out', whereas the former is represented by 'For some ϕ, both I am thinking of ϕs and there are ϕs'.[30] This will in fact be the case if, for example, I am thinking of blue roses and there are blue roses, or if I am thinking of an omnipotent God and there is an omnipotent God. There is no need to posit some blue roses which mysteriously preserve their identity throughout the passage from possibility to actuality, across the gulf (than which no greater could be conceived) from *esse in intellectu* to *esse in re*.

These confusions averted, Kant's argument from the fact that the real contains no more than the possible may be reconstructed in some such way as this: what we think of (our concepts) and what actually exist (objects) are quite different. They may or may not correspond to each other. But their correspondence, if they do correspond, is a matter of the determinations, the predicables, that specify the content of our thought being exactly the same as those which determine and can be truly predicated of what in fact exists. Since our thought is specified by these determinations and is independent of the existence of any object corresponding to it, the determinations, the predicables, that have to specify both the content of thought and the object which corresponds to it, if anything

---

[29] Pronouns amount to quantification, and quantification, so it is said, brings 'ontological commitment'. Chs. VI and VII below are devoted to the disentangling of the conceptual knots that are involved here.

[30] Cf. my remarks about correspondence in n. 23, p. 32.

does, cannot themselves include existence. Again, it is one thing to entertain the thought of some object—a blue rose, for instance—and quite another thing to judge that such an object exists. But it must be possible for me to pass from merely thinking of an object to actually judging that there *is* such an object. What I am thinking of and what I later come to believe exists is completely specified by some predicable or set of predicables: as we might say, the substitutable expressions for ϕ in ' I used to entertain the thought of ϕs, but now I believe there are ϕs' must be predicables. But since my thought of ϕs was quite independent of any belief in the existence of ϕs, 'exists' itself cannot occur as one of the predicables substitutable for 'ϕ' in this context. Existence, as Kant would say, belongs to the positing of ϕs as things in themselves, not to what is posited. This is why it cannot be, as he would say, 'a real predicate'.

Kant's argument, perhaps, remains obscure. We feel that there is sense in what he says, but the attempt to make it exact has limited success. This is why Kant's claim that existence is not a real predicate is so much less effective than the Fregean doctrine, which we are shortly to examine.

7. *Plato's Beard*

There is one more classical argument to show that existence is not a predicate which deserves consideration. This argument, because it is foreshadowed by puzzles that Plato draws attention to in the *Sophist* and elsewhere, has been called by Quine 'Plato's Beard'.[31] Its ancestry may in fact go back beyond Plato to Parmenides' *Way of Truth*. Suppose I say, exasperated after hunting through advertisements and telephoning motor dealers, 'The car we need doesn't exist'. On the face of it, this proposition looks like many others we could utter, e.g. 'The car we bought doesn't use much petrol'. This latter proposition might be said to be about something, namely, the car we bought. If we never bought a car, the status of the sentence is distinctly odd. How could it be true that the car we bought doesn't use much petrol if we never bought a car? How could it even be false? The car we bought must exist if we are to say something about it. What, then, of the car we need? Does *it* have to exist

---

[31] Cf. W. V. Quine, 'On What There Is', in *From a Logical Point of View*, 1963, p. 2.

if we are to say anything about it? In particular, does it have to exist if we are to say of it, meaningfully, that it doesn't exist? Wouldn't this be to condemn the proposition as self-contradictory?

Actually, the expression 'The car we need' behaves differently from 'The car we bought' even if 'doesn't use much petrol' is appended to it (see below, Ch. IX, § 3). The car we need doesn't have to exist even for us to be able to say truly that it doesn't use much petrol. Perhaps there are no cars whose petrol consumption is small enough to meet our needs. If, however, we substitute 'The car we bought' for 'The car we need' in 'The car we need doesn't exist', the sentence we produce is not one for which we can readily imagine a use. If we were to add the words 'any longer', it would become intelligible, but that would involve introducing the topic of temporal existence rather earlier in this book than is intended (see below, Ch. V).

In fact, definite descriptions like 'The car we bought' or 'The king of France' do not combine very easily with 'exists' or 'does not exist'. (Russell's ear for English idiom let him down when he thought that 'The king of France exists' was a sentence for which it was necessary to lay down a meaning.) More natural is the construction which attaches 'exist' or 'do not exist' to nouns in the plural without the definite article. 'Aristocratic Australians exist' is readily intelligible, and a use for it, or its negation, can be imagined without difficulty. The problem can be raised more simply with this example. 'Aristocratic Australians drink gin' might be said to be about aristocratic Australians, and the same holds for 'Aristocratic Australians don't drink gin'. If there are no Australian aristocrats the status of both these sentences is odd. How could it be true that aristocratic Australians don't drink gin if there are no Australian aristocrats?[32] So what of the sentence 'Aristocratic Australians don't exist'? Can this be true only if there are Australian aristocrats? If so, can it ever be true, can it ever

[32] Alvin Plantinga has objected that it is true that dragons do not have fur despite the fact that there are no dragons (see, *God and Other Minds*, 1967, p. 40). But in the same way that it is true that dragons do not have fur it is also true that there are dragons (see below, Ch. X, § 3). Plantinga's other example 'Dragons are beasts of fable' was discussed by me in 'Baier on the Equivocal Character of "Exists" ', *Mind*, 78, 1969, pp 222 ff. See also Jonathan Barnes, *The Ontological Argument*, 1972, pp. 42 f. Barnes' point (i) is answered in my Ch. V, his point (ii) in Ch. X, his point (iii) in Chs. VI and VII.

escape from being self-contradictory? The existence of aristocratic Australians begins to look like a logical necessity. And what is true of them would be true of any class we liked to specify. It can be stated quite generally: for any A, the proposition that A's exist and the proposition that A's don't exist can be true only if there are A's. All propositions of the form 'A's don't exist' are, on this showing, self-contradictory; and all propositions of the form 'A's exist' are accordingly tautological.

The self-contradictions (and tautologies) involved are, however, of a peculiar character. Suppose I say 'This equilateral triangle is scalene'. We recognize this as being self-contradictory because we see that it entails two propositions each of which is the contradictory of the other: 'Every side of this triangle is equal to every other' and 'Not every side of this triangle is equal to every other'. But nothing is amiss with either of *these* propositions. Each can, in appropriate circumstances, be true. The first can truly be asserted of every equilateral triangle and the second of every isosceles and every scalene triangle. Not so with 'Aristocratic Australians do not exist', in the view that what this says is self-contradictory. If we hold that this is self-contradictory, it will be because we see it too as entailing two propositions each of which is the contradictory of the other. But what will these propositions be? Presumably, 'Aristocratic Australians do not exist' and 'Aristocratic Australians exist'. But we cannot say that nothing is amiss with either of these propositions—in the view we are considering. There are, on this view, no appropriate circumstances in which the first could be true, and all circumstances are appropriate to the truth of the second. Moreover, the first just *is* the proposition said to be self-contradictory. If any proposition p is recognized as self-contradictory it will normally be because, for some proposition q, we see that it entails both q and 'not-q'. The self-contradictory character of p will be shown in the fact that q is entailed as well as 'not-q'. But in this case 'not-q' *is* the proposition whose self-contradictoriness is claimed. It looks as though the disease which, in this view, negative existential propositions contract is bound to have complications.

That some disease or other would attack all negative existential propositions if the account of them we have been considering were correct constitutes a *reductio ad absurdum* of the account in question. We need not waste more time in attempting a precise diagnosis of the disease, because it is an obvious fact that some negative existential propositions are healthy. 'Aristocratic Australians don't exist' is not in the least self-contradictory, even if it is false. What was wrong was the view that it could only be true if there were Australian aristocrats, that it was in this respect similar to propositions like 'Aristocratic Australians don't drink gin'.[33] Kant, as we have seen, made a sharp distinction between affirmative existential propositions like 'Aristocratic Australians exist' and propositions like 'Aristocratic Australians drink gin'. 'Exist' for him was not a real predicate like 'drink gin'. Plato's Beard forces us to make a similar distinction in the case of the negations of these propositions, although the emphasis is on the 'grammatical' subject of the propositions rather than the 'grammatical' predicates. 'Aristocratic Australians don't drink gin' says something about Australian aristocrats, whereas we get into difficulties if we suppose that anything is said about Australian aristrocrats by 'Aristrocratic Australians don't exist'. But it makes no difference whether we say that in this latter proposition 'Aristocratic Australians' is not a 'real' subject or whether we say that 'don't exist' is not a 'real' predicate. 'Subject' and 'predicate' are correlative terms, and if there is no predicate in a proposition there can be no subject either.[34] Nor does it make any difference whether it is 'exist' or 'don't exist' that we say is not a 'real' predicate. We learn the use of a concept simultaneously with the use of its negation: indeed an expression and its negation express the same concept. There is not one concept of light and another concept of dark: *eadem est scientia oppositorum*, as medieval Aristotelians put it. And, finally, it makes no difference whether we say that existence is not a real, but merely a logical, predicate, or that 'exist' is not a logical, but merely a grammatical, predicate. Kant used

---

[33] For a comment on the logical form of this proposition, see below, Ch. VI, p. 155, n. 5.

[34] On the strict interpretation of 'predicate', if this is understood as 'first-level predicate', the converse of this is true, i.e., there can be no predicate in a proposition if there is no subject. This is the interpretation which requires that we use another word like 'predicable' to do the work forbidden to 'predicate'. See § 4 of this chapter.

the word 'logical' in a dismissive way to refer to the same superficial type of classification which Russell and others have referred to as 'grammatical'. It is a measure of the change of attitude amongst philosophers towards logic that since the work of Frege and Russell 'logical' could not be used to signify the trivial and unimportant in contradistinction to the 'real'. Similarly, since Wittgenstein and Chomsky have restored grammar to the forefront of intellectual activity, 'grammatical' has become an unsuitable word for the rejection of some feature as insignificant. The difference should now perhaps be stated in terms of the distinction between 'surface' and 'depth' grammar. It is at the deeper levels of grammar that 'exist' is being said not to be a predicate. But more precise terminology is available, and for this we must turn to Frege.

III
Frege's Doctrine of Existence

1. *Frege's account of statements of number*

The light which Frege throws on the notion of existence is reflected from the concept of number, which it is his principal concern to illuminate. The first systematic exposition which he gave of his theory of number is found in *Die Grundlagen der Arithmetik*, which appeared in 1884.[1] The first part of this book is devoted to demonstrating that absurd consequences can be drawn from commonly held opinions about number, and in particular from the view that numbers are properties of objects. The sort of proposition which Frege regards as basic to our understanding of number are answers to questions of the form 'How many *A*'s are there?'. These could easily be misconstrued as ascribing a property to an object or group of objects. 'There are twelve signs of the Zodiac' looks superficially as though it were of the same form as 'There are yellow lilies of the valley'. 'Venus has 0 moons' resembles 'Saturn has very large moons'. 'The King's carriage is drawn by four horses' looks the same as 'The King's carriage is drawn by thoroughbred horses'. 'Venus has 0 moons' and 'The King's carriage is drawn by four horses' express possible answers to questions of the form 'How many *A*'s are there?', although not perhaps the most natural way of expressing such answers. The most natural way is, no doubt, as in the first example, to use a sentence beginning with 'There is' or 'There are'; and here the structure of the sentence is ambiguous even on the superficial level. Does 'There are twelve signs of the Zodiac' split up thus: 'There

---

[1] Published with Eng. tr. by J. L. Austin *en face* as *The Foundations of Arithmetic*, 1952.

are / twelve signs of the Zodiac', as does 'There are / yellow lilies of the valley', or like this: 'There are twelve / signs of the Zodiac'? The latter is suggested by the fact that 'There are twelve of them' is a possible transformation of 'There are twelve signs of the Zodiac', whereas 'There are yellow of them' cannot similarly be derived from 'There are yellow lilies of the valley'. 'Twelve', though occupying the same position in a sentence as an adjective, is not felt in this sentence to be entirely adjectival. In the propositions about the King's carriage, however, the distinction between the role of 'four' and 'thoroughbred' is less easy to perceive at the superficial level. Frege observes (§ 52) that we can even put both words together with 'horses' to produce the phrase 'four thoroughbred horses'—a construction which, as he puts it, 'fosters the illusion that "four" modifies the concept "thoroughbred horse" in just the same way as "thoroughbred" modifies the concept "horse"'.

Having satisfied himself that number is not a property of objects, he still needs to answer the question, What is that of which we assert something when we make a statement of number? His answer, in the *Grundlagen*, is that number statements ascribe properties to concepts.

While looking at one and the same external phenomenon, I can say with equal truth both 'It is a[2] copse' and 'It is five trees', or both 'Here are four companies' and 'Here are 500 men'. Now what changes here from one judgement to the other is neither any individual object, nor the whole, the agglomeration of them, but rather my terminology. But that itself is only a sign that one concept has been substituted for another. This suggests as the answer to the first of the questions left open in our last paragraph, that the content of a statement of number is an assertion about a concept. (§ 46)

Frege's next argument to show that this is indeed the correct answer to his question makes use of the example 'Venus has 0 moons'. If I say this, there 'simply does not exist any moon or agglomeration of moons for anything to be asserted of; but what happens is that a property is assigned to the *concept* "moon of Venus", namely that of including nothing under it'. Frege is here invoking a version of Plato's Beard. If we regard the number 'one' as a property that can be ascribed to an object (to any object) and numbers greater than one as properties

[2] German uses the same word for 'one' and for the indefinite article.

which can be ascribed to agglomerations of objects, the number 'nought' will have to be regarded as ascribable to non-existent objects. But to ascribe something to a non-existent object is to ascribe it to nothing at all, and to ascribe something to nothing at all is not to ascribe it to anything. Judgements ascribing the number 'nought', in this view, just could not be made, just as, according to an argument of Plato's,[3] there could be no such thing as false judgement.

2. *Geach's criterion for predicables and Prior's criterion for predicates*

In Frege's view, then, 'Venus has 0 moons' is a proposition in which a property is ascribed to a concept. This distinction between ascribing properties to objects and ascribing them to concepts was anticipated by a distinction which Aristotle drew between general propositions, like 'No man is just', and singular propositions, like 'Aristides is just'.[4] Aristotle's distinction has been developed by Geach and Prior. The similarity between 'Venus has 0 moons' and 'No man is just' is closer than might appear at first sight. We may wonder, for a start, why Frege used the somewhat unnatural sentence 'Venus has 0 moons' as his example, rather than 'Venus has no moon'. No doubt his reason was that he wished to emphasize that what we have here is an answer to the number question 'How many moons has Venus?'. Most of the possible answers to this question are expressible by a numeral. By using the numeral '0', therefore, he shows how this proposition is covered by his thesis about statements of number more clearly than he would have done by using the word 'no'. Frege in fact makes no difference between '0' and 'no' in this context. He would not even have allowed 'Venus has no moon' and 'Venus has 0 moons' to be related as *definiens* and *definiendum*: they are too close for that. In the first paragraph of the next chapter he writes 'It is tempting to define 0 by saying that the number 0 belongs to a concept if no object falls under it. But this seems to amount to replacing 0 by "no", which means the same'. (§ 55). We need not hesitate, therefore, to attribute to him the view that

---

[3] *Theaetetus* 188-9, where he argues that if to judge falsely is to judge what is not, it is to judge nothing, which is not to judge anything at all; so that there is no such thing as false judgement. See below, Appendix A, pp. 327 f.

[4] See *De Interpretatione*, Ch. 7.

in 'Venus has no moon', just as much as in 'Venus has 0 moons', a property is assigned to the concept 'moon of Venus'.

'Venus has no moon' can be rephrased as 'No moon belongs to Venus', which is explicitly of the form of an Aristotelian categorical. Aristotle saw that such propositions—propositions like 'No man is just'—behave differently under negation from propositions like 'Aristides is just'. The negation of the latter is equivalent to 'Aristides is unjust', which is obtained by negating its predicate.[5] In the case of 'Aristides' there is no difference between 'Aristides is unjust' and ' It is not the case that Aristides is just', between negating the predicate and negating the proposition as a whole. In the case of 'No man', however, the negation of the predicate produces 'No man is unjust', whereas the negation of the proposition as a whole produces 'It is not the case that no man is just'. The former is obviously false, whereas even the most obstinate Calvinist believer in the total depravity of the human race would have to admit that the latter is true, even if verified only by the justice of Christ.

This difference between general and singular propositions can be explained in the light of doctrines propounded by Geach and Prior. Geach's doctrine concerns syntactic categories, the category of names and that of predicables. A 'predicable', as we have seen, is an expression which can be used as a predicate, even though in any given proposition it may not be being so used. Predicables can be negated. Like 'just' and 'unjust' they come in contradictory pairs.[6] No name, however, can significantly be negated. 'Not Aristides' is not a syntactically coherent string of expressions. 'Unjust' can be defined as that predicable which is true of a subject if, and only if, the result of predicating 'just' of that subject is false. But there is no name which can be defined as that which, if attached to a given predicable, produces a true proposition if, and only if, the proposition which results from attaching 'Aristides' to that predicable is

---

[5] I am neglecting the fact that it is possible for a person, an idiot, for instance, to be neither just nor unjust. The reader, if he likes, may take me to be stipulating a new meaning for 'unjust', as the contradictory of 'just'. Perfect contradictories are hard to come by in ordinary language. An old-fashioned example would be 'covered', to describe someone wearing a hat or a cap, as opposed contradictorily to 'uncovered'.

[6] See above, Ch. II, p. 24; and cf. *Reference and Generality*, § 27; cf. also Geach's more recent remarks in 'Names and Identity', in *Mind and Language*, ed. S. Guttenplan, 1975, pp. 143 ff.

false. However much Themistocles may be opposed to Aristides, it cannot be said that a proposition of the form 'Themistocles ϕ's' is true if, and only if, the corresponding proposition of the form 'Aristides ϕ's' is false. Themistocles and Aristides are, after all, both men.

Following points made by Prior, we can generalize this thesis to take account of the fact that it applies, not only to negation, but to all operators on propositions. The proposition 'People say that Aristides is just' is constituted by attaching the proposition 'Aristides is just' to the operator 'People say that—'. Just as 'unjust' was defined as the predicable which is true of a subject if, and only if, the result of predicating 'just' of that subject is false, so 'allegedly just' can be defined as the predicable which is true of a subject if, and only if, the proposition which results from first predicating 'just' of that subject and then attaching the proposition thus formed to the operator 'People say that —' is true. It is not possible, however, to introduce a complex name 'Allegedly Aristides' by a similar method. (If 'Allegedly Aristides' were a name, 'Allegedly Aristides is just' and 'Allegedly Aristides is unjust' would be contradictories.) In general, a complex predicable may be formed by attaching any operator which forms propositions out of propositions to a relatively simple predicable, whereas it is not possible to form complex names in this, or any other way.

We have so far been talking about the difference between names and predicables, two syntactic categories defined by the roles their members are *capable* of playing. To be a predicate, or to name something, is *actually* to perform a role in language. We need the term 'predicable' as well as 'predicate' because not every meaningful use of an expression which *can* serve as a predicate is a case of its *actually* being predicated of something. We have noted Geach's rule for determining whether an expression is a predicable: can a further predicable be formed such that the result of predicating it of something is equivalent to the negation of the result of predicating the original predicable of that thing? From Prior we obtain an analogous rule for determining whether a predicable is actually being predicated of something in a given proposition: is the proposition formed by substituting for the predicable its own contradictory equivalent to the negation of the original proposition? Thus in 'Aristides is just' the predicable '— is just' is actually predicated of something, because the proposition formed by substituting for it its contradictory, '— is unjust', is equivalent to 'It is not the case that Aristides is just'. But in 'No man is just' the predicable '— is just' is not being actually predicated of anything, because the proposition formed by substituting '— is unjust' for it is not equivalent to 'It is not the case that no man is just'.

Prior's rule does not apply only to negation. An expression is actually being used as a predicate in a proposition if, and only if, the result of substituting for it the complex expression formed from the original expression and some operator on propositions is equivalent to the result of attaching the original proposition to this same operator. Thus '— is just' is shown to be actually predicated of a subject in 'Aristides is just' by the fact that the result of attaching '— has to be just' to 'Aristides is the same as the result of attaching 'Aristides is just' to 'Necessarily —'. In 'No man is just', on the other hand, '— is just' is not so predicated, since attaching '— has to be just' to 'No man' does not produce the same result as attaching 'No man is just' to 'Necessarily —'.

Similar arguments could be used to show that '— is just' is not predicated of every man in 'Every man is just' or of some man in 'Some man is just'. In these propositions '— is just' is a predicable but not a predicate.

A more striking consequence of Prior's rule is that in these propositions 'No man —', 'Every man —' and 'Some man —' are predicates—and therefore, wherever they occur, predicables. It is a sufficient, as well as a necessary, condition of an expression's being used as a predicate in a given proposition that the result of substituting for it the complex expression formed by attaching it to some operator on propositions is equivalent to the result of attaching that proposition to this operator. The relation of 'Some man —' to 'No man —' is the same as the relation of '— is unjust' to '— is just'. Just as the result of attaching 'Aristides' to '— is unjust' is the same as that of attaching 'Aristides is just' to 'It is not the case that —', so the result of attaching '— is just' to 'Some man —' is the same as that of attaching 'No man is unjust' to 'It is not the case that —'. And, of course, the result of attaching '— is just' to 'No man —' is the same as that of attaching 'Some man is just' to 'It is not the case that —'. We may say therefore that 'some man —' is a complex predicable formed out of 'No man —' and negation; or, more naturally, that 'No man —' is a complex predicable formed out of 'Some man —' and negation. In 'No man is just' the expressions 'No man —' and '— is just' are equally *predicables*, because each is capable of negation, as 'Aristides' and 'Themistocles' are not; but in this sentence it is only 'No man —' which is a *predicate*, i.e. which is actually being predicated of something.

Prior used the symbolism of brackets to state the criterion for something's being used as a genuine predicate. To say that in 'Aristides is just' the predicable '— is just' is being used as a genuine predicate is the same, for Prior, as saying that 'Aristides' is a genuine proper name, a Russellian proper name.[7] Frege had included definite descriptions, like 'The man who has been ostracized', in the class of proper names, so that '— is just' would in Frege's view have been used as a genuine predicate in 'The man who has been ostracized is just' as much as in 'Aristides is just'. But Russell would now allow this. Propositions incorporating definite descriptions admit, for Russell, of both internal and external negation—the definite descriptions can have either primary or secondary occurrence. Propositions formed by attaching a predicable to a genuine proper name do not, in Russell's view, allow room for the distinction between internal and external negation. Prior's symbolism provides a criterion for recognizing a genuine Russellian proper name. Prior writes: 'an expression is being used as a Russellian name only if, where "δ" is an expression that forms sentences from sentences and predicates from predicates, e.g. "Not", "allegedly" or "possibly", $(\delta\phi)N$ is indistinguishable in sense from $\delta(\phi N)$.'[8] Again,

---

[7] Russell and Prior both thought that the logical criteria for an expression's being a genuine proper name had epistemological consequences which would exclude 'Aristides', in its ordinary use, from this category. These consequences seemed, in the end, to leave only 'This', for Russell, and 'I' for Prior, in the category of genuine proper names. (Cf. W. Godfrey-Smith, 'Prior and Particulars', in *Philosophy*, 53, 1978, 335-42. I have criticized the argument by which Prior sought to draw these epistemological conclusions in 'Prior and Ontology', *Ratio*, 15, 1973, 299 f.)

[8] *Objects of Thought*, edd. P. T. Geach and A. J. P. Kenny, 1971, p. 150; NB that Prior here uses N instead of x to stand for proper names. He usually uses N to express negation; and N is used to express negation usually in this book, in particular at pp. 50 ff. For the meaninglessness of brackets in this context, cf. Geach in *Mind and Language*, ed. S. Guttenplan, p. 145.

using Vp as short for Cpp (and $V\phi x$ as short for $C\phi x\phi x$),
If x is a name in the Russellian sense, it makes no difference whether we mentally bracket this [the formula $V\phi x$] as $V(\phi x)$ and read it as 'If x ϕ's then x ϕ's', or bracket it as $(V\phi)x$ and read it as 'x ϕ's-if-it-ϕ's (or x does-not-ϕ-without-ϕing)'. But if we allow 'Not every man —' to count as a name, then when we substitute this for x we must read $V(\phi x)$ as 'If not every man ϕ's then not every man ϕ's', which is a logical law, but $(V\phi)x$ must be read as 'Not every man ϕ's-if-he-ϕ's', which is not a logical law and is even the contradictory of one.[9]

Prior is here using brackets to distinguish between (a) the result of first attaching a predicable ϕ to δ to form a complex predicable and then attaching some expression E to the complex predicable thus formed and (b) the result of first attaching E to ϕ to form a proposition and then attaching the proposition thus formed to δ. The fact that the resultant formulae are indistinguishable when E is a proper name is what shows that the E is a genuine name and the ϕ actually being predicated here of what E stands for. The brackets are in this case unnecessary. Where E is an expression like 'Not every man —', brackets became essential, if we insist on writing our formulae this way. The distinction between 'Aristides is just' and 'No man is just' can be expressed in the same way. Reading 'ϕ —' as '— is just, and 'δ —' as 'It is not the case that —' and N as 'Aristides', there is no difference between $(\delta\phi)N$ and $\delta(\phi N)$. Reading 'ϕ—' and 'δ —' as before but N as 'No man', we find it necessary to insist on the difference between $(\delta\phi)N$ and $\delta(\phi N)$. The former will be equivalent to 'No man is unjust', the latter to 'Some man is just'.

3. *The philosophical significance of logical notations*

It is worth while standing back a little from this argument of Prior's to get a good view of the role of brackets, and possible alternatives to them, in logical and mathematical symbolism. Brackets in logic, as in mathematics, serve to express distinctions of scope. The formula $(p \lor q)\&r$ needs to be distinguished from the formula $p \lor (q \& r)$, just as $(3 + 4) \times 5$ needs to be distinguished from $3 + (4 \times 5)$. But Łukasiewicz showed that distinctions of scope could be expressed by adopting as a universal rule the practice of writing symbols for functions to the left of symbols for their arguments. Thus in the Łukasiewicz (Polish)

---

[9] From 'Nonentities' in *Analytical Philosophy* (1st Series), ed. R. J. Butler, 1962, pp. 122 f.; reprinted in Prior's *Essays in Logic and Ethics*, 1976.

notation the above distinction can be expressed without brackets: $KApqr$ (or $\times+3,4,5$) needs no bracketing to distinguish it from $ApKqr$ ($+3\times 4, 5$), since the order of the function and argument-symbols has already distinguished the two formulae.[10] Similarly—and Russellian symbolism expresses this as well as Polish—what '$(N\phi)$ some man' tries to express can be adequately expressed by $\Sigma x N\phi x$, where x ranges over men, and what '$N(\phi$ some man)' tries to express can adequately be expressed by $N\Sigma x\phi x$. Brackets are no longer needed to make the required distinctions. Here, however, the alleged distinction between '$(N\phi)$ Aristides' and '$N(\phi$ Aristides)' ceases to be parallel to the distinction between '$(N\phi)$ some man' and '$N(\phi$ some man)', since there is no distinction to make. When it is said that what brackets express are distinctions of scope, what is meant is that they make clear to us *which* expressions are arguments to *which* expressions as functions. $(p \vee q) \mathbin{\&} r$ shows that p and q are arguments to the function $\vee$, and that the value of this function for these arguments together with r constitute the arguments for the further function $\&$. But, as we have said, Polish notation shows which expressions are arguments to which expressions as functions by always writing all arguments to the right of their functions. Thus, in $\Sigma x N\phi x$ ϕ — is argument to the function N —, and the value of this function for that argument, namely $N\varphi$ — is itself argument to the function Σx — x. '$(N\phi)$ some man' is a crazy way of expressing the same thing—crazy because in '$(N\phi)$ some man' ϕ — is argument to N — and is written to the right of it, but $N\phi$ — is argument to '— some man', though written to the left of it. Incompatible conventions are similarly observed in '$N(\phi$ some man)'. Again, if Prior has to use brackets to distinguish '$V(\phi$ not every man)' from '$(V\phi)$ not every man', this is a sign that by the Polish convention this order of writing V and ϕ and 'not every man' produces an ill-formed formula. If the expressions were written in correct Polish order we should have 'V not every man ϕ's' corresponding to the true proposition 'If not every man ϕ's, then not every man ϕ's', and 'Not every man $V\phi$'s' corresponding to the false proposition 'Not every man ϕ's-if-he-ϕ's'. The Polish symbolism

---

[10] It may help to read $KApqr$ as 'The conjunction of the alternation of p and q and r' and $ApKqr$ as 'The alternation of p and the conjunction of q and r', just as $\times+3,4,5$ is 'The product of the sum of 3 and 4 and 5' and $+3\times 4,5$ as 'The sum of 3 and the product of 4 and 5'.

for quantification of course produces just this result: $V N \Pi x \phi x$ is distinct from $N \Pi x V \phi x$. And in this, though not in its symbolism for binary truth-functions or dyadic predicates, Russellian symbolism is as economical and perspicuous as Polish. However, whereas '$N\phi$ some man' and '$V\phi$ not every man' are misleading modes of expression and need to be disambiguated by brackets only because they are misleading, '$N\phi$ Aristides' is not misleading and needs no disambiguation. Here 'Aristides' is argument to the function ϕ — and 'ϕ Aristides' to the function N —. No other arrangement is possible. 'Aristides' cannot be argument to the negation function, nor vice versa, nor can ϕ — be argument to 'Aristides' or N — argument to ϕ —.

It may be felt that the fact that the rules of a given calculus prevent a distinction from being made is of no significance for establishing a truth of philosophical logic. This is a mistake. The fact that left-right ordering can perform, as well as brackets can, the task of expressing scope distinctions, tells us something about scope distinctions. Wittgenstein makes the general point in the *Tractatus* (3.3421-3.441):

> A particular mode of signifying may be unimportant, but it is always important that it is a *possible* mode of signifying. And that is generally so in philosophy: again and again the individual case turns out to be unimportant, but the possibility of each individual case discloses something about the essence of the world.
>
> Definitions are rules for translating from one language into another. Any correct sign language must be translatable into any other in accordance with such rules: it is *this* that they all have in common.
>
> What signifies in a symbol is what is common to all the symbols that the rules of logical syntax allow us to substitute for it.
>
> For instance, we can express what is common to all notations for truth-functions in the following way: they have in common that, for example, the notation that uses '$\sim p$' ('not p') and '$p \vee q$' ('p or q') can *be substituted* for any of them.
>
> (This serves to characterize the way in which something general can be disclosed by the possibility of a specific notation.)

One might say, in accordance with Wittgenstein's remarks in 3.441, that what is common to all scope-indicating notations is that Łukasiewicz's left-right ordering notation can be substituted for any of them. What is wrong with the attempt to distinguish '$N(\phi$ Aristides$)$' from '$(N\phi)$ Aristides' is shown by the fact that the distinction cannot be made in Polish notation.

Perhaps it will be said: So much the worse for Polish

notation. This would be a shallow response. The differences which force us to use bracketing are inescapable differences. $(3 + 4) \times 5 \neq 3 + (4 \times 5)$. The truth-table for $(p \lor q) \& r$ is different from that for $p \lor (q \& r)$. These are not differences that can be denied. And these differences can be expressed in Polish notation. But the alleged difference between 'It is not the case that Aristides is just' and 'Aristides is unjust' can certainly be denied. It is a controversial philosophical thesis. We cannot be sure that the distinction between '$N(\phi$ Aristides$)$' and '$(N\phi)$ Aristides' is not a distinction without a difference. Moreover, the difference between $(3 + 4) \times 5$ and $3 + (4 \times 5)$ can be explained. It is a difference between the order in which certain operations are performed. We have here three numbers and two operators. The only difference between them is the order of the operations. The same is true in the truth-functional case, where we have three propositional variables and two truth-functions. The differences in the order of these arithmetical and logical operations, which is expressed by brackets, can perfectly well also be expressed by the left-right ordering of Polish notation. What the brackets purport to express in the case of '$N\phi$ Aristides' is quite different. What we have here are two operators and a name. But the operators, unlike '+' and '×', are of different categories: one forms propositions from names, the other forms propositions from propositions. This gives us no choice in the order of operations: the proposition 'ϕ Aristides' has to be formed first by the operation of ϕ on 'Aristides' in order for the operator N to have anything to operate on. If it is objected that N is an operator that can form predicates from predicates as well as propositions from propositions, we can ask in reply, how do we know that the operator which allegedly forms predicates from predicates is *the same* as the operator which forms propositions from propositions. The only reason we could have for supposing that we have the same operator N in '$(N\phi)$ Aristides' as we have in '$N(\phi$ Aristides$)$' is that the one is definitionally equivalent to the other. But this is what those who introduce bracketing here are concerned to deny. If they are right, the use of N here is equivocal and ought in a logically adequate language to be replaced by two distinct operators.[11] But then we should have no need of brackets.

[11] Cf. Wittgenstein, *Tractatus* 5.451.

PHILOSOPHICAL SIGNIFICANCE OF LOGICAL NOTATIONS 53

Prior then is surely right to regard expressions like '$N(\phi$ Aristides)' as being indistinguishable from expressions like '$(N\phi)$ Aristides', and right to regard their indistinguishability as a criterion for identifying expressions like 'Aristides' as Russellian names. His criterion is of immense value for clarifying our ideas about the role of predication, and it is for this reason that we have spent so much time on it in this chapter. But it has further implications, and I shall return to it at a later stage in my argument (Ch. V, § 7).

4. *The relevance of Prior's criterion to Frege's doctrine*

Prior's criterion for determining when a predicable is actually being used in a proposition as a predicate can, however, be set out without any reference to symbolism. He talks of our wanting to know of the component parts of propositions like 'Aristides is just' and 'No man is just' which is functor and which argument, which 'wraps round' which.[12] His instruction for answering this question is to see what happens when the proposition is subjected to a further operator or placed in a wider context. If the result of taking, say, '— is just' as context for 'Aristides' and combining it with the wider context 'It is not the case that —' to form the context '— is unjust' for 'Aristides', produces the same result as taking 'It is not the case that —' as context for the proposition 'Aristides is just', we know we were right to take '— is just' as the context (the function) for 'Aristides' (the argument). If, on the other hand, the result of taking '— is just' as context for 'No man' and combining it with the wider context 'It is not the case that —' to form the context '— is unjust' for 'No man' produces a different result from taking 'It is not the case that —' as context for the proposition 'No man is just', we know that we were wrong to take '— is just' as the context (the function) for 'No man' (the argument). We should have regarded 'No man' as being wrapped round 'is just', not vice versa. 'No man —' represents the function and '— is just' the argument. We might say that in this proposition 'No man —' is predicated of what 'is just' stands for,[13] although in 'Aristides is just' '— is just' is predicated of Aristides. The difference noted by Aristotle between

---

[12] In 'Is the Concept of Referential Opacity Really Necessary?', *Acta Philosophica Fennica*, 16, 1963, 195-6.

[13] Later in this chapter I will show that this way of speaking is misleading and has to give place to a different one.

propositions like 'Aristides is just' and propositions like 'No man is just' is now explained.

How does this tie up with Frege's doctrine that in number statements a property is ascribed to a concept, not to an object? Instead of 'No man is just' Frege would have preferred us to write 'The number of just men is 0' or 'Nothing is a just man'. In each of these versions, according to Frege, a property is being assigned to a concept. In the previous paragraph we suggested that in the proposition 'No man is just' the predicable 'No man —' might be said to be predicated of what the predicable '— is just' stands for. We might similarly say that in 'Nothing is a just man' the predicable 'Nothing —' is predicated of what '— is a just man' stands for. A concept, in Frege's logical theory, is precisely what a predicable stands for. In this terminology then 'Nothing is a just man' predicates something of the concept *just man*. So does 'The number of just men is 0', and any proposition which tells us what the number of just men is. Prior's criterion, interpreted as a way of determining what in a given proposition is predicated of what, together with Frege's understanding of 'concept', yields Frege's doctrine about number statements.

5. *Statements of number and statements of existence*

Having given his account of the structure of statements of number like 'Nothing is a just man', Frege moves swiftly to apply the same analysis to statements of existence. 'In this respect', he says, 'existence is analogous to number. Affirmation of existence is in fact nothing but denial of the number nought. Because existence is a property of concepts the ontological argument for the existence of God breaks down.' (§ 53.) The statement that existence is a property of concepts needs careful interpretation, as we shall see; but the statement that existence is analogous to number is easily justified. It might even have been strengthened: if existence as such can only be said to be *analogous* to number, *statements* of existence can surely be said to *be* statements of number. Statements of number are possible answers to questions of the form 'How many A's are there?' and answers to such questions are no less answers for being relatively vague. Nor do they fail to be answers because they are negative. In answering the question

'How many A's are there?' I need not produce one of the Natural Numbers. I may just say 'A lot', which is tantamount to saying 'The number of A's is not small', or 'A few', which is tantamount to saying 'The number of A's is not large'. If I say 'There are some A's', this is tantamount to saying 'The number of A's is not 0'. Instead of saying 'There are a lot of A's' I may say 'A's are numerous', and instead of saying 'There are some A's' I may say 'A's exist'. All these may be regarded as statements of number.

'Affirmation of existence is nothing but denial of the number nought.' So 'Just men exist' means the same as 'The number of just men is not nought', and both mean the same as 'Something is a just man'. 'Something is a just man' is the negation of 'Nothing is a just man'. As we have seen, 'Something —' and 'Nothing —' in these propositions are predicates, and as such they are contradictories, just as '— is just' and '— is unjust' are contradictories. We also established earlier (Ch. II, § 7) that a predicate and its contradictory are expressions of one and the same concept, where a concept is viewed, not in Frege's fashion, but as a capacity to make a certain sort of judgement. In this sense of concept, 'Something —' expresses the same concept as 'Nothing —'. If, therefore, the latter is used to ascribe a property to a concept, the former must be used in the same way. Immediately before the passage we have just quoted Frege says 'the proposition that there exists no rectangular equilateral rectilinear triangle does state a property of the concept "rectangular equilateral rectilinear triangle"; it assigns to it the number nought'. If a proposition of the form 'There exists no A' states a property of a concept, so must its contradictory 'There exists an A'. This argument of Frege's would be difficult to fault.

6. *The difference between* existing *and* being instantiated

But *what* property of the concept 'rectangular equilateral rectilinear triangle' does 'There exists a rectangular equilateral rectilinear triangle' state? When Frege says that 'existence is a property of concepts', he is open to misinterpretation. He tries, in the essay 'On Concept and Object',[14] to prevent this. He says

[14] *Translations from the Philosophical Writings of Gottlob Frege*, ed. Peter Geach and Max Black, pp. 48 ff.

that the sentence 'There is at least one square root of 4' expresses the same thought as the sentence 'The concept *square root of 4* is realized'. In the first sentence the words 'There is at least one' stand for the property that is being assigned to the concept: the words 'square root of 4' stand for the concept to which it is assigned. But in the second sentence the words 'The concept *square root of 4*' do not stand for this concept, or for any other—cf. 'The concept horse is not a concept' (ibid., p. 46). What they stand for is an object—necessarily, because in Frege's terminology the expression 'The concept *square root of four*' is a proper name. Nor do the words 'is realized' in the second sentence stand for the same concept that the words 'There is at least one' stand for in the first. The expression 'is realized' stands for a concept under which falls an object, namely the object referred to by the proper name 'The concept *square root of 4*'. Such concepts are called by Frege first-level concepts. The expression 'There is at least one' stands for a concept within which falls a concept, namely the concept which the expression 'square root of 4' stands for. Such concepts are called by Frege second-level concepts. The distinction between first- and second-level concepts is as much to be respected as that between concepts and objects.

So when Frege says that existence is a property of concepts he must not be understood to be countenancing sentences of the form 'The concept *A* exists'. To suppose this would be to invite the interpretation of negative existential propositions as asserting something of the form 'The concept *A* does not exist'. Frege cannot mean this. It would simply be a way of bringing back Plato's Beard. In a negative existential statement like 'There is no moon of Venus' the property of non-existence is assigned to a concept; but it is the words 'There is no' which assign the property, and the words 'moon of Venus' which stand for the concept to which it is assigned.

This is not quite what Frege says in the *Grundlagen* when he tells us what property a negative existential proposition assigns to a concept. In § 46 he says 'If I say "Venus has 0 moons", there simply does not exist any moon or agglomeration of moons for anything to be asserted of [This is Plato's Beard again]; but what happens is that a property is assigned to the *concept* "moon of Venus", namely that of including nothing under it'. This seems inconsistent with what he was to say later in 'On Concept and Object'. Something possesses the property of including nothing under it, presumably, if the predicate '— includes nothing under it' is truly predicable of it. But the form of words required to complete the predicate '— includes nothing under it' so that it forms a true proposition is not a predicable, but what Frege insists is a proper name, e.g. 'The concept *moon of Venus*'. In 'The concept *moon of Venus* includes nothing under it', therefore, a property is not assigned to a concept by the words '— includes nothing under it', but rather to an object. When Frege says that the property of including nothing under it is assigned to the concept 'moon of Venus', he is speaking inaccurately, by the standards of 'On Concept and Object'. This property could be assigned in this context only to the object named by 'The concept "moon of Venus"', not to the concept for which 'moon of Venus' stands.

Russell stated his very similar position by saying that 'existence is essentially a property of a propositional function'.[15] To this G. E. Moore objected[16] that when Russell said in this passage that 'it is of propositional functions that you can assert or deny existence' and that it is a fallacy to transfer 'to the individual that satisfies a propositional function a predicate which only applies to a propositional function', he was making a mistake. If what Russell said was taken literally, we should have to suppose that he thought that 'Some tame tigers exist' means the same as '"x is a tame tiger" exists'. And this is a valid objection to Russell's way of stating his position. For Russell would have no objection to saying that in 'The propositional function "x is a tame tiger" exists', just as in 'The propositional function "x is a tame tiger" is sometimes true', something is properly said to be predicated of a propositional function. The statement 'The propositional function "x is a tame tiger" is a propositional function' is true for Russell, as the statement 'The concept *horse* is a concept' is not true for Frege. For Frege no concept can be referred to or picked out by a form of words which begins 'The concept —'. So when Frege says that existence is a property of a concept he is not

---

[15] 'Lectures on the Philosophy of Logical Atomism' in *Logic and Knowledge*, ed. R. C. Marsh, 1966, pp. 232 ff.
[16] 'Is Existence a Predicate?' in *Logic and Language* (2nd Series), ed. A. G. N. Flew, 1961, pp. 90 f.

countenancing sentences of the form 'The concept *A* exists'. But when Russell says that existence is a property of a propositional function, he immediately adds 'It means that that propositional function is true in at least one instance.' He would have difficulty in resisting the inference that 'The propositional function "x is a man" is not true even in one instance' means the same as 'The propositional function "x is a man" does not exist'; and that again is Plato's Beard. Russell should have stuck to his own advice and given only a 'definition in use' of 'exist', indicating only which complete sentences about propositional functions mean the same as sentences containing the verb 'exist'. Sometimes he does this: 'To say that unicorns exist is simply to say that "(x is a unicorn) is possible"'.[17]

To return to Frege, the two sentences 'There is at least one square root of 4' and 'The concept *square root of 4* is realized' express the same thought, but how else are they related? Are we to think, as some writers have supposed,[18] that the second is capable in some way of elucidating the first? Was this Frege's view?

If we were to give a generous interpretation of § 46 of the *Grundlagen*, we should suppose that there too he was maintaining merely that the two sentences, 'Venus has 0 moons' and 'The concept "moon of Venus" has the property of including nothing under it', express the same thought. We may infer that an alternative paraphrase of 'There is at least one square root of 4' is 'The concept *square root of 4* has the property of including something under it'. What we have here is a proposition of the same form as 'Susan has the property of being married to someone', i.e. the form $\Sigma x \phi a x$. This may be abbreviated to 'Susan is married', which is of the form ψa, just as the proposition 'The concept *square root of 4* has the property of including something under it' may be abbreviated to 'The concept *square root of 4* is realized'. But the abbreviations should not make us overlook the fact that the same propositions can be

---

[17] 'Logical Atomism', p. 233.
[18] e.g. J. L. Mackie and W. Bednarowski in 'The Riddle of Existence', *Proceedings of the Aristotelian Society*, Supp. Vol. 50, 1976. Cf. P. F. Strawson's 'two models' for interpreting sentences like 'King Arthur never existed', *Freedom and Resentment*, 1965, p. 191, and Milton K. Munitz, *Existence and Logic*, 1974, pp. 86 ff., who wishes to distinguish *instantiation* (which $\Sigma x - x$ expresses) from *existence (wirklichkeit)*.

analysed *either* as attaching the first-level predicables '— is married' (= '— has the property of being married to someone') and '— is realized' (= '— has the property of including something under it') to 'Susan' and 'The concept *square root of 4*', respectively, *or* as attaching the second-level predicables '— someone' and '— something' to the first-level predicables 'Susan has the property of being married to —' (= '— is married to Susan') and 'The concept *square root of 4* has the property of including — under it' (= '— is included under the concept square root of 4'), respectively. Propositions of the form $\Sigma x \phi a x$ are substitution instances both of the form ψa and of the form $\Sigma x \chi x$.

Frege makes this point explicitly in 'On Concept and Object':
Language has means of presenting now one, now another part of the thought as the subject; one of the most familiar is the distinction of active and passive forms. It is thus not impossible that one way of analysing a given thought should make it appear as a singular judgement; another, as a particular judgement; and a third, as a universal judgement. It need not surprise us that the same sentence may be conceived as an assertion about an object and also as an assertion about a concept; only we must observe that what is asserted is different.[19]

What is asserted of the concept, Frege means to say, is existence. It is the expression 'There is at least one —' which does this job. What is asserted about the object is realization. It is the expression '— is realized' which does *this* job. ('But notice carefully', Frege says, 'that what is asserted here is not the same thing as was asserted about the concept.' (ibid.)) He would surely wish to have retracted the remark in the *Grundlagen* that what happens when I say 'Venus has 0 moons' is that 'a property is assigned to the *concept* 'moon of Venus', namely that of including nothing under it' (§ 46).

'The concept *square root of 4* is realized' means the same as 'There is at least one thing that realizes the concept *square root of 4*'. Can it therefore—to repeat our previous question—be taken as *elucidating* the sentence 'There is at least one square root of 4'? Frege says earlier in 'On Concept and Object' (p. 47) that 'someone falling under the concept *man*' means the same as 'a man'. Would he not also wish to say that 'thing that realizes the concept *square root of 4*' means the same as 'square root of 4'? Is not the former simply a 'fluffed up' version of

[19] *Philosophical Writings*, p. 49.

the latter? The notion of *being realized*, or *being instantiated*, or *not being empty*, or *having the property of including something under it*, cannot therefore be taken as clarifying the notion of existence, not unless we take those ways of talking as obscure ways of saying something that can be expressed with greater precision in another way. If these expressions had been used by Frege to provide definitions of 'exist' or 'there is' he would have been guilty of *circulus in definiendo*.

7. *Predication and 'being wrapped round'*

According to the doctrine we have been expounding, in 'There exists an even prime number' or 'Something is an even prime number' the expressions 'There exists —' and 'Something —' function as predicates. We have seen that confusion can arise if we ask what it is that is here predicated: *being realized* or *being instantiated* is the answer that all too dangerously suggests itself. But we can avoid this danger by insisting that the first term of the relation '*x* is predicated of *y*' is always a linguistic expression. In 'Charles is fat' it is '— is fat' which is predicated of Charles. This usage has good authority.[20] But there is no established usage which permits the second term of the predication to be a linguistic expression. In 'Charles is fat' the predicate '— is fat' is predicated, not of the name 'Charles', but of what the name 'Charles' stands for, namely, the man Charles. So, if we say that in 'Something is an even prime number' the predicate 'Something —' is predicated of something, it will have to be what '— is an even prime number' stands for. This, in Frege's view, is a concept. Here, however, we find ourselves slipping back into the dangerous way of talking that we have recently been trying to hard to avoid: the sort of expression that we find it natural to talk about as being predicated of concepts is '— is realized', '— has instances'. Moreover, there are many who see no reason for accepting Frege's view that a first-level predicable like '— is an even prime number' stands for, or refers to, anything at all. Concepts, in so far as they are introduced into logical theory as the references of predicative expressions, are to be avoided if possible. How, though, are they to be avoided if we call expressions like 'Something —'

[20] Cf. Geach, *Reference and Generality*, § 17.

and 'There exists —' predicates? There must be an answer to the question 'What are these expressions predicated *of*?'

A way of side-stepping this question is to give up the relation '*x* is predicated of *y*' altogether. It may be wondered how this relation can be given up without at the same time giving up the notions of 'predicate' and 'predicable'. But this can in fact be done. We can give a definition of 'predicable' which makes no use of the relation *being predicated of*. It is necessary first to define 'first-level predicable'. A first-level predicable is an expression which, when attached to one or more occurrences of one or more proper names, yields a proposition. (Alternatively, a first-level predicable is what is obtained by removing from a proposition one or more occurrences of one or more proper names.) A second-level predicable is an expression which, when attached to one or more occurrences of one or more first-level predicables, yields a proposition. The way of defining predicables of higher order is now obvious. These definitions work admirably for 'Two is an even prime number' and 'Something is an even prime number', for example. The expression '— is an even prime number', when attached to the proper name 'Two', yields a proposition, and so does the expression 'Something —' when attached to the first-level predicable '— is an even prime number'. When a predicable actually is attached to an expression of the appropriate category to form a proposition, it is a predicate. 'Something —' may not be recognizable as a predicate in the traditional grammatical sense, but the definition of 'second-level predicable' which we have just given provides a clearly intelligible extension of this traditional sense. The traditional sense needs in fact to be corrected as well as extended: its identification of '— is an even prime number' as predicate in both 'Two is an even prime number' and 'Something is an even prime number' is positively misleading. It invites us to regard 'Something is an even prime number' and 'Something is not an even prime number' as contradictories. Prior made a similar point using the example 'Every animal is not a man'. If we treat '— is not a man' here as a context for 'Every animal' in the same way as it is a context for 'Satan' in 'Satan is not a man', we make trouble for ourselves. But this is what we are encouraged to do by traditional grammar, which regards '— is not a man' as predicate in both propositions. Traditional grammar is deceived in this case by the superficial structure of ordinary English sentences. If, however, we rewrote the sentence 'Every animal is not a man' in what Prior called 'a structure-indicating pidgin',[21] we should not be misled. We should then have '(Every animal (not (is a man)))', where 'is a man' is first attached to the negation operator 'not' to form a complex first-level predicable, and this is then attached to the second-level predicable 'Every animal' to form a proposition. 'Satan is not a man' in this pidgin would come out as '(Not (is a man (Satan)))'. This artificial language, like Polish logical notation, always writes function-expressions to the left of their argument-expressions. So long as we use this 'structure-indicating pidgin', an expression will be a predicate in a given proposition only if, in that proposition, it has something (other than brackets) occurring to the right of it.

In stating these definitions of first- and second-level predicables we have used the word 'attach'. In the case of second-level predicables particularly, this was ambiguous. A proposition is formed by attaching 'Every animal —' to the first-level predicable '— is not a man', and 'Every animal —' is thus a second-level predicable. A proposition is formed by attaching '— is not a man' to the proper name 'Satan', and '— is not a man' is thus a first-level predicable. But the same proposition is formed by attaching 'Satan' to the first-level predicable '— is not a man'—*being attached to* is a symmetrical relation—so 'Satan' ought to be regarded as a second-level predicable as much as 'Every animal —'. This result is undesirable for many reasons, and it can be avoided by substituting for the symmetrical relation *being attached to* the asymmetrical *being wrapped round*. This amounts to elevating into a piece of formal jargon the phrase 'wrap round' which we quoted from Prior earlier in this chapter (§ 4). We can then say that a second-level predicable is an expression which yields a proposition by being wrapped round a first-level predicable. 'Satan' in 'Satan is not a man' will not qualify as a second-level predicable although it yields a proposition by being attached to '— is not a man', because it is not wrapped round the expression it is attached to. Prior, in the passage cited earlier, provides us with a criterion for deciding whether, when one expression is attached

[21] *Objects of Thought*, p. 151.

to another to form a proposition, the first is wrapped round the second or vice versa. The criterion makes it clear that 'Every animal —' in 'Every animal is not a man' *is* wrapped round '— is not a man', in exactly the same way as it was proved that in 'No man is just' it is 'No man —' which is wrapped round '— is just', not vice versa. But we can avoid saying that 'Every animal —' is predicated of what '— is not a man' stands for, as '— is not a man' is predicated of what 'Satan' stands for. We can do this, because instead of the *being predicated of* relation, which holds between linguistic expressions and things that need not be linguistic expressions, we make use of the *being wrapped round* relation, which holds only between linguistic expressions. We can thus avoid the dangers of having to talk of 'assigning properties to concepts'; nor do we have to leave off the explanation of existential propositions at the point where they are said to predicate *being instantiated* of concepts. The danger of circularity in our explanation is averted.

The relation in which 'No man —' stands to '— is just', which Prior called *being wrapped round* must be carefully distinguished from one which was recognized by Frege. Frege used the function-argument relation twice over in explaining the structure of a proposition like 'No man is just'. We are familiar with his view that '— is just' stands for a first-level concept, which is here argument to the second-level concept for which 'No man —' stands. Here we have a truth-value which is the value of a second-level function for a first-level function as argument. Neither the truth-value nor the functions, which in this case are concepts, are linguistic entities. But Frege also held that the proposition 'No man is just' is the value of the function 'No man —' for '— is just' as argument; and here the value of the function, the proposition, is a linguistic entity, in the sense of being a string of words. For Frege, predicables, whether first-level predicables like '— is just' or second-level like 'No man —', are not identifiable with strings of words. So in our case the argument of the function, and the function itself of which the proposition, rather than the truth-value, is the value for this argument, are not identifiable as strings of words. But it does not follow that they are identifiable with what such strings of words signify. We have not, in Geach's phrase, 'shifted from the domain of language to the domain of what language signifies'.²² What they are is a feature of language, something that different propositions may have in common. This distinction between bits of language and features of language is required by the recognition of a different predicable in 'Brutus killed Brutus' and 'Caesar killed Caesar' from any to be found in 'Brutus killed Caesar'. There is no bit of language to be found in the first two of these propositions which is not present in the third. But the feature they have in common with each other, but not with the third, is itself a predicable—the same thing is being predicated of Brutus in the first as is being predicated of Caesar in the second.

Not every case of predication, therefore, will consist in a word or phrase being wrapped round another. But some cases will; and in 'No man is just' and the other examples used in this chapter, the predicable in Frege's sense, a common linguistic pattern, is identifiable with the presence of a particular word or phrase. Prior's relation of *being wrapped round* is a relation which obtains between words and phrases of this sort, between bits of language, not features of language. It is to be distinguished from Frege's second, linguistic, application of the relation between function and argument. It is arguable that wherever a predicable in Frege's sense, an identifiable feature of propositions, occurs in language, a symbolism can be constructed in which a predicable in our sense can be seen to be wrapped round another linguistic expression. This need not be argued now. The predicables with which I am concerned all involve bits of language which can be wrapped round other bits of language. Translation into Fregean terminology would be possible, but is not necessary.

8. *Extension of the meaning of 'second-level predicable'*

If the phrase 'second-level predicable' is interpreted strictly, according to the definition just given, '— exists' is not a second-level predicable. 'Something —' in 'Something is an even prime number' can be regarded as being wrapped round '— is an even prime number', which is a first-level predicable. But what '— exists' is wrapped round in 'An even prime number exists' is not a first-level predicable, although it could be converted into

---

²² Geach, 'Names and Identity', in *Mind and Language*, ed. Guttenplan, p. 141.

one by the addition of the copula. Even, if instead of 'An even prime number exists', we say 'There exists an even prime number' or 'There is an even prime number', we do not have, superficially, a case of a second-level predicable being wrapped round a first-level predicable. Since 'an even prime number' is not a first-level predicable, neither 'There exists —' nor 'There is —' meets the strict requirement for being a second-level predicable. Not that the expressions capable of filling the gaps in 'There exists —' and 'There is —' are normally proper names:[23] what is required to fill these gaps is a noun or noun-phrase introduced by the indefinite article. 'There exist —' and 'There are —' similarly require completion by a plural noun or noun-phrase. Frege remarks 'As soon as a word is used with the indefinite article or in the plural without any article, it is a concept word'.[24] Frege thus uses his term of art *Begriffswort* (concept-word)' to cover a wider range of expressions than is covered by my 'first-level predicable' in the strict sense. We may note that an expression which Frege would classify as a *Begriffswort* is similarly required in contexts like 'All — are even numbers': 'numbers divisible by two' will fill this gap, 'thirty-three' will not. Again we may note that the job done by 'numbers divisible by two' in filling the gap in 'All — are even numbers' is the same as the job done by '— is a number divisible by two' in filling the gap in 'Whatever — is an even number'. In classifying both 'numbers divisible by two' and 'is a number divisible by two' as *Begriffswörte* Frege is taking a logical point of view, whereas in allowing the latter but not the former to be a first-level predicable in the strict sense I am taking a narrowly grammatical point of view: Frege is attending to the deep structure, I to the surface structure of language. But it is the contrast between deep structure and surface structure that is my present concern.

The trouble is that what 'There exists —' or 'There is —' is wrapped round in 'There exists an even prime number' is not, superficially, a first-level predicable. Superficially, 'There exists —' and 'There is —' themselves resemble first-level predicables. They would resemble them more closely still, if it were not for the fact that in English these verbs precede their grammatical

---

[23] For apparent exceptions see below, Ch. XI, § 7.
[24] *Foundations of Arithmetic*, § 51.

subjects and need the prefix 'There'.[25] These features, however, are relatively local phenomena of no logical significance. 'There is an even prime number' might just as well have had 'An even prime number is' as a variant, in the same way as 'An even prime number exists' is a variant of 'There exists an even prime number'. In Greek *'esti'* can equally well come before or after its grammatical subject. Where the superficial grammar of 'There exists —' and 'There is —' corresponds better to the underlying logic of the sentences in which they occur than does that of '— exists' is in this: the expressions required for filling the gaps in 'There exists —' and 'There is —' have to be *Begriffswörte*. This requirement is one of superficial grammar as well as of logic. 'There exists the number two' or 'There is thirty-three' are grammatically ill-formed,[26] where 'The number two exists' and 'Thirty-three exists' are not. But even if limited to completion by *Begriffswörte*, 'There is —' and 'There exists —' are still superficially similar to first-level predicables: superficially 'There is —' in 'There is an even prime number' is related to 'an even prime number' in the same way as '— has no rational square root' is related to it in 'An even prime number has no rational square root'. Just so 'There are aristocratic Australians' and 'Aristocratic Australians exist' have the same superficial structure as 'Aristocratic Australians drink gin'.

How then are we to avoid saying that 'An even prime number exists' has, from the point of view of logic, the same form as 'An Australian aristocrate drinks gin'? If we are to say that '— exists' is a second-level, whereas '— drinks gin' is a first-level, predicable we shall have to use something like the old formula: the grammatical form is misleading as to the logical form. There seem certainly to be occasions when we can properly apply this formula: 'Disraeli and Beaconsfield are identical' superficially has the same form as 'Robert and Lucy are musical'. But whereas the latter is equivalent to 'Robert is musical and Lucy is musical', the former is not equivalent to 'Disraeli is identical and Beaconsfield is identical', but rather to 'Disraeli is the same as Beaconsfield'. Just as it is said that

---

[25] The linguists' explanation of this has been stated in Ch. I, § 2.
[26] Except in contexts like 'Is there a multiple of eleven between thirty and forty?' which are examined below, Ch. XI, § 7. The sentences there examined, however, cannot by themselves, without help from context, be regarded as expressing complete propositions.

the logical form of 'Disraeli and Beaconsfield are identical' is exhibited better by 'Disraeli is the same as Beaconsfield', so we may wish to say that the logical form of 'An even prime number exists' is exhibited better by 'Something is an even prime number', in which a second-level predicable is wrapped round a first-level predicable in the strict interpretation of the term. How could the latter proposition have this structure without the former proposition, which has the same meaning as it, having it too? It is not that we have here two different ways of dividing the same proposition, as 'Susan is married to someone' can be divided into 'Susan' (name) and '— is married to someone' (first-level predicable) or into 'Susan is married to —' (first-level predicable) and '— someone' (second-level predicable). In splitting 'An even prime number exists' into 'An even prime number' and '— exists' and 'Something is an even prime number' into 'Something —' and '— is an even prime number' we are dividing what is fundamentally the same proposition at what is fundamentally the same point. Logical differences are all big differences, as Wittgenstein said. How could the differences between these sentences and these divisions be *big* differences?

Even if we were unwilling to admit that 'Something is an even prime number' exhibits the true logical form of 'An even prime number exists', we should have to admit that there *are* expressions which superficially resemble first-level predicables, but which are really second-level. 'Small cacti abound' looks on the face of it as though it were of the same logical form as 'Small cacti store moisture'. 'Aristocratic Australians are numerous' has superficially the same form as 'Aristocratic Australians are rude', and 'The American Indians are disappearing' the same form as 'The American Indians are underprivileged'. These propositions all share the same superficial form as 'Aristocratic Australians exist'. And corresponding to 'There are (exist) aristocratic Australians' we have 'There are many aristocratic Australians', 'There are lots of small cacti' and 'There are fewer and fewer American Indians'. Just as we should wish to say that 'Something is an even prime number' exhibits the true logical form of 'An even prime number exists' or 'There exists (is) an even prime number', so we shall wish to say that 'Many people are aristocratic Australians' and

'Fewer and fewer people are American Indians' exhibit the true logical form of these other propositions.

As we saw at the beginning of this chapter, one of the great merits of Frege's analysis of existential propositions is that it not *ad hoc*. It does not provide a category to which existential propositions and they alone belong, but places them in a category for which an antecedent need has been shown, the category of possible answers to number-questions. In all these cases Frege's analysis reveals the proposition as resulting from a second-level predicable being wrapped round a first-level predicable. But in all these cases sentences of the form 'n objects ϕ', where replacements for 'n objects —' are recognizable as second-level predicables and replacements for 'ϕ —' as first-level predicables, are transformable into sentences of the form 'There are n A's', where 'A's' is not replaceable by a first-level predicable in the narrow sense. Thus 'Five people are surviving ex-Prime Ministers' is transformable into 'There are five surviving ex-Prime Ministers'. The expression '— are surviving ex-Prime Ministers' is a first-level predicable, so 'Five people —' is a second-level predicable. But 'surviving ex-Prime Ministers' is not a first-level predicable in the strict sense, so 'There are five —' is not a second-level predicable in the strict sense. So, since there are infinitely many pairs of expressions of the form 'n objects —' and 'There are n — ' which correspond in this way, the need to extend the sense of 'first-level predicable' so that it corresponds to Frege's '*Begriffswort*', and correspondingly to extend the sense of 'second-level predicable', is obvious, without reference to the status of '— exists'. The role of 'Something —' and '— exists' and that of '— is an even prime number' and 'An even prime number', respectively, are so obviously the same in the sentences 'Something is an even prime number' and 'An even prime number exists', that the extension of the class of second-level predicables to include '— exists' is in any case amply justified. And so far from being *ad hoc*, it is an extension which will take in '— are numerous', '— are few', '— are disappearing', etc., as well as infinitely many expressions of the form 'There are n —', for every natural number, n.

9. Can '—exist' ever function as a first-level predicate?

In the case of '— are numerous', '— are few', '— abound', etc., a cogent reason for regarding them as second-level predicables in an extended sense is that it is clear that they can never function as first-level predicates. 'Aristocratic Australians are numerous', 'Aristocratic Australians are few', 'Aristocratic Australians abound' all make equally good sense. 'Aristides is numerous', 'Aristides is few', and 'Aristides abounds' are all obvious nonsense. We can point up the contrast between '— are rude', which is a first-level predicable, and '— are numerous', which is a second-level predicable, by contrasting the following valid syllogism,

(A) 1. Aristocratic Australians are rude
2. Aristides is an aristocratic Australian
3. *Ergo* Aristides is rude

with this travesty of a syllogism

(B) 1. Aristocratic Australians are numerous
2. Aristides is an aristocratic Australian
3. *Ergo* Aristides is numerous.

Similarly, it has been claimed,[27] the valid syllogism

(C) 1. Aristocratic Australians drink gin
2. Aristides is an aristocratic Australian
3. *Ergo* Aristides drinks gin

can be contrasted with the only superficially valid syllogism

(D) 1. Aristocratic Australians exist
2. Aristides is an aristocratic Australian
3. *Ergo* Aristides exists.

Philosophers have hoped that once people have seen the absurdity of B, and have recognized that 'Aristocratic Australians exist' like 'Aristocratic Australians are numerous' is an answer to the question 'How many aristocratic Australians are there?', they would quickly come to see that '— exist' like '— are numerous' is a second-level predicable.

But those who insist that '— exist' can function as a first-level predicate have a way of escape. They admit that D may be construed as an invalid syllogism; but they attribute this, not to the fact that D3, like B3, is unintelligible, but to an

---

[27] The comparison between 'exist' and 'are numerous' is made by Russell. See *Introduction to Mathematical Philosophy*, pp. 164 f.; *Logic and Knowledge*, p. 223.

equivocation between the sense of 'exist' in Dl, and the sense of 'exists' in D3. They would grant that '— exist' in D1, if this proposition were viewed in isolation, would be most naturally understood as a second-level predicable, with D1 understood as a not very precise answer to the question 'How many Australians are aristocrats?' But they would insist that it could be taken as a first-level predicable, as it has to be taken in D3, if D3 is to be intelligible; and if so taken, D as a whole is a perfectly valid inference. Existence, they would hold, like the habit of drinking gin, is a property which each and every aristocratic Australian, Aristides included, possesses. The predicable '— exist', in this sense, is not like the predicable '— are numerous' at all.

Geach is one philosopher who has maintained that as well as the sense, established by Frege, in which '— exist' is a second-level predicable, there is another sense in which it is a first-level predicable. We shall be examining his claim at some length in Chapter V. Against this claim Dummett has argued, quite generally, that no expression can have a use both as a first-level predicable and as a second-level predicable without being simply, or as the medievals would say 'accidentally', equivocal.

If this doctrine were correct, the verb 'exists' would be simply equivocal: after all, what difference of sense could be greater than one involving a difference of logical type, that between a quantifier and a first-level predicate? This is enough to show that the doctrine, as stated, cannot be correct: for, even if there are two distinguishable senses of 'exists', these senses are evidently connected.[28]

What Dummett says is evident is that if, as Geach believes, there are two senses of the word 'exist', this is a case of analogy, not pure equivocation (see Ch. I. § 6). Even if there are two senses in which 'exist' is used, there must be some connection of meaning between them. The way in which the word is used in one sense must enter into the explanation of the way in which it is used in the other sense. This, I think, Geach would not deny. What he would deny is that it is impossible for a word to be used analogically in this way and still be in one sense a first-level predicable and in another sense a second-level predicable. Clear examples can be found of this occurring. I have already used such a word in the example 'The American

[28] Michael Dummett, *Frege: Philosophy of Language*, 1973, p. 386.

Indians are disappearing'. The usefulness of the word 'disappear' as an example rested on its ability to function, as in this sentence, as a second-level predicate. But it can equally well be used as a first-level predicate.[29] As I watch him retreating into the misty distance I may say 'Hiawatha is disappearing'. A pool of water on a hot and sunny terrace may shrink to nothing, may become smaller and smaller until it finally disappears.[30] Now it is not difficult to show connections between these different uses. In each case we have a phenomenon which can be expressed by the phrase 'less and less': the American Indians are becoming less and less numerous, my view of Hiawatha is becoming less and less clear, the area of terrace covered by water is becoming less and and less extended. The element of equivocation is due to the applicability of the notions of *greater* and *less* both to continuous and to discrete quantity. The Indians are becoming fewer, while the pool is becoming smaller. We have alrady seen that '— are few' is a second-level predicable: '— is small' is obviously a first-level predicable. The fact that both are concerned with quantity explains why the same expression can be used, now as a first-level, now as a second-level predicable without prejudice to the connection between the two senses. Dummett's rhetorical question 'What difference of sense could be greater than one involving a difference of logical type?' is easily answered. The familiar cases of pure equivocation, 'bank', 'race', etc., involve greater difference of sense than that between these two senses of 'disappear'.

Dummett regards difference of logical type, as between a quantifier and a first-level predicable, as precluding analogy and requiring pure equivocation. But differences of logical type can exist between expressions that are second-level and expressions that are third-level predicables, and so on, just as much as between expressions which are first-level and expressions which are second-level predicables. An expression which both Geach and Dummett have discussed in their writings

[29] This example was drawn to my attention by Professor Geach.
[30] It may be objected that by allowing that the pool of water—an individual—disappears, I have committed myself to non-existence, and thus to existence, as a property of individuals. Hiawatha disappears from view, but the pool of water disappears from the Nature of Things. This, however, would be over-hasty. When the pool of water disappears it is not so much true that it *doesn't exist* as that it *no longer exists*. Chapter V is devoted to explaining how '—no longer exists' can be a first-level predicable without '—exists' being one.

is 'There is something which —'. This can occur both as a second-level predicate, as in 'There is something which George bought and Mary gave away', and as a third-level predicate, as in 'There is something which every great general is' and in 'There is something which George and Mary both are'. It can also occur in a context where it is not a predicable of any level: 'There is something which George and Mary both believe'. In the first case 'There is something which —' is symbolizable as Σx—x, in the second case as '$\Sigma \phi$—ϕ—', and in the third case as Σp—p. The differences of type of the variables in these symbolizations mark the differences of syntactic category of the quantificational expressions taken as a whole. The ordinary language expression which they all represent has a different sense corresponding to each symbolization. But it is not purely equivocal. That it is used analogically is shown by the occurrence in each of the symbolizations of the quantifier Σ together with a variable, though the category of variable changes from case to case. It is also shown, without benefit of symbols, by the fact that each proposition introduced by the ordinary-language phrase 'There is something which —' can be regarded as an existential generalization of some other proposition. 'There is something which George bought and Mary gave away' is related in this way to 'George bought Arkle and Mary gave him away', 'There is something which every great general is' to 'Every great general is patient', 'There is something which George and Mary both are' to 'George and Mary are both extravagant' and 'There is something which George and Mary both believe' to 'George and Mary both believe that Richard is going to die'. These connections between the quantifier and instantiation will be spelled out at greater length later in the book (Ch. XI, § 6). Enough has been said, however, to show that in the case of 'There is something which —', as in the case of 'disappear', we have an expression which in different senses can be seen to belong to different logical types, but which is not purely equivocal. Dummett's argument against Geach will not stand up.

We cannot then in principle rule out the possibility that 'exist' can have different senses, in one of which it is a first-level and in another of which it is a second-level predicable. But if it is held to be used analogically, now as a first-level, now as a second-level predicate, the person who holds this owes us an account of the connection between its two senses. The connection we saw between the different senses of 'There is something which —' also serves to bind this expression, and the simple 'Something —', to '— exist' used as a second-level predicate. Our claim that the role performed by 'Something —' in 'Something is an even prime number' is the same as that performed by '— exists' in 'An even prime number exists' is borne out by the fact that the latter as well as the former proposition can be regarded as the existential generalization of 'Two is an even prime number'. In contrast to this, where the gap in '— exist' is filled by a proper name, the result cannot be regarded as the existential generalization of anything. If a sense of '— exist' is allowed in which it is a first-level predicable, this link between '— exist' and 'Something —' is clearly broken. What links are there which remain to bind the supposed first-level sense of '— exist' to the second-level sense?

10. *An explanation of the illusion that 'Aristides exists', etc., make sense*

'There is something which George and Mary' and 'Something Aristides' are fairly obviously ill formed. 'George and Mary exist' and 'Aristides exists' not so obviously. Russell indeed would have claimed that in so far as each incorporated a proper name or names (and he would not easily have conceded this) each lacked significance in just the same way as 'George and Mary abound' or 'Aristides is numerous' lacks significance. Against this it has been objected recently[31] that the parallel between 'exist' and 'numerous' or 'rare' is not as close as Russell thought it was:

> ... it is not clear how, if it is genuinely a mistake to treat '*x* exists' as a genuine first-level predicate, we are in a position to say what the consequences would be of treating it as one. In this respect, 'exist' contrasts clearly with a predicate like 'rare'. The evident absurdity of inferring from 'Women who stammer are rare' that this woman stammerer is rare reveals that the logical form of sentences of the form '*F*'s are rare' is unlike that of a large class of sentences which are superficially similar, and the difference will no doubt turn out to be that 'rare' is not a first-level

---

[31] By Michael Woods, 'Existence and Tense', *Truth and Meaning*, edd. G. Evans and J. McDowell, 1976, p. 249. Woods attributes his objection to Dummett, but I can find no trace of it in the place cited by Woods.

predicate, true of individuals. But for precisely this reason, there is no sense in asking what the truth conditions of sentences containing it *would be, if* it were construed as a first-level predicate. Because 'numerous' is not a first-level predicate, we do not know what to make of a sentence like 'Sadie is numerous'. The parallel between 'exist' and 'numerous' has commonly been thought to be fairly close, but there are not the same surface indications that 'exist' is not a predicate true of individuals.

Woods is arguing that people who deny that 'exist' is a first-level predicable *both* assimilate it to 'numerous' *and* tend to appeal 'to the idea that, if "exist" is construed as a (first-level) predicate, certain sentences which in fact express contingent truths or falsehoods will no longer do so' (ibid.). The appeal he has in mind is of course to the argument we have referred to as 'Plato's Beard'. Enough has been said already to show that we must disavow any appeal that involves having a *clear* idea of what the consequences would be of treating 'exist' as a first-level predicate (see Ch. II, § 7). Plato's Beard is tangled. It is a name for the muddle that we get ourselves into if we attribute to sentences like 'Aristocratic Australians exist' or 'Aristides exists' a meaning which they do not have, either because they have quite a different meaning or because they have no meaning at all. We do not get into these muddles by drawing consequences that are clearly seen to follow from propositions expressed by sentences understood in this way. Understood in this way they do not express propositions and can have no clear consequences. But philosophers should not be surprised that there is no way of stating clearly, but several ways of indicating obscurely, what the consequences are of holding a false view of the logical form of a proposition. Such views are necessarily incoherent, and one of the ways of showing them to be incoherent is to show what absurdities seem to follow from them. Ryle indeed claimed that there is no other way of showing this, when he argued that it was precisely this which Plato was engaged in in the more tangled passages of the *Parmenides*:

Now when we treat a formal concept as if it were a non-formal or proper concept, we are committing a breach of 'logical syntax'. But what shows us that we are doing this? The deductive derivation of absurdities and contradictions shows it, and nothing else can. Russell's proof that, in his code-symbolism, ϕ cannot be value of x in the propositional function ϕx is only another exercise in the same genre as Plato's proof that 'Unity' cannot go into the gap in the sentence frame '. . . . exists' or '. . . . does not exist'.[32]

Nevertheless, Woods has a point when he says that there are not the same 'surface indications' that 'exist' is not a first-level predicable as there are that 'numerous' is not one. 'Sadie is numerous' is patent nonsense. 'Aristides exists', and indeed 'I exist', *sound* all right. Frege reminded us that affirmation of existence is nothing but denial of the number nought. If we regard this as establishing that '— exist' is a predicable of the same level as '— are numerous', we must explain why we have the illusion that '— exist' can function as a first-level predicate, whereas we have no such illusion in the case of '— are numerous'. People are not easily persuaded that Descartes was uttering an ill-formed formula when he said '*Je suis*'. If the view that '— exist' is a first-level predicable is an illusion, it is a deep-seated illusion, comparable with what Kant called the transcendental illusions of metaphysics. How, then, are we to explain this illusion, the illusion that 'Aristides exists' makes better sense than 'Sadie is numerous'?

An oblique thrust is best here. It is the Fregean discovery that answers to questions of the form 'How many A's are there?' are given by wrapping a second-level predicable round a first-level one. The correct answer to the question 'How many moons has the Earth?' is 'One'. The proposition for which this word 'One' is elliptical should not therefore be regarded as one which ascribes a property to an object. But it is by no means unheard of for philosophers to hold that *being one* is a property possessed by objects, not to say a property possessed by *all* objects. In this view, filling the gap in '— is one' by a proper name produces a proposition, and indeed a necessarily true proposition. The same is maintained for '— exists': *ens et unum convertuntur*. Since everything is one and nothing is more than one, plurality, in this view, exists only in the mind. Things are not many in themselves, but acquire 'manyness' only in so far as we think of them together. Number is an idea to which nothing corresponds in reality.[33] Such is the disastrous result of construing oneness as a property of objects.

[32] Gilbert Ryle, 'Plato's "Parmenides"', *Collected Papers*, 1971, 1, 33.
[33] Cf. Bertrand Russell, *A Critical Examination of the Philosophy of Leibniz*, 1958, § 63.

But it would be difficult to maintain that no sense at all can be made of a sentence like 'Allah is one'. No doubt the truth which those who utter this sentence are anxious to proclaim is better expressed by the sentence 'There is only one God'. But the connection between such propositions, in which a second-level predicable is wrapped round a first-level predicable, and proper names, which do not occur in them at all, is close. For the word 'Aristides' to be a genuine proper name there must be just one man answering to a certain description. When people were first taught the use of the name 'Aristides' it is very likely that their friends pointed to a man on the other side of the Agora and said 'That's Aristides'. If it had not been for the fact that there was *just one man* (and one just man, of course) who could be identified as the man at whom they were pointing, the use of the name could not have been taught. It is easy to imagine that this fact, which consists in the possession by some concept of the property of being uniquely instantiated, is expressed by 'Aristides is one'. Similarly, if it had not been for the fact that *there was* a man who could be identified as a man at whom these people were pointing, the use of the name 'Aristides' could not have been taught. It is easy to imagine that this fact, which consists in the possession by some concept of the property, simply, of being instantiated, is expressed by 'Aristides exists'. There is indeed a connection between existence and the use of a proper name. Unless some property is instantiated, and indeed uniquely instantiated, an expression cannot acquire the significance of a proper name. But this does not legitimize the formation of propositions by attaching '— exists', or for that matter '— is one', to the proper name in question. There must *be* something if 'Aristides' is to be a proper name, but that does not entitle us to say that Aristides *is*. The illusion that 'Aristides exists' has significance comes, perhaps, from the mistaken feeling that it does so entitle us.

If we can explain the illusion that some genuine proposition is expressed by the words 'Aristides exists' by pointing to a confusion between these words and a sentence which asserts the unique instantiation of some property, we may also be able in this way to explain our ability to reject certain alleged analyses of 'Aristides exists'. On the face of it, this ability accords ill with our claim to find 'Aristides exists' as unintelligible as 'Aristides is numerous'. But a natural reaction to the suggestion that 'Aristides exists' means the same as, for example, 'For some x, x is identical with Aristides' is to say 'Oh no! Its meaning is quite different. "Aristides is identical with Aristides" is a tautology, and "For some x, x is identical with Aristides" is entailed by it, so it too must be a tautology.' Propositions of the form Iaa and $CIaa\Sigma xIxa$ are held to be truths of logic, so propositions of the form $\Sigma xIxa$ must be truths of logic too. But how could 'Aristides exists' be equivalent to a truth of logic? It surely expresses a contingent truth. Or rather, if we take seriously the present tense of 'exists' and are using 'Aristides' to refer to someone now dead, we shall want 'Aristides exists' to express a contingent falsehood, although once it expressed a contingent truth. But how could 'For some x, Aristides is identical with x', entailed as it is by any true identity statement about Aristides, pass from being true to being false? 'Augustus is identical with Octavian' did not cease to be true when Augustus died. How could 'For some x, Augustus is identical with x' do so?

No doubt there are philosophical objections to the view that propositions of the form $\Sigma xIxa$ are entailed by corresponding propositions of the form Iaa, or that propositions of the latter form are logically true,[34] but that need not delay us now. The point is that we find ourselves objecting to a suggested analysis of 'Aristides exists' on the grounds that it fails to preserve its status as a contingent truth (or falsehood). But how, if 'Aristides exists' is held by us to be unintelligible, can we simultaneously insist that what it states is contingent? Only, it seems, if we surreptitiously confuse 'Aristides exists' with a form of words suitable for asserting the unique instantiation of some property whose instantiation is a condition of our using the word 'Aristides' as a proper name.

However we are to explain it, we have in some measure the

[34] Cf. Leonard Linsky, *Names and Descriptions*, 1977, pp. 24 ff. We may take this opportunity of noting Wittgenstein's view of this matter in the *Tractatus*. To say that propositions of the form $\Sigma xIxa$ are tautological is, in Wittgenstein's terms, to say that they are *sinnlos*—i.e. that they lack 'true-false' poles. Wittgenstein in fact regarded them as *unsinnig*—nonsensical. This is a consequence of his view that identity is not a relation. At *Tractatus* 5.534 he explicitly says that $(\exists x).x=a$ is a pseudo-proposition. For further comments on this, see below Ch. V, p. 139; Ch. XI, pp. 286 ff.; Appendix B, p. 339.

illusion that 'Aristides exists' expresses a proposition; but although we are more inclined to accept this than to accept that 'Sadie is numerous' expresses one, we should not despair entirely of finding 'surface indications' that '— exists' is not a first-level predicable. First-level predicables, that is, expressions which yield propositions when wrapped round proper names, will also yield propositions when attached to definite descriptions—Frege indeed was prepared to include definite descriptions in the category of proper names. But whereas attaching '— drinks gin' to 'the Albanian who understands Gödel's Theorem' yields an acceptable proposition, attaching '— exits' to it produces a weird result. If we change the definite to the indefinite article and then embed our phrase in this same context, we produce a sentence that is quite in order: 'An Albanian who understands Gödel's theorem exists'. In Frege's terms what we have done is to substitute a *Begriffswort* for an *Eigenname*, a predicable for a proper name. The context '— exists' calls for indefinite rather than definite descriptions, and this is something that is apparent to the ear of the ordinary speaker (or hearer). It constitutes a 'surface indication' that '— exist' is not a first-level predicable.

Mr Bailey is our grocer. If I say to someone out of the blue 'Mr Bailey exists', he will not have the least idea what I am playing at. Only a special context can give intelligibility to such a string of words. We need here to make use of the contrast Wittgenstein drew between what we say 'outside philosophy' and what we say when we are 'doing philosophy'. In 'ordinary language' we have no use for strings of words like 'Mr Bailey exists'. Those who object to Wittgensteinian appeals to ordinary language often seem to miss the motivation behind such appeals. It is that when we are doing philosophy we tend to fall into ways of using language which are distortions of language; unawares we break the rules for the use of words which alone give the words their meaning. It is inside philosophy that words tend to 'idle' in this way. Outside philosophy our words take care of themselves. While they are employed in ordinary life to do the jobs for which they were invented, they obey the rules which alone enable them to do these jobs. When there is doubt, therefore, whether a given locution is intelligible, it is sensible to ask whether it is used outside philosophy, i.e. in ordinary language. If it is, the claim that it is unintelligible, ill formed, the product of some category mistake, is inadmissible. If it is not, the champions of its intelligibility had better look to their defences.

Put in these terms, what I am claiming is that the result of embedding a proper name in '— exists' is, in general, a meaningless string of words. Outside philosophy we have no need of 'Mr Bailey exists' or '*Je suis*'. If someone wishes to persuade me that '— exist' can function as a first-level predicate, he will have to show me a sentence which I can recognize as usable outside philosophy and which is formed by wrapping '— exists' round a genuine proper name. Until this is done, I protest that I simply do not understand what is meant by filling the gap in '— exists' with a proper name. Most of what follows in this book will be devoted to examining sentences which are obviously intelligible, and which can plausibly be held to result from wrapping '— exists' round a proper name. 'President Ford does not know that David Pears exists',[35] 'Arkle no longer exists' and 'Lady Catherine de Bourgh never existed' are such sentences. They have a perfectly good use outside philosophy. It would be absurd to claim that they were ill formed or unintelligible. The point at issue is rather whether they are to be analysed, in the way that their surface structure suggests, as the result of wrapping a predicable '— exists' round a genuine proper name, used as such. It will be my aim to deny this in each case. But for the vast majority of sentences in which '— exists' is attached to a proper name, I am content to assert that I do not understand what anyone could be saying who uttered them.

Those who wish to prove that '— exist' has a use as a first-level predicate have more to do than simply to produce a meaningful sentence formed by filling its gap with a proper name. We are not talking now about the mark on paper 'exist' or the sound it represents. Of course it is possible for a given mark or sound to be allotted any meaning that is desired. What we are talking about is the word 'exist' which already has a use as a second-level predicate in sentences like 'Aristocratic Australians

---

[35] This example, introduced into the discussion by J. L. Mackie in his paper 'The Riddle of Existence', *Proc. Arist. Soc.*, Supp. Vol. 50, 1976, will be discussed in the next chapter.

exist'. The suggestion is that, while in this sentence 'exist' is a second-level predicate, in other sentences it is a first-level predicate. But this is the view that 'exist' is used analogically. If it were purely equivocal it would indeed be merely the *mark* or the *sound* which was said to have two uses. If it is the *word* 'exist' which is said to have two senses, there must be some connection between the two. This was the point insisted on by Dummett and acceptable, surely, to Geach. As we saw, 'disappear' can have a use both as a first-level and as a second-level predicate, but here it is possible to give some explanation of the twofold use: the connection can be spelt out. Those who claim that 'Aristides exists' makes as good sense as 'Aristocratic Australians exist' owe us, therefore, as we have said, an explanation of the twofold use. They must not only convince us of the intelligibility of the former but spell out its connection with the latter. The onus of proof is on them—twice over.

IV
Embedded Existential Propositions

1. *Propositions in which singular existential propositions are apparently embedded*

If '— exist' can never function as a first-level predicate, strings of words like 'Aristides exists' must be regarded as unintelligible. They do not amount to propositions. And indeed we have declared ourselves willing to jettison these pseudo-sentences along with 'Aristides is numerous' and 'Sadie abounds'. However, it seems prima facie that we can form propositions by embedding strings of words like 'Aristides exists' in contexts like 'It might not have been the case that —' or 'President Ford does not know that —'. 'It might not have been the case that Socrates existed' and 'President Ford does not know that David Pears exists' are strings of words which clearly are intelligible, are genuine propositions; and they have every appearance of having been formed by embedding 'Socrates existed' or 'David Pears exists' in wider contexts. But what has to be embedded in contexts like 'It might not have been the case that —' and 'President Ford does not know that —' to form a genuine proposition in the way described is itself a proposition. If the examples given are indeed formed in this way, 'Socrates existed' and 'David Pears exists' will have to be genuine propositions after all. We need therefore to examine whether they are formed in this way. We need in any case to explain why our examples are intelligible, whereas 'It might not have been the case that Socrates was numerous' and 'President Ford does not know that David Pears abounds' are nonsense.

The examples we have just looked at are due to G. E. Moore,

Alvin Plantinga, and J. L. Mackie. G. E. Moore[1] saw that Russell's interpretation of propositions like 'Some tame tigers exist', which is no different from Frege's interpretation, has this consequence: If you were to point at something and 'say the words "This exists", and if you were using "exists" merely as the singular of "exist" in the sense in which it is used in "Some tame tigers exist", what you did would not express a proposition at all, but would be absolutely meaningless'. But Moore 'could not help feeling' that there were other significant uses of 'exists', that 'in the case of anything to point at which and say "This is a tame tiger" is significant, it is also significant to point at it and say "This exists", *in some sense or other*'. His reason for thinking this was that it seemed to him 'that you can clearly say *with truth* of any such object "This *might* not have existed"'. He did not see 'how it is possible that "This might not have existed" should be true, unless "This does in fact exist" is true, and therefore also significant'.

Moore complicated the issue by proceeding at this point to say that he 'could not help thinking' that in such a case 'This' refers to 'some sense-datum, or some set of sense-data'. It is possible to develop Moore's point without introducing these complications. It is difficult to imagine anyone having occasion to assert what is supposedly asserted by 'I exist'. If this string of words does express a proposition, the proposition it expresses is at best trivial and uninformative. But the more complex proposition 'I might not have existed', into which 'I exist' appears to enter as a component, is non-trivial, obviously true, and something which any human being has good reason to assert. 'I might not have existed' seems to be formed by embedding 'I exist' in the context 'It is not the case that —' and embedding the result of *this* in the context 'It is possible that —'. These contexts can be amalgamated and expressed as 'It might not have been the case that —'. (Using Prior's symbols for modal and truth-functional operators, we can say that 'I might not have existed' is apparently the result of substituting 'I exist' for p in MNp.) If 'I exist' is not already a well-formed formula, it is hard to see how embedding it in a wider context can make it so.

[1] In 'Is Existence a Predicate?', *Logic and Language* (2nd Series), ed. A. G. N. Flew, p. 91.

Alvin Plantinga has endorsed this view of Moore's and elaborated it. Talking of 'Socrates does not exist', conceived as the negation of a proposition formed by attaching the first-level predicable '— exist' to the name 'Socrates', Plantinga says:

> We can also consider possible worlds in which it is true and assert conditionals in which it functions as antecedent or consequent. For example, if no persons had existed, then Socrates would not have existed. And if Socrates had not existed, then at least one essence which *is* instantiated would not have been. Furthermore, any world in which Socrates does not exist is one in which he did not teach Plato. If Socrates had not existed, Plato would not have been his student, the Athenians would not have executed him, Plato would not have recounted his views in the *Dialogues*, and histories of philosophy would contain no reference to him.[2]

Plantinga's first point amounts to the claim that we can obtain a significant proposition by embedding the proposition 'Socrates exists' in the context 'It might not have been the case that —'. His next point is that we can do the same by embedding it in contexts of the form 'If it had been the case that p it would not have been the case that —' or 'If it had not been the case that —, it would have been the case q'. 'If Socrates has not existed, Plato would not have been his student' is not a clear example of embedding 'Socrates exists' in a context of the latter form, since 'Plato was not his student' is not a complete proposition, so cannot properly be substituted for q. The pronoun 'his' is anaphoric and cannot be understood independently of the name 'Socrates' in the antecedent of the proposition, to which it has backwards reference. But we can easily adjust Plantinga's remarks so that they make cleanly the point he wished to make: we need only substitute 'Socrates' for 'his', or 'Socrates' for 'him', in what Plantinga wrote, to produce propositions which do seem prima facie to be the result of embedding 'Socrates exists' in contexts of the form 'If it had been the case that p, it would not have been the case that —' and 'If it had not been the case that —, it would have been the case that q'. And we may accept as plausible the argument that, if 'Socrates exists' is not already a well-formed proposition, it is difficult to see how embedding it in contexts of these sorts can make it so.

Yet another such argument has been put forward by J. L.

[2] *The Nature of Necessity*, 1974, p. 148.

Mackie.[3] Those who doubt whether '— exist' can ever be used as a first-level predicate will not be persuaded by the suggestion that it is so used in 'David Pears exists'. They will feel perfectly able to forgo the opportunity of using this string of words as a proposition. More troublesome for them will be the string of words:

(1) President Ford does not know that David Pears exists.

'David Pears exists', if it were a proposition, would be one that could not help being true, and if true would be trivially so. Some philosophers might think that its status as a genuine proposition is thereby called in question, even if they are unmoved by the arguments of the last chapter about '— exist' only ever functioning as a second-level predicate. Others would regard these considerations, labelled as belonging to 'pragmatics', as of little weight in assessing the significance of 'David Pears exists'. But (1) at any rate, cannot be impugned in this way. There is just a very faint possibility that (1) is false; and therefore, if, as is overwhelmingly probable, (1) is true, it is not trivially true. There is no doubt that it makes perfectly good sense, and it is not difficult to imagine circumstances in which someone would have reason to assert it. Again, if 'David Pears exists' by itself is an ill-formed formula, it seems impossible that it should be turned into a well-formed one by being embedded in the wider context 'President Ford does not know that —'.

All these arguments proceed by first requiring us to admit that some string of words like 'I might not have existed' or (1) is an obviously or plausibly true proposition, then persuading us to accept the prima-facie analysis of the proposition as formed by embedding a singular existential proposition in a wider context, and finally concluding that the singular existential proposition thus embedded is perfectly in order. A proposition of the form δp, where δ is an operator forming sentences out of sentences, can hardly be true, or for that matter false, if the string of words corresponding to p is not a genuine proposition. Singular existential propositions, if there are such things, are propositions formed by wrapping a first-level predicable round a proper name or something which performs a

[3] 'The Riddle of Existence'.

similar role to a proper name. 'Socrates exists' and 'David Pears exists' and 'I exist' would be examples of such propositions. Clearly there can only be such propositions if '— exist' can play the role of a first-level predicate.

There is no doubt that 'I might not have existed', the propositions Plantinga sets out, and (1) are all genuine propositions. Are they, however, of the form δp? That is the link in the chain of argument which needs to be examined. Are there really three propositions, 'I exist', 'Socrates exists' and 'David Pears exists' embedded in these wider propositions?

2. *How to relieve President Ford's ignorance of David Pears's existence*

Something unusual may, for a start, be noticed about (1). It does not behave in quite the same way as, for instance, 'President Ford does not know that Mr Reagan won the 1976 California primary'. If President Ford does not know *this*, let us tell him. 'Mr President, Mr Reagan won the 1976 California primary.' 'Oh, thanks a lot. I didn't know.' But what happens if we try the same method with the David Pears example? 'Mr President, David Pears exists.' 'Oh, thanks a lot. Who's David Pears?' If we want to relieve Mr Ford's ignorance of David Pears's existence we shall have to try a different tactic. We might make an attempt on these lines: 'Mr President, there is a teacher of philosophy at Oxford who has written books on philosophers called "Russell" and "Wittgenstein",[4] and who . . ., etc.' Generalizing, we can say that if *a* does not know that *b* exists we can put this right by telling him something of the form 'There is someone who ϕ's'. This might lead us to say that what *a* does not know is properly expressible, not by a sentence of the form '*b* exists', but rather by a sentence of the form 'For some x, ϕx'. It would follow that any proposition of the form '*a* does not know that *b* exists' can be paraphrased, and its meaning thereby clarified, by a proposition of the form '*a* does not know that, for some x, ϕx'.

The first assumption that is made by someone who argues in this way is that, if telling someone that p will not alter the

---

[4] We mustn't take any further risks in supposing an ability on Mr Ford's part to understand the use, as opposed to the mention, of names well known in philosophy.

fact that he does not know that p, it cannot really have been the fact that p of which he was ignorant. This assumption is false. Some creatures who are capable of ignorance are so ignorant that they would not understand what I said if I told them the fact of which they are ignorant. Talking of my dog I may say, 'Poor thing, she doesn't know that Williams is going away for six months'. Now I can no more remove my dog's ignorance by telling her that Williams is going away for six months than I can remove President Ford's ignorance by telling him that David Pears exists. But it does not follow that what my dog does not know is not, properly speaking, the fact that Williams is going away for six months. What she doesn't know is perfectly well expressed in this way, and there is no call to paraphrase the sentence 'She doesn't know that Williams is going away for six months' in any way whatsoever. So if I cannot relieve a person's ignorance of a particular fact by telling him that p, it doesn't follow that the ignorance in question was not precisely his not knowing that p.

However, there is nothing I can do that would relieve my dog's ignorance; but, as we have seen, there is something I can do to relieve President Ford's ignorance. To remove his ignorance of David Pears's existence we shall no doubt have to tell him something of the form 'For some $x, \phi x$'. If we tell him that 'There is a teacher of philosophy in Oxford . . ., etc.', does it follow that *this* was what he was ignorant of? Should we say that (1) was misleadingly expressed and that what should have been said by someone more attuned to the exigencies of logic was something of the form 'President Ford does not know that, for some $x, \phi x$'? If I *can* relieve someone's ignorance of a particular fact by telling him that p, does it follow that the ignorance in question *was* precisely his not knowing that p?

What if it turns out that I could equally well have relieved his ignorance by telling him that q? There is not just one proposition of the form 'For some $x, \phi x$' that would serve to remove President Ford's ignorance: many would do. Perhaps David Pears met Dr Kissinger at a holiday resort in Mexico in 1972. We might in that case be able to apprise President Ford of David Pears's existence by saying to him 'There's an Englishman whom Henry Kissinger met on holiday in Mexico in 1972 and with whom he played poker every night and . . ., etc.'. In

David Pears's case there is not just one existential proposition of which we are saying President Ford is ignorant when we say that he does not know that David Pears exists. Ignorance of David Pears's existence is a more complicated business than not knowing who won the 1976 California primary.

3. *Examples where the embedded proposition is formed by attaching '— exists' to a definite description*

In rejecting the view that propositions of the form '*a* does not know that *b* exists' can be paraphrased by propositions of the form '*a* does not know that, for some $x, \phi x$', I am disagreeing with Russell. Russell at one time[5] maintained that proper names like 'David Pears', which fall short of being logically proper names, could be paraphrased by definite descriptions and could accordingly, on Russell's theory, be attached to the verb 'exists' to produce acceptable propositions. I do not accept this account in the case of the majority of those proper names which Russell thought logically improper; but it is worth noting that if the view were correct it would put (1) in the same category as another example Mackie gave of an embedded existential proposition in which 'exists' allegedly functions as a first-level predicate. Mackie's example, slightly simplified, is:

(2) Hardly anyone knows that the sheltered bay we found yesterday exists.

Here 'exists' is attached to what is already explicitly a definite description. If the Russellian account of names like 'David Pears' is true we shall be able to paraphrase (1) by a proposition having the same logical form as (2).

But now let us suppose that we have the deplorable intention of removing the ignorance that exists on the part of most of our fellow human beings about the existence of the sheltered bay we found yesterday. We are not likely to set about it by placing a large advertisement in the newspapers saying boldly 'The sheltered bay we found yesterday exists'. It will not do even if we substitute for this the Russellian *analysans* of propositions of the form 'The ϕ'er exists', which in this case will be 'There is just one x such that x is a sheltered bay and x was found by us yesterday'. The fact of which hardly anyone is

---
[5] See 'Logical Atomism', *Logic and Knowledge*, ed. R. C. Marsh, VI, 242 f.

aware has nothing to do with our discoveries of yesterday. It is only to be expected, and a matter of indifference, that people for the most part are ignorant of our movements: it is thoroughly surprising, and subject for rejoicing, that so few people know of the existence of this sheltered bay.

What we feel inclined to say in response to these considerations is that the phrase 'the sheltered bay which we found yesterday' has, as Russell would say, 'primary occurrence' in (2).[6] This can be appreciated by taking the somewhat similar, though more straightforward, proposition, 'Hardly anyone knows that the sheltered bay we found yesterday was the scene of a bloody battle in 1645'. Russell would say that in principle there are two ways of understanding this proposition. If we take the definite description ' The sheltered bay we found yesterday' as having primary occurrence, the proposition according to Russell is equivalent to 'For some x, both x alone is a sheltered bay found by us yesterday and hardly anyone knows that x was the scene of a bloody battle in 1645'. If, on the other hand, the definite description is taken as having secondary occurrence, the proposition comes out as equivalent to 'Hardly anyone knows that, for some x, both x alone is a sheltered bay found by us yesterday and x was the scene of a bloody battle in 1645'. The second alternative is most unlikely to represent what someone who uttered the original sentence would intend to assert by it.[7] We can scarcely suppose that in this context 'the sheltered bay we found yesterday' has secondary occurrence. Since, then, it has to be interpreted as having primary occurrence, it must be supposed that, in its

---

[6] Mackie is aware of the need for the definite description in (2) to have primary occurrence ('The Riddle of Existence', pp. 252 f.). However, he thinks that this points to a difference between the unembedded propositions 'The sheltered bay we found yesterday exists' and 'A unique sheltered bay that we found yesterday exists'. Russell would not have recognized such a difference. His analysis of 'The sheltered bay we found yesterday exists', which would represent it as being of the form $\Sigma x \Pi y E I x y \phi y$, would leave no room for distinguishing primary and secondary occurrence when it is embedded in a wider context.

[7] If we want an example where both interpretations are plausible, we might amend the proposition so that it reads 'Hardly anyone knows that the present holiday camp for Quakers was the scene of a bloody battle in 1645'. What hardly anyone is being said to know, in this case, might be *either* the fact of the occurrence of the bloody battle on the site in question *or* the fact that the same site on which a bloody battle was fought in 1645 is now occupied by the only Quaker holiday camp.

deep structure, the description it contains falls outside the scope of the operator represented by 'Hardly anyone knows that —'. The Russellian analysis makes this clear. When giving the *analysans* of the proposition that is appropriate if the definite description is taken as having primary occurrence, it postpones the words 'hardly anyone knows that' until after the description 'a sheltered bay which we found yesterday'. The latter falls within the scope, and is therefore written to the right, of the operator 'For some x', but it falls outside the scope, and is therefore written to the left, of the operator 'hardly anyone knows that'. Put less linguistically, the fact that we found a sheltered bay yesterday is no part of what we are saying hardly anyone knows. It is near-universal ignorance of the location of the bloody battle that we are remarking, not the slightness of public knowledge of our holiday adventures.

Without committing ourselves to all the details of Russell's doctrine of primary and secondary occurrence, we can see that there is something obviously right about the view that the definite description 'the sheltered bay we found yesterday' has wider scope than the operator 'Hardly anyone knows that' in 'Hardly anyone knows that the sheltered bay we found yesterday was the scene of a bloody battle in 1645'. But if we say that the same definite description has primary occurrence in (2) we seem committed to the following analysis: 'For some x, both x alone is a sheltered bay which we found yesterday and hardly anyone knows that x exists'. How is this last proposition to be understood? Clearly, it can only be understood if a corresponding proposition, shorn of the quantifier, 'For some x', and with a name substituted for the remaining occurrences of x, can also be understood. (We are not here talking about truth-conditions, but conditions for understanding the proposition.) In that case, we must have a way of understanding propositions like ' Both St. Giles's Bay is a sheltered bay which we found yesterday and hardly anyone knows that St. Giles's Bay exists'. But the second conjunct of this conjunctive proposition is the same in form as (1). The Russellian aim of giving an illuminating paraphrase of (1) by substituting a definite description for 'David Pears' faces a dilemma. Either the definite description has secondary occurrence, in which case the analysis fails for the reasons given in the last paragraph but one; or it has primary occurrence, in which case the proposed *analysans* can be understood only if the *analysandum* is already understood. Furthermore, if we accept the second horn of the dilemma, we can no longer see any important difference between (1) and (2). Each was introduced by Mackie in order to present a type of counter-example to the thesis that 'exists' is always a second-level predicable. The suggestion was that the type of counter-example represented by (2) was interestingly different from the type represented by (1). But the form represented by (1) is presupposed by (2). The proposition about the sheltered bay falls essentially into the same category as the proposition about David Pears.

For the proposition about President Ford *is* also a proposition about David Pears. It can just as well be regarded as saying of David Pears that he is one of the people of whose existence President Ford is unaware as it can be regarded as saying of President Ford that he is unaware of David Pears's existence. Just as (2) needed to be understood as equivalent to 'Concerning the sheltered bay we found yesterday, hardly anyone knows that that bay exists', so (1) can be paraphrased 'Concerning David Pears, President Ford does not know that that man exists'. So any Russellian attempt to analyse (1) by taking 'David Pears' as the abbreviation of a definite description would have to give that definite description primary occurrence. The second horn of the dilemma is unavoidable. This shows that a vicious regress is lurking in any such attempt. Using Russell's symbolism, we may say that such an attempt would involve assigning to (1), which superficially has the form '$\sim a$ knows that ϕb', the deeper-level form '$\sim a$ knows that $\phi(\imath x)(\psi x)$'. But this itself has the still deeper-level form '$(\exists x)(y)[(x=y \equiv \psi y)$ & $\sim a$ knows that ϕx]'. This latter form, however, is intelligible only if propositions of the form '(y) $[(b=y \equiv \psi y)$ & $\sim a$ knows that ϕb]' are intelligible. This is because we cannot suppose that someone understands an existentially quantified proposition if he does not understand a proposition which would count as a substitution instance of it: 'Some number is an even prime' will not be understood by someone to whom 'Two is an even prime' is unintelligible. But the square brackets in '(y) $[(b=y \equiv \psi y)$ & $\sim a$ knows that

ϕb]' are idle, and when they are removed we have a conjunctive proposition of which '$\sim a$ knows that ϕb' is a conjunct. The conjunctive proposition will certainly not be understood if one of its conjuncts is not understood. So propositions of the form '$(\exists x)(y)[(x=y \equiv \psi y) \mathbin{\&} \sim a$ knows that ϕx]' are intelligible only if we know how to understand propositions of the form '$\sim a$ knows that ϕb'—which is where we came in.

4. *Preliminary analysis of 'President Ford does not know that David Pears exists'*

The need to interpret (1) in the sense 'Concerning David Pears, President Ford does not know that that man exists' suggests that we say that the name 'David Pears' has primary occurrence in (1). But how can we understand this idea? 'Primary occurrence' is defined in terms of definite descriptions, not in terms of proper names, and our present position is that 'David Pears' is a proper name and cannot be 'reduced' in any way to a definite description.

Let us see whether a broader meaning can be given to 'primary occurrence' than that which Russell originally gave it in 'On Denoting'. On Russell's view, a definite description has primary occurrence in a proposition if, in the analysis of that proposition, the open sentence which corresponds to the definite description falls within the scope of the quantifier which governs the proposition as a whole, but outside the scope of some other operator which governs only the second conjunct of the conjunctive matrix governed by the quantifier. In other words, the proposition as a whole will be analysed as a conjunctive open sentence, each conjunct containing an occurrence of a variable bound by a single quantifier governing the conjunctive open sentence as a whole. The second of the conjuncts, but not the first, will be within the scope of some sentential operator, which may be negation, or something of the form 'President Ford does not know that', or any of a number of other possibilities. It is essential that the open sentence which corresponds to the definite description, while remaining outside the scope of the sentential operator which governs the second conjunct—for this is what gives the definite description primary occurrence—be bound to this second conjunct by sharing with it a variable bound by a quantifier governing the proposition as a whole.

The propositions Russell was concerned with required analyses of the form $\Sigma x K\phi x\delta\psi x$[8], where δ represents a sentential operator of the kind we have described, and where the variable which appears in each conjunct is an individual variable. Russell, however, unlike some of his disciples, was perfectly willing to use predicative variables and bind them with quantifiers; and it is easy to construct a formula which answers to the general description given in the last paragraph, but where the variable bound by the quantifier is of the predicative category. The simplest formula containing a predicative variable and answering to this description would be $\Sigma\phi K\phi a\delta\phi b$. Can we give a sense to the suggestion that 'David Pears' has primary occurrence in (1) by analysing (1) in such a way that it is seen to be a proposition of this form? I think not. Propositions of this form contain two proper names, symbolized by a and b in the formula. (1) does indeed contain two proper names, but the name 'President Ford' occurs as part of the phrase 'President Ford does not know that' which looks the most likely candidate for the role of sentential operator providing a substitute for δ in the formula. That leaves no proper name to act as substitute for b. But there are other formulae which would answer to the description given, and which would not require a proper name in the operand clause of the second conjunct: for instance, $\Sigma\phi K\phi a\Sigma x\phi x$. It is possible to obtain an open sentence, not only by attaching a proper name to a predicative variable, but by attaching the predicative variable to a second-level predicable, e.g. 'For some x, — x'. Since the verb 'exists' occurs in the operand clause of our *analysandum*, it is tempting to suppose that a proposition of just this form will supply the correct *analysans*. We should then be able to account for (1) without having to admit that it constituted a counter-example to the thesis that 'exists' is never a first-level predicate. On this view, the meaning of (1) would be given by:

(3) For some ϕ, both David Pears ϕ's and President Ford does not know that, for some x, ϕx.

[8] It is unimportant for our purposes that substitutions for ϕx have to be of the form $\Pi y E I x y \phi y$.

This bears some resemblance to an ordinary-language variant of (1), namely, 'President Ford does not know that there is such a person as David Pears'. But it will not do. All that (3) says is that there is something which David Pears is doing and President Ford does not know that anyone is doing it. This could perfectly well be true of President Ford, even if he knew that David Pears existed. It is likely to be true of David Pears's best friends. What is essential to the knowledge that David Pears exists is, surely, there being some concept that David Pears *alone* instantiates, something which David Pears and nobody else does. Let us try, therefore,

(4) For some ϕ, both David Pears alone ϕ's and President Ford does not know that, for just one x, ϕx.

This will not do either. Again, it could perfectly well be true even though President Ford was fully aware of the fact that David Pears existed. Suppose, for example, that David Pears is at this moment the only person in the Hall at Christ Church in Oxford and that President Ford does not know that there is just one person there. In that case (4) would be true. But it does not follow that (1) is true.[9] There is more adjusting to be done.

Where we have been going wrong is in supposing that in the deep structure of (1) the phrase 'President Ford does not know that' must hang together as a single logical item. Certainly this phrase *can* function as a complex sentential operator, and as such is capable of being substituted for δ in our formula. But when negation occurs in a complex proposition it is often a moot question whether the scope of the negation operator is to be regarded as being the proposition as a whole, or only part of it. This question is the obverse of the question originally posed by Russell, whether the definite description 'The King of France' has primary or secondary occurrence in the proposition 'The King of France is not bald'. If 'The King of France' is taken as having primary occurrence in this proposition, 'not' must be taken as having in its scope only the predicable '— is bald'. If, on the other hand, 'The King of France' has secondary occurrence, 'not' will have the whole proposition in its scope.

[9] I am grateful to Mr Mackie for pointing this out to me at the meeting at which his paper was originally presented.

So it is possible that the 'not' which occurs in (1) should be regarded as having widest scope; though here, since there are three operators, negation, the quantifier, and 'President Ford knows that', this is perfectly compatible with 'David Pears' having, in our extended sense, primary occurrence. If 'not' is taken in this way the required *analysans* of (1) will be:

(5) It is not the case that, for some ϕ, both David Pears alone ϕ's and President Ford knows that for just one x, ϕx.

This indeed accords with the intuitions which were given expression earlier in the chapter. There are many different propositions which will serve to remove the President's ignorance of David Pears's existence. I can remove it by telling him that there is just one teacher of philosophy at Oxford who has written books on philosophers called 'Russell' and 'Wittgenstein', and who is a Student of Christ Church, and who . . ., etc. Or I can remove it, in the circumstances envisaged, by telling him that there is just one Englishman whom Henry Kissinger met on holiday in Mexico in 1972, and with whom he played poker every night, and who . . ., etc. So to be in a position to assert (1) I must know that President Ford has been told none of these things, i.e. that there is nothing that David Pears alone does, of which it is also true that President Ford knows that just one person does it. And to know this is to know that (5) is true.

5. *Restriction on the sort of predicables required for the range of ϕ in this analysis*

Can all this be paralleled for (2)? One way to remove the ignorance about the sheltered bay would be by telling people that there is a sheltered bay (we need hardly add 'just one') ten miles due west of Fishguard. We could also remove it by telling them that there is such a bay fifteen miles north of St. David's. There are many ways of directing people to a given place. To say that hardly anyone knows that the bay exists is to say that for most people there is no suitable description such that both the bay alone fits that description and they know that there is just one bay which fits that description. 'Hardly anyone knows that' requires more careful unpacking than

'President Ford does not know that' because it involves negation, the operator 'x knows that' and the quantifier 'For most x'. The order in which these operators occur is important. If, as in (5), we give widest scope to the negation operator, we shall produce a proposition which denies that those who know that the sheltered bay we found yesterday exists are in a majority. This would be true if they represented 50 per cent of the population. But what we want is to *assert* that those who do not know that the sheltered bay we found yesterday exists *are* in the majority, i.e. represent *more* than 50 per cent. This will be achieved if (2) is given the following analysis:

(6) For most x, it is not the case that, for some ϕ, both the sheltered bay we found yesterday alone ϕ's and x knows that, for just one y, ϕy.

I leave the unpacking of the definite description 'The sheltered bay we found yesterday' as an exercise for the reader.

But would (6) ever be true? Amongst the descriptions that can truly be given of the sheltered bay we found yesterday are those provided by map readings in terms of longitude and latitude, or perhaps the National Grid. If ϕ is of the form 'is situated $m^{\circ}N$, $n^{\circ}W$', can it really be maintained that hardly anyone knows that, for just one y, ϕy? Everyone who knows about map references knows that any map reference, if sufficiently precise, will pick out a single point on the surface of the earth. So everyone who can understand predicates of the form 'is situated $m^{\circ}N$, $n^{\circ}W$' knows that there is always just one place of which such an expression can truly be predicated. Or is the point that hardly anyone *can* understand predicates of this kind? But that was not what we had in mind when we asserted (2).

The same difficulty arises for (1).[10] It is no doubt true that, for some n, both David Pears is the nth tallest person in England and President Ford knows that there is someone who is the nth tallest person in England. Let us suppose that this proposition is verified by substituting 'six millionth' for nth at each occurrence. In that case (5) is shown to be false by the fact that 'is the six millionth tallest person in England' can be substituted for ϕ in the matrix of (5) to yield a true proposition.

[10] I am again grateful to Mr Mackie for having drawn my attention to this point.

But we should not in that case say that (1) was false. It does not matter whether six million or some other number is the correct substitution for n here, provided it is a number such that President Ford knows that there are at least that many people in England. But this piece of general knowledge, like the piece of general knowledge that is constituted by most people's knowing that any map reference will individuate some one place, is not sufficient to constitute a person's knowledge of an individual.

A minimal requirement for the substitutions for 'For some x, ϕx' and 'For some y, ϕy' in (5) and (6) is that the propositions formed by substituting constants for the variable ϕ be contingent. Some will hold that no special provision need be made for this, since all existential propositions are contingent; but I do not accept this view. Some propositions of this form are necessary; perhaps even, *pace* Kant, analytic. Thus substituting 'is an even prime number' for ϕ may produce a necessary or even analytic truth. But a true proposition of this kind will not provide a basis for the introduction of a proper name. Names of numbers are best thought of as abbreviations for definite descriptions. In other words, what Russell said about 'Julius Caesar' is appropriate enough in the case of 'π' or 'thirty-three'. These can indeed be regarded as shorthand for 'The ratio of the circumference of any circle to its diameter' and 'The successor of thirty-two (which is the successor of thirty-one ... etc.)'. So knowing that thirty-three exists just *is* knowing that for some n, n alone is a successor of thirty-two, and not to know that π exists is not to know that, for some n, n alone is a ratio of the circumference to the diameter of any circle. What is known or not known in this sort of case is a necessary truth, but knowledge of necessary truths of this sort does not play a part in the introduction into discourse of genuine proper names. This sort of ignorance does not require so complicated an analysis as those which (5) and (6) provide. But, in any case, there is no question here of a counter-example to the thesis that existence is a second-level predicate. If President Ford is unaware of the existence of π, what he is unaware of can quite simply be expressed by a proposition of the form 'For some n, ϕn'.

So a constraint must be placed on possible substitutions

for ϕ in (5) and (6). Such substitutions must be predicables such that it is not necessary that they can truly be predicated of just one individual. Indeed we must be still more restrictive. The proposition 'For just one x, x is the six millionth tallest person in England' may not be a necessary truth, but its truth is deducible, with the help only of logical truths, from a contingent proposition which is a piece of 'general knowledge', namely that the population of England exceeds six million. Propositions of this sort must not be allowable as substitution instances of 'For just one x, ϕx' and 'For just one y, ϕy' in (5) and (6). Accordingly we must disallow as possible substitutions for ϕ in (5) and (6) predicables standing for concepts whose unique instantiation is deducible, with the help only of logical truths, from facts of general knowledge. The existence of President Ford may be a fact of general knowledge, but the existence of David Pears is not. Propositions of the form '*a* knows that *b* exists' are in general false: we are all ignorant of the existence of the majority of our fellow human beings.

6. *Difficulties involving opacity*

The success of (5) in providing an analysis of (1) could be challenged also in this way. Suppose President Ford is watching on television a programme about Wyoming. At one point a man is shown fishing from a small boat on Jackson Lake with the Tetons in the background. There was just one man shown fishing from a boat on that lake on that programme on that evening. The man in fact was David Pears. President Ford was greatly impressed by the beauty of the photography and, if asked several weeks later whether he knew that there was just one man who was filmed fishing from a small boat on Jackson Lake and who appeared on television on that programme on that particular night, he would reply 'Yes'. So it seems that (5) would be false. But if asked at the same time if he knew whether David Pears was fond of fishing, he would say that he had never heard of David Pears. So we should be inclined to say that (1) was true. Nobody had told him that the man in the boat was called 'David Pears'. For that matter, when Henry Kissinger told him about the man with whom he played poker every night during his holiday in Mexico in 1972, he never told him that the man was called 'David Pears'. Would we be right in these cases in saying that (1) is true? Does President Ford have to know that someone is called 'David Pears' in order to know that David Pears exists?

To this question there is no correct answer. In Quine's terminology, there is a use of expressions like 'President Ford does not know that — exists' which treats them as transparent contexts, and in analysing (1) as equivalent to (5) we have been treating the expression in this way. But no doubt there is another use of such contexts which treats them as opaque. If 'President Ford does not know that — exists' is understood as an opaque context, (5) will not provide an analysis of (1). Indeed, someone's refusal to allow that the falsehood of (5) is a sufficient condition for the falsehood of (1) shows that he is treating the context as opaque. But in that case we can analyse what he *does* mean by (1) by inserting 'both' before ϕx and 'and x is called "David Pears"' after ϕx in (5).[11] All that has been shown is that (1) is ambiguous. We do not always apply the same rules for allowing that someone knows that someone else exists. On some occasions, when we are strict, we require that a man know the name of a person before we allow that he knows that that person exists. On other occasions we will admit that he knows very well that the other person exists, although he has not the least idea of his name. But on neither understanding of (1) do we have to agree that '— exists' is there being used as a first-level predicate.

Another difficulty may be felt with propositions like (5) as analyses of propositions like (1). Let us suppose, with many modern scholars, that the author of Chapters 40 and following of the Book of Isaiah was not the Isaiah who lived in the year that King Uzziah died. And let us suppose, with St. Augustine, that Mary the sister of Martha and the 'woman who was a sinner' of Luke 7:37 were the same person as Mary Magdalen. Let us further suppose that President Carter, whose background is that of conservative Protestantism, believes that all the chapters of the Book of Isaiah were written by one person, and that the sister of Martha and the woman who was a sinner and Mary Magdalen were three different women. Now Isaiah alone wrote Chapter 6 of Isaiah and President Carter knows that just one man wrote that chapter, so on our showing he

---

[11] Cf. the treatment of (19) and (20) in Ch. IX below.

knows that Isaiah existed. But Deutero-Isaiah alone wrote Chapter 40 of Isaiah and President Carter knows that just one man wrote that chapter, so on our showing he knows that Deutero-Isaiah existed. And Mary was the only sister of Martha and President Carter knows that Martha had just one sister, so he knows that Mary existed; and similar considerations show that he knows both that 'the woman who was a sinner' existed and that Mary Magdalen existed. So the President knows that both Isaiah and Deutero-Isaiah existed, but thinks that a single man wrote all the chapters of Isaiah. And he knows that Mary Magdalen, who *was* a sinner *and* the sister of Martha, existed, but thinks that three women existed, where, with St. Augustine, we say there was only one. Can we really say that President Carter has knowledge of all these things? He certainly does not know that there were at least two authors responsible for the Book of Isaiah or that just one woman is talked about in John 11: 1, Luke 7: 37, and John 20: 1.

These are, I believe, only apparent difficulties. No one but an Absolute Idealist need believe that x knows that y exists only if x knows all there is to know about y. It is quite possible for x to know that y exists even if he is in grave error about y's identity. He may think that y is the same as z, when he isn't, and still know that both y and z exist; and he may think that y is different from z, when he isn't, and it still be true both that he knows that y exists and that he knows that z exists. *This* sort of opacity, if such we should call it, is certainly involved in propositions asserting knowledge of a person's existence. There is no need to amend (5) as an analysis of (1), or to suppose a variety of senses of (1), in order to take account of these considerations.

7. *Indeterminacy in claims about* a's *knowledge of* b's *existence*

It is important to emphasize that there is considerable indeterminacy in our use of sentences of the form 'a knows that b exists'. As appeared in the need to distinguish an opaque from a transparent interpretation of this construction, it is by no means certain that a's knowledge of b's existence implies an ability on a's part to use the proper name 'b'. So the various theories that philosophers have put forward to explain a person's ability to use a proper name—the 'cluster' theory, the causal theory, etc.—are not necessarily relevant to an understanding of the form 'a knows that b exists', at least transparently interpreted. Different people may indeed have different requirements about how much a must know if he is to know that b exists, just as different people have different requirements about how much knowledge of b it is necessary for a to have if he is to be said to know b. President Ford's sincere denial that he had ever heard of David Pears may or may not count against a claim that he does nevertheless know of David Pears's existence. We manage fairly well to make ourselves understood without settling these matters.

This indeterminacy does not affect my claim to have, in (5), at least a schematic analysis of (1). The indeterminacy is entirely concentrated in the range of possible substitutions for ϕ in this formula. The arguments advanced before the formula was introduced are sufficient to establish that any analysis that is given of (1) must conform to this scheme. These were arguments from analogy. We saw an analogy between the role of 'the sheltered bay we found yesterday' in 'Hardly anyone knows that the sheltered bay we found yesterday was the scene of a bloody battle in 1645', where it has primary occurrence, and the role which the same expression plays in (2). The role which this definite description plays in (2) is again analogous to the role the name 'David Pears' plays in (1). There must be some sense of 'primary occurrence' in which these expressions all have primary occurrence in these propositions. I produced an extended sense of primary occurrence: an expression has primary occurrence in a proposition if, in a complete analysis of the proposition, it is attached to a variable to form a conjunct of a conjunctive matrix whose other conjunct is governed by some sentential operator and contains a further occurrence of the same variable, both variables being bound to an initial existential quantifier. The only way a proper name like 'David Pears' can appear in the first conjunct of a conjunctive matrix of this sort is by being attached to a predicative variable. The predicative variable can only appear in the second conjunct as argument to a second-level predicate, since there is no available proper name to attach to it to turn it into an open sentence. It is thus that we arrived at (3). The considerations which required (3) to be changed to (4) were compelling: if knowledge of David Pears's existence consists in knowing that some property is instantiated, it must consist in knowing that it is uniquely instantiated. The emendation of (4) to produce (5) was simply a matter of the correct placing of the negation operator. These considerations all hold good, even if uncertainty remains over the range of substitutions possible for ϕ in the formula. They suffice to show that 'exist' in (1) is not to be construed as a first-level predicate.

8. *Analysis of 'I might not have existed'*

We are now in a position to return to the points raised by Moore and Plantinga at the beginning of the chapter. Moore cited the truth of any proposition formed by pointing at something and saying 'This might not have existed' as evidence of the significance in some sense of 'This does in fact exist'. Plantinga suggested that it might be possible similarly to infer the meaningfulness of 'Socrates exists' from the undoubted truth of 'Socrates might not have existed' and 'If Socrates had not existed Plato would not have been his student'. Both argued from this to a sense of 'exist' in which it could properly be predicated of individuals. Let us now take the proposition 'I might not have existed'. It will be interesting to see if this proposition is amenable to an analysis along similar lines to that given to (1) and (2) above.

As a start, let us try,

(7) For some ϕ, both I alone ϕ and it might not have been the case that, for just one x, ϕx.[12]

Suppose that David Pears says this while he is standing all alone in the Hall of Christ Church. What he says is true because no one else is in the hall and it might well have been the case, either that no one at all, or that more than one person, was in the hall. But that can scarcely amount to the statement of a sufficient condition of the truth of his statement that he, David Pears, might not have existed. The contingency of his existence is quite another matter than the possibility that more or less than one person is standing in Christ Church Hall.

[12] An almost identical analysis of 'I might not have not have been existing now' is put forward by H.-N. Castañeda in 'On the Phenomeno-Logic of the I', *Proceedings of the XIVth International Congress of Philosophy*, Vienna, 1968, p. 265.

It is sometimes held that there are facts about a person which are necessarily true of that person and of no one else—what might be called 'individuating facts' about the person. A likely candidate for the role of individuating fact is the fact that the person came into existence as the result of the union of a particular sperm with a particular ovum; or, in the case of identical twins, triplets, etc., as the result of the separate development of one spatially distinguishable part of a particular fertilized ovum. For any person x, there must be some predicable ϕ, such that the proposition ϕx states an individuating fact of this kind. In my case, since I am an only child, the predicable ϕ in question will be of the form '— is the result of the union of such-and-such a sperm and such-and-such an ovum'. I do not of course know how to fill out completely the dummy description 'such-and-such' on each of its occurrences in this predicable, but they are capable in principle of being filled out. A scientist might 'mark' a particular sperm and a particular ovum by radioactivating them and know that the one had fertilized the other, and thus be able to trace the resultant embryo and human being. It is not impossible to lay down conditions that a predicable must satisfy in order to yield the statement of an individuating fact of this sort.[13]

We do not usually attribute to Locke the view that individuals as such have essential properties: quite the contrary. 'Essential and not essential relate only to our abstract ideas, and the names annexed to them.'[14] But as Mackie has pointed out, when Locke is dealing with the idea of identity, he lets slip a remark that supports this view that a person's origin is essential to him. 'That, therefore, that had one beginning, is the same thing: and that which had a different beginning in time and place from that, is not the same, but diverse.'[15] Mackie gives an illuminating account of the reasons we have for this view. Unless we are committed to a complete determinism, in which case the proposition 'I might not have existed' will have no

---

[13] This view of the individuating facts about a person is adopted by Saul Kripke in 'Naming and Necessity', *The Semantics of Natural Languages*, edd. D. Davidson and G. Harman, 1972, pp. 312-14; it is argued for by Colin McGinn in 'The Necessities of Origin', *Journal of Philosophy*, 73, 1976, No. 5.
[14] *An Essay Concerning Human Understanding*, Book III, Ch. 6, § 4.
[15] Ibid., Book II, Ch. 27, § 1. Mackie's discussion is in *Problems from Locke*, 1976, pp. 150-60.

interest for us, we shall be prepared to allow that at any stage in a person's life the future holds a number of different genuine possibilities. In 1810 is was a genuine possibility that Napoleon might never have invaded Russia, in 1789 that he might never have been the ruler of France, in 1775 that he might never have been a soldier. But these were only possibilities about Napoleon in so far as they presuppose that up to the date in question what we know happened to Napoleon did in fact happen to him. There has to be some, however brief, segment of the actual history of Napoleon for the name 'Napoleon' to latch on to. Otherwise we should not be talking about *him,* but about someone else. Possibilities relate to the future; and, unless there is some time when the counterfactual possibilities about Napoleon which we are envisaging could have been regarded by him, or his friends, as ways in which his life could develop in what for him then was the future, there is no sense in which we can say that it is *he* who might have been otherwise than he in fact was. But if we do not leave him at least the fact of his conception we shall have removed from our scheme of things the Napoleon about whom we are speculating.

That is to assume that Napoleon's conception is in fact the *terminus ante quem non* for such speculations. It is to rule out the possibility of a pre-existent Napoleon such as Plato would have posited. It is to rule out the possibility of transmigrations of Napoleon's soul of a kind which would regard its incarnation in the body of a Corsican as a reward or punishment for its actions in a previous life. Suppose that Napoleon had a previous existence as Molière's kitchen-maid; we could not in that case identify the possibility that he never existed with the possibility that Letizia Buonaparte should never have conceived a son in 1768. But this does not affect the issue. Whether or not these Platonic or Buddhist beliefs are intelligible is a philosophical question that can leave aside. For, even if they were intelligible, we should still have to look to some fact about the ultimate origin of the transmigrating soul to be an individuating fact about it. It may be that the vanishing point of intelligibility of Plato's views about souls is not their immateriality or their immortality so much as their ungenerability. Perhaps there is no sense in which many different individual beings could each have existed throughout eternity.

Whatever else might have been true of me, it seems that my origin could not have been other than it was. These facts about my origin may be expressed by the ascription to me of certain biological properties, as that I am the result of the union of such and such a sperm with such and such an ovum; or by the ascription of properties of some quite different, e.g. psychological, kind. But whatever the category appropriate for these essential properties, this will be expressed by limitations on the range of predicables which are permitted as substitutions for the variable ϕ in (7). The predicable 'stands at this moment in Christ Church Hall' will fall outside the range: the predicable 'results from the union of such-and-such a sperm with such-and-such an ovum' may well fall within it. So again the analysis provided of a recalcitrant proposition turns out only to be a schematic one. (7) will not be a complete analysis of 'I might not have existed' until the limitations on the range of permitted substitutions for ϕ are determined. But again, I can claim that I have dealt with the alleged counter-example to my claim that 'exist' is never a first-level predicate, even if I am unable to provide more than a schematic analysis of the counter-example in question. 'I might not have existed' is intelligible only if there are some facts about me that are essential to my existence. If no facts were essential in this way, no counter-factual supposition could be tantamount to supposing my non-existence. If they are individuating facts about *me*, they must be statable by some proposition of the form 'I alone ϕ'. If the property thus ascribed is, not only individuating, but essential to me, the supposition that that property is not uniquely instantiated is the supposition that I never existed. This is expressed by a proposition of the form 'It is not the case that, for just one x, ϕx'. When I say that I might not have existed, I do not commit myself in any way to any particular property as the property which thus individuates me and is essential to me. If I were entirely ignorant of my origins, as I might well be, I should in fact have no idea what this property was. But that there is some such property is certain, and my assertion that I might not have existed is the assertion that there is some such property; that is, that there is some property essential to me, which I alone possess, and which might never have been uniquely instantiated; that is, that some proposition of the form of (7), with a suitable limitation on permissible substitutions for ϕ, is true. Accordingly there is no need, on account of the intelligibility, and indeed truth, of 'I might not have existed' to postulate a sense of 'exist' in which it is a predicate of individuals, a first-level predicate. The prima-facie analysis of 'I might not have existed' which derived it from the embedding of 'I exist' in the context 'It might not have been the case that —' is to be rejected.

Moore's proposition 'This might not have existed' and Plantinga's 'Socrates might not have existed' are obviously capable of a similar analysis, although Moore's stipulation that 'This' refers to a sense-datum might give rise to a frustrating hunt after 'individuating facts' about sense-data. Plantinga's 'If Socrates had not existed, Plato would not have been his student' is amenable to analysis on much the same lines. Let us first amend it, as already suggested, to 'If Socrates had not existed, Plato would not have been Socrates' student'. The same recipe as that which provided (7) as a paraphrase of 'I might not have existed' then yields 'For some ϕ, both Socrates alone ϕ's and, if it had not been the case that, for just one x, ϕx, Plato would not have been Socrates' student' as a paraphrase of the amended counter-factual. Similarly we can obtain for 'If no persons had existed, Socrates would not have existed' the paraphrase 'For some ϕ, both Socrates alone ϕ's, and , if no persons had existed, if would not have been the case that, for just one x, ϕx'.

9. *General form of analyses of propositions apparently involving embedded singular existential propositions*

The arguments put forward by Moore, Plantinga, and Mackie were based on the claim that propositions which were obviously in order resulted from embedding in wider contexts propositions formed by predicating '— exist' of objects. So to predicate '— exist' is to treat '— exist' as a first-level predicable; and if the propositions to which these philosophers draw our attention were constructed in the way they allege, their claim that existence is, or can be, a property of objects would have to be allowed. My discussion in the preceding pages has been designed to rebut these arguments by showing that none of the unexceptionable propositions to which they draw our attention is analysable as the result of embedding in a wider context a proposition of the form 'a exists'. We have argued that another analysis should be given in each case. The analyses offered have been in one way different and in another way the same. The propositions brought to our notice by Mackie were concerned with knowledge of someone or something's existence. Those presented by Moore and Plantinga concerned the possibility of someone's non-existence. The question of what a person has to know if he is to know that someone exists is different from the question of what would have to be the case if the possibility of someone's not existing were realized. These are different questions, but they are both philosophical questions of extreme difficulty. There is no reason to suppose that a single answer, or method of answering, can be found for both of them. It is not claimed that either of them has been adequately answered in this chapter.

What I have claimed is that answers to both questions will involve the unique instantiation of some property, or set of properties, belonging to that person alone. What has to be the case for it to be known that a exists, or for it to be possible that a doesn't exist, is for something of the form 'For some ϕ, both a alone ϕs and δ for just one x, ϕx' to be true. Different substitutions for δ here require different ranges of possible substitutions for ϕ. If I am to know of your existence I do not have to know any of your essential properties. I may know that you exist in virtue of knowing that there is just one person who is the manager of my local supermarket. But it does not follow that you would not have existed if you had not become manager of my local supermarket (or that you did not exist until you became manager of my local supermarket). However, despite the different restrictions required on substitutions for the predicative variable in the sort of analysis given by (5) and (6), on the one hand, and (7) on the other, both sorts of analysis make use of the quantification of predicative variables. These philosophers' objections to the claim that '— exist' is never a first-level predicable are to be met by invoking expressions of the form 'For some ϕ —' 'For no ϕ —', which are third-level predicables. Whatever the variations in the analyses provided by (5), (6), and (7), this binding of predicative variables by a quantifier remains constant.

Higher-order quantification, as it is called, will very often provide us with a means of answering objections to Frege's doctrine of existence. At a naïve level it has been felt that the ground can be cut from under Frege's feet by drawing attention to the fact that there are all sorts of things which do not exist: hobgoblins and female popes and prime numbers which are both even and greater than two. The paradox of non-existence seems, on this view, not to get started (see above, Ch. II, § 7). This can be resisted by saying that the proposition 'There are things which do not exist' is to be analysed as 'For some ϕ, it is not the case that, for some x, ϕx'. For want of a third-level predicable, all Frege's gains might have been lost. In the next chapter I shall make further use of an analysis which involves higher-order quantification in rebutting claims that '— exist' is sometimes a first-level predicable. I shall have to wait for the sixth chapter before attempting to deal with radical objections to, and misunderstandings of, the practice of binding with quantifiers variables other than individual variables. These objections, though radical in the sense that they strike at the root of the methods of analysis that I am now employing, will turn out to be from another point of view, surprisingly conservative.

V
Tensed Existential Propositions

1. *Tensed existential propositions as involving embedded existential propositions*

The strongest case for there being at least some contexts in which 'exist' is a first-level predicable can be made by directing attention to propositions in which 'exist' is subordinated to expressions like 'comes to' and 'no longer'. It is difficult not to believe that in 'Arkle came to exist in 1945' or 'Arkle no longer exists' something is predicated of a particular racehorse. Why should we differentiate between the form of 'Arkle no longer exists' and that of 'Arkle no longer races'? The proposition 'Arkle no longer races' is the result of performing some tense-logical operation on the proposition 'Arkle races'. The proposition 'Arkle no longer exists' must surely be the result of performing the same operation on the proposition 'Arkle exists'. But if 'exists' is not a first-level predicable there will be no such proposition for the tense-logical operator to operate on. This analysis of 'Arkle no longer exists', however, has other difficulties to face besides that of requiring that 'exist' be a first-level predicable. Let us examine these difficulties.

2. *'Arkle no longer exists' and Plato's Beard*

Negative existential propositions, as we have seen, give rise to the paradox of Plato's Beard—if, that is, the grammatical subject of the proposition is taken as a true logical subject. 'Aristocratic Australians don't exist' would be in some way self-defeating if we took it as saying something *about* aristocratic Australians. It is partly for this reason that the expression 'Aristocratic Australians', as it occurs in this proposition, is to be construed as a first-level predicable, in the wide sense, rather than a genuine logical subject. The sentence 'Aristocratic Australians don't exist' means the same as 'Nobody is an aristocratic Australian', where the correctness of this categorization of '— is an aristocratic Australian' as a predicable is apparent. But 'Arkle' in 'Arkle does not exist', as much as in any other context,[1] can only be construed as a logical subject. 'Arkle does not exist' must either be a proposition about a particular racehorse or fail to be a proposition at all. There is no side-stepping the paradox of reference in this case: Arkle must exist for 'Arkle does not exist' to be significant.

Arkle, however, need not exist *now* for propositions about him to be true or false. Arkle does not have to be alive in 1987 if we are to be able to say of him in that year that he won the Derby in 1967. 'When Mr N. N. dies one says that the bearer of the name dies, not that the meaning dies. And it would be nonsensical to say that, for if the name ceased to have meaning it would make no sense to say "Mr N. N. is dead".'[2] So one of the things that we seem to be able to say of a racehorse after he is dead is precisely that he is dead, i.e. that he no longer exists. 'Arkle does not exist' may give rise to paradox, but 'Arkle no longer exists' seems to be entirely in order.

3. *The Tensed or Qualified Version of Plato's Beard*

On reflection, however, there is a class of things which we do not seem to be able to say of the dead, and it is not obvious that their having ceased to exist is excluded from this class. We cannot say of those who no longer exist that they are at this moment engaged in any activity. The dead are not now up and doing. How much is included in the scope of 'activity' and 'doing' here? There is a sense of 'do' in which it is a mere dummy verb, a predicative variable, as 'thing' is a dummy noun or individual variable. In this sense of 'do' we might enunciate as a general law that if a is truly said to do anything at time t there must be such a thing as a at time t. Metaliguistically this can be expressed thus: if any predicate is truly applicable to (holds of) an object at a given time there must at that time be

---

[1] Except those in which the word 'Arkle' is being mentioned rather than used. See below, Ch. X, for my account of propositions like 'King Arthur existed'.
[2] Ludwig Wittgenstein, *Philosophical Investigations*, 1953, I, § 40.

such an object. It is difficult to avoid ambiguity in the statement of this claim, but steps can be taken to avoid misinterpretation. It is not being claimed that if a person at time t ascribes a predicate ϕ to an object a there must be such an object as a at time t. Rather, the claim is that if a person at any time says truly of an object a that at time t it ϕ's, there must at time t be such an object as a. If Queen Anne died in 1714 we cannot at any time truly say of her that she yawned in 1715.

The proposition 'Arkle no longer exists', which at first sight seemed to be entirely in order, on closer inspection appears to fall foul of this law. Propositions of the form 'a no longer ϕ's' are exponible into conjunctive propositions of the form 'Both it was the case that a ϕ'ed and it is not the case now that a ϕ's'. If 'Arkle no longer exists' is explicated in this fashion the second conjunct of its explication will be 'It is not the case now that Arkle exists'. The simple 'Arkle does not exist' can be regarded as equivalent to this, if, that is, we take its present tense seriously. The present tense of 'Aristocratic Australians do not exist' was not taken very seriously; we did not expect the sentence to be understood as saying that aristocratic Australians do not exist now, i.e. that they are extinct. Rather, the trouble with taking '— do not exist' in 'Aristocratic Australians do not exist' as a first-level predicate is that it requires us to take 'Aristocratic Australians' as a name, although there is not *and never has been* anything for 'Aristocratic Australians' to name. 'Aristocratic Australians do not exist' was regarded as tenseless, rather than as present-tensed. It becomes entangled in Plato's Beard because it seems at once to name something and to say that there never has been anything which could bear this name. The version of Plato's Beard that 'Arkle does not exist' is entangled in is a modified version of this. It does not rest on the unqualified premiss that if an expression is used as a name there must at some time have been something which was the bearer of the name: the version of Plato's Beard which rests on this we may call 'The Unqualified Version of Plato's Beard'. It rests rather on the qualified premiss that if a predicate is said to hold at some particular time of something named, the thing named must exist at the time in question: we may call the version of Plato's Beard which uses this premiss 'The

Qualified Version of Plato's Beard'. Since 'Arkle does not exist', with its present tense taken seriously, falls foul of the Qualified Version of Plato's Beard in this way, so does 'Arkle no longer exists' which can be explicated as containing it as a conjunct. 'Arkle no longer exists', therefore, can only be understood if 'Arkle does not (now) exist' is intelligible, and this we have seen reason to doubt.

However, the rule that, if a person is truly to say of an object a that it ϕ's at time t, there must be such an object as a at time t, is a rule which seems to have obvious exceptions. Frege died in 1925 but he did not receive the full honour due to his genius until, perhaps, the 1950s. Henry VIII died in 1547, but he is responsible for a state of religious disunity that still exists today. The evil that men do lives after them; and although posthumous fame is believed by some to be a substitute for, it is not in any literal sense a kind of, survival after death.

4. *Intentional exceptions to the rule*

These exceptions, however, and many others which readily suggest themselves, fall into two classes. The predicates which are thus said to hold of individuals at a time when those individuals no longer exist seem to be either intentional or causal. By 'intentional' I mean involving in some way or other what Russell called 'propositional attitudes', e.g. believing, approving, fearing, wanting, admiring. If Frege was admired in 1977 it was because people in 1977 thought that Frege was a great logician. But what people in 1977 admired Frege for was not anything that Frege had done in 1977. And if Frege comes to be despised in the 1980s the change will not be anything that actually occurs in Frege: it will be a change that occurs in people living in the seventies and eighties, a change, namely in what they think about Frege.

It is sometimes said that the object of an intentional verb, unlike the object of, for example, the verb 'lift', or 'hurt', need not exist—indeed need not ever have existed. If this were admitted, we might regard the intentional type of exception from the rule that a predicate can hold of an object only at a time when there is such an object as a type of exception only to be expected: if what I admire needn't exist at all, *a fortiori* it needn't exist at the time when I admire it. This, I believe, would be a mistake. I shall argue later (Ch. IX, § 5) that where a person or thing really is the object of an intentional verb its existence is as necessary as the existence of a thing lifted or a person hurt. If it is really General Amin whom I fear, there must really be such a person as General Amin for me to be fearing. 'Williams is afraid of Amin' can express a genuine relation between two persons, just as 'Amin has hurt Williams' can. If 'Williams is afraid of Jack the Ripper's ghost' does not similarly presuppose the existence of a ghost of Jack the Ripper, it is because this last proposition is not to be regarded as expressing a relation between two individuals. Its underlying logical form must be something like 'Williams believes that there is something which is the ghost of Jack the Ripper and which is likely to hurt him'. More of this later. What needs to be said here is that an intentional proposition requires to be unpacked in such a way that it is seen to contain a subordinate as well as a principal clause. First of all we may concede that 'Williams is afraid of Amin' can express a genuine relation between Williams and Amin, even if, unbeknownst to Williams, Amin has recently been killed and is no more to be feared. Suppose that Amin has threatened that on Friday he will torture Williams, but has in fact, without Williams knowing it, died on Wednesday: it can still be true, desperately true, that Amin is feared by Williams on Thursday. It could thus be true of Amin on Thursday, even if he no longer existed them, that he was feared by Williams. But this predicate '— is feared by Williams' which is true of Amin on Thursday must be capable of being unpacked into something like 'Williams fears that — will hurt him'. I cannot fear something without believing that it is or will be, in some perhaps quite unspecified way, harmful to me. And what is true of 'fear' is true of intentional verbs generally. If ϕ is an intentional verb, any proposition of the form ϕab will be capable of being unpacked into another of the form $\delta \psi b$ where δ is a sentence-forming operator on sentences. The individual named by b will thus be the subject not only of the original unanalysed predicable 'ϕa —' (' — is feared by Williams') but also of the subordinate predicable or predicative expression of the *analysans* ('— will hurt him'[3]). What we

---

[3] As this example shows, the subordinate clause of the *analysans* may be formed, not only by attaching a straightforward predicate to the name of the person whom

may require in these cases is that the object of which something is predicated should exist, or should be thought to exist, at the time when the predicate is said to hold; but this requirement applies only to predicables or predicative expressions corresponding to ψ, i.e. to those which occur in a subordinate clause. There is no prohibition on complex predicables of the form $\delta\psi$ —, which represent the original intentional predicable of the form ϕa —, holding of the subject at a time when the subject does not exist. If Frege is admired in 1981, it is because people in 1981 think that Frege, before his death in 1925, did work which finally set logic 'on the sure path of a science'. That people think this of him is true of Frege in 1981, but what they think of him was true of him only prior to his death. Their admiration may be posthumous, but what they admire him for must be or at least be believed to be contemporary. In the proposition 'People think that Frege did good work' we may distinguish two predicables. The first, relatively simple, predicable ascribes to Frege the property of having done good work. We may say that this predicable, '— did good work', is *directly* predicated of Frege in this proposition. The other, relatively complex, predicable ascribes to Frege the property of being thought by people to have done good work, which is what the property of being admired amounts to in this case. We may say that this predicable, 'People think that — did good work', is *indirectly* predicated of Frege. A predicable is indirectly predicated of a subject if it is a complex predicable one of whose components is a predicable which, in the proposition in question, is itself predicated of that subject. A predicable is directly predicated of a subject if, and only if, it is predicated of it, but not indirectly. We can cover the intentional type of exceptions to our thesis by saying that the thesis applies only to predicables directly predicated of a subject. Because '— is admired' is analysable as a predicable of the form

we describe as the intentional object, but also by attaching an expression formed by filling up one place of a two-place predicate by a reflexive pronoun referring back to the subject of the main clause. Such an expression (e.g. '— will hurt him') is not a predicable, because it is not capable by itself of forming a proposition out of a proper name ('Amin will hurt him', where 'him' is reflexive, is not a complete proposition, since it requires a further context in which to be embedded in order to provide 'him' with an antecedent). I have accordingly used the phrase 'predicable *or predicative expression*' to cover cases of this kind, which are very frequent in intentional contexts.

$\delta\psi$, it is never directly predicated of anything. We can therefore allow that it can be truly said to hold of an object at a time when there is no such object. But '— does not exist', if predicable of an object at all, will be directly predicable of it. We have difficulty in seeing how it can be truly predicated of an object at a time when there is no such object.

5. *Causal exceptions to the rule*

There is another main class of exception to the principle that a predicable can hold of an object only at a time when the object exists. Predicables of this class are causal. A flood can cause the collapse of a building whose foundations it has undermined long after the flood waters have subsided. I can make a will designed to cause the maximum ill feeling amongst my relations after I am dead. Louis XV by his action or inaction was held to be responsible for the French Revolution, but he did not live to see what he had brought about: *après moi le déluge*. But in these cases too the predicables which are truly applicable to no longer existing objects admit of being unpacked. The relatively simple predicable '— caused this building to collapse by undermining the foundations' can be explicated by the more complex 'This building collapsed because — undermined the foundations', '— will stir up trouble amongst my relations by making such-and-such a will' expands into 'My relations will quarrel because — made such-and-such a will', and '— caused the fall of the French Monarchy by his action or inaction' into 'The French Monarchy fell because — did or failed to do so-and-so'. In each case a predicable of the form ϕ is shown to be applicable in virtue of the applicability of a more complex predicable of the form 'p, because ψ —'. In each case the time at which the proposition represented by p is true is a time at which the subject of which the whole complex predicable is predicated no longer exists. It is this time that is appropriate to the exponible predicable represented by ϕ, which applies, to use the terminology of the last paragraph, indirectly to its subject. But the predicable represented by ψ, which applies directly to that subject, can apply to it only at a time when the subject exists. The flood will not cause the building to collapse until next summer, but the undermining was done last spring; the quarrel amongst my relations is not yet stirred up, though I have made my will; the Revolution did not break out until 1789, but Louis XV was beyond action and inaction by 1776.

In this case, since the causal predicable ϕ has to be unpacked into the complex predicable 'p, because ψ —', it is in some cases impossible to say at what time it holds of a given subject a. The complex proposition 'p because ψa', is obtained by attaching a as subject-term to the complex predicable into which ϕ is analysed. If the relatively simple propositions p and ψa out of which 'p, because ψa' is formed are true at the same time, this time may be regarded as appropriate to the whole proposition 'p, because ψa' or to its unanalysed form ϕa. If, however, p is true at one time and ψa at another, there does not seem to be any time at which 'p, because ψa' or ϕa can properly be said to be true. To ask when it is true is like asking whether the whole conjunctive proposition 'It rained yesterday and it will rain tomorrow' is a past- or future-tensed proposition. It is our custom to extend any time reference there may be in p to ϕa: because the house has not yet collapsed we say that the flood *will* cause it to do so, even though the flood has now subsided; I *will* stir up trouble amongst my relations, though I won't be there to see it; and George III, reminiscing in 1776 about the follies of his dead rival, could have said 'A revolution *will* be caused by that man'. *Actio agentis est in patienti*. But where the cause of the change in the patient is some non-simultaneous change in the agent, the tensing of these propositions must be regarded as a mere convention. They do not, properly speaking, yield predicables which hold of their subjects at a time when the subjects no longer exist. The only predicable in these cases which holds of the subject at a determinate time is that represented by ψ in the formula 'p, because ψa', and this can only hold of a at a time when there is such an object as a. What we have here is not, properly speaking, a counter-example to the thesis that a predicable can hold of its subject only while that subject exists. There is no need in this case to make distinctions between predicables that apply directly and those that apply indirectly, since the latter too hold of the subjects either at a time when their subjects exist or at no determinate time at all.

We may indeed wonder whether these considerations about the time at which causal predicables hold of their subjects can illuminate the intentional predicables which, in my terminology, apply indirectly to their subjects. If President Amin satisfies the predicable 'Williams fears that — will hurt him', this is because Williams's expression of his fear involved a direct reference to Amin. This will be so only if Williams has a thought expressible by 'Amin will hurt me' in which Amin is referred to by some proper name, 'Idi Amin', or whatever other proper name is used for the same person. Now, on one currently popular view of proper names, a genuine proper name can be used as such by a speaker (or thinker) only if there is some causal account of the use of that name stretching back from the speaker to the bearer of the name. If I am really to have the thought that Amin will hurt me, Amin must already have exercised some causal influence, of an innocuous kind, on me to enable me to use his name. I must have heard people talk who have heard people talk who . . . have been sensibly affected by Amin's body, and have set up a use for a name in association with this affection. If this account of proper names, which is perhaps not entirely unconnected with the name of Kripke, is accepted, 'Williams fears that Amin will hurt him' has to be explicated in some such way as this: For some name, N, Williams has a fear which is expressible by him by attaching the predicable '— will hurt me' to N, and N has the sense it does for Williams because Amin affected certain people in certain ways. Here again the time at which Williams has the fear may well be different from the time at which Amin affected people. If so, the whole proposition cannot be said to be true at any particular time, although this can be said of different clauses in it. Nor can the predicable 'Williams fears that — will hurt him', strictly speaking, hold of Amin at a time when he no longer exists.

If we are able to take care in this way of the apparent exceptions to the rule that a predicable can hold of an object only at a time when there is such an object, the rule reintroduces paradox into the claim that Arkle does not exist in 1981 where '— does not exist' is regarded as predicating something of Arkle. This can be true only if there is such a horse as Arkle in 1981: i.e. it can be true only if it is false. We cannot, therefore, predicate '— does not exist' of Arkle. Nor can '— exist' be predicated of Arkle in the more complex proposition 'Arkle no longer exists'. 'Arkle no longer exists' is indeed entangled in the Qualified Version of Plato's Beard.

6. *Is 'Arkle no longer exists' entangled in the Unqualified Version of Plato's Beard as well?*

A further argument might be directed against the view that in 'Arkle no longer exists' we are using '— exist' as a first-level predicate, an argument which makes no reference to the existence of Arkle at a particular time. If 'Arkle no longer exists' is true, 'Arkle at one time existed' is true, where 'exist' is used in the same sense. But if this proposition is true its contradictory must be false, and therefore significant. Its contradictory is 'Arkle never existed'. The significance of this, however, is doubtful, when we consider that it could not be true without making 'Arkle' devoid of reference. Construing 'exist' in 'Arkle never existed' as a first-level predicable seems to raise again the original paradox of reference (the Unqualified Version of Plato's Beard). If this makes it impossible so to construe 'exist' in this context, it must also be impossible so to construe it in 'Arkle no longer exists'. For surely what the latter says Arkle is no longer doing is the same as what Arkle is said to have done in 'Arkle at some time existed' and what he is said not to have done in the contradictory of this, 'Arkle never existed'. Just so, 'Henry no longer beats his wife' says that Henry has stopped doing precisely what 'Henry at one time beat his wife', which it implies or presupposes, says he once did, and what the contradictory of this, 'Henry never beat his wife', denies that he ever did. 'Exist', it seems, can no more be construed as a first-level predicable in 'Arkle no longer exists' than it can in 'Aristocratic Australians exist'.

Commenting on this argument, but taking as his examples 'Socrates has never existed' and 'Socrates at some time has existed', Professor Geach wrote:

The latter is necessarily true-if-it-says-anything, but it is only contingently the case that by uttering this sentence we succeed in saying anything. If Socrates had never come to be, we could not have set up the use of 'Socrates' that we have: just as nobody *was* able to use the name that way before Socrates *did* come to be. But it is (in Arthur Prior's terminology) now-unalterably-the-case that Socrates did exist and that the name 'Socrates' did come to be used of him. To quote Prior again: Whereof one cannot speak, thereof one must be silent; but it doesn't follow that whereof one could not have spoken yesterday, thereof one must be silent today. It might never have been the case that 'Socrates has existed' is true; but it never could have been the case that 'Socrates has existed' was false; and before Socrates did exist. *'Gegonen ho Socrates'* with the proper name where we now use 'Socrates' was unsayable. All this depends on the view that you can't name the not-yet-existent: you can have a name (ready) for it, but not a name *of* it. If one denied this, then indeed there might be difficulties about 'Socrates never has existed and never will exist': but that is surely a good reason not to deny it![4]

Geach here admits that it never could have been the case that 'Socrates has existed' was false, which seems tantamount to saying that 'Socrates never existed' cannot be true. I suggested earlier that this might be thought to raise again the Unqualified Version of the paradox of Plato's Beard. It should be noted, however, that the original version of the paradox, applying as it did to *general* existential propositions, rested on the fact that some negative general existential propositions are evidently true. If 'Aristocratic Australians don't exist' is not a good example of a proposition which is evidently true, 'Men who can run a mile in ten seconds don't exist' is perhaps better. Plato's Beard causes trouble because, on the view that this true proposition states something about men who can run a mile in ten seconds, it appears to be in some way self-contradictory. The trouble is, if anything, exacerbated if we take 'Aristocratic Australians have *never* existed' or 'Men who can run a mile in ten seconds have *never* existed' as our examples. But no proposition which attaches '— never existed' to a genuine proper name is evidently true: on the contrary, if there are any such propositions they are all evidently false. It does not look as though the paradox can arise so simply for singular existential propositions.

However, yet another version of the paradox might seem to arise at this point. We might feel that, if, as Geach says, it never could have been the case that 'Socrates has existed' is false, we could no longer truly say 'Socrates might not have existed'. In fact, of course, the analysis of propositions of this

---

[4] See my 'On Dying', in *Philosophy*, 44, 1969, 227 f., where these privately communicated remarks of Geach are quoted.

last type given in Chapter IV would permit us to say 'Socrates might not have existed', even if 'Socrates has existed' could never have been false. It might be suggested that the distinction between primary and secondary occurrence would enable us to reconcile these positions. 'Socrates' in 'Socrates might not have existed' could have primary occurrence, in our extended sense of 'primary occurrence', in which case the proposition would be true; or it could have secondary occurrence, in which case it would be false. In the light of what we said in Chapter IV we can paraphrase the proposition taken in this latter sense by:

(8) It could have been the case that, for some ϕ, both Socrates alone ϕ's and it is not the case that, for just one x, ϕx.

where what is said to be possible is in fact self-contradictory. This might be what was meant by saying that it could never have been the case that 'Socrates has existed' is false.

Nevertheless, we do not suggest that in saying 'It never could have been the case that "Socrates has existed" is false' Geach was in any sense asserting that it could never have been the case that Socrates did not exist. He was saying something, not about Socrates, but about the words 'Socrates has existed', namely, that these words could never have been used, in their normal sense, to say something false. What they seem to say could have been false, but in that case they could never have been used to say it. Given that '— exist' can be used as a first-level predicate, it is true that Socrates existed, false that Socrates never existed, and true that it might never have been the case that Socrates existed. There is no paradox here, since all this is compatible with the fact that the word 'Socrates' could not play the role in language which it does play if there had been no such person. All this can be true, even if we regard 'Socrates existed', 'Socrates never existed', and 'It might never have been the case that Socrates existed' as the result of embedding 'Socrates exists' in tense and modal contexts.

G. E. Moore would have put this another way. Instead of saying that if Socrates had never existed the words 'Socrates never existed' could not have been used with the meaning they normally have, he would have said that in this case there could have been no such Proposition as 'Socrates never existed'.⁵ What it means to say 'There could have been no such Proposition as "Socrates never existed"' is, however, obscure. What is it for a Proposition to exist or not to exist? We are not likely to solve problems about the non-existence of a person at some time or in some possible world by appeal to the non-existence of a Proposition at that time or in that possible world. But Prior, who praises Moore's treatment of this issue,⁶ makes a distinction which amounts to the same thing. Prior talks, not of Propositions, but of facts, existing and not existing.

There are no possible states of affairs in which is is the case that $NE!x$, and yet not all possible states of affairs are ones in which $E!x$. For there are possible states of affairs in which there are no facts about x at all; and I don't mean ones in which *it is the case that there are not* facts about x (for that would itself be one, if true), but ones such that *it isn't the case in them that there are* facts about x.⁷

Using M to represent 'It is possible that' and L to represent 'It is necessary that', Prior claims that $NLE!x$ can be true without its following that $MNE!x$ is true. Since there are worlds in which there are no facts about x, x's existence is not necessary; but, since there are no worlds in which x's non-existence is a fact, x's non-existence is not possible. Where we drew a distinction between propositions like (7), where 'Socrates' has primary occurrence, and propositions like (8), where it has secondary occurrence, Prior queries the equivalence of NL with MN, and therewith the possibility of having just one primitive modal operator. It is a high price to pay.

Prior's reasons for thus distinguishing $NLE!x$ from $MNE!x$ seem to be out of harmony with what he normally has to say

⁵ Cf. *Lectures on Philosophy*, 1966, p. 129, where Moore says that 'There might have been no such thing as this sense-datum' is equivalent, not to '"There is no such thing as this sense datum" might have been true', but to 'There *might have been* no such proposition as "There is such a thing as this sense datum".' One may compare Castañeda's view that a proposition expressible by 'I exist' is 'though contingently existing, necessarily true' ('Phenomeno-Logic of the I', pp. 265 f.). So to speak is to treat propositions as abstract entities which indicative sentences express. Following Geach (*Reference and Generality*, § 19) I write 'Proposition' with an initial capital when it refers to non-linguistic entities of this sort, reserving 'proposition' (with a lower-case initial) for the ordinary use to refer to linguistic entities.

⁶ Prior, *Past, Present and Future*, p. 150 n. 1.

⁷ Ibid., pp. 150 f. $E!x$ is Prior's abbreviation of 'x exists' and $NE!x$ the negation of this.

about modal operators. Prior holds, and we have seen (in Ch. III, § 2) that this doctrine of his is central to much of his philosophy of logic, that an operator which forms a sentence out of a sentence also forms a predicable out of a predicable. If we regard 'Arkle exists' as formed by wrapping the predicable '— exists' round the proper name 'Arkle', we can regard 'Arkle does not exist' as formed *either* by wrapping the truth-functional expression 'It is not the case that —' round the sentence 'Arkle exists' *or* by wrapping the complex predicable '— does not exist' round the proper name 'Arkle'. It makes no difference which way we take it. Proper names, unlike definite descriptions, offer no purchase for distinctions of scope. So, if 'Arkle exists' is a proposition in which something is predicated of Arkle, the same must be said about 'Arkle does not exist'. But Prior regards the modal operators 'It is possible that —' and 'It is necessary that —' as belonging to the same syntactical category as 'It is not the case that —'. Accordingly, if 'Arkle does not exist' says something about Arkle, so does 'It is possible that Arkle should not exist' ($MNE!x$). This is saying something, not about the Proposition that Arkle does not exist, still less about the sentence 'Arkle does not exist', but about the horse, Arkle. When we say that it is possible that Arkle should not exist we are not saying of the Proposition 'Arkle does not exist' that it could be true, still less of the string of words that they could be used with the sense they now have to express a true Proposition: rather, we are saying of Arkle that it is possible he should not exist. This may truly be said of him even if it may not be truly said of him that he does not exist. All this, of course, is on the supposition that 'Arkle exists' predicates something of Arkle, which Prior is willing to admit, although I am not. It could all have been said of the application of modal or truth-functional operators to a proposition like 'Arkle is fast', which everyone will admit to be formed by attaching a first-level predicable to the proper name 'Arkle'. If we say 'It is possible that Arkle should not be fast' we are not saying anything about the Proposition 'Arkle is not fast', nor about what could or could not be said by using this string of words with the meaning they normally have: we are saying something about Arkle. If it is possible that Arkle should not be fast, it is, of course, possible that the words

'Arkle is not fast' should be used having the meaning they normally have to state something true, as it is not possible for the words 'Arkle does not exist', having the meaning they normally have, to be used to state something true. But neither of these claims is made by the corresponding statements of the form *MNp*. Statements of this form are not statements about statements, but are statements about whatever the statement represented by *p* is about.

Prior's distinction between *MNE!x* and *NLE!x* seems to be unwarranted. My distinction between a sense of 'Arkle might never have existed' in which 'Arkle' has primary occurrence, as in (7), and one in which it has secondary occurrence, as in (8), can perhaps be sustained; but it is not clear from anything that has been said in the course of this section that 'Arkle might never have existed' has to be understood in either of these ways. I had recourse to the first of these ways of understanding it in Chapter IV. This was because it allowed us to avoid having to regard 'Arkle might not have existed' as the result of embedding 'Arkle never existed' in the context 'It might be the case that —'. We are now examining another reason for resisting this analysis, namely, that 'Arkle never existed' seems to raise again the unqualified version of the paradox of reference. But we need not have allowed ourselves to be frightened by this spectre. 'Arkle never existed' might raise a paradox of reference if there were some reason to suppose it, or some other proposition of the same form, true. But neither it nor any proposition of this form could be true.[8] And even though 'Arkle has existed' could never have been used to say something false, we are not therefore debarred from saying that it might never have been the case that Arkle existed. No paradox need arise in this area, and there is so far no need to challenge the equivalence of *MN* and *NL*. The second set of arguments against the view that 'exists' in 'Arkle no longer exists' is a first-level predicable, which we have been examining in this section, seems to have had no success.

[8] Propositions like 'Mr Micawber never existed' are not of this form, as will be argued in Ch. X.

7. *Attempts by Miller and Plantinga to avoid the qualified version of the paradox*

The first argument of this chapter rested on the premiss that it is impossible to assert a predicable of an object as holding of that object at a time when the object doesn't exist. This argument, which we called the Qualified Version of Plato's Beard, has not so far been faulted. It has ancient origins. There is a problem, not only about ceasing to exist, but also about coming into existence. Prior[9] quotes the following passage from Aristotle's *Physics*:

> What comes to be must do so either from what is or from what is not, both of which are impossible. For what is cannot come to be (because it *is* already), and from what is not nothing could have come to be (because something must be present as a substratum).[10]

By substratum (*hypokeimenon*) Aristotle means here that from which, or out of which, a thing comes to be. But 'that from which', in this context, is ambiguous. Aquinas has to make clear, when he is talking of creation, that what is created *comes to be from* nothing (*ex nihilo*), not in the sense in which something *comes to be* hot *from* being cold, but in the sense in which a cake *comes to be out of* its ingredients.[11] To say that something is created from nothing is to say that there isn't anything out of which God creates the thing. That is clear enough. But, as Aquinas allows, there is another sense of 'from' in which the thing that is hot comes to be so from being cold and in which noon comes from morning (*ex mane fit meridies*), and in this sense of 'from' the created thing comes to be *from being nothing*. But how can this be, unless we can say that during the period up to its creation '— does not exist' was truly predicable of it? It is a parallel difficulty, of course, which arises from the notion of ceasing to exist. If Adam came into existence because he came to exist from not existing, Arkle no longer exists because he came not to exist from existing. It begins to look as though the only escape is to deny that things do come into existence or cease to exist, to postulate, with the Atomists and Kant, substances which are ungenerable and imperishable.

---
[9] *Past, Present and Future*, p. 139.
[10] *Physics*, 191ᵃ 23-32.
[11] *Summa Theologiae*, Iᵃ, Qu. 45, a. 1 ad 3um.

In the following pages we shall examine some less drastic attempts that have been made by philosophers to escape the paradox we are investigating. The failure of these attempts drives home the deep character of the paradox itself. The attemps themselves are important and merit consideration. But there is an added reason for looking at them closely. The solution of the paradox which will eventually be proposed in this chapter is unlikely to win easy acceptance. Only if the full force of the paradox has been felt, and the failure of more obvious ways of evading it recognized, will this solution begin to look plausible. The idea of something beginning or ceasing to exist, the ideas of death and birth, are so familiar to us that they appear utterly simple. It is only after experiencing the struggle involved in dealing with the paradoxes to which these apparently simple ideas give rise that we become willing to recognize their full complexity.

Must we then admit that, if Arkle no longer exists, he has passed from a state of existing to a state of not existing? One way out of this difficulty—so it has been thought—is to make a distinction between saying that non-existence is truly predicable of Arkle and saying that the proposition that Arkle exists is false. 'Arkle does not exist' is thus supposed to be ambiguous in that the negation can be regarded as either internal or external to the proposition as a whole. This distinction is made by Barry Miller,[12] who sees in it the answer to the problem about dying. 'Arkle no longer exists' is true, not because the predicate '— does not exist' is now, though earlier it was not, truly predicable of Arkle, but because the proposition 'Arkle exists' is now, though earlier it was not, false. The same manoeuvre is executed by Alvin Plantinga to deal with the problem of possible non-existents.[13] Red Rum still runs, but he might have died, indeed he might never have existed. This proposition, Plantinga claims, must be understood, not as saying that it is possible that it should always have been the case that the predicate 'does not exist' was truly predicable of Red Rum, but that it is possible that the proposition 'Red Rum exists' should always have been false.

Plantinga believes that this distinction between internal

---

[12] In 'In Defence of the Predicate "Exists"', *Mind*, 84, 1975, pp. 338-54.
[13] *The Nature of Necessity*, pp. 149 ff.

and external negation applies, not merely to singular existenial propositions, but to singular propositions in general. He alleges, for instance, that a distinction must be drawn between 'Socrates is non-snubnosed' and 'It is false that Socrates is snubnosed'. This distinction is thought of as analogous to the distinction between 'Someone is non-snubnosed' and 'It is false that someone is snubnosed'. The latter distinction is obvious: the first proposition of the pair is true, the second false. But the former distinction is not obvious. Indeed Prior, as we have seen,[14] made the impossibility of making such distinctions a criterion for an expression's being a Russellian name. In the case of a proposition of the form $\delta\phi N$, where N is such a name, there is no possibility of distinguishing $(\delta\phi)N$ from $\delta(\phi N)$. To say that a proposition is a singular proposition is to say that it is formed by attaching a predicable to a Russellian name. A singular existential proposition would thus be a proposition formed by attaching a predicable '— exists' to such a name. If Prior is right, the supposition that a distinction can be drawn between internal and external negation of such a proposition contradicts the supposition that it is a singular proposition. The distinction between 'Someone is non-snubnosed' and 'It is not the case that someone is snubnosed' is a distinction of scope which, like all distinctions of scope, can be expressed by the difference in the order of operators in the formulae which give the logical form of these propositions, $\Sigma x N\phi x$ and $N\Sigma x\phi x$. The order of the operators in $N\phi a$, which gives the logical form of 'Socrates is non-snubnosed' and 'It is not the case that Socrates is snubnosed' alike, cannot be varied. It seems that the distinction between internal and external negation can get no hold on singular propositions.

Plantinga has attempted to explain the applicability of the distinction to singular propositions by contrasting a proposition which predicates non-snubnosedness of Socrates with a proposition which predicates falsehood of the Proposition that Socrates is snubnosed. Propositions of the first sort he calls 'predicative', those of the second sort 'impredicative'.[15] He would quite properly, distinguish 'The Proposition that Socrates

---

[14] The cogency of our present argument against Plantinga depends on what was said in sections 2 and 3 of Ch. III.

[15] *The Nature of Necessity*, p. 149. It is confusing of Plantinga to use the terms 'predicative' and 'impredicative' to mark this contrast, when they were given by

is snubnosed is false' from 'The sentence "Socrates is snubnosed" expresses something false'. The latter does indeed say something different from 'Socrates is non-snubnosed'. It says something about a string of English words, whereas the subject of 'Socrates is non-snubnosed' is nothing except Socrates. If Plantinga's distinction had been the distinction between 'The sentence "Socrates is snubnosed" expresses something false' and 'Socrates is non-snubnosed', there would have been no reason to dispute it. It is easy to see how the one could have been true and the other false: if the English word 'snubnosed' had meant what 'stupid' now means, the truth-values of the two propositions would indeed have been different. But Plantinga is concerned to distinguish a proposition about a Proposition, rather than a proposition about a sentence, from the proposition about Socrates.

How then can this distinction be made? We may be told that in 'Socrates is non-snubnosed' a property (a negative one) is ascribed to Socrates, while in 'It is false that Socrates is snubnosed' a proposition is negated. But when a singular proposition is negated a property is *ipso facto* ascribed to an object. Properties are what predicables stand for, and predicables are obtained by removing proper names from propositions. Removing a proper name from a negative proposition automatically produces a predicable which stands for a negative property; and, equally, ascribing such a property to an object is done by attaching a negative predicable thus obtained to the name of that object and thus producing a negated proposition. Those who deny that properties are what predicables stand for, or that predicables are what are obtained by removing proper names from propositions, owe us alternative accounts of *property* and *predicable*.

Perhaps it will be said that 'It is false that Socrates is snubnosed' expresses, not the negation of a proposition, but the predicating of falsity of a Proposition. What is it to say of a Proposition that it is false? My view would be that the meaning of 'The Proposition that Socrates is snubnosed is false' is given by 'For some p, both the Proposition that Socrates is snubnosed is the same Proposition as the Proposition that p

---

Russell a technical sense which is quite different and which has become classical. See Bertrand Russell, *Introduction to Mathematical Philosophy*, p. 188.

and it is not the case that p'. In this the sentence 'Socrates is snubnosed' is used, not mentioned, whereas in 'The sentence "Socrates is snubnosed" says something false' it is mentioned, not used. The difference between *sentence* and *Proposition* is always to be explained in terms of the distinction between *mention* and *use*.[16] This means, for a start, that 'It is false that Socrates is snubnosed' says something about Socrates, since the word 'Socrates' is used here, not mentioned. In 'The sentence "Socrates is snubnosed" says something false', on the other hand, the word 'Socrates', together with the words 'is' and 'snubnosed', is mentioned, not used. If a property is what a predicate stands for, we can recognize even the *analysans* we have just given for 'It is false that Socrates is snubnosed' as predicating something of Socrates: 'For some p, both the Proposition that — is snubnosed is the same Proposition as the Proposition that p, and it is not the case that p' is a predicable which is here attached to the proper name 'Socrates'. Indeed this predicable is indistinguishable from the predicable '— is not (or non-) snubnosed'. 'For some p, both the Proposition that Socrates is not snubnosed is the same Proposition as the Proposition that p and it is not the case that p' is equivalent to 'Both the Proposition that Socrates is snubnosed is the same Proposition as the Proposition that Socrates is snubnosed and it is not the case that Socrates is snubnosed'. In this, however, the first conjunct is trivially true and redundant: all that is non-trivially asserted by the proposition as a whole is that it is not the case that Socrates is snubnosed. There seems therefore to be no significant difference between 'It is false that Socrates is snubnosed' and 'It is not the case that Socrates is snubnosed'. We cannot say that the first predicates falsity of a Proposition while the second negates it, and that these operations result in two distinct propositions. And I have already argued for the equivalence of 'It is not the case that Socrates is snubnosed' and 'Socrates is not snubnosed'.

The illusion that 'It is false that Socrates is snubnosed' says something different from 'Socrates is non-snubnosed', that the first predicates falsehood of a Proposition and nothing of

---

[16] See my *What is Truth?*, pp. 56-7. The analysis of 'It is false that Socrates is snubnosed' given above is a development of what is said about falsehood in Ch. IV of that book.

Socrates, whilst the second predicates non-snubnosedness of Socrates and nothing of a Proposition, is produced by confusion between 'It is false that Socrates is snubnosed' and 'The sentence "Socrates is snubnosed" says something false'. Propositions and sentences are too often confused. Indeed there has been much confusion about what the two things *are* that are being confused here. As I have said, my own view is that what we have here is merely an instance of a more general confusion, that between use and mention, which is a constant source of philosophical error. The confusion between Propositions and sentences can persist even where an author, like Plantinga, is emphatic that he is talking, not about sentences, but about Propositions. It is the oldest philosophical mistake to claim to make a distinction, e.g. between what is actual and what is potential, and yet to persist in talking of one of the things distingished in language appropriate only to the other.

Plantinga wants the distinction between 'Socrates is non-snubnosed' and 'It is false that Socrates is snubnosed' because he wishes to distinguish two senses of 'Socrates might not have existed'. 'It might have been the case that non-existence was truly predicable of Socrates' is, he thinks, false. 'It might have been the case that the Proposition that Socrates exists is false' is, he thinks, true. This distinction cannot be made; and what we have said in Chapter IV shows that it *need* not be made in order to solve the problem about possible non-existents. Barry Miller wants to use the same distinction to solve the problem about coming into existence and ceasing to exist. In Miller's view, if Arkle came into existence, we do not have to say that the predicate '— does not exist' held of Arkle at a certain time and did not hold of him at a later time: instead we can say that at the earlier time the Proposition 'Arkle exists' was false and at a later time true. 'Arkle no longer exists' can be interpreted in the same fashion, *mutatis mutandis*. Plantinga and Miller's purported distinction has been shown to be a distinction without a difference, so it will not solve the problems they want it to solve. Plantinga's problem is one for which I believe we have an alternative solution (that given in Chapter IV). Miller's problem is our present concern: how to make sense of the notions of coming into existence and ceasing to exist. So far we have arrived at no solution of it.

Miller's solution requires that we make a distinction between $(NE!)x$ and $N(E!x)$, which, as we have shown, cannot be made. This distinction can be attempted only by the use of brackets, but by brackets whose role cannot be preformed by altering the order of operators in accordance with the conventions of Polish notation. This shows that the distinction is illusory.[17] Prior, however, tried to make a distinction that is expressible by altering the order of operators, and if we are to object to this distinction it will have to be on other grounds. Prior too intended his distinction to solve the problem of coming into existence and ceasing to exist. We must now examine this attempt.

8. *A similar attempt by Prior*

We have seen in section 6 how Prior based his distinction between $MNE!x$ and $NLE!x$ on certain observations of Moore's. Moore commented, not only on the relation of possibility to existence, but on that of time to existence as well; and this too is noted by Prior. But Moore's comment[18] seems in fact to be concerned with sentences rather than Propositions. He says that 'I don't exist now' is self-contradictory, but that there will be no contradiction in my saying of myself in the future 'I didn't exist at t_1'. This imples that while I can now utter without self-contradiction the sentence 'I didn't exist at t_1', I could not at t_1 have uttered without self-contradiction the bare and unadorned sentence 'I don't exist'. These observations of Moore's seem perfectly justified. Prior, however, goes on to interpret them in a way which involves talk, not about sentences, but about Propositions, not about what words we can or cannot utter without self-contradiction, but about what is the case. He contrasts 'It was the case at t_1, that (I don't exist)', which he regards as false, with 'It was not the case at t_1, that (I exist)', which he regards as true; and he sums this up by saying 'it *now is not* the case that my existence was the case then—it's not that my *non-existence* then was the case'.[19] Moore's point is that I couldn't have said of myself in 1900 that I didn't exist then, though I can say of myself now that I didn't exist

---

[17] See above, Ch. III, § 3.
[18] *The Commonplace Book of G. E. Moore*, ed. Casimir Lewy, 1962, p. 329.
[19] Prior, *Past, Present and Future*, p. 151.

in 1900. But it doesn't follow from that, as Prior seems to think, that it wasn't the case in 1900 that I didn't exist then. It was; and I have just said that it was. The remark which Geach attributed to Prior can be turned against himself: 'Whereof one cannot speak, thereof one must be silent; but it doesn't follow that whereof one could not have spoken yesterday, thereof one must be silent today.'[20] If one says that it was the case in 1900 that (I don't exist), one is not mentioning the sentence 'I don't exist' and remarking on what one could or could not have done with it in 1900: one is *using* the sentence 'I don't exist' to say something now. The fact that one could not be using the sentence *unembedded in any wider context* to say something true does not mean that one cannot use it *embedded in such a context* to say something true. Whatever we may think of the possibility of embedding sentences like 'I don't exist' in wider contexts—and this is the point that has been principally at issue in this and the previous chapter of this book—there is no doubt that there are sentences which we cannot use unembedded in a wider context to say something true, which can be so used *embedded in a context*. Any sentence which expresses a self-contradiction is an example, 'That than which no greater can be conceived is something than which a greater can be conceived' by itself cannot be used to express something true. It does not follow that, embedded in a proposition of the form 'If p, then that than which no greater can be conceived is something than which a greater can be conceived', it cannot be used to say something true. If this sort of thing were impossible it would be impossible ever to state a *reductio ad absurdum* argument. Pragmatic paradoxes also provide examples: 'I am not thinking' can never be used to express something true, but 'It was the case twelve hours ago that (I am not thinking)' can often be so used.

Prior generalized the contrast between 'It was the case at t_1 that (I don't exist)' and 'It was not the case at t_1 that (I exist)'. In standard tense logical systems PN, which means 'It has been the case that (it is not the case that (—))', and NH, which means 'It is not the case that (it has always been the case that (—))', are equivalent (so that P and H are interdefinable). But just as Prior was prepared to deny the standard equivalence in modal

---

[20] See above, p. 118.

A SIMILAR ATTEMPT BY PRIOR

logic of MN and NL,[21] so, in this context, he is prepared to deny this standard equivalence in tense logic. Similarly he denies the equivalence in metric tense logic between PnN = 'It was the case n time units ago that (it is not the case that (—))' and NPn = 'It is not the case that (it was the case n time units ago that (—))'. This last equivalence, $PnN = NPn$, is a way of asserting that differences between the scope of Pn and that of N are insignificant. In every tense logical system a difference has to be recognized between the complex non-metric operators PN and NP. PN symbolizes 'It has at some time been the case (it is not the case that (—))', and NP symbolizes 'It is not the case that (it has at some time been the case that (—))' = 'It has never been the case that (—)'. $PN = \Sigma nPnN$, and this is clearly different from $NP = N\Sigma nPn$, even if PnN is taken as equivalent to NPn. This latter equivalence would give us $\Sigma nPnN = \Sigma nNPn$, but $\Sigma nNPn$ would still be different from $N\Sigma nPn$. The difference between PN and NP is therefore one in which the difference of scope is impossible to disregard. Not so the difference between PnN and NPn. Intuitively these seem equivalent: 'Three years ago it was the case that (it is not the case that (George is married))' means the same as 'It is not the case that (three years ago it was the case that (George is married))'. It is because PnN and NPn are equivalent that PN is standardly taken to be equivalent to NH. $PN = \Sigma nPnN = \Sigma nNPn = N\Pi nPn = NH$. Not all differences of the scope of operators import a difference of truth value: $\Sigma n\Sigma mIn\sqrt{m}$ is no different from $\Sigma m\Sigma nIn\sqrt{m}$.[22] If Prior is going to deny $PnN = NPn$ he will have to give good reasons for doing so.

He has reasons, but we may doubt whether they are good. Let us take the case where it is claimed, not that George was not married three years ago, but that George, who is our contemporary, was not married three hundred years ago. Three hundred years ago, when George did not yet exist, there was, according to Prior, no such Proposition as 'George is married' nor yet such a Proposition as 'It is not the case that George is married'. (Prior is with me and against Plantinga and Miller in recognizing no distinction between $N(\phi x)$ and $(N\phi)x$.)

---

[21] See above p. 120.
[22] Either formula can be paraphrased by 'There are numbers which are related to each other as square and square root'.

Accordingly Prior holds that 'Three hundred years ago it was the case that (it is not the case that (George is married))' is false. Three hundred years ago there was no such Proposition as 'George is not married', so *a fortiori* no such proposition was then true—it was *not* then the case. On the other hand, precisely because there was no such true Proposition as this three hundred years ago, 'It is not the case that (three hundred years ago it was the case that (George is married))' is true: there *was* no such (true) Proposition three hundred years ago.

Although Prior's distinction can be represented as a distinction between the scope and order of operators, and is thus more plausible than the alleged distinction between $N(\phi x)$ and $(N\phi)x$, it is in fact based on the same mistake. Prior himself, except when he is dealing with this topic, is insistent that a proposition *Pnp* is not a proposition about a Proposition, but is about whatever the corresponding proposition *p* is about. *Pnp* no more predicates pastness of the Proposition that *p* than *Np* predicates falsehood of it. '*Pn* —', like '*N* —', is regarded by Prior as an adverb, an expression which forms sentences out of sentences. Now we may grant that, for any *p*, if it is either true or false that *p*, is is also either true or false that *Np* (if 'George is married' is either true or false, so is 'It is not the case that George is married'). Nevertheless, we cannot similarly assert that, for any *p*, for any *n*, if it is either true or false that *p*, it is also either true or false that *Pnp* (if 'George is not married' is either true or false, it does not follow that the same holds for 'Three hundred years ago it was the case that George was not married'). If someone were to say to me 'George was not married three hundred years ago', I should not reply 'That's false'. If I did reply in this way I should be taken to imply that George *was* married three hundred years ago. The normal reply to such a remark would be, not 'That's false', but 'That's absurd: George wasn't alive then'. But such claims need not be absurd. People often have a hazy idea about the age of people they are talking to. In conversation with someone who has lived in Coventry all her life I may say 'Were you frightened during the bombing raids?', only to regret my lack of tact when she replies 'I wasn't born then'. She could not, without misleading me, have replied either 'Yes' or 'No'. Prior would have her reply 'No', on the grounds that it was not the case during the bombing raids that this person was frightened: there was no such Proposition then as 'Susan Jenkins is frightened', and so we cannot say that the Proposition 'Susan Jenkins is frightened' was true at the time of the bombing raids on Coventry. This is what Prior would say, and we already begin to see the genesis of his mistake. It can readily be agreed that no one during the bombing raids on Coventry could have used the words 'Susan Jenkins is frightened', having the meaning they normally have and referring to our Susan Jenkins, to say something true. It is false that these words could then have been so used. But this does not make it false that, during the bombing raids on Coventry, Susan Jenkins was frightened. We can *mention* the sentence 'Susan Jenkins is frightened' and say that it could not have been used during the bombing raids to say something true: we cannot *use* the sentence to say of Susan Jenkins that it was not the case that she was frightened during the bombing. These are the alternatives: either I am speaking about the sentence and saying what it could or could not have been used to say; or I am using the sentence in an attempt to describe Susan Jenkins's state of mind during the raids on Coventry. This attempt would be bound to fail, since it is impossible to state that some predicate held of Susan at a time when she did not yet exist. The remark about the sentence, on the other hand, is assured of success. A sentence type, which is what we are talking about, does not come into existence or cease to exist, and there is no difficulty about saying what could or could not have been said by its means at any moment in history. Prior's mistake is to have claimed to have been speaking about Propositions when all the time he was speaking about sentences. The distinction between Propositions and sentences can only be brought out in terms of a distinction between use and mention. If I say that a sentence S was true n time units ago, I mean that someone could then have used this string of words to say something true. If I say that a Proposition p was true n time units ago, I am using some words to say something now about a state of affairs n time units ago. $NPn\phi S$ may be true, where S names a form of words that can be used to state that p, and ϕ means 'can be used to say something true', and yet $NPnp$ fail to say anything true or false. Let S' name a sentence that can be used to deny what S asserts. Prior's view that *NPnp* can be true and *PnNp* false can then be described as the result of confusing these with *NPnϕS* and *PnϕS'*, respectively.

9. *Aristotelian accounts of coming into existence and ceasing to exist*

Prior's attempt to solve the problem of *coming into existence* rested on the view that we could say of x, if it came into existence n time units ago, that for any $m>n$, *NPmE!x*, although we could never say of x, for any n, that *PnNE!x*. This distinction, we believe, cannot be made. But even if it could, it would not help us with our problem about *ceasing to exist*. If x at some time has come into existence, according to Prior, we express this by saying that Σ*nKNPnE!xE!x* (though not by saying that Σ*nKPnNE!xE!x*). If, however, x no longer exists, we should still have to say that Σ*nKPnE!xNE!x*, and there seems to be no way here of separating the *N* from the *E!*. This will not do. We have to be able, after all, to give an account, not only *de generatione*, but also *de corruptione*.

Aristotle's own account of coming and ceasing to exist in Book I, Chapter 3 of *De Generatione et Corruptione* relies heavily on the notion of substantial form. This account has been adopted more recently by A. J. P. Kenny, G. E. L. Owen,[23] and M J. Woods.[24] Substantial forms are, in a realist's view, referred to by a peculiar category of predicable—predicables, that is, which hold of a subject as long as that subject exists. Arkle is a living being, and cannot cease to be alive without ceasing to exist. *Vivere viventibus est esse*.[25] Similarly his beginning to be alive was his beginning to exist. This category includes predicables of the kind Strawson called 'sortal', predicables referring to natural kinds and predicables which are now referred to as 'count nouns'. Aristotle's term 'second substance' is another way of delimiting this area. Let us call these predicables 'essential predicables'.

The Aristotelian account is sometimes expressed by saying that 'exist' in the complex expressions 'cease to exist' and 'come to exist' is a dummy verb, a proxy for some essential

[23] 'Aristotle on the Snares of Ontology', *New Essays on Plato and Aristotle*, ed. R. Bambrough, 1965. Cf. A. J. P. Kenny, *The Five Ways*, 1968, Ch. V.
[24] 'Existence and Tense', *Truth and Meaning*, edd. G. Evans and J. McDowell.
[25] Aristotle, *De Anima*, II, 415^{b}13.

predicate.[26] To say that Arkle has ceased to exist is to say that Arkle has ceased to be alive, or that he has ceased to be a horse. To say that my wireless has ceased to exist is to say that it has ceased to be a wireless. This has been put in the form of an explicit definition by M. J. Woods. He classifies predicables into three types.[27] Type 1 predicables are those we have been speaking of. They are predicables which hold of an object as long as it exists and no longer. Type 2 predicables can hold of an object only while it exists, but they do not have to hold of it all the time that it exists. Both Type 1 predicables and Type 2 predicables conform to the rule enunciated at the beginning of this chapter, the rule that if a is truly said to ϕ at time t there must be such an object as a at time t, the rule that gives rise to the Qualified Version of Plato's Beard. Not so Type 3 predicables. These are the predicables we looked at earlier which provide prima-facie exceptions to the rule. Type 3 predicables are exemplified by '— is famous', '— is admired', etc. From the point of view of our rule, the important distinction is the distinction between Type 1 and Type 2 predicables on the one hand, and Type 3 predicables on the other. From the point of the Aristotelian analysis of *ceasing to exist*, the important distinction is the distinction between Type 1 predicables on the one hand, and Type 2 and Type 3 predicables on the other. Let us use a particular style of variable, f, g, etc., to stand for Type 1 predicables. We can then state the following explicit definition, which is that given by Woods,[28] of 'exist' as a first-level predicable capable of being tensed:

(W) $\Pi x E(x \text{ exists at } t)(\Sigma f(fx \text{ at } t))$.

Before looking at Woods's method of picking out essential or Type 1 predicables it is necessary to set out the difficulties, to my mind fatal, with which this whole Aristotelian account of singular existential propositions is beset. We had difficulty in understanding 'Arkle no longer exists', because it seemed to be exponible into 'Both Arkle used to exist and Arkle does not now exist', and 'Arkle does not now exist' brought us back to Plato's Beard. If the verb 'exist' here is held to be standing

---

[26] Cf. Munitz, *Existence and Logic*, pp. 110 f.
[27] 'Existence and Tense' p. 256.
[28] Ibid., p. 262. I have translated the symbols into Polish notation.

proxy for, e.g. 'is a horse', we are invited to regard 'Arkle is no longer a horse' as an explanatory paraphrase of 'Arkle no longer exists'. But, by the same token, 'Arkle is no longer a horse' is exponible as 'Both Arkle used to be a horse and Arkle is not now a horse'; and yet 'Arkle is not now a horse' is at least as paradoxical as 'Arkle does not now exist'. The Aristotelian paraphrase of 'Arkle no longer exists', if it is intended to be explanatory, is a striking case of *obscurum per obscurius* explanation. In delimiting the class of predicables called 'Type 1 predicables' we used an expression of the form 'cannot cease to be *f* without ceasing to exist'. This, superficially, is of the same form as 'cannot cease to be a minister of religion without ceasing to be exempt from military service'. This last example presents no problems. We have a clear idea of what it would be like for someone to cease to be a minister of religion (not every minister of religion has an indelible mark on his soul), and we have an even clearer idea of what it would be like for someone to cease to be exempt from military service. But, *ex hypothesi*, we have no clear idea of what it would be like for something to cease to exist; and the idea we have of what it would be like for something to cease to be a horse is if anything still more obscure.

The difficulties are well enough known. They are the difficulties of the notion of substantial change. Let us suppose, for dramatic effect and for virtual instantaneousness, that Arkle's stable catches fire and that he and all the things that are in the stable are suddenly consumed and turned to ashes. Can we say that Arkle is no longer a horse, that Arkle has ceased to be a horse and is now ash? No doubt we do talk, carelessly and flippantly, in this way about animals, including human beings. But it is surely a muddled way of talking. What is now ash is not Arkle, even if some of the matter which composed Arkle has now rearranged itself and become ash. For the matter which composed Arkle, even if it is all preserved in an incinerated form, was never the same thing as Arkle, even if it is now the same thing as a heap of ash. The identity of Arkle was never dependent on the identity of the particles of matter which composed him. During the course of his life he was composed of many different particles of matter, which passed through the organism that was Arkle rather as particles of water pass through the arrangement of flowing water which is a river. If the river ceased to flow it would cease to be a river. But there too there would be nothing, no collection of water molecules, which was once a river and is now an elongated stagnant pond. The collection of water molecules that constituted the river the moment before it ceased to flow were not even then *the river*. For at each earlier stage the river was composed of quite different molecules, and its identity as a river was quite different from the identity of the water that was in it at any time. Just so with Arkle. Arkle was never the same as the matter of which he was composed: and even if the matter of which he was composed on his last day had ceased to be horseflesh and has become ash, we cannot say that Arkle himself has ceased to be a horse and has become something else. We can make no sense of the idea that Arkle has ceased to be a horse and has become something else. We can indeed make no sense of the idea that Arkle has ceased to be a horse. So it will certainly not serve to explain, or provide us with an analysis of, the notion of ceasing to exist. This is true of Type 1 predicables in general. Using f to stand for predicables of this type we may say that 'a has ceased to f' is true if and only if $KPfaNfa$ is true. Nfa, however, is unintelligible: only if fa is true is there anything for a to refer to. Plato's Beard is not avoided by substituting $KPfaNfa$ for $KPE!aNE!a$.

It is worth looking into Woods's method of delimiting the class of permissible substitutions for f, i.e. the class of Type 1 predicables. Woods notes that there are two ways in which logicians have suggested that the temporal determinations of propositions should be categorized: either they are sentential operators of the form 'It was the case at t that —', or they are the result of substituting an $(n+1)$-place predicable for an n-place predicable in a temporally undetermined clause and filling the extra argument-place with a time reference. Thus Arkle's being asleep at midnight might be expressed by 'It was the case at midnight that (Arkle is asleep), or by 'Arkle is asleep at midnight', where '— is asleep at . . .' is a two-place predicable one of whose argument-places is filled by 'midnight'. Woods's method of delimiting Type 1 predicables is this: Type 1 predicables are monadic predicables which, according to Woods, do not need relativization by the addition of a further argument-place converting them into two-place predicables. Since '— is asleep' is something which is true of Arkle at some times but not at others, it has to be converted into '— is asleep at . . . .', in which the second argument-place must be filled by the designation of a time. But '— is a horse' is something which is true of Arkle as long as he exists. Woods claims that 'all predicables which are represented formally as being monadic will be Type 1, since they will lack internal relativization to a time'.[29] But any two-place predicable can be converted into a monadic one by having one of its argument-places filled. Thus '— is famous at time t_1' is represented formally as being monadic and is not of Type 1, nor does it lack internal relativization to a time. Type 1 predicables are true of objects only while they exist (p.256), but if '— is famous at time t_1' is ever true of Arkle it is always true of him, provided that 'is' is understood tenselessly. And the time designated by 'time t_1' may be later than Arkle's death. Woods seems simply to have overlooked complex predicables.

We may ignore the infelicities of Woods's attempt to delimit the class of Type 1 predicable and still feel that we have some intuitive grasp of the type of predicable intended, as we have some intuitive grasp of the notion of essential predicables or Aristotle's second substance. Even so it does not seem that (W) can provide us with a viable analysis of coming into existence or ceasing to exist. Letting a stand for 'Arkle', we should get the following substitution for 'Arkle no longer exists' by using definition (W) and standard truth-functional and tense-logical symbols: $KP\Sigma ffaN\Sigma gga$. The second conjunct here says that no Type 1 predicable holds at the present time of Arkle. Odd. Arkle is neither a horse, nor a man, not a plant, nor . . . He begins to sound like Aristotle's prime matter. $N\Sigma gga$ is equivalent to $\Pi gNga$. If '— is a horse' is a substitution instance of 'g —', we can infer from $\Pi gNga$ that Arkle is not a horse. So the attempt to interpret Arkle's no longer existing in terms of definition (W) inherits all the absurdities which accrued to the attempt to explain Arkle's ceasing to exist in terms of Arkle's ceasing to be a horse.

If (W), with its predicative variable taking as substitution instances only Type 1 predicables, produces this *inconvénient*, so will the better-known definition of '— exist' given by

[29] Ibid.

Leśniewski, which is the same as (W) except for having an unrestricted predicative variable.³⁰ For Leśniewski, 'x exists' is defined as $\Sigma\phi\phi x$, where any predicable whatsoever is substitutable for ϕ. On this definition 'Arkle no longer exists' will be translatable into $KP\Sigma\phi\phi a N\Sigma\psi\psi a$. But since '— is a horse' is as much a substitution instance of 'ψ —' as of 'g —', this too entails the absurd consequence that Arkle is not a horse.

Similar *inconvénients* result from defining '— exists' as ΣxI—x.³¹ 'Arkle no longer exists' will come out on this definition as $KP\Sigma xIaxN\Sigma yIay$. The latter conjunct of this is equivalent to $\Pi yNIay$, which entails $NIaa$. This, however, is a prima-facie self-contradiction. To say that Arkle has died is hardly to say that Arkle used to be Arkle, but is so no longer.

10. *Analysis of 'Arkle no longer exists'*

It is time to attempt some positive account of 'Arkle no longer exists'. All the accounts so far given have regarded the fundamental structure of this proposition as the embedding of a proposition 'Arkle exists', or some proposition like $\Sigma f fa$ thought to provide an analysis of it, in the context 'It is no longer the case that —' (i.e. substituting 'Arkle exists', or its analysis, for p in $KPpNp$). 'Arkle exists' on this analysis is thought of as the result of attaching a first-level predicable, '— exists', or some first-level predicable like 'Σff —' held to have the same meaning, to the proper name 'Arkle'. The arguments of Chapter III, and the answers to objections to the conclusion of these arguments which were contained in Chapter IV, provide ample reason for calling in question this assumption about the fundamental structure of 'Arkle no longer exists'. The pattern of analysis used in Chapter IV may again prove useful here.

Let us try a paraphrase of 'Arkle no longer exists' along the lines of the paraphrases of (1) and (2) that were given in Chapter IV:

(9) For some τ, for some n, both it was the case n time units ago that Arkle occupied τ, and (now) it is not the case

---

³⁰ Cf. Prior, *Formal Logic*, 1955, pp. 294, f.
³¹ As Quine often does: cf. *Ontological Relativity and Other Essays*, 1969, p. 94. Cf. my remarks in Ch. 3, above, p. 77. The fundamental objection to this is that it involves taking identity as a first-level concept. I argue against this in 'Is Identity a Relation?', *Proc. Arist. Soc.*, 80, 1979-80.

that, for some x, x has reached the place where it now is by a continuous route over n units of time from τ, and x is an animal,

where τ is a variable whose substitution instances are designations of places. 'Place' here is understood in such a way that the place which Arkle occupies at any given moment is precisely that portion of space delimited by the surface of Arkle's body. It must be understood with some willingness to give and take. If Arkle's mane is trimmed or if he loses an ear in an accident, there will strictly speaking be no one thing which has reached the place it is now occupying by a continuous route over a given period of time from a place occupied by Arkle before the operation or the accident at the beginning of that period; for the place occupied by Arkle minus his mane or ear at that time was smaller than that occupied by the whole of Arkle. This will, however, be so small a difference as to be negligible. Arkle will still exist despite the fact that he has been slightly diminished. But had Arkle been an amoeba and undergone fission, we might well have denied that he still existed, and that on formally similar grounds. There would be nothing which had reached the place it was at by a continuous route over a period of time from some place occupied at the beginning of that period by Arkle; for each of the results of fission would have reached the place it occupied by a continuous route from only a part, and that not a preponderant part, of some place once occupied by Arkle.

The clause 'and x is an animal' rules out the case where Arkle dies and his corpse is, say, immediately frozen so that it does not disintegrate. The corpse no doubt has reached the place it now occupies by a continuous route from some place once occupied by Arkle. The corpse, however, is not Arkle; nor is it, except in some equivocal sense,[32] an animal. These are points for which I was arguing in the last section. Since there is no *animal* which has reached the place it now occupies by a continuous route from some place once occupied by Arkle, Arkle no longer exists.

[32] Cf. Aristotle, *De Anima*, Book II, Ch. I, and *passim*.

11. Generalization of the analysis and solution of the Qualified Version of Plato's Beard

No such clause will be needed in the case of an object the criterion of whose identity is purely material, e.g. a rock. Criteria of identity of course differ for different kinds of object. What it is for this to be the same seminar as the one I was conducting last term is different from what it is for this to be the same thunderstorm as the one that passed over your town two hours ago. Seminars can be disbanded and thunderstorms can die away, and what it is for each of them to cease to exist is different in accordance with the difference between their respective criteria of identity. (9) therefore is incapable of giving us a general analysis of all propositions of the form 'a no longer exists'. Something more schematic is required.

If we possess some criterion of identity for A's we must know that there are some predicables, ϕ and ψ, and some number, n, such that, for every x and for every y, necessarily, if it has been the case n time-units ago that x ϕ's and is now the case that y ψ's, x is the same A as y; there must be some predicables, that is, satisfying the following formula for a given n:

(10) $\Pi x \Pi y L C P n \phi x C \psi y I^A xy$,

where $I^A xy$ means 'x is the same A as y'. Let us call predicables satisfying (10) for some particular n and A 'n-A-reidentifying predicables', and predicables which satisfy any formula obtained by substituting any name of a kind for A and any number for n 'reidentifying predicables'. Reidentifying predicables stand for properties of reidentification. To say that a no longer exists is to say that there are two such properties, one of which belonged to a at some time in the past and the other of which now belongs to nothing. Alternatively we may say that there are two reidentifying predicables and some number, n, such that n time-units ago the first predicable held of a and now the second predicable holds of nothing. Formally, we get:

(11) $\Sigma \phi \Sigma \psi \Sigma n K (\Pi x \Pi y L C P n \phi x C \psi y I^A xy) K P n \phi a N \Sigma z \psi z$,

where the part of the formula in brackets is the same as (10), or, more simply,

(11A) $\Sigma \phi \Sigma \psi \Sigma n K P n \phi a N \Sigma x \psi x$, where ϕ and ψ are n-A-reidentifying predicables. The only non-logical constants in these formulae are a and A. a was introduced as an abbreviation of 'Arkle', but it can stand for any proper name. Given that we know what a proper name names, we know to what kind it belongs. Only if we know this can we know how to make repeated use of the same proper name, for a repeated use of a proper name is always equivalent to the use of an expression of the form 'the same A' where A is the name of a kind. So given a we know what A is.

'Arkle still exists, is, of course, the negation of (11), and this is equivalent to

(12) $\Pi\phi\Pi\psi\Pi nC(\Pi x\Pi yLCPn\phi xC\psi yI^A xy)CPn\phi a\Sigma z\psi z$,

or, more simply,

(12A) $\Pi\phi\Pi\psi\Pi nCPn\phi a\Sigma x\psi x$,

where ϕ and ψ are, again, n-A-reidentifying predicables. What (12) and (12A) say is that, for any two predicables satisfying (10) for any number n of time-units, if n time-units ago the first predicable held of a, then the second predicable now holds of something (which must of course be a). In less formal language we can express this as follows: if a had one member of any pair of properties of reidentification at some time in the past, the other member now belongs to something.

The same considerations will yield the following analysis of 'Arkle came into existence':

(13) $\Sigma nN\Sigma\phi\Sigma\psi K(\Pi x\Pi yLCPn\phi xC\psi yI^A xy)KPn\Sigma z\phi z\psi a$,

or, more simply,

(13A) $\Sigma nN\Sigma\phi\Sigma\psi KPn\Sigma x\phi x\psi a$,

where, once more, ϕ and ψ are n-A-reidentifying predicables. (13) and (13A) say that, for some n, there are no two predicables satisfying (10), such that both the first held of something n time-units ago and the second holds of a now. In less formal language: there is a time in the past such that no pair of properties of reidentification has one member which then belonged to something and another member which belongs to *a* now. Our theory thus makes this a treatise *'De generatione'* as well as a treatise *'De corruptione'*.[33]

The theory also allows us to solve the paradox of the Qualified Version of Plato's Beard. The paradox arose because the proposition 'Arkle no longer exists' seemed to require analysis as the conjunction of two propositions, 'Arkle at one time existed' and 'Arkle does not exist now'. The latter apparently attributes to Arkle a property, non-existence, at a time when

---

[33] Mr Simon Orde has presented the following difficulty for these analyses. Let us suppose that the first moon landing took place exactly ten years ago. Then, with the following substitutions for variables, and taking years as our time-units:

$$a = \text{Neil Armstrong}$$
$$\phi = \text{is a man on the moon}$$
$$\psi = \text{is the only man ever to have been on the moon}$$
$$n = \text{ten}$$
$$A = \text{man}$$

we have (10) true, so that ' — is a man on the moon' and '— is the only man ever to have been on the moon' are ten-man-reidentifying predicables. However, since no one is now the only man to have been on the moon (since more than one man has visited it), (11) is also true. But, with these substitutions, (11) should mean that Neil Armstrong no longer exists, which is false. Similarly (12), which should be true, comes out false.

The point to notice here is that, with ϕ read as 'is a man on the moon', 'y is the only man ever to have been on the moon' is equivalent to $\Pi w \Pi m C P m \phi w I A w y$. With the above substitutions for ϕ, ψ, and A and any substitution for n, (10) is accordingly equivalent to

$$(10^{\text{Orde}}) \; \Pi x \Pi y L C P n \phi x C \Pi w \Pi m C P m \phi w I A w y I A_{xy},$$

which says that anyone who was on the moon n years ago is the same man as anyone who is the only man ever to have been on the moon. But (10^{Orde}) is a truth of logic. Not only is it true with any substitution for n, it is true for any substitution for ϕ and A. It is true solely in virtue of the logical constants which occur in it. The predicable which Orde asks us to substitute for ϕ occurs in it, as Quine would say, 'non-essentially'.

Orde's objection requires us, therefore, to make the following qualification to our explanation of the term n-A-reidentifying predicable. A pair of predicables ϕ and ψ are n-A-reidentifying predicables if they satisfy (10) without being exponible in such a way that (10) becomes a logical truth. The predicables substituted for ϕ and ψ will not be n-A-reidentifying if either of them is definable in such a way as to make (10) equivalent to a theorem of any system of tense logic.

This restriction should not be regarded as a mere *ad hoc* bit of machinery designed to enable us to side-step Orde's objection. The notion of properties of re-identification is intended to capture the criterion of identity which is implicit in the concept of a substance which persists through time. Such substances develop according to natural laws appropriate to their own kind; and the necessity which makes a man now answering to such-and-such a description the same as one who n years ago answered to another such description is a natural necessity derived from these natural laws. It is not, therefore, to be confused with logical necessity, and no laws of logic are sufficient to generate n-A-reidentifying predicables.

it says itself that he does not exist. Similarly, the Qualified Version of Plato's Beard might be thought to prevent us from making sense of ' Arkle came into existence'; for this too is prima facie exponible. It seems to be equivalent to 'Either Arkle at some time did not exist and Arkle now exists, or it has been the case that (Arkle at some time did not exist and Arkle now exists)'; and the first conjunct of each of the disjuncts of this proposition says that there was a time when Arkle possessed a property, *non-existence*, although by the same token he did not at that time exist. Whether it is generation or corruption that we are analysing, trouble arises because something is predicated of Arkle in each conjunct of the *analysans* and something is thus said to hold of him at a time when he does not exist. My analysis of these propositions is different. It does not make them conjunctions of two distinct propositions, but quantified propositions with conjunctive matrices—in each case the initial quantifier binds variables occurring in a conjunctive open sentence. The proper name 'Arkle', or the *a* which stands for it, occurs in only one conjunct of this conjunctive open sentence. In each case the time reference proper to the conjunct in which the name 'Arkle' occurs refers to a time when Arkle is alive. There is no question therefore of a property being said to hold of Arkle at a time when there is or was no such horse.

To say that Arkle no longer exists is to say that there are two 'properties of reidentification' one of which belonged to Arkle at some time in the past and the other of which now belongs to nothing. To say that Arkle came into existence is to say that it is or has been the case that there are no two properties of reidentification one of which belonged to something at some time in the past and the other of which belongs to Arkle now. Part of what we say when we say that Arkle no longer exists is that a property belonged to him; but it belonged to him in the past when he was alive. No part of what we say when we say that Arkle came into existence is that any property belonged to him at any time. The proposition that Arkle no longer exists, on this analysis, is no more entangled in the Qualified Version of Plato's Beard than were the causal propositions we examined in section 3 of this chapter. 'Ill feeling has been stirred up amongst the Williams family by Williams's making a will' is a proposition which may only become true after Williams's death. We should not naturally say of him therefore that he possessed the property of *having stirred up ill feeling amongst his relations by making a will* at a time when he no longer existed. The time when he made the will was before his death; the time when the trouble broke out was after his death. If we are to talk of his having such a property we cannot say that he had it at one of these times rather than the other. The only property that can properly be said to belong to him at a definite time is the property of *being engaged in making a will*. He possessed that property at some time when he was alive. The effect of his having possessed this property, namely, the ill will stirred up amongst his relations, is not itself, and does not involve, any property belonging to Williams. That the Williams family are at loggerheads with each other at time t does not even seem to imply the existence of Williams at time t. Similarly, if there are two properties of reidentification, ϕ and ψ, such that ϕ belonged to Arkle some time in the past and ψ now belongs to nothing, the only property that can properly be said to belong to Arkle at a definite time in virtue of this fact is ϕ; and he possessed this property when he was alive. The fact that the other property, ψ, now belongs to nothing, does not involve any property's now belonging to Arkle.[34] Arkle, therefore, can cheerfully come into existence and cease to exist without getting entangled in Plato's Beard, even in its modified form. The paradox is disposed of. Nor do we have to countenance '— exist' as a first-level predicable.

12. No longer existing *a property, and a temporal property, of individuals*

We have learned how to avoid treating existence as a property of individuals: none of the propositions which seemed to force us to treat '— exist' as a first-level predicable turned out in the long run to have this power. What we can admit, however, is that *no longer existing* and *having come into existence* are genuine properties of individuals. As with propositions (5) and (6) of Chapter IV, propositions (11) to (13) of this chapter

---

[34] We may recall the difficulty of saying that 'John is tall and Mary is married' says something false of Mary when, though Mary *is* married, John is short. Cf. O. R. Jones, 'Truth and Predication', *Analysis*, 32, No. 3, 1972, and my *What is Truth?*, pp. 21 f.

are singular propositions, and so do justice to the insight expressed by Geach as follows:

> It would be quite absurd to say that Jacob in uttering these words ['Joseph is not and Simeon is not'] was not talking about Joseph and Simeon but about the use of their names. Of course he was talking about his sons; he was expressing a fear that something had happened to them, that they were dead. We have a sense of 'is' or 'exists' that seems to me to be certainly a genuine predicate of individuals.[35]

'Joseph is not' and 'Simeon is not' are elliptical for 'Joseph no longer is (exists)' and 'Simeon no longer is (exists)', and thus (11) should provide an analysis of each of them.[36] So it does, if *a* is taken in turn as standing for 'Joseph' and 'Simeon'. (11) will in this way say something about Joseph or Simeon, and (11) minus *a* will be 'a genuine predicate of individuals'. But what (11) minus *a* represents will not be the negation of '— is' or '— exists', but the negation of '— still exists', i.e. '— no longer exists'. Geach is wrong therefore in thinking that we are forced to admit a sense of '— exists' itself as a genuine predicate of individuals. It has been the aim of this chapter to give an analysis of propositions of the form '*a* no longer exists' or '*a* still exists' which treats them as genuine singular propositions, but which does not permit them to be regarded as the result of attaching the operators 'It is no longer the case that —' or 'It is still the case that —' to corresponding propositions of the form '*a* exists'.

This claim, that there are singular propositions of the form '*a* no longer exists' but no singular propositions of the form '*a* exists', may be compared to a thesis of Dummett's. Dummett's thesis, like my own, is an attempt to give sense to obviously meaningful sentences like 'Arkle no longer exists' without having to concede Geach's position that there is a sense of 'is' or 'exists' that is a genuine predicate of individuals. According to this thesis 'Cleopatra no longer exists' ascribes to Cleopatra not the loss of the temporal property of existence, but an atemporal property of *not existing at this time*. There are, how-

---

[35] Geach, *God and the Soul*, p. 58. Cf. above, Ch. I, p. 15, n. 25, for an earlier comment on this biblical example.
[36] Just so 'an existing politician' means 'a politician who still exists', and 'The pool of water has disappeared' implies 'The pool of water no longer exists' (see above, Ch. II, p. 22, and Ch. III, p. 71, n. 30).

ever, important differences between myself and Dummett. Dummett writes:

> Temporal existence is thus no more a property than atemporal existence: if 'Cleopatra no longer exists' is taken to ascribe a property to Cleopatra, then the property in question is not that of non-existence, which she is being said to have at this time, but rather the property of not existing at this time.... Properties, thus understood, are atemporal, that is, things of which it can make no sense to say that one acquires them or loses them.[37]

In the preceding paragraph he has drawn an analogy between saying that Cleopatra no longer exists and saying, of a particular road, 'The road no longer exists here'. Just as *beauty* is a property which Cleopatra may first have acquired and later lost, so *narrowness* is a property which a road may be thought of as acquiring and later losing. And as an alternative to saying that *narrowness* is a property which a road begins to have at a certain point we may say that the road has the property of *being narrow from this point*. Similarly we can say that the road has the property of *not existing beyond this point*; but here the option of saying that *non-existence* is a property which the road begins to have at a certain point is not open to us. Similarly, we are to conclude, we may ascribe to Cleopatra the property of *not existing after a certain date*, but may not say of her that after a certain date she acquired the property of *not existing*.

Analogies between spatial and temporal ways of speaking are notoriously dangerous. It seems that, while there is just the same reason for denying that Cleopatra acquired the property of *non-existence* as there is for denying that the road does so, the reasons for allowing each of them the property of *not existing after a certain point* are different. The property of *not existing after a certain point* in the case of the road can be identified with its occupying a certain geographical position. Position is not the same as existence. The Fosse Way, for instance, stretches from Seaton to Lincoln. We do not need the existential 'is' to describe this fact: The Fosse Way is in Devon but not in Cornwall. This is the copulative 'is'. Admittedly we do need the existential 'is' to express the fact that the Fosse Way does not exist north of Lincoln, but it is not needed in predicative

---

[37] Frege: *Philosophy of Language*, p. 387. By 'atemporal existence' Dummett has in mind what is frequently held to be expressed by the quantifier: 'There *exists* an *x* such that ...'

position after 'the Fosse Way'. To say that the Fosse Way does not exist north of Lincoln is to say that there *is* nowhere north of Lincoln where the Fosse Way *is*. The first of these italicized occurrences of 'is' is existential, but the second is the copula. Neither involves the use of 'is' as a first-level predicable. But 'There is nowhere north of Lincoln where — is' is here a first-level predicate of the Fosse Way. It is because '— does not exist beyond Lincoln' can be interpreted in this way that it too is a first-level predicable.

We cannot give an exactly parallel analysis of 'Cleopatra did not exist after 30 BC'. We cannot say 'There is no time after 30 BC at which Cleopatra was', because temporal phrases such as 'in 29 BC', unlike locative phrases such as 'in Cornwall', cannot serve as complements to the copula.[38] What we can say is 'There is no time after 30 BC at which Cleopatra still existed'. This proposition is the negation of a generalization of propositions like 'Cleopatra still existed in 29 BC' which can be analysed by means of a metrically tensed version of (12). If b is an abbreviation of 'Cleopatra', B the name of the kind to which Cleopatra belonged and χm stands for '30 BC is more than m time-units ago' the following will be the analysis of 'Cleopatra did not exist after 30 BC':

(14) $\quad N\Sigma m K\chi m Pm\Pi\phi\Pi\psi\Pi n C(\Pi x\Pi y LCPn\phi x C\psi y I^B xy)C\text{-}Pn\phi b\Sigma z\psi z,$

or, more simply,

(14A) $N\Sigma m K\chi m Pm\Pi\phi\Pi\psi\Pi n CPn\phi b\Sigma x\psi x,$

where ϕ and ψ are $n\text{-}A$-reidentifying predicables. (14) and (14A) say there is no time subsequent to 30 BC at which every pair of properties of reidentification is such that if Cleopatra had one member of the pair at any previous time something has the other member. On this analysis '— did not exist after 30 BC' is properly said to be predicated of Cleopatra, and the property of *not existing after 30 BC* can properly be said to belong to her, without its following that in 30 BC the property of *existing* ceased to belong to her or that she then acquired the property of *non-existence*.

[38] Cf. John Lyons, *Introduction to Theoretical Linguistics*, 1971, pp. 346 ff. For locative complements to the copula, cf. above, Ch. I, p. 15, and below, Ch. XII, pp. 319 ff. Appendix A, pp. 328 f.

NO LONGER EXISTING A PROPERTY

Can it be said of Cleopatra, however, that in 30 BC she lost the property of *still existing* and acquired that of *no longer existing*? Is Dummett mistaken when, in the passage quoted, he says that, if 'Cleopatra no longer exists' is taken to ascribe a property to Cleopatra, this property is one of which it makes no sense to say that one acquires it or loses it? Dummett's reason for saying this is that the property which, in his view, may be ascribed to Cleopatra by this proposition is that of *not existing at this time*. This, he says, is atemporal; and this is so if 'not existing at this time' is taken as synonymous with, say, 'not existing in 1981'. No property expressible by a phrase of the form 'not ϕ-ing in 1981' could be said to be acquired or lost. But this does not imply that no property expressible by a phrase of the form 'no longer ϕ-ing' can be said to be acquired or lost. I cannot at any time acquire the property of *not being overweight in 1981*, but I should like in 1981 to acquire the property of *no longer being overweight*. Similarly, Cleopatra could not at any time have acquired the property of *not existing in 29 BC*, although this is a property she—atemporally—has; but it does not follow that she did not acquire in 30 BC the property of *no longer existing*. The properties of *no longer existing* and of *still existing* are what the predicates in (11) and (12) express. The propositions (11) and (12) are present-tensed, and it is by no means the case that if they are true they always have been or always will be true. They do not in this sense ascribe atemporal properties to anything.

It may well be that Dummett is misled at this point by his own analogy between 'Cleopatra no longer exists' and 'The road no longer exists here'. The fact which the latter proposition states is one which concerns the way the road is spread out in space rather than the way in which it persists or fails to persist through time. We are particularly tempted to talk about the spatial properties of roads in language appropriate to the temporal properties of journeys. This is because our experience of roads is typically successive, so that we naturally transfer what we say about ourselves, the travellers, to the routes by which we travel. Walking through Lincolnshire, we may say, at a particular point, 'The Fosse Way no longer exists here'. What we say, equivalent as it is to 'The Fosse Way is not at the place at which we have now arrived', is something tensed, something which though true now was not true an hour ago. But it is we who have changed, and have thus changed the truth-value of what we say; it is not the Fosse Way which has changed. Again, moving my pencil across the map I may say 'The Fosse Way is no longer here', meaning 'The point on the map which my pencil is now touching does not represent any place where the Fosse Way is'. If I had said what I just said half a second earlier it would have been false: but it is the position of my pencil that has changed, not the map or the facts represented on the map. These connections allow us to use a phrase like 'no longer', which is primarily applicable to changing conditions correlated to a series of times related by the before–after relation, to describe an object in terms of a series of positions related by, e.g. the north–south relation. The proposition that the Fosse Way no longer exists north of Lincoln is one whose truth-value is not, in any relevant way, subject to change. This is because the use of 'no longer' is being extended here from its original temporal application, so that it now applies analogically to a spatial dimension. But in 'Cleopatra no longer exists' the phrase is being used in its original sense, a sense which can be explicated in terms of tense operators and is in no way atemporal. Dummett is not justified in arguing that because the property which 'The road no longer exists here' ascribes to the road is an atemporal property, the property which 'Cleopatra no longer exists' ascribes to Cleopatra is also atemporal.

We have still, however, to answer the question whether *no longer existing* is a property which Cleopatra can be said to have acquired. The proposition 'Cleopatra no longer exists' is one which became true in 30 BC and is thus not itself atemporal. So much has been established. But does it follow that *no longer existing* is a temporal property, in the sense that it can be acquired (and the property of *still existing*, by the same token, lost)? If Cleopatra acquired the property of *no longer existing*, she acquired it only when she died. But we have seen reason in section 3 of this chapter for denying that any property could belong to an object, or any predicate be true of it, at a time when the object no longer existed. On my analysis, to say that Cleopatra no longer exists is to say that there are two 'properties of reidentification' one of which belonged to Cleopatra at some time in the past and the other of which now belongs to nothing. To say this is to say something about the present but also something about the past, about a property's belonging to Cleopatra when she was alive. We have seen that this escapes unscathed from the entanglements of Plato's Beard. Whenever it became true that Cleopatra no longer existed, the property ascribed to her by saying at that time that she no longer existed is not itself a datable property. It implies that some datable property did once belong to her, but only at a time when she was alive. Despite the fact that the proposition 'Cleopatra no longer exists' has only been true since her death, and only became true then, we speak misleadingly if we attribute to her now the property of *no longer existing*, or say that she acquired it in 30 BC. It would be no less absurd than saying of Williams that he acquired the property of *having stirred up ill feeling amongst his relations by making a will* only at a time when he was already dead.

We can thus see that although a given proposition only became true at a certain date, and although that proposition is a singular proposition which says something about a certain object, it does not follow that the object acquired a property at that date. But neither can we infer from the fact that a proposition ascribes to an object a property which cannot be acquired that the proposition is atemporal or can properly be said to ascribe an atemporal property to the object. *Being overweight in 1981* may be an atemporal property which can be ascribed to Williams by a tenseless proposition which, if ever true, is always true. *No longer being overweight* is certainly not such a property. Nor is *no longer existing*. If it is a property at all, it is certainly not one which can be ascribed to Cleopatra by a proposition which, if ever true, is always true. It is misleading, therefore, to call such a property an atemporal property, and in this I disagree with Dummett. I agree with him that 'Cleopatra no longer exists', despite its being a singular proposition about Cleopatra, does not imply that Cleopatra lost the property of existence or gained that of *non-existence*. It does not, however, ascribe an atemporal property to Cleopatra, nor is it to be identified with a tenseless proposition which asserts Cleopatra's non-existence in 1981.

To sum up, then, it can be said that both Geach and Dummett

agree with me in allowing that a proposition like 'Arkle no longer exists' can be said to be a singular proposition about a particular object, although Dummett wrongly regards it as ascribing an atemporal property to this object, and Geach wrongly regards it as implying loss of the supposed property of *existence*. Geach is therefore properly credited with the insight that someone who utters the words 'Joseph is not and Simeon is not' or 'Arkle no longer exists' is talking about Joseph or Simeon or Arkle. These are genuine singular propositions, although this does not force us, as he thinks, to recognize a first-level predicable '— exist'. The concept of existence does, nevertheless, enter into (11), which is our analysis of 'Arkle no longer exists'; but it is not there expressed by a first-level predicable embedded in the context, 'It is no longer the case that —'. It is expressed by the quantificational expression Σz—z, whose argument place is filled, not by an individual but by a predicative expression. It is thus expressed by a second-level predicable, and we are able to do justice to the other important insight, which applies to 'Arkle no longer exists', as much as to the propositions examined in Chapter III. It applies also to those examined in Chapter IV, which again prima facie involve the embedding of singular existential propositions in wider contexts. This Fregean insight, that despite appearances the concept of existence, taken neat, can never be expressed by a first-level predicable, has been classically formulated by W. V. Quine in the dictum 'Existence is what the existential quantifier expresses'.[39] It is to Quine's dictum and his interpretation of it that we must turn in the next chapter. What has been done in this chapter is essentially the same as what was done in the last: we have examined certain singular propositions, which appear to predicate existence of individuals, and given an analysis of them which preserves their singularity but allows their existential character to be expressed by the quantifier. We thus have the best of both worlds.

[39] Quine, 'Existence and Quantification' p. 97.

VI
Quantification, Reference, and Ontological Commitment

1. *Quantification of non-individual variables*

In the last two chapters I have been concerned with propositions in which 'exists', coupled with a proper name, seems to be embedded in an epistemic, modal, or tense context. My analyses of these propositions rely heavily on a repeated predicate variable bound by the existential quantifier. They all involve the form 'For some ϕ, both — ϕ's and — ϕ's'. But quantifying variables of categories other than the individual is a practice which, in the eyes of some philosophers, requires justification. Some even go so far as to deny that they understand what is meant by sentences like 'For some ϕ, both David ϕ's and Jonathan ϕ's' or 'For some p, both Percy says that p and p'. Others, like Quine, admit that they understand these expressions, but regard them with alarm, since they believe that on one interpretation at least they commit their users to unwelcome metaphysical doctrines, to the view that universals and other abstract entities exist. So far I have followed Frege in categorizing 'For some x, — x' as a second-level predicable. I have used, but not discussed or attempted to categorize, expressions of the form 'For some ϕ, — ϕ's'. The quantifier, I have assumed, is not tied to individual variables like that which is bound by it in the expression 'For some x, — x'. It can equally well bind predicative variables, as in the sentence 'For some ϕ, both David ϕ's and Jonathan ϕ's', or propositional variables, as in the sentence 'For some p, both Percy says that p and p'. The quantifier itself, as Aristotle said of *being*, is outside all categories, and can be used to bind variables of any category. Combined with a variable in this way it can constitute a second-level predicable like 'For some x, — x', a first- or third-level predicable, like 'For some ϕ, —ϕ's', or an expression like 'For some p, — p', which is not to be categorized as a predicable of any level.¹ And there are other possibilities. It is time to defend these assumptions, and in particular to refute certain doctrines of Quine which would call them in question. Quine's views, which have been influential, are in any case worth refuting, since they embody a fundamental misunderstanding of the concept of existence.

No philosopher is more emphatic than Quine in his professed acceptance of Frege's account of existence. 'Existence is what the existential quantifier expresses.' His famous essay 'On What There Is'² aims to do for singular propositions generally what Russell did for propositions containing definite descriptions, namely, reduce them to an existentially quantified form in order to free us from the difficulties of Plato's Beard. However, even in this essay Quine makes remarks which show that he is not completely emancipated from the illusion that 'exist' is a first-level predicable; and in later works he elaborates a view of quantification, as 'objectual' or 'referential', which can only be understood if we regard him as covertly treating existence as a property of objects.

2. *Reference and the variables of quantification*

Describing the result of Russell's analysis of a proposition like 'The author of *Waverley* was a poet' in 'On What There is'³ Quine says that 'the burden of objective reference which had been put upon the descriptive phrase is now taken over by words of the kind that logicians call bound variables, variables of quantification, namely, words like "something", "nothing", "everything"'. We can understand what he means by talk of removing the burden of objective reference from the descriptive phrase. There is a temptation to regard the sentence 'The author of *Waverely* was a poet' as significant only if some object is referred to by the phrase 'The author of *Waverley*'. To think in this way is to think of definite descriptions of this sort as analogous to proper names—classifiable together with

---

[1] I have already drawn attention to this fact: see above, Ch. III, pp. 73 ff.
[2] *From a Logical Point of View*, Ch. 1.
[3] Ibid., p. 6.

REFERENCE AND VARIABLES OF QUANTIFICATION 155

proper names, perhaps, as 'singular terms' or 'referring expressions'. In Russell's view, proper names, if they are genuine proper names and not just abbreviations of definite descriptions, contribute to the meaning of a sentence in which they occur only if they have in fact something to stand for or refer to. But definite descriptions can contribute to the meaning of the sentences in which they occur in quite another way. They can be regarded in effect as functioning as second-level predicates.[4] To say 'The author of *Waverley* was a poet' is to say 'There was just one man who wrote *Waverley* and he was a poet'. Here '— was a poet' is a first-level predicable and 'There was just one man who wrote Waverley and he —' is functioning as a second-level predicate, so that it ranks as an expression of the same category as 'something —', 'nothing —' and 'everything —'. Russell's failure to understand that his own theory implies that definite descriptions are second-level predicables shows only in the symbolism he chose for its expression. Propositions like 'The author of *Waverley* was a poet' are analysed by Russell as being of the form $\Sigma x \Pi y K E I x y \phi y \psi x$. Here $\Sigma x \Pi y K E I x y \phi y$—$x$ gives the form of a second-level predicable, but this is obscured by Russell's use of $\psi(\imath x)(\phi x)$ to abbreviate $\Sigma x \Pi y K E I x y \phi y \psi x$, thus making $(\imath x)(\phi x)$ appear as argument to ψ, rather than vice versa. Prior's use of $\imath x \phi x \psi x$ as the abbreviation for $\Sigma x \Pi y K E I x y \phi y \psi x$ avoids any such appearance. $\imath x \phi x$—x is clearly a second-level predicable, just as $\Pi x C \phi x$—x and Πx—x are.[5] In this way there is no question of definite

---

[4] This point was probably first made by Geach in a footnote to his translation of Frege's 'On Concept and Object', *Translations from the Philosophical Writings of Gottlob Frege*, p. 51, n. A. It should be noted that it only applies to definite descriptions as they occur in propositions like 'The author of *Waverley* is a poet'. In 'The author of *Waverley* exists', on the other hand, the phrase 'The author of *Waverley*' functions as a first-level predicable, on Russell's analysis, as does the phrase 'Aristocratic Australians' in 'Aristocratic Australians exist' (see next footnote). For Russell's analysis of propositions like 'The author of *Waverley* exists', see above, Ch. IV, p. 88, n. 6.

[5] See Prior, 'Is the Concept of Referential Opacity Really Necessary?', *Acta Philosophica Fennica*, 16, 1963, and my *What is Truth?*, pp. 36 ff. Since expressions of the form $\Pi x C \phi x$-x are to be recognized as second-level predicables, the phrase 'Aristocratic Australians' will have to be so recognized in 'Aristocratic Australians drink gin', if this proposition is of the form $\Pi x C \phi x \psi x$. It will thus play a different role from that which it plays in 'Aristocratic Australians exist' (see last footnote, and cf. Ch. II, p. 38, and Ch. III, p. 69). If, on the other hand, 'Aristocratic Australians drink gin' is taken as in some sense presupposing the existence of aristocratic Australians, as was assumed in Ch. II, its structure will

descriptions having to refer to objects in order to contribute to the significance of the sentences in which they occur. We do not suppose that 'Nothing' has to refer to something in 'Nothing is red and green all over', if that sentence is to be significant. If 'The author of Waverley —' is to be categorized as a second-level predicable on a par with 'Nothing —', we can readily see that there is no longer any question of 'putting upon it the burden of objective reference'.

The odd thing is that what Quine immediately goes on to say is that, as a result of Russell's analysis, the burden of objective reference is taken over from definite descriptions by words like, *inter alia*, 'nothing'. What prompts him to say this is no doubt the fact that, for instance, 'It is not the case that the author of *Waverley* was a poet' is paraphrased on Russell's theory by 'Nothing was sole author of *Waverley* and a poet'. But surely we cannot say that what 'the author of *Waverley*' was wrongly supposed to do, what we were tempted to think that it did, namely, refer to something, is now done by 'Nothing'?

Quine may be expressing himself carelessly here. The words which are said to be like 'something', 'nothing', 'everything', are otherwise described by him as 'bound variables, variables of quantification'. But in the formula $N\Sigma x \Pi y K E I x y \phi y \psi x$ the last occurrences of x, which are bound variables, are not by themselves what corresponds to 'Nothing' in the sentence of ordinary language, but the initial expression $N\Sigma x$ together with these. Does Quine really mean to say that in propositions of this form the whole expression $N\Sigma x - x - x$ is what 'takes over the burden of objective reference' or only that the last two occurrences of x do this? It is not only in this passage that Quine seems to be calling expressions like $\Pi x - x$ and $\Sigma x - x$ bound variables. He says (p. 12) '*there is something* (bound have to be recognized as being more complex than is expressed by the formula $\Pi x C \phi x \psi x$. In the same way, if 'The author of *Waverley* is a poet' is taken as presupposing that just one man wrote *Waverley*, its structure will be more complex than is expressed by $\imath x \phi x \psi x$. For this reason I suggested, in Ch. IV of *What is Truth?*, that the structure of sentences like 'The author of *Waverley* is a poet' is expressible by something for which I invented the shorthand formula $\vdash_2 \Sigma x \Pi y E I x y \phi y$, $\Pi z C \phi z \psi z$. A similar suggestion might be made for using the somewhat simpler formula $\vdash_2 \Sigma x \phi x$, $\Pi y C \phi y \psi y$ to express the structure of sentences like 'Aristocratic Australians drink gin'. If these suggestions were adopted we should have to say that 'Aristocratic Australians' and 'The author of *Waverley*' each had to play a double role in these sentences, once as a first-level predicable which is argument to a second-level predicate, and once as itself a second-level predicate.

variable) which red houses and sunsets have in common', and (p. 13) 'The variables of quantification, "something", "nothing", "everything", range over our whole ontology'. On the previous line he says 'Pronouns are the basic media of reference'. Since Russell's analysis of 'The author of *Waverley* was a poet' gives 'Something was sole author of *Waverley* and it was a poet' as its equivalent, and 'something' and 'it' are pronouns, Quine, perhaps, is thinking of such expressions as these when he talks of 'the variables of quantification'. There are many places in his works where he compares pronouns like 'it', which refer back to an antecedent 'something' or 'everything', with bound variables.[6] And in so far as 'Something — it —' corresponds to $\Sigma x - x - x$, 'something' here does the job done by the first bound variable as well as that done by Σx. Perhaps this could be thought to justify calling 'something' a bound variable. But it is all very unclear; and we should probably not press too hard for an answer to the question of exactly which expression Quine is referring to as a 'bound variable'.

The most important point is that, whichever of the possible candidates for the role of 'bound variables' in this context is actually intended by Quine, he is surely wrong in thinking it can take over the burden of referring to objects. Quine is explicit in his claim that this is what bound variables do. 'They refer to entities generally, with a kind of studied ambiguity peculiar to themselves.'[7] This remark of Quine's was criticized by Geach in 1951. Geach suspects that Quine is misled by the use both of the word 'pronoun' and of the word 'variable'. Pronouns are too easily thought of as doing the same work as nouns, i.e. naming, even as doing it better than ordinary names:

If I call an object 'Jemima' or 'cat' I may be mistaken; but surely not if I just call it 'this' or 'something'! If I answer the question 'what is there?' by giving a list, I may go wrong; but surely not if I reply 'everything'![8]

Russell, after all, had thought that demonstrative pronouns were the only logically proper names, and Quine, after saying (p. 13) that 'pronouns are the basic media of reference', adds, 'nouns might better have been named propronouns'. In his reply to

---

[6] Cf. *Mathematical Logic*, 1962, p. 70.
[7] *From a Logical Point of View*, p. 6.
[8] Geach, 'On What There Is', *Proc. Arist. Soc.*, Supp. Vol. 25, 1951, p. 129.

Geach, Quine indignantly rejects the charge that he treats pronouns or variables as quasi-names: 'I have nowhere spoken of bound variables as naming' (ibid., p. 150). No; but he had certainly spoken of them as referring. He does so in the sentence just quoted: 'they refer to entities generally, with a kind of studied ambiguity peculiar to themselves'. This 'studied ambiguity' can easily be thought of as implied by the use of the word 'variable' to describe part of the quantificational apparatus. As Geach remarks, Frege had pointed out[9] how the whole terminology of 'variables' and 'values of variables' leads to endless confusion.

Bound variables perform two functions. First, they provide cross-referencing between the prenex quantifiers and the argument-places of the functional expressions within their scope. 'Someone is loved by everyone' is distinct from 'Everyone is loved by someone'. The first entails that everyone is a lover, the second that everyone is a beloved. But whom does the first say that everyone loves, and by whom does the second say that everyone is loved? Here there is ambiguity in ordinary language, which the variables of quantification can dispel. If ϕxy is taken as an abbreviation of 'x is loved by y', the first may be interpreted either as $\Sigma x \Pi y \phi xy$ or as $\Pi y \Sigma x \phi xy$ and the second either as $\Pi x \Sigma y \phi xy$ or as $\Sigma y \Pi x \phi xy$. Here there are four possibilities where ordinary language only had two.[10] But this function can be performed by other devices than variables, as we know them. It could perfectly well be performed by vincula like this: $\overline{\Sigma \Pi \phi}, \overline{\Pi \Sigma \phi}, \overline{\Pi \Sigma \phi}, \overline{\Sigma \Pi \phi}$.'[11] There would be little temptation to regard such vincula as quasi-nouns, or variable or ambiguous names.

Secondly, variables perform the function of indicating what

---

[9] In 'What is a Function?' in *Translations from the Philosophical Writings of Gottlob Frege*, pp. 107 ff.

[10] The four formulae as given are equivalent to $\Sigma y \Pi x \phi yx$, $\Pi x \Sigma y \phi yx$, $\Pi y \Sigma x \phi yx$, and $\Sigma x \Pi y \phi yx$ respectively. These are not distinct possibilities.

[11] This point is made by Quine himself (*Mathematical Logic*, pp. 69 f.). He has also pointed out, in his paper 'Variables Explained Away' (Quine, *Selected Logic Papers*, pp. 227-35) that the function of variables could be performed by operators that form predicables out of predicables. Inversion ('Inv') is such an operator, forming 'Invϕxy' which has the same sense as ϕyx. We can thus express the four possibilities by $\Sigma x \Pi y \phi xy$, $\Pi x \Sigma y \phi xy$, $\Sigma x \Pi y \text{Inv} \phi xy$ and $\Pi x \Sigma y \text{Inv} \phi xy$. Since here the order in which the variable occur is always alphabetical, both when they are attached to the quantifiers and when they occur in argument position after ϕ, they no longer serve to make necessary distinctions and can be omitted.

category of expression is required to provide an existential or universal instantiation of the quantified formula in question. For instance, if I have formulae of the type $\Sigma x \phi x$ or $\Pi x \phi x$, their instantiations will have to be of the form 'ϕ John' or 'ϕ James': x is a style of variable that requires replacement by proper names. If I have formulae of the type $\Sigma \phi \phi a$ or $\Pi \phi \phi a$, *their* instantiations will have to be of the form 'a yawned' or 'a laughed': ϕ is a style of variable that requires replacement by predicables. And if I have formulae of the type $\Sigma p \delta p$ or $\Pi p \delta p$, *their* instantiations will have to be of the form 'δ grass is green' or 'δ twice two is four': p is a style of variable that requires replacement by propositions.

It might be thought that this last function was unnecessary because the category of the expression not bound by the quantifier would show what category of constant was needed to provide instantiation of the quantified proposition. Thus 'Σ yawned' would express what '$\Sigma x\ x$ yawned' expresses, since the only constant expression that '— yawned' can take in the argument position is a proper name. Similarly 'Σ John said that' will express what 'Σp John said that p' expresses: only a propositional expression can complete 'John said that —' to produce a proposition. But this argument overlooks the fact that it is possible to produce quantified propositions which contain nothing but quantifiers and variables. $\Pi x \Sigma \phi \phi x$ is a perfectly good proposition meaning, roughly, 'Something is true of everything'. This could not be adequately expressed by $\Pi \Sigma$, which might equally well stand for $\Pi \phi \Sigma x \phi x$, i.e. 'Everything is true of something'. It is not, however, necessary for each variable to be repeated in the expression of these propositions. $\Pi x \Sigma \phi$ is adequate for expressing what $\Pi x \Sigma \phi \phi x$ expresses, since there is no alternative to the order in which the predicative and individual variables occur in the matrix. Either we have a convention by which predicative variables precede individual variables in the matrix, or we have the opposite convention: it makes no difference to the sense. Thus $\Pi x \Sigma \phi$ and $\Pi \phi \Sigma x$ are all we need in order to disambiguate $\Pi \Sigma$. We need not think of ϕ and x here as 'variables' particularly: the same function could be performed by subscripts added to the quantifiers. Π_1 could be used to express what is now expressed by binding an individual variable with the universal quantifier, Π_2 and Π_3

similarly for predicative and propositional variables, respectively. Thus our two readings of $\Pi\Sigma$ would come out as $\Pi_1\Sigma_2$ and $\Pi_2\Sigma_1$. Clearly the work done by the subscripts here is quite different from the work done by the vincula in the alternatives to $\Sigma x \Pi y \phi xy$, etc. set out on page 158 above. This should enable us to appreciate the difference between the work done by variables in so far as they are repeated once or more in the matrix after their first appearance attached to the quantifier (work done equally well, if less conveniently, by vincula) and the work they do simply in virtue of being attached to the quantifier (this last work being equivalent to that done by '-body', '-where', etc. when attached to pronouns like 'every' and 'some' to produce 'everybody', 'somewhere', etc.). It seems to be a mere convenience of symbolism that both sorts of work are done by what we call variables, though the fact that variables *can* do this is of the utmost importance.[12] But, in any case, variables, or some equivalent symbols, are needed to show what would count as substitution instances, whose denials would falsify $\Pi x \Sigma \phi$ and $\Pi \phi \Sigma x$ respectively. The first of these, $\Pi x \Sigma \phi$, in the language which dispenses altogether with variables, would have 'Σ Anthony' as a substitution instance; so that '$N\Sigma$ Anthony' ('Nothing is true of Anthony') would falsify it—a thing difficult to achieve. But an appropriate substitution instance for the second, $\Pi \phi \Sigma x$, would be 'Σ is a round square' ('Something is a round square'), which enables us to see how easily *it* could be falsified.

We do not understand a quantified proposition unless we understand what propositions would be substitution instances of it, irrespective of whether these propositions are true or false. Not that we need to be in a position to give a complete list of all the propositions which could count as substitution instances. Where the expression to be substituted for the quantified variable is a proper name, for instance, our understanding of the quantified proposition does not depend on our understanding all the names that could occur in substitution instances of it. Each one of us is only ever acquainted with a small proportion of the names that there are for objects. But unless we know some name whose substitution for the variable in the quantified proposition would yield a substitution

---

[12] See above, Ch. III, § 3, and below, Ch. XI, § 2.

instance of it, true or false, it is hard to see how we could understand the proposition. And to understand the use of a name is to know who its bearer is. So in the case of propositions in which individual variables are bound by quantifiers we must be able to pick out some objects whose names could be substituted meaningfully[13] for the variables, if we are to understand the proposition.[14] In this rather weak sense we might concede Quine's claim that words like 'something' and 'everything', when they correspond to quantifiers binding individual variables, 'refer to entities generally, with a kind of studied ambiguity peculiar to themselves'. But it is *only* individual variables which are connected in this way to proper names and to entities (= the things which proper names name). Predicative variables and propositional variables, whose substitution instances are not proper names but predicables and propositions, have nothing to do with 'reference' to 'entities'. If there were no such variables, variables of a category distinct from the category of individuals, and we used vincula to perform the task of cross-reference, we should not need variables at all; for we should not require to distinguish propositions like $\Pi x \Sigma \phi$ (= $\Pi x \Sigma \phi \phi x$) from propositions like $\Pi \phi \Sigma x$ (= $\Pi \phi \Sigma x \phi x$). It is all the more strange that Quine should regard it as the peculiar property of bound variables, as such, to 'bear the burden of reference'.

3. 'Quantifying over' and 'ontological commitment'

Where we have talked of 'substitution instances' of variables, some philosophers[15] have talked of 'values'. Quine does not use 'value' in this way. If I say 'For some x, x is bald' the singular proposition 'Charles is bald' may be a substitution instance of this quantified proposition, and the name 'Charles' a substitution instance of the variable bound by the quantifier; but

[13] See above, Ch. IV, § 4.

[14] Dr John Mayberry has pointed out to me that a proposition of the form $\Pi x \phi x$ is intelligible even if the domain of discourse of the quantifier is that whose only members are formally indefinable real numbers. But a proposition in which the quantifier is given restricted interpretation in this way is, I think, intelligible only because it is equivalent to one of the form $\Pi x C \psi x \phi x$ in which the quantifier is given relatively unrestricted interpretation—one, for instance, in which the domain of discourse is the class of numbers in general and where ψx represents 'x is a formally indefinable real'. For such a proposition my claim holds good.

[15] See the view attributed to Gilbert Ryle by Quine in *The Ways of Paradox*, 1966, p. 180.

it is the man, Charles, not the name, 'Charles', whom Quine would call a value of this variable. Again, we may speak of the class of proper names, a class of expressions, as the class of possible substitution instances for the variable. But the range of values of the variable is not, in Quine's terminology, a class of expressions, but the class of objects. It is these which the quantifier is said to 'quantify over'. It is a solecism to speak of a quantifier 'quantifying over', not the values of variables, but the variables themselves; and when it is a variable of a category other than individual which the quantifier binds, there is nothing for it to quantify *over*. Variables have values over which we can quantify only when the possible substitution instances for those variables are names. To speak of 'quantifying over' properties, or Propositions, or times, is to imply that substitution instances of predicative or propositional or time-variables, such as '— barked' or 'Mice eat cheese' or 'on Thursday' are expressions which name things, or 'refer' to 'entities'. And that is not the sort of question which ought to be begged. We must accordingly view with suspicion the assumption that wherever a quantifier is used there is something that is being 'quantified over', or the practice of talking, whenever variables occur, of the 'values' of those variables.

Still more suspect is Quine's particular jargon, 'committing ourselves to an ontology'. Granted, when Quine first introduces this phrase on p. 8 of *From a Logical Point of View*, he is primarily concerned to deny that in saying, e.g., that the author of *Waverley* 'is *not*' we commit ourselves to an ontology containing the author of *Waverley*. Definite descriptions, which seemed to bear a burden of reference, need not be regarded as doing any such thing. Soon, however, Quine is using the language of ontological commitment to frighten us off other quite harmless ways of speaking. 'We can very easily involve ourselves in ontological commitment by saying, for example, that *there is something* (bound variable) which red houses and sunsets have in common.' (p. 12.) It is not the fact that red houses and sunsets are here said to *have* something in common, suggesting as it does the instantiation 'Houses *have* redness and sunsets *have* redness', which Quine finds dangerous: he was equally nervous of the formulation which Geach later suggested: 'If A and B are both red, then there is something that they both are'.[16] We do not commit ourselves, in Quine's view, to an ontology containing attributes, such as redness, by saying simply that houses are red and sunsets are red; but when we existentially generalize, by inferring that there is something which houses and sunsets are, we immediately fall headlong into Platonism: 'One may admit that there are red houses, roses, and sunsets, but deny, except as a popular and misleading manner of speaking, that they have anything in common.' (p. 10.) (One might wonder what it is that those who speak popularly or misleadingly want to assert, or how they could manage to say it in a more scientific and less misleading way.)

Quine thus makes a difference between two relations: on the one hand, the relation between (A) 'There is someone who alone wrote *Waverley*' and (B) 'Scott alone wrote *Waverley*', and, on the other hand, the relation between (C) 'There is something which houses and roses and sunsets are' and (D) 'Houses and roses and sunsets are red'. (A) commits us to an ontology containing values of what Quine calls a 'bound variable', namely, 'someone'. Scott (not 'Scott') would be a value of this type. (A) therefore does not commit us to any type of thing which we are not already committed to by (B).[17] (C), on the other hand, commits us to an ontology containing values of another 'bound variable', namely 'something'. Such values, on Quine's view, would be redness, whiteness, purpleness, etc. And no value of this type is even apparently mentioned in (D). (D) commits us to houses and roses and sunsets, but not to redness and the like. It seems, therefore, that the relation of (A) to (B) is quite different, on Quine's view, from the relation of (C) to (D). (A) is entailed by (B). But since he says that 'one may admit' (D), but 'deny, except as a popular and misleading manner of speaking, (C), we cannot similarly suppose that in Quine's view (C) is entailed by (D). Contrary to what we might have expected, (C) is *not* the existential generalization of (D), otherwise it *would* be entailed by it.

Quine's doctrine of ontological commitment is this: where

[16] 'On What There Is', p. 132.
[17] Quine, of course, would not regard (B) as committing us to *Scott*. (B) would be replaced by (B') 'Something Scottizes and alone wrote *Waverley*'. But the values of the variable which occurs in (B') would be *of the same type* as the values of the variable which occurs in (A).

there is quantification (any use of expressions like 'everything', 'nothing', 'something') there are bound variables; where there are bound variables there are values of those variables; values of variables are not expressions but things, objects, entities; to be an entity is to be; to be, therefore, is to be the value of a variable. So we commit ourselves ontologically by making things the values of our variables.

When philosophers use the word 'entity' we should immediately be on our guard. If an oddity is a thing which is odd, an entity is a thing which is. So much is guaranteed by the etymology of 'entity'. But, whereas '— is odd' is a first-level predicable which can serve to delimit a class of objects, the class, namely, of those objects of which '— is odd' can truly be predicated, '— is' is not a first-level predicable, and thus is incapable of delimiting any class of objects at all. 'Being is not a genus.'[18] Quine, however, goes further than merely making a carefree use of the dangerous term 'entity'. 'To be,' he says, 'is to be the value of a variable.' Now the sort of thing which is a value of the variable contained in our proposition (A) is the sort of thing which can be a writer: Scott, for example, or Keats. Such things are, in Frege's terminology, objects. Expressions which can be used to predicate something of objects —expressions, that is, which can be attached to the proper names of such objects to form propositions—are first-level predicables. The expression '— is the value of a variable', since it can truly be predicated of Scott, is therefore a predicable of this level. If '— is the value of a variable' is a first-level predicable so, on Quine's view must '— is' be, since 'to be is to be the value of a variable'. 'On What There Is' is thus a most peculiar philosophical document. It starts out in an attempt to disentangle Plato's Beard, to free us from our apparent commitment to the round square cupola on Berkeley College and to Pegasus, following in Russell's footsteps by recognizing 'there is' and 'there are', 'something' and Σx—x, as second-level predicables. But it finishes by re-establishing a notion of existence as a first-level predicable, as something which we might find ourselves, by a careless use of the existential quantifier, attributing to such prima-facie undesirables as attributes, classes, Propositions, or numbers.

[18] Aristotle, *Posterior Analytics*, 92^{b}14.

4. 'Nouns might better have been named propronouns'

Quine denied hotly that he ever described bound variables as names, or quasi-names, or anything namelike.[19] But what he undoubtedly did again and again was to describe bound variables as 'referring'. 'To be is to be in the range of reference of a pronoun. Pronouns are the basic media of reference.' (p. 13.) The pronouns he has in mind are those which he also calls bound variables: 'everything', 'nothing', 'something'. 'A theory is committed to those and only those entities to which the bound variables of the theory must be capable of referring.' (pp. 13 f.) 'Intuitionism . . . countenances the use of bound variables to refer to abstract entities . . . .' (p. 14.) What *is* reference? In any other context than that of Quine's philosophy of language one would think of explicating the *referring* relation in terms of the relation between a proper name and its bearer. Frege, notoriously, thought that expressions of logical categories other than names, predicables, for example, and sentences, referred to something, had references. But the explication of this idea leaves Frege's philosophy of language in fragments unless the referring relation of name to its bearer is taken as paradigmatic for the wider notion of reference.[20] Quine, however, regards proper names, not only in the wider sense understood by Frege but in the narrower sense understood by Russell, as eliminable from our language. They are not to be regarded as amongst the elementary tools which we need in order to say what we have to say. In particular, he does not regard proper names as the basic medium of reference. It is 'the bound variables of quantification' which are fundamental in this regard. 'Nouns might better have been named propronouns.' (p. 13.)

What sense can be made of this notion of reference which is supposedly independent of the name-bearer relation? What are the things which 'bound variables' refer to 'with a kind of studied ambiguity peculiar to themselves?' The answer, I think is 'their values'. The notion of *value* is absolutely crucial here.

'Variable' and 'value' were of course originally technical terms of mathematics. The variable x in the function $2x^2 + 3x - 7$ was something whose different values yielded different

---

[19] Cf. *Proc. Arist. Soc.*, Supp. Vol. 25, p. 150. The quotations are from *From a Logical Point of View*.

[20] Cf. Michael Dummett, *Frege: Philosophy of Language*, Ch. 7.

values for the function. Thus we might talk of determining what the value of the function $2x^2 + 3x - 7$ is if the value of x is 5. No doubt it is the number 5 not the numeral '5', which is properly said to be the value of x in this problem. But we can hardly divorce the notion of 5's being a value of x here from the practice of obtaining the value of the function for this value of the argument by substituting a numeral for the variable letter 'x' in the expression of the function, and calculating the result. Similarly, when Frege extended the notion of function to include concepts, and spoke of a truth-value as being the value of such a function for a given value of its argument, his meaning can only be grasped in so far as we understand the possibility of substituting a proper name for the variable included in the predicative expression which stands for the function and thus obtaining a complete sentence. We cannot understand the role of x as variable in the functional expression 'x went to the cinema' without being able to recognize 'Stephen went to the cinema' as a possible substitution instance of it. Stephen is a value of the variable because 'Stephen' is a possible substitution for the variable letter in the predicate. Values were first introduced as what are nameable by possible substitutions for variables of this kind. The idea of what constitutes a legitimate substitution explains the idea of value of the variable, not vice versa.

Frege thought that the possible substitutes for variables of every category would be expressions having reference. Thus substituting 'Today is Friday' for p and '$6 \times 6 = 36$' for q in 'If p then q' would yield a complex name formed by a truth-functional expression from two other names. The values of p and q and the value of 'If p then q', for given values of p and q, would all alike be truth-values. Similarly, if, in $\Pi x \phi x$, Πx—x stands for a second-level concept which yields different truth-values for different values of the variable ϕ, these values can themselves be regarded as first-level concepts which predicative expressions like 'went to the cinema' stand for. Quine, however, would not agree that an expression like 'went to the cinema' has to stand for anything. He would not be entitled to call the concept for which 'went to the cinema' stands a value of the variable ϕ in $\Pi x \phi x$, and, indeed, he would call ϕ, not a variable, but a schematic letter. But he can hardly avoid recognizing 'went to the cinema' as a legitimate substitution instance for the schematic letter ϕ in $\Pi x \phi x$, or 'Today is Friday' and '$6 \times 6 = 36$' as legitimate substitutions for p and q in 'If p then q'. The notion of having a *substitution instance* must therefore be wider than that of having a *value*, in the way Quine understands 'value'. So for Quine 'substitution instance' and 'schematic letter' have to be understood in cases like p and ϕ, independently of 'value' and 'variable'; and if either pair is to be explanatory of the other, it is the former which must be explanatory of the latter.

If the notion that Stephen is a value of x in the functional expression 'x went to the cinema' is to be explained in terms of meaningful substitutions for x in this open sentence, it is, after all, to be explained in terms of the notion of proper name. It is as a proper name that 'Stephen' is a meaningful substitution for x in 'x went to the cinema'. To know what count as meaningful substitutions for 'x' here just is to know which expressions are proper names. Quine, of course, explicitly denies this.[21] He believes that we can only understand the notion of 'singular term' or 'proper name' by appealing implicitly to 'classical or objectual quantification'.[22] We know that 'Stephen' in 'Stephen went to the cinema' is a singular term because it can occupy the position occupied by 'For some x, x' in 'For some x, x went to the cinema'. Singular terms, in Quine's view, are substitutes for the variables of referential quantification —poor substitutes, no doubt, but having their referential function only because they are thus substitutable. They refer to objects because they can be taken to name values of quantified variables, and because these are what primarily and ultimately *exist*. Thus names (nouns) are explained in terms of quantified variables (pronouns) and these again in terms of existence. I shall be arguing later[23] that this order of explanation is back to front. Quine's thesis that nouns are propronouns is what is appears to be: a clear case of *hysteron proteron*, the cart before the horse.

[21] *Ontological Relativity*, p. 106, where he refers back to p. 95.
[22] For an explanation of this terminology, see Ch. VIII below.
[23] In the next chapter, and Ch. VIII, § 9.

5. *Quine's inadequate view of proper names explains his confusion of reference with quantification*

The difference between Quine's view of this matter and the view of, for example, Russell comes out well from Quine's most recent exposition of his doctrine.[24] Here he is speculating about the mechanisms by which a child learns certain elementary linguistic devices. His account of the genesis of singular predications is strange. He gives different accounts of what he calls 'occasion sentences' and 'standing sentences'. Assent to occasion sentences is prompted by what is currently observable. Thus 'Mama is smiling' is assented to when Mama is present and is smiling. Quine assimilates this to a compound term 'yellow paper', which is assented to when the responses 'yellow' and 'paper' are both prompted by some salient element of the observational field. Such sentences are available for those who have already learned 'Mama' and 'smiling', or 'yellow' and 'paper', as observation terms. The further technique that is needed to achieve mastery of the compound idiom is called by Quine 'attributive composition', and this, he says, is one of many dyadic constructions on terms. Just as 'Mama is smiling' is a dyadic construction on 'Mama' and 'smiling', so 'Mama is in the garden' is a dyadic construction on 'Mama' and 'the garden'.

> The learning of $\ulcorner \alpha$ in $\beta \urcorner$ is thus just like the learning of attributive composition, $\ulcorner \alpha\beta \urcorner$, except that there it was a matter merely of a partial coincidence or overlapping of the two relevant masses, while now it is a matter more specifically of the embedding of the first in the second.[25]

What could be further removed from the standard view of the proposition 'Mama is smiling' as being of the form ϕx and 'Mama is in the garden' as being of the form ψxy? The difference emerges, as usual, under negation. Quine's child, presumably, will dissent from 'Mama is smiling' if either no Mama is present or nothing smiling is present or if two 'revelant masses' that are parts respectively of the Mama-mass and the smiling-mass are present but do not overlap. Again 'Mama is in the garden' will not win assent if either Mama or the garden is absent or if, though present, the one is not embedded in the other. But for Russell, if 'Mama' is a proper name, as it

---

[24] Quine, *The Roots of Reference*, 1973. My comments are on § 16 and § 17.
[25] Ibid., pp. 61 f.

QUINE'S INADEQUATE VIEW OF PROPER NAMES 169

must be if either of these propositions is to be a singular predication, 'Mama is smiling' wins dissent only if Mama is unsmiling, and 'Mama is in the garden' only if the garden does not contain Mama. As Prior rightly saw, it is a criterion for an expression N being a Russellian proper name that there be no difference between $(\delta\phi)N$ and $\delta(\phi N)$. Negation is the simplest operation capable of exemplifying δ here, and dissent from p is identifiable with assent to 'not-p'.[26]

Quine's account of the learning process by which the child acquires command of those singular predications which are 'standing sentences' is quite different. His example is 'Fido is a dog'. The mechanism is this: the child has learned to assent to 'A dog?' in the presence of dogs. An association has been set up in his mind between the word 'Fido' and a mental image of Fido. When he hears the word 'Fido' in the sentence 'Fido is a dog' presented for his assent, the mental image of the dog Fido pops up and prompts assent to the whole sentence. Quine gives exactly similar accounts of the learning of 'Snow is white' and 'A dog is an animal', which are not singular predications. The latter, indeed, is regarded by Quine as an instance of the universal categorical form 'Every α is β ', and this account has to serve for an explanation of our mastery of this linguistic device, eventually to be chosen as one of the parents of the all-important construction, objectual quantification.[27] This device, though not itself referential, is one of 'the roots of reference'.

But what, we may once again ask, is to count as the negation of these propositions? Presented with the mental image of Fido we can only, one supposes, assent to or dissent from 'dog'. But presented with a mental image corresponding to α in some sentence of the form 'Every α is β' we may assent to β or to 'not-β', but yet again we may incline to the response 'Some are, some aren't'. This is good enough for dissent from the proposition of the form 'Every α is β'. Just this was our reason for refusing to say that in 'No man is just' it is ' — is just' which is predicated of what 'No man' stands for;[28] and what goes for 'No man is just' goes for 'A dog is an animal' and 'A triangle

---

[26] For Prior's criterion, see above Ch. III, § 2.
[27] Cf. Quine, *The Roots of Reference*, p. 101.
[28] See above, Ch. III, § 2.

is equilateral'. Quine's imagist account of the mastery of singular propositions like 'Fido is a dog', though far-fetched, does nothing to violate the criteria we have adopted for 'Fido''s being a proper name. But his assimilation of this singular proposition to 'Snow is white' and 'A dog is an animal' shows that he does not mean what we mean by 'singular proposition', that is, proposition containing a proper name.

Quine's story about the birth of the referential apparatus of theoretical language places the acquisition of the techniques just described before even its conception. Reference is 'out of' the relative clause 'by' the categorical 'Every α is β'. So long as we are with 'Mama is in the garden' and 'Fido is a dog', sire and dam have not yet become acquainted. So Quine concludes that the mere mastery of proper names like 'Mama' and 'Fido' has nothing to do with reference. Reference, on the other hand, has everything to do with quantification. But when we see what Quine understands by the mastery of singular predications, we feel no surprise. Russell, Geach, and Prior, on the one hand, and Quine, on the other, are not talking about the same thing when they talk about the use of a word as a proper name. The alternative to regarding names as propronouns, for Quine, is to regard them as one-word observations sentences. The criteria Geach and Prior have set out for distinguishing and identifying names and predicables should have saved Quine from dragging in quantification to give reference a firm basis. We have no need of his hypotheses.

Sadly, when quantification is dragged in to explain reference, it is disabled from serving the wider ends for which it was designed. Ontological commitment, for Quine, is achieved by the use of the bound variables of quantification. What we commit ourselves to, what alone we need make reference to, are the values of our variables. But this represents an arbitrary and unjustified limitation on the sense of 'value' and 'variable'. Our variables only have values, in Quine's sense, if the appropriate substitution instances for them are proper names. In so far as the notions of variable and substitution instance extend farther than the category of proper names, there is in fact no connection between bound variables as such and what Quine means by 'values', or between bound variables and reference. So far from quantification being of its nature referential, it can only be understood as referential at all when the variables quantified occupy the position of proper names. Quantification is essentially neutral with regard to ontology.

To speak in this way is to assume some connection between reference and ontology, even if the Quinian connection between reference and quantification is rejected. Quine, as we shall see, is willing to admit a variety of quantification which is not referential, which does not, in his terminology, carry ontological commitment. But Quine nowhere envisages a separation between reference and ontology. To do so would require the abandonment of some of the deepest presuppositions of his philosophy. It is my view, however, that these should be abandoned. And to explain why, it is necessary to look more closely and critically at what, if anything, is meant by 'ontology' and 'ontological'. This iconoclastic aim is my aim in the next chapter.

VII
Ontology called in Question

1. *'Ontological' has different senses corresponding to the different senses of 'be'*

The topic of these pages is existence, or being: and so the discussion they contain might be thought to belong to ontology. So much seems to be secured by etymological considerations. But what is ontology, or what is meant by the word 'ontological'? Independently of the concepts of being and existence, the concept of ontology is unintelligible. We are more likely to discover what people have meant by 'ontological' by inquiring into the meaning of 'is' or 'exist' than vice versa. And yet a recent author has sought to illuminate the concept of existence by talking of an 'ontologic' sense of 'exist'.[1] That is a clearer case than Quine's of putting the cart before the horse. Indeed, it is my view that the words 'ontology' and 'ontological' are almost always the sign of confused thinking, that they serve only to introduce muddle into the practice of philosophy. There is nothing surprising in this. Philosophy is bedevilled with technical jargon whose use embodies confusion—as often as not, several different sorts of confusion. Such words have no clear sense, but they are liable to have several unclear senses. The only way to dissipate the obscurity they bring with them is to attempt an explanation rather than a clarification of the way or ways in which they are used. What follows is intended simultaneously to account for the senses that 'ontology' and 'ontological' have and to give reasons for thinking that these words are best avoided. Philosophy would benefit from a campaign to extirpate them from its vocabulary.

[1] Milton K. Munitz, *Existence and Logic*, p. 91.

Etymologically the word 'ontology' has connections with the Greek equivalent of the verb 'be', not with any exact synonym of the English word 'exist'. As we saw in Chapter I, some uses of the Greek *'einai'* are indeed translatable by 'exist' in English, but some are not. In particular the Greek *'einai'*, like the English 'be', can be used as copula. Is it possible that the word 'ontological' derives part of its meaning from the copulative sense of *'einai'* rather than the existential? Is it possible, in fact, that 'ontological' has different senses, just as *'einai'* and its English equivalent, 'be', have different senses?

2. *The vacuity theory of* actualité

This possibility is, I think, realized. Let us look first at the sense of 'ontological' which corresponds to the copulative sense of 'be'. It is not immediately apparent that there is such a correspondence. Before arguing that there is, I shall try to isolate the sense of 'ontological' that is in question. Philosophers tend to contrast ontological claims with epistemological claims on the one hand, and with evaluative claims on the other. Epistemological questions are questions about what we can *know* to be the case, ontological ones are about what *is* the case. Similarly, a question of value concerns what *ought* to be the case, a question of ontology concerns what *is* the case. 'Ontological' stands to 'epistemological' and 'evaluative' rather as 'actual' stands to 'necessary' and 'possible'. 'It is known that p', 'It ought to be the case that p', 'It is necessary that p', and 'It is possible that p' all contrast with 'It is the case that p'. But 'It is the case that p' is simply a blown-up version of p. When we contrast 'It is known that —' or 'It is necessary that —' with 'It is the case that —' what we are really doing is contrasting complex propositions which are yielded by operators forming propositions out of propositions with simple propositions involving no such operators.

The point is one which Arthur Prior never tired of making with respect to the present tense.[2] 'The building up of complexes like Findlay's "(*x* past) future" requires that tensing be an operation of which the subjects are themselves tensed sentences, and when we have got inside all other tensing to the

[2] Prior, *Past, Present and Future*, pp. 14 f.

"kernel" of the complex, *its* tense will have to be the present.'[3] Prior regards Findlay's '(x past) future' as exemplified by something like 'It will be the case that it was the case that he is sick', which merely spells out what ordinary language represents by the future perfect: 'He will have been sick'. For grammar 'He is sick' is just as much tensed as 'He was sick'; but for tense logic 'He is sick' is a simple proposition, unaffected by any tense operator, whereas 'He was sick' is equivalent to the result of subjecting the simple 'He is sick' to the past tense operator 'It was the case that —'. Prior makes his point about the present tense by adapting Findlay's formulae to enunciate the general law 'x present = x'; and in his own symbolism he uses the complex Pp and Fp to represent propositions like 'He was sick' and 'He will be sick', but has nothing further than the simple p to represent 'He is sick'. Just so, modal logicians represent 'Necessarily p' by Lp, 'Possibly p' by Mp, but 'Actually p' by simple p. The meaning of the French word *'actuel'* spans both 'present' and 'actual'. Prior could have used this to illustrate the point he makes about the so-called 'no-truth' theory of Ramsey and Ayer (that 'It is true that p' = 'It is the case that p' = p) and his own 'no-present' theory of tense. He writes:

Nor do these two 'vacuity' or 'omnipresence' theories—the one about 'truly' and the one about the present—constitute a mere parallelism. They are in a sense the same theory—in the sense that they merely assert the vacuity of one and the same phrase, 'It is the case that —' or 'It is true that —', considered against different non-vacuous contrasting phrases. It is, on the one hand, the vacuous member of the pair of which the non-vacuous member is 'It is not the case that —' or 'It is false that —'. But it is also the vacuous member of a set of which other members are 'It has been the case that —' (or 'It has been true that —') and 'It will be the case that —' (or 'It will be true that —').[4]

Prior might have added that it is the vacuous member of the pairs of which 'It is known that —' and 'It ought to be the case that —' are the non-vacuous members, and that 'Actually p' is the vacuous member of the set of which 'Possibly p' and 'Necessarily p' are non-vacuous members. Given the twofold sense of the French word *'actuel'*, the theory might, in its generalized form, be called the vacuity theory of *actualité*.

[3] Ibid., p. 15; and see above, Ch. I, p. 8.
[4] Prior, *Papers on Time and Tense*, 1968, pp. 21 f.

3. Actual and possible worlds, fact and value, ontology and epistemology

This point is missed by those who regard 'ontological' questions, questions about what is the case, as just a different species of a genus of which epistemological questions and questions of value are further species. The point is missed equally by those who talk about what is the case in 'the actual world' as co-ordinate with what is the case in 'other possible worlds'. What is the case in the actual world is just what is the case. But some philosophers have wanted to make a distinction between, for instance, the property of *knowing Chinese* and the property of *knowing Chinese in the actual world*.[5] This distinction, however, makes sense only if one forgets how such locutions as 'in another possible world' were originally understood. If I say 'There is a possible world in which Smith might have known Chinese' I mean 'If things had been otherwise (if, for example, Smith had been brought up in Shanghai), Smith might have known Chinese'. If, on the other hand, I say 'In the actual world Smith does not know Chinese', I mean 'Things being as they are, Smith does not know Chinese'. 'Things being as they are' contrasts with 'If things had been otherwise', but, like 'It is the case that —' as described by Prior, it is the vacuous member of this pair of contrasting phrases. Similarly, when I say 'In another possible world Smith might have known Chinese but in the actual world he does not know Chinese', all that 'in the actual world' does is to emphasize the lack of any condition on what is asserted in the second conjunct of the proposition: 'in the actual world' emphasizes the categorical character of the proposition which follows by contrast with the hypothetical character of the proposition expressed by 'In another world Smith might have known Chinese'. Categorical propositions are opposed to hypothetical as present tense propositions are to past and future, and as assertoric propositions are to problematic or apodeictic propositions:[6] they are the simple case of which the others are modifications. It is wrong

---

[5] Cf. Plantinga, *The Nature of Necessity*, Ch. IV, § 11.

[6] It is interesting to note that what corresponds in Kant's Table of Categories to 'Assertoric' in his Table of Judgements (*Critique of Pure Reason*, A70, 80, B95, 106) is 'Existence'. The same ambiguity is at work as that which we are tracing in 'ontological'. See below, Ch. XI, § 1.

to think of them, together with hypothetical or past tense or apodeictic propositions, as co-ordinate species of a common genus. Nor is 'the actual world' just one world amongst others. How things are in the actual world is just how things are, in the same way as what is the case now is just what is the case. The idea that *knowing Chinese in the actual world* is a different property from *knowing Chinese* is a confusion. To say that in the actual world Smith does not know Chinese is simply a way of contrasting the plain fact of Smith's ignorance with the possibility of his knowledge. But plain facts are not another modality to be listed alongside necessities and possibilities. They are what the unmodified sentences state whose various modifications tell us what can or what must be the case.

Just so 'ontological' does not specify an interest or enquiry of a special kind, to be contrasted perhaps with 'epistemological' or 'axiological' interests and enquiries. It would only signify, if it had a worthwhile use at all, the absence of any special interest or manner of enquiry. Ontology is the zero case of a particular science.

If, failing to recognize this, we treat 'ontological' as a *differentia specifica*, we are liable to create an illusion of distinctions where none are to be had, or at least none to be got in this way. Just as the past is the past present (if it was the case that p, it was the case that it is the case that p) so the past is the present past (if it was the case that p, it is the case that it was the case that p). Similarly, what is known is known to be the case, and its being known to be the case is itself the case. What epistemological research uncovers is automatically a result for ontological enquiry. What there is to know is part of what there is. More controversially we may hold that, if it ought to be the case that p, it is the case that it ought to be the case that p. Our judgements about how things ought to be cannot be simply contrasted with our judgements about how things are, because they are included in our judgements about how things are. We cannot judge anything without judging it to be the case. So if we wish to give sense to a distinction between factual questions and evaluative questions we must interpret 'factual' as meaning something like 'empirical'. To understand 'factual question' as 'question about what is the case' is to make all questions factual. So much is quarenteed by the redundancy of 'It is the case that —'. Evaluative theory may or may not be distinguishable from empirical theory, but it is not distinguishable from ontology, conceived as the theory of what is the case. Or, if someone wishes to identify empirical theory with 'ontological' theory, *what is the case* with *what can in principle be established empirically as being the case*, he must argue for it. He cannot assume that 'the empirical'—something positively characterized—is identical with the vacuous member of the 'what ought to be the case/what is the case' contrast—something only negatively characterized.

The use of 'ontology' to contrast with 'epistemology' encourages people to think that investigating what is, or can be, known to be the case is an alternative to investigating what is the case; and using it to contrast with 'value theory' encourages them to assume, without argument, that what ought to be the case is not part of what is the case. In so far as we are led by it to think that we have established distinctions when we have done no such thing, the word 'ontology' in this use is not merely unhelpful, but damaging.

4. *The connection between this use of 'ontological' and the copula*

Why does the word 'ontological' have this use? The reason lies, I think, in the emphatic use we make of the verb *to be* when we contrast, for example, the way things are *known* to be, or *ought* to be, or *would* be in other circumstances (possible worlds), with the way they *are*. The Greeks used their synonym of the verb *to be* in this way even more extensively than we do. Speaking the truth was described by them as 'saying what is', speaking falsely as 'saying what is not'. This use of the verb 'be' and its synonyms is, I believe, a special case of its use as copula. It derives from contexts like 'The Earth was not known to be round, but it *was*', 'Jones ought to be relieved and grateful, but he *isn't*'. Instead of repeating the copula with its complement, which were together subordinate to 'known' or 'ought', we, as did the Greeks before us, merely repeat the copula. The verb 'is', or *'esti'*, and its modifications thus become dummy verbs, which enable us to refer back to a verbal expression previously used without actually repeating it. Just so pronouns enable us to refer back to previously used nouns without actually repeating them. In 'Jones ought to be grateful, but he isn't' the word 'he' is a pronoun of laziness[7] and 'isn't' —or the 'is' which is part of it—is a 'pro-verb of laziness'. What we are intending to do is to deny, in an unmodified, simple form just what was asserted in a complex form, modified by the deontic operator 'It ought to be the case that —', in 'Jones ought to be grateful'. Instead of saying 'It ought to be the case that Jones is grateful but it is not the case that Jones is grateful', we save our breath and spare our audience by using the pronoun 'he' and the pro-verb 'is'. And we emphasize the 'is' to show that it is not modified by 'ought to' or 'is known to' or the like. Since *'onto-'* is the participial stem of the Greek synonym of the verb 'be', we call questions about what *is* the case, as opposed to what *ought* to be or is *known* to be the case, 'ontological' questions. This is the justification for saying that there is a sense of 'ontological' which corresponds to the copulative sense of the verb 'be'. We can understand how the word 'ontological' came to be used in this way, but we can still deplore the fact that it is so used, and believe that more people are misled than are enlightened by its being used in this way.

5. *Ontology and what there is*

The other main use of the word 'ontological', which is equally to be deplored, derives from the use of the synonym of 'be' not as copula, but as equivalent to 'exist'. To use a famous phrase of Quine's, an ontological treatise is a treatise 'on what there is'. Quine is explicit about the connection between existence and ontology in the following passage:

The question of deviance in the logic of quantification is relevant to ontology—to the question what there is. What there are, according to a given theory in standard form, are all and only the objects that the variables of quantification are meant in that theory to take as values. This is scarcely contestable, since (x) and $(\exists x)$ are explained by the words 'each object x is such that' and 'there is an object x such that'. Some languages may have no clear equivalent of our existential phrase 'there is', nor of our quantifiers; but surely there is no putting the two asunder.

Consequently some philosophical interest, ontological interest, attaches to deviations in quantification theory. They can affect what is to count as there being. The intuitionist's deviant quantification (if 'quantification' is still a good word for it) carries with it a deviant notion of

[7] Cf. Geach, *Reference and Generality*, § 76. Cf. below, Ch. XI, § 7.

existence (if 'existence' is still a good word for it). When he says he recognizes there to be just such and such objects, we may not even agree that he recognizes there to be just those (much less that he would be right in so doing). It is only relative to some translation of his language into ours (not necessarily into our logic, but into our inclusive language) that *we* can venture to say what he recognizes there to be (in *our* sense of 'there to be').[8]

Quine's use of 'there are', 'there being', and 'there to be' in this passage is confusing. The question what there is, is a non-philosophical context, will only occur restricted by some, usually locative, qualification. For instance, I may ask 'What is there in the parcel?' and the answer may be 'Books'. This fits in with Frege's doctrine that questions about existence, like questions about number, are questions about whether a given property should be assigned, not to an object, but to a concept. A common noun in the plural, like 'Books', is, according to Frege,[9] a suitable way of referring to a concept. If we say 'There are books in the parcel' we assign a property to the concept *book in the parcel*. But in the passage under consideration Quine envisages, as an answer to the locatively unqualified question 'What is there according to a given theory?', the elliptical answer 'All and only the objects that the variables of quantification are meant in that theory to take as values'. Let us suppose that the objects that the variables of quantification are meant in theory T to take as values are ϕ-objects. The answer to the question 'What is there, according to T?' will then be 'All and only ϕ-objects'. But this phrase, unlike the word 'Books', is not a suitable expression for signifying a concept. The answer to the question, if the ellipsis is filled in, will now be 'There are, according to T, all and only ϕ-objects'.

Now it is odd in English to take the verb of a sentence whose subject term is qualified by 'all and only' and advance it to the front of a sentence and prefix 'There' to it. 'All and only Australian citizens vote in Australian General Elections' cannot comfortably be transformed into 'There vote in Australian General Elections all and only Australian citizens'. But even if 'There are all and only ϕ-objects' were accepted as an idiomatic form, it would mean the same as 'All and only ϕ-objects

---

[8] Quine, *Philosophy of Logic*, 1970, p. 89.
[9] Frege, *The Foundations of Arithmetic*, tr. J. L. Austin, § 51. See above, Ch. III, § 8.

are'. Any proposition containing the phrase 'all and only' will have the sense that whatever fits the description following the phrase fits some other description, and vice versa. So 'All and only ϕ-objects *are*' must mean that whatever fits the description 'ϕ-object' is describable as *being*, and vice versa. But 'being' here must refer not to a property of concepts, but to a property of objects, as 'ϕ-object' does. The only way to construe what Quine says here is to take 'are' in the phrase 'What there are' as a first-level predicable, disregarding the prefixed 'there' as camouflage. 'What there are are all and only ϕ-objects' must have the same form as 'What breathe are all and only animals'. To borrow from Austin, it is the old business of treating existing as rather like breathing, only quieter.

Quine's following sentences confirm this. Deviations in quantification theory, he says, 'can affect what to count as there being'. What would be an example of this? Presumably something which Quine would regard as a deviant quantification theory,[10] namely, 'Substitutionalism', would on his view quantify predicate variables without counting properties as objects. What Quine has in mind then is a theory which 'affects what to count as there being' by *not counting properties as there being*. But this is a very curious phrase. The expression 'count properties as . . .' requires for its completion a predicative expression in participial or adjectival or nominal form. We could count properties as belonging to something, or as objects, or as real. Grammatically, there would be no objection to the phrase 'count properties as existing, or being'. But 'count properties as *there* being' is ill-formed. If the phrase 'count as there being' is to mean anything at all, it must mean the same as 'count as being'. But so to talk is, once again, to treat 'be' or 'exist' as a word which can be predicated of objects.

Twice in the second of the paragraphs quoted above Quine uses the phrase 'there to be just . . .'. But 'there to be just such and such objects' is simply the *oratio obliqua* form of 'there are just such and such objects', which is tantamount to 'there are all and only such and such objects'. So what we have said about 'There are all and only ϕ-objects' applies here too. Quine tells us that existence is what the existential quantifier expresses.

[10] For a discussion of what Quine calls 'substitutional quantification' and deals with in *Philosophy of Logic* under the heading 'Deviant Logics', see below, Ch. VIII.

To say, using the existential quantifier, 'For some x, x is an even prime number', is to say that there is an even prime number, or that the concept *even prime number* is instantiated. Perhaps the form 'There are just such and such objects' is to be interpreted as meaning 'Only the concept *such and such object* is instantiated—just it, and nothing else'. 'Such and such objects' is, of course, so schematic that we can make little or nothing of such a claim. But a similar interpretation might be given to the claim that according to a given theory there are 'all and only the objects that the variables of quantification are meant in (the theory in question) to take as values'. That is to say, if the theory is T and the objects in question ϕ-objects, only the concept *ϕ-object* is instantiated. In other words, the concept *ϕ-object*, and no other concept at all, is instantiated: there are just ϕ-objects. But this is absurd. If ϕ-objects include numbers, the concept *ϕ-object which is a number* will be instantiated, as will the concept *ϕ-object which is a prime number*. The suggestion that the only concept which is instantiated is that of *ϕ-object* could not possibly be what Quine means, since it is obviously false. But the other alternative, that he means that all and only ϕ-objects have the property of existing, will only make sense if '— are' or '— exist' is understood as predicable on the same level as '— growl'.

Quine's account of ontology thus presupposes that '— exist' or '— is' has a use as a first-level predicable. His view that existence is what the existential quantifier expresses is incompatible with this, but we must simply regard this as an inconsistency in his teaching. Much of this book is devoted to showing that '— exist' or '— is' cannot be a first-level predicate. If this view, the view that existence cannot be a property of objects, is correct, the way in which Quine and others explain the meaning of 'ontology' is incoherent. There cannot be a science whose object is to tell us what things, or what sorts of things, *are*. The search for what a theorist 'counts as there being' or 'what he really recognizes there to be' is a futile one. Or, if it has point, it can only be because there is some other way of describing it, some other way of specifying what it is that the ontologist is searching for.

6. *Ontology as the use of Ockham's Razor*

If we look at what ontologists, so called, actually do, we shall see, I think, that they are concerned with ultimate subjects of predication. They wish to know whether, in addition to the concrete objects, such as spades, butterflies, and angels, which there are in the universe, there are abstract objects such as eloquence, cousinship, hockey, utilitarianism, and Mozart's Coronation Mass. They wish to know whether 'Saxe blue is lighter than Navy blue' states a relation between colours (concrete or abstract objects?) which cannot be stated by any statement about relations between coloured objects. Does the sentence 'Ryle's eloquence surpassed Russell's eloquence' mean any more than the sentence 'Ryle was a better speaker than Russell'? Does 'Plato believed that all learning was recollection' assert a relation between Plato and something called 'The Doctrine of *Anamnesis*'? Are there such things as sets, and if so does every well-formed predicable determine one?

Let us take what I hope is an uncontroversial example of a type of entity which is clearly unnecessary. If we were desribing the order of people in some seating arrangement we might say 'There is a lady between Richard and Lawrence'. Here we assert a three-term relation as existing between Richard, Lawrence, and some unspecified lady. Again, we might say 'There is a difference of age between Richard and Lawrence', and prima facie we seem to be asserting another three-term relation as existing between Richard, Lawrence, and something called 'a difference of age'. But we are uneasy about this. Who wants his 'ontology' cluttered up with such dubious items as *differences of age*? This unease can be justified when we reflect that instead of saying 'There is a difference of age between Richard and Lawrence' we need only have said 'Richard is either older or younger than Lawrence'. Here it is only a two-term relation which is said to hold between Richard and Lawrence, and there is no question of a third term. The fact which we originally stated with the help of an expression standing for a three-term relation can perfectly well be stated with an expression which stands only for a two-term relation. Ockham's Razor is all set to remove the unwanted, because unnecessary, *difference of age*.

An ontological question which is more debatable is that which concerns the existence of attributes, properties, qualities, of the like. It was touched on in the previous chapter. The existential generalization 'There is something which houses and sunsets have in common' suggests an original which also makes use of the two-place predicable '— have ....', namely, 'Houses have redness and sunsets have redness'. The relation expressed by 'have' here is the converse of that expressed by 'inheres' in 'Redness inheres in houses and redness inheres in sunsets'. 'Have' thus expresses the same relation as that of *standing under*, which Hume found implicit in the notion of *substratum*, and by which he was so greatly puzzled.[11] The metaphysical realist insists that these relations, or this relation —because a relation and its converse go together[12]—have to be taken seriously. His opponent believes that 'Redness inheres in houses' and 'Houses have redness' say no more than 'Houses are red'. We have no need of singular abstract terms like 'redness' in order to say how things are coloured. The realist, who maintains that 'Houses have redness and sunsets have redness' states something that is missed out by, or is only implicit in, 'Houses are red and sunsets are red', is already committed to including redness in his 'ontology' before ever he proceeds to the existential generalization 'There is something which houses and sunsets have in common'. The anti-realist, who thinks that 'Houses are red and sunsets are red' adequately expresses the facts in question, does not acquire any new commitment by existentially generalizing to 'There is something which houses and sunsets both are'. He believes that what the realist states with the help of the two-place predicable '— have ....' can perfectly well be stated with the help only of the one-place predicable '— are red'. Ontological commitments are incurred by insisting on the use of n-place predicables and refusing to allow that the same things which are said with their help could be said just as well by using only $(n-1)$-place predicables. Ontological commitments are shed by realizing that what seemed to need an n-place predicable in order to be said can be said adequately with an $(n-1)$-place predicable.

[11] Hume, *A Treatise of Human Nature*, Book I, Part IV, § V.
[12] *Eadem est scientia oppositorum* again. See above, Ch. II, p. 40.

7. *Aristotle's* 'ousia': *substance and existence*

But what has this to do with ontology, with existence? The explanation of this is historical, and requires us to look at least as far back as Aristotle. The difference between an *n*-place predicable and an (*n*−1)-place predicable lies in the number of individual expressions which are required in order to turn the predicable into a complete sentence. Ontology is a matter of how many, or how many types of, individual expressions we need in our language. Do we need names for attributes like 'redness' as well as names for objects like 'house'? If we introduce new types of individual expressions we shall, of course, need to introduce correspondingly new predicative expressions: a language which includes nouns like 'redness' will also have to include verbs like 'inheres'. Both will seem superfluous to ontological minimalists like the anti-realist. But it is the fact that individual expressions are involved that explains why the issue is said to be an 'ontological' one. Aristotle introduced a category of 'substance' which was defined in terms of predication and inherence: substances were primarily those things of which other things were predicated, but which were neither predicated of other things nor 'in' other things.[13] (Since being in, or inhering in, something is, as the anti-realist believes, explicable in terms of predication, these two conditions amount to the same thing.) Substances then are the ultimate subjects of predication, that is to say, they are what individual expressions stand for. The question, what substances are there, is thus the same as the question, what individual expressions do we need in order to say the things we have to say. But Aristotle was also interested in the question 'What exists?'; and his initial answer to this question is that it is substances which, in the primary and fullest sense *are*, or exist. Whatever else exists, exists only in a secondary and analogical sense, to the extent that it has relation to substance. The word which is traditionally translated 'substance', namely *'ousia'*, is a verbal noun from the verb *'einai'*, equivalent of 'to be', from which 'ontology' is also derived. So the ontological question 'What is there?' is answered automatically by the one word *'Ousiai'*, meaning 'Substances'; but the question 'What substances are

---

[13] Aristotle, *Categories*, Ch. 5, 2^{a}12-13.

there?' is the same as the question 'How many individual expressions do we need?' This is how we determine our 'ontological' commitment.

Quine's notion that existence has some intimate connection with reference, that any variables we bind with quantifiers must be regarded as ranging over values, i.e. as individual variables, is thus a residue of Aristotelianism. The doctrine that to be is to be the value of a variable and the doctrine that it is substances which in the primary and fullest sense *are* are at bottom the same. It is a muddled doctrine, in its Quinian as well as in its Aristotelian dress. Questions about how many individual expressions we need, or what is the smallest n for which we need an n-place predicable, if we are to say what we need to say about the world, have nothing to do with *being*, or existence. These are the questions that have been traditionally called 'ontological'; but it is a misnomer. In so far as 'ontology' is thought of as being concerned with existence it has nothing to do with such Ockhamist interests. It is not *entities* but *individual expressions* which should not be multiplied beyond necessity. I can bind what expressions I like with the existential quantifier: unless the expressions have already been categorized as individual, I am in no way 'committed'. The issue between the realist and the anti-realist must be fought out in terms of the possibility of reducing 'Houses have redness and sunsets have redness' to 'Houses are red and sunsets are red'. It will then already have been settled before we pass to 'There is something which houses and sunsets have in common' or 'There is something which houses and sunsets are'.

8. *Strawson on the 'ontological-categorial' and the 'logico-grammatical'*

P. F. Strawson has had some interesting comments to make on the relations between logic or grammar and ontology. They touch on the position I have just outlined, but seem to me to miss the main point. Speaking of Quine's views about 'ontological commitment', Strawson[14] says:

Is it ontological? Why should it be more than grammatical? or grammatico-logical? Quine says we are committed to a certain class of *objects*. It

[14] P. F. Strawson, 'Positions for Quantifiers', *Semantics and Philosophy*, edd. Milton K. Munitz and Peter K. Unger, 1974, p. 72.

would be more to the point, at least at first, to say that we are committed to a certain class of subjects; where 'subject' is the logico-grammatical correlate of the logico-grammatical 'predicate'.

The interesting thing here is that Strawson thinks there is a genuine contrast between an 'ontological' and a 'grammatico-logical' commitment. He returns to this with a look at what is meant by commitment to 'objects'—Quine, after all, had talked about 'objectual' quantification. He asks (on pp. 73 f.),

> What of the doctrine that all subjects stand for objects and hence that all quantification into subject position is quantification over objects? Surely 'clarity is served' by distinguishing two senses of 'object', one merely relative, logico-grammatical sense and the other a sense which might not inaptly be called ontological.

We need not linger over Strawson's contention that the 'logico-grammatical' sense of 'object' is 'merely relative'. He thinks that the same—what?—can be 'presented as an object' in one proposition and not as an object in another. Frege's doctrine of the absolute distinction between concept and object is thus rejected. But the other, 'ontological' sense of the word 'object' is, in Strawson's view, in play when we 'distinguish objects from qualities, properties, relations, events, processes, species, types, and whatnot'. In this sense 'we use the word for ontological classification or categorization; for distinguishing one ontological category from others. Never mind that it is not a particularly well-defined category. Few categories are.'

Against this I would claim that 'object' in this context has only one sense, and that a logical one. It serves to distinguish names from predicative expressions by means of the admittedly misleading statement that objects are what names stand for, while concepts are what predicative expressions stand for. The distinction is not relative, but absolute; and the categories distinguished are as well defined as any categories could be. They are logical categories, and 'all logical differences are big differences'.

Strawson's notions of 'ontological classification' and 'ontological category' are peculiarly old-fashioned. They seem indeed to belong to a literally interpreted Aristotelianism. His distinction between objects, qualities, relations, and whatnot is practically a repetition of Aristotle's distinction between substances, qualities, relations, and whatnot. But what are Aristotle's categories categories of, and what is Strawson's ontological classification a classification of? Of *what there is—ta onta* —no doubt. It is odd that Strawson should thus ignore the Wittgensteinian discovery, which his predecessor as Waynflete Professor had used to such good effect,[15] that concepts such as substance (which is closely related to Frege's *object*), quality, relation, etc., are formal concepts. They are *Scheinbegriffe*, for which the proper sign is the appropriate variable.[16] The 'ontological' distinction between object (substance) and concept (quality, relation) is not to be contrasted with, but reduced to, the logical distinction between subject-expression and predicate-expression. 'Clarity is served' only by translating this material-mode talk about ontological classification into formal-mode talk about syntactical categories. By failing to make this move Strawson immediately creates a difficulty for himself. His attempt to distinguish two roles of predicate-expressions, 'the indication of propositionality' and 'concept-specification',[17] is a remarkable piece of *obscurum per obscurius* explanation. Having, as he thinks, sufficiently distinguished the role of the predicate, as the specifier of general concepts, from the role of the subject, as the specifier of particulars, he is left with the unexplained fact that the verb, or predicate-expression, has the function of indicating propositional combination. How it does this, or why it should even be thought to do this, remains a mystery. How much more illuminating is Frege's doctrine that the predicate just *is* what is obtained by removing one or more occurrences of one or more names from a proposition!

Strawson would hardly have found himself in this position if he had not uncritically accepted the notions of *general concept* and *particular* as 'ontological categories'. Oddly enough he comes very near to seeing that the 'ontological' notion of object is to be explained in terms of the 'logical' notion of subject. 'Of course,' he says, 'there is a link between the two senses of "object". For objects in the ontological-categorial sense are the basic objects in the logico-grammatical sense.' He does not elaborate here (p. 74) what he means by 'basic'. Let us do it

[15] Cf. G. Ryle, 'Categories', *Collected Papers*, 1971, 2, 170 ff.
[16] Wittgenstein, *Tractatus*, 4.126-4.1272.
[17] Strawson, 'Positions for Quantifiers', p. 78. He develops this at greater length in *Subject and Predicate in Logic and Grammar*, 1974, particularly pp. 20-35.

for him. The proposition 'The fact that Robert is dyslexic implies that he needs special attention from his teachers' has the appearance of predicating something of a fact. But facts, we may feel, unlike Robert, are not 'basic objects'. This feeling, if articulated, amounts to recognition of the following contrast. We can paraphrase the sentence in question thus: 'Since Robert is dyslexic, he needs special attention from his teachers'. We thereby eliminate the non-basic predicate 'implies' and the non-basic object which is its subject. But the predicate '— is dyslexic' and the object of which it is predicated are not so easily eliminated. This is what claims about 'basic objects' amount to. The 'ontological' question whether facts are basic objects, in the way boys are, is a question about the sorts of subject-expression we can and cannot eliminate by reductive analysis of this sort. If the only legitimate 'ontology' is, as I believe it is, the search for objects which are basic in this sense, it is in fact what Strawson would describe as a 'logico-grammatical' enterprise, despite the contrast which he draws between the 'ontological-categorial' and the 'logico-grammatical'. But its being called 'ontology' is a disaster.

This book is not concerned with 'ontology' in this sense. It has nothing to do with the supposed question of *what there is*. If the word 'ontology' had not been spoiled in the ways outlined, it would have been reasonable to describe the inquiry I am undertaking as 'ontological'. It has to do with the verb 'be', particularly in so far as it is synonymous with the verb 'exist'. It does not aim to answer the questions 'What exists?' or 'What sort of things exist?', for such questions are almost bound to be misconceived. Even if they were straightforward questions, the question 'What is existence?' would differ from them, just as the question 'What is truth?' differs from the question 'What things (or propositions) are true?', i.e. 'What is *the* truth?'. What the present enquiry does is rather to seek to understand the meaning of propositions of the form 'As exist' or 'There is an A'. Such an aim is not, perhaps, altogether alien from the purposes of old Father Parmenides. But those who were looking for a comprehensive account of Being *qua* Being will no doubt feel themselves to have been cheated.

VIII
Objectual, Substitutional, and Prioresque Quantification

1. *Quine's two ways of defining the quantifier*

Chapter VI was devoted to an attempt to break the connection between reference and quantification, and, in a bad sense of a bad word, between 'ontology' and quantification. If what we have been arguing in Chapter VII is accepted, we can dismiss all talk about 'ontology' as confused and irrelevant. The issue is whether quantification is essentially referential. That it is, that quantification is indeed definitive of reference, is the doctrine of Quine's earlier writings, of 'On What There Is' and *Word and Object*. In Chapter VI I was arguing that quantification need be understood referentially only when the variables quantified occupy the position of proper names. By the time Quine wrote 'Existence and Quantification'[1] he had half come round to this point of view—but only half. He had seen that there was an interpretation of quantification in which it had nothing to do with 'ontological commitment'. He called this 'substitutional quantification'. But he thought that there was another interpretation of quantification, regarded by him as in some way the superior and genuine interpretation, which allowed him to think of it in the old way as the vehicle of reference, as the means by which we 'commit ourselves ontologically'. This he called 'objectual' or 'referential' quantification.

The supposed difference between the substitutional and the objectual interpretations of quantification emerges if we set out two ways of stating the truth-conditions of a quantified proposition:

(O) $\Sigma x \phi x$ is true if, and only if, 'ϕ —' is true of some object

[1] *Ontological Relativity*, Ch. 4.

(S) $\Sigma x\phi x$ is true if, and only if, some proper name substituted for x in ϕx yields a true proposition.

This version (O) of the truth-conditions for objectual quantification is very much simpler than that normally given by logicians setting up a theory of truth. Since they are concerned, not only with one-place predicables like 'ϕ —', but with n-place predicables for every n, what in their versions of (O) the predicable is said to be true of (i.e. what is said to satisfy the predicable) is not an object but a sequence of objects. Furthermore, what they are concerned to define is not the truth of $\Sigma x\phi x$, but its satisfaction by such a sequence. But there is no need for us to become involved here with these complications. We are not concerned with securing generality, but with pointing up the contrast between (O) and (S). Again, our statement (S) of the truth conditions for substitutional quantification requires comment, since it too is a simplified version of the standard statement of these conditions. It relates only to the case where the quantified variable is an individual variable, and does not attempt to explain the generalized notion of a 'substitution class'. Even so there is room for misunderstanding of what is meant in this context by 'substituting a proper name for x in ϕx'. The role of x here is to indicate that the expressions to be substituted for it should not only be proper names but be performing the function of proper names. A proper name is not properly said to have been substituted for x in ϕx if in the resulting proposition it is mentioned rather than used. Thus we should not say that ' "Cicero" has six letters' results from substituting 'Cicero' for x in 'x has six letters'. The role of 'Cicero' in ' "Cicero" has six letters' is no different from that of 'Sneeze' in ' "Sneeze" has six letters'. Indeed we cannot allow the notion of substituting a proper name for x in ϕx to cover cases where the proper name is mentioned *as well as being* used. 'Giorgione was so called because of his size' does not result from substituting 'Giorgione' for x in 'x was so called because of his size', because the name 'Giorgione' is not only being used here to name someone, namely, Barbarelli, but is also being mentioned: only in this way do we have an antecedent for 'so'. The supposed peculiarities of substitutional quantification into opaque contexts depend on failure to make these distinctions.[2]

[2] See below, § 5, and Ch. IX, § 7.

It must first be remarked that neither (O) nor (S) provides a definition of existential quantification in the traditional sense of 'definition'. What I mean by 'traditional' here may be explicated with the help of an example. The expression 'x is square' may be defined as 'x is equilateral and x is rectangular'. Here we are licensed to replace an expression whose form is relatively simple by an expression whose form is relatively complex: we may thus speak of ourselves as producing an 'analysis' of the *definiendum*. The *definiens* is not a simple synonym of the *definiendum*, as 'commence' is of 'begin'.[3] There is no circularity in the definition. Someone who knew the meaning of 'square' might still be enlightened by the definition, since it has the effect of showing how an expression could be dispensed with in favour of more primitive expressions. Thus those who construct axiomatic systems aim by means of such definitions to reduce all expressions used in the system to a very small set of primitive, undefined expressions. But Euclid, when he gives his definition of 'circle', is not assigning meaning for the first time to a previously insignificant expression. He is enabling those who already know how to use the world 'circle' to see how it is equivalent to an overtly complex expression constructed out of more primitive terms. (O) and (S) do not provide anything of this sort. Someone who knew the meaning of $\Sigma x \phi x$ would not have its use explained in terms of expressions with a different and simpler meaning by being told that it is true if, and only if, 'ϕ —' is true of *some object*. The word 'some' is, for the purposes of the definition, synonymous with the expression Σ, which is supposed to be being defined. And it is the same with (S). A purported analytic definition of Σ which had recourse to the phrase 'some proper name' would be viciously circular. We may say, then, that (O) and (S) provide stipulative definitions rather than definitions of the traditional analytic kind. The difference between (O) and (S) does not emerge at this point.

If, on the other hand, (O) and (S) are thought of as providing interpretations for the previously meaningless expression $\Sigma x \phi x$ there is no question of circularity. Definitions of this kind, which are thought of as *giving* meaning to an expression which those to whom the definition is given do not know how to use,

[3] Cf. Locke, *Concerning Human Understanding*, Book III, Ch. IV, § 6.

cannot incur the charge of circularity. There is no objection to using synonyms for this purpose. If a Frenchman were to be told that 'station' was the English equivalent of '*gare*', it would in no way frustrate the purpose of his instruction that '*gare*' and 'station' are synonymous.

(O), in effect, is little more than a simple translation of the symbolic expression $\Sigma x - x$ into English: the truth conditions of a proposition containing $\Sigma x - x$ are given by means of a proposition containing 'some object'. The domain of $\Sigma x - x$, the range of values of the quantified variable which appears in the *definiendum*, is exactly the same as that picked out by the word following 'some' in the *definiens*. In stating (O) we have used the quantifier without restriction. What we thus quantify over are objects in general, and this is why the word 'object' follows the word 'some' in the *definiens*. So this statement of the truth conditions for $\Sigma x \phi x$ is a statement about just the same things as $\Sigma x \phi x$ is about.

The *definiens* of (S), on the other hand, primarily says something not about objects but about proper names. If it says anything about objects also, it says it indirectly, by way of implication. The *definiens* of (S) is metalinguistic where that of (O) remains in the object language. (O) does indeed talk metalinguistically of the predicate 'ϕ —' just as (S) talks metalinguistically of the open sentence ϕx. What is important, though, is the fact that the *definiens* of (S) quantifies, not over objects in general, but over proper names, which, if they *are* objects of a kind, are nevertheless a very restricted kind of object. It is the expression 'proper name', not the word 'object', which here follows the word 'some'.

It might be thought that since the *definiens* of (S) was metalinguistic the *definiendum* had to be as well. Such a conclusion would be hasty, although eventually, we believe, it has to be accepted. As (O) has been stated here, its *definiens* is metalinguistic too, so far as the mention of the predicate 'ϕ —' is concerned; and in stating it this way we have merely followed normal practice, a practice dictated by the ulterior motive of providing a recursive definition, not of the quantifier, but of truth or satisfaction.[4] No one, however, wishes to maintain

---

[4] We could of course have stated (O) without mentioning any predicate. We could have said: '$\Sigma x \phi x$ is true if, and only if, some object ϕ's'. What we were doing

that, when $\Sigma x\phi x$ is interpreted along the lines of (O), it is given a meaning which makes it metalinguistic. Statements of truth-conditions such as (O) and (S) do not aim to provide something in the *definiens* which means what the *definiendum* means: *definiendum* and *definiens* are connected, not by 'means the same as', but by the biconditional 'if, and only if', which is intended as expressing only material equivalence. All (O) says is that '$\Sigma x\phi x$ is true' and ' "ϕ —" is true of some object' have the same truth value (for all substitutions for ϕ, of course). What applies to (O) applies also to (S). We cannot, therefore, assume that simply because (S) states the truth conditions of $\Sigma x\phi x$ in metalinguistic terms it gives $\Sigma x\phi x$ a meaning which is metalinguistic.

Some of those who have explained quantification by 'objectualist' definitions like (O) have also, without awareness that any new interpretation was involved, use 'substitutionalist' interpretations like (S) in the next breath, as it were.[5] Such philosophers clearly regarded what are now called 'objectualist' and 'substitutionalist' interpretations as alternative ways of explaining one and the same meaning of $\Sigma x\phi x$. It would not have occurred to them that explanations like (O) gave it a meaning as part of the object language whereas explanations like (S) gave it a metalinguistic meaning.

2. *The two main differences between objectual and substitutional quantification*

However, it has been claimed, notably by Quine, that the truth-conditions stated by (O) make certain propositions of the form $\Sigma x\phi x$ true, where the truth-conditions stated by (S) would make them false. This is the first of the two main differences between the interpretations. The difference arises from the possibility of there being objects which do not have names. For example, a possible substitution for 'ϕ —' in $\Sigma x\phi x$ is '— is a pigeon in Trafalgar Square which has never been named'. With this substitution for 'ϕ —', $\Sigma x\phi x$ comes out true on the

would thus be seen more clearly as the translation of symbolic notation into ordinary English. But the appearance in the *definiens* of 'true', or some analogous term such as 'satisfies', is familiar from Tarskian contexts, and necessary for Tarskian purposes.

[5] See Leslie Stevenson, 'Frege's Two Definitions of Quantification', *Philosophical Quarterly*, 1973, pp. 207-23.

objectualist statement of the truth-conditions if, and only if, '— is a pigeon in Trafalgar Square which has never been named' is true of some object—as it almost certainly is. But if we follow the substitutionalist statement of the truth conditions of quantified formulae, $\Sigma x \phi x$, with this substitution for 'ϕ—', is true only if some proper name substituted for x in 'x is a pigeon in Trafalgar Square which has never been named' produces a true proposition. And this it clearly cannot do.

Not every pigeon in Trafalgar Square has a name, but any pigeon there or anywhere else could have a name if we chose to give it one. It might therefore be suggested that (S) be amended so that it no longer talked about actual but only about possible names. $\Sigma x \phi x$ would then be held to be true if, and only if, there *could* be a name which, if substituted for x in ϕx, would produce a true proposition. But even this is impossible where substitutions for 'ϕ—' are, or include, the predicate '— has never been named'. More generally, it has been thought improper to introduce modality into an interpretation of quantification, particularly in the light of difficulties Quine himself has found in the combination of modality and quantification in a single system. Moreover, while any pigeon in any square can be given a name if occasion arises, in the theory of real numbers it can be proved that there are numbers which cannot be specified or designated. Granted the force of these objections, it will simplify matters if we understand the *definiens* of (S) as talking about proper names that have actually been given to objects. We must therefore admit that (S) imposes a necessary condition on the truth of some prima-facie true propositions of the form $\Sigma x \phi x$ which they cannot meet. Although there are certainly pigeons in Trafalgar Square which no one has ever named, there is no true proposition to be found in which a proper name takes the place of x in 'x is a pigeon in Trafalgar Square which no one has ever named'. (O) and (S) state different truth-conditions for the truth of propositions of the form $\Sigma x \phi x$. Some propositions of this form come out as true on (O) but false on (S). So the form $\Sigma x \phi x$, as interpreted by means of the truth-conditions given by (S), clearly has a different meaning from that which it has when interpreted by means of the truth-conditions given by (O). And since the truth of such a proposition on the (S) interpretation

OBJECTUAL AND SUBSTITUTIONAL QUANTIFICATION

is dependent on the existence of proper names, it is hard to deny that the proposition thus interpreted is about proper names, i.e. is metalinguistic. But this is a controversial point to which I shall have to return.

Such then is one difference between the interpretations given of $\Sigma x \phi x$ by (O) and (S) respectively. Another and perhaps more important difference concerns categories of variable. Analogues of (S) can be found for cases where other than individual variables are bound by the quantifier. Thus:

(S') $\Sigma \phi \phi a$ is true if, and only if, some predicable substituted for ϕ in ϕa yields a true proposition

(S'') $\Sigma p \delta p$ is true if, and only if, some proposition substituted for p in δp yields a true proposition.

The *definientia* of (S') and (S'') quantify over predicables and propositions respectively: like the *definiens* of (S) itself, they are about linguistic expressions. In terms of 'ontological commitment' we can say that (S), (S'), and (S'') are committed to a single type of entity, namely, linguistic expressions. Someone who is prepared to 'countenance' the proper names of (S) will not shrink back from the predicables of (S') or the propositions of (S'').

The corresponding analogues of (O) are different in this respect. They are:

(O') $\Sigma \phi \phi a$ is true if, and only if, some property belongs to a

(O'') $\Sigma p \delta p$ is true if, and only if, 'δ —' is true of some Proposition.

An example of (O') would be '"$\Sigma \phi (\phi \text{Peter})$" is true if, and only if, some property belongs to Peter'. An example of (O'') would be '"$\Sigma p(\text{John believes that } p)$" is true if, and only if "— is believed by John" is true of some Proposition'.[6] The Propositions of (O'') are thus comparable with the properties of (O'). Correlative to Propositions conceived as abstract entities are predicables like '— is believed by John' which are true or false of these Propositions. The expressions symbolized by 'δ —' in (S'') and the *definiendum* of (O'') are sentential operators, expressions which form propositions out of propositions. Such are 'John believes that —', 'It is not the case that —',

---

[6] For the use of 'Proposition' with an initial capital to refer to Propositions as abstract entities, see above, Ch. V, p. 120, n. 5.

'Necessarily —', 'Allegedly —'. Corresponding to any such substitution instance of 'δ —' is a substitution instance of 'δ' —', which is conceived as a predicable true or false of Propositions. As well as '— is believed by John' we have '— is false', '— is necessary' and '— is alleged'.

We thus have the following contrast between the (S)'s and the (O)'s. (S') and (S'') involve ontological commitment, if we may continue to talk for a moment in this way, only to members of the class of linguistic expressions, to which (S) was already committed. (O') and (O''), on the other hand, commit us to classes of entities which those who use (O) may not be prepared to countenance. (O') commits us to properties and (O'') to Propositions. There are those who use (O) as the preferred analysis of existential quantification, and who, as nominalists, or reluctant realists, would be unhappy having to admit properties and Propositions into the class of objects spoken of in (O). But we must also note that properties and Propositions have to be thought of as objects of a sort. The truth-conditions which (O') and (O'') state for propositions of the form $\Sigma\phi\phi a$ and $\Sigma p\delta p$ can be thought of simply as resulting from restricting the range of x in statements of the condition for the truth of propositions of the form $\Sigma x\phi x$. Corresponding to '$\Sigma\phi(\phi$ Peter)' we have '$\Sigma x(x$ is a property belonging to Peter)'. and corresponding to 'Σp(John believes that p)' we have '$\Sigma x(x$ is a Proposition believed by John)'. Many philosophers would wish to give the first member of each of these pairs of propositions as a reductive analysis of the second, to regard '$\Sigma x(x$ is a property belonging to Peter)' and '$\Sigma x(x$ is a Proposition believed by John)' as saying nothing that was not already said, more economically, by '$\Sigma\phi(\phi$ Peter)' and 'Σp(John believes that p)'. But if the truth-conditions of the two latter propositions can only be given by the two former, which are what the *definientia* of (O') and (O'') amount to, the prospect is dim for reductive analyses of this kind. Quine fears that existential generalization from propositions like 'Peter is red-haired' and 'John believes that grass is green' to propositions like 'Peter is something' and 'John believes something' involves commitment to undesirable abstract entities. His fear would in this view be justified.

Where the objectualist 'definitions' of $\Sigma\phi\phi a$ and $\Sigma p\delta p$ are ontologically spendthrift the corresponding substitutionalist ones are parsimonious. This is not surprising. What is expressed in '$\Sigma x(x$ is a property belonging to Peter)' and '$\Sigma x(x$ is a Proposition believed by John)' with the help of the two-place predicables '— is a property belonging to . . . .' and '— is a Proposition believed by . . . .' is expressed in '$\Sigma \phi(\phi$ Peter)' and 'Σp(John believes that p)' with the help only of the one-place predicables '$\Sigma \phi(\phi$ —)' and 'Σp(— believes that p)'. As we saw in section 7 of Chapter VII, ontological commitments are shed by realizing that something which seemed to be sayable only with the help of an n-place predicable can in fact be said adequately with the help only of $(n-1)$-place predicable. Furthermore, the difference between an n-place predicable and an $(n-1)$-place predicable lies in the number of individual expressions which are required in order to turn the predicable into a complete sentence. The *definientia* of (O') and (O'') use individual expressions where the *definienda* use predicative or propositional expressions. Since these *definientia* are, for relevant purposes, couched in the object language, they are ontologically committed in a way that the *definientia* of (S') and (S''), which are metalinguistic, are not. (S') and (S'') avoid ontological commitment by the device that Quine calls 'semantic ascent'.[7] They use no individual expressions which are not already used in the singular statements of which their *definienda* are the generalizations, except for those whose range is linguistic expressions like predicables and propositions. So (S') and (S'') enable us to bind predicative and propositional variables with quantifiers without becoming metaphysical realists about properties and Propositions.

The objectualist and substitutionalist interpretations of the existential quantifier each possess some failing that the other lacks. The objectualist commits us to metaphysical realism—a failing at least in Quine's eyes. The substitutionalist preserves neutrality on this matter. The substitutionalist gives us an account of existential propositions which produces the wrong truth-value for them when we are dealing with objects which lack names. (For there *are* pigeons in Trafalgar Square which lack names.) The objectualist gets the truth-values right. (Analogous

[7] Described by him on p. 16 of *From a Logical Point of View*, on pp. 10–13 of *Philosophy of Logic*, and, most comprehensively, in § 56 of *Word and Object*, 1950.

difficulties beset the substitutionalist with respect to true existential statements about unspecificable properties or unexpressed Propositions, which by (S′) and (S″) will come out as false.) Faced with the dilemma of choosing between the two, we look for some way out. Is there some *tertium quid*, an interpretation of quantification which is neither objectualist nor substitutionalist, but preserves the virtues and escapes the vices of each?

3. *The 'Prioresque' interpretation of quantification*

A. N. Prior has normally been regarded as belonging to the substitutionalist school[8] in matters of quantification. But the account he gives of the existential quantifier in *Objects of Thought* (pp. 34–7) differs in a most important respect from the account given by (S), (S′), and (S″). The latter state sufficient and necessary conditions for the truth of propositions governed by the existential quantifier: they contain the biconditional, 'if, and only if'. Prior's account of existentially quantified propositions is metalinguistic, in the way (S), (S′), and (S″) are, but it provides only sufficient conditions for the truth of existentially quantified propositions. Prior's account simply drops 'and only if' from (S), (S′), and (S″): for the rest it does not differ from them significantly.

This has the effect of freeing the 'substitutionalist' account from the danger of changing the truth-value of propositions like 'There are pigeons in Trafalgar Square which have never been named'. This proposition would still be true if, *per impossibile*, there were a true proposition formable by substituting some proper name for x in 'x is a pigeon in Trafalgar Square which never has been named'. But we do not have to say that it would be true *only if* there were such a proposition. Even Quine would admit that an existentially quantified proposition of the form $\Sigma x \phi x$, 'objectually' interpreted, is true *if* a true proposition is produced by substituting some proper name for x in ϕx. If all that the (S)'s were doing was stating sufficient conditions for the truth of existential propositions, the true propositions thus determined would all be included amongst those shown to be true by the (O)'s.

What the (S)'s thus interpreted would not do is give us

[8] See L. J. Cohen's review of Prior's *Objects of Thought* in *Mind*, 82, 1973.

sufficient conditions for the falsity of existential propositions. In order to have sufficient conditions for falsity we need to have necessary conditions for truth. And so Prior's version of the (S)'s would be no use to us if we were looking for definitions of existentially quantified formulae which would give us the semantics of the quantifier for use in a formal system. If the existentially quantified formulae were thought of as totally uninterpreted, a version of the (S)'s which omitted the words 'and only if' would not serve to give us an interpretation of them. We should not understand a formula if we knew only that it was true on some occasions when it was true, and were never able to know when it was false.

But need we look to Prior's version of the (S)'s to provide us with a semantics for the existential quantifier of the sort that is required in a formal system? Need we regard Prior's account of the meaning of the existential quantifier as an interpretation of a previously uninterpreted symbol? It is clear that Prior did not intend it in this way. He says (p. 35) 'I do not think that any formal definition of "something" is either necessary or possible, but certain observations can usefully be made about the truth-conditions of statements of this sort' (statements like 'Something is red-haired'). Note that he is talking, not about the logical symbol Σ, nor about the logicians' jargon 'for some x', but about the ordinary-language expression 'something'. He has just said 'Consider, for instance, the sentence "For some x, x is red-haired". The colloquial equivalent of this is "Something is red-haired".' Colloquial expressions like 'something' are not uninterpreted symbols for which it is necessary to 'give a semantics'. They are expressions which we all know how to use. What is in question is whether we can give them an analytic definition, whether we can pass from knowing how to use them to knowing how we use them, and that without circularity. Such definitions are possible in some cases. 'Female fox' is an analytic, non-circular definition of 'vixen'. But Prior denies that this sort of definition is possible for 'something'. The other sort of definition, the sort that 'gives the semantics' for a previously uninterpreted symbol, is what he says is not necessary.

What *is* possible is to give an account in metalinguistic terms of a sufficient condition for the truth of 'Something is red-haired'. This is not only possible but necessary—necessary to enable us to extend our understanding from the colloquial 'Something is red-haired' to the non-colloquial, semi-formal, 'For some ϕ, Peter ϕ's', and 'For some p, James believes that p'. We do this via 'For some x, x is red-haired', which is introduced as the equivalent of the colloquial 'Something is red-haired'. It is a sufficient condition for the truth of what these two last sentences express that there be some proper name which, when substituted for x in 'x is red-haired' or for 'Something' in 'Something is red-haired', produces a true proposition. Similarly, if substituting a predicable for ϕ or a proposition for p in 'Peter ϕ's' or 'James believes that p' produces a true proposition, the corresponding existentially quantified propositions are true. So we have the materials for an analogy. We know that the truth of a proposition like 'Peter is red-haired' is a sufficient condition for the truth of 'For some x, x is red-haired'. It is also a sufficient condition for the truth of 'For some ϕ, Peter ϕ's'. We know that, as 'For some x, x is red-haired' is to x and its substitution instances, so 'For some ϕ, Peter ϕ's' is to ϕ and its substitution instances. We know the meaning of 'For some x, x is red-haired'. (It is equivalent to 'Something is red-haired'.) We can say, then, that the meaning of 'For some ϕ, Peter ϕ's' is related to that of 'For some x, x is red-haired' as ϕ and its substitution instances are to x and its substitution instances. This is an adequate account of the meaning of 'For some ϕ, Peter ϕ's'. A similar account could be given of the meaning of 'For some p, James believes that p'. It is not a formal account, if by 'formal account' is meant a statement of the necessary and sufficient conditions for the truth of the proposition. But meaning can be informally explained. And the account we have given is in fact more formal than is absolutely required. The sort of analogical extension of the meaning of 'For some' from contexts like 'For some x, x is red-haired' to contexts like 'For some ϕ, Peter ϕ's' can quickly be made by anyone who has grasped the notion of variables of different categories. It has been spelled out here in what would otherwise be superfluous detail, because there have been sceptics who have doubted whether sense could be given to expressions like 'For some ϕ' and 'For some p'.

Prior gives the analogical explanation we have just expounded with the help of the semi-formal expressions 'For some x', 'For some ϕ', and 'For some p'. He also points out that colloquial language itself has quantificational expressions which correspond to the use of the quantifier to bind variables other than individual expressions. Just as we require a word like 'Peter' to stand as a substitute for 'Something' in 'Something is red-haired',[9] so we require a phrase like 'in New York' to stand as a substitute for 'somewhere' in 'I saw that film somewhere', a phrase like 'at Christmas' to stand as substitute for 'sometime' in 'I'll write to him sometime', or a phrase like 'by hitch-hiking' to stand as a substitute for 'somehow' in 'I'll get there somehow'. None of these expressions belongs to the category of individual expressions to which 'Peter' and 'Something' belong. We should regard 'in New York', 'at Christmas', and 'by hitch-hiking' as adverbial phrases, and it seems reasonable to call 'somewhere', 'sometime', and 'somehow' quantificational adverbs or adverbial quantifiers. The point Prior wants to make is that colloquial language itself is richer in quantifiers than the nominal quantifiers which are all that Quine, in his more strictly 'objectualist' moments, is willing to admit. We have 'For some t' as a semi-formal equivalent of 'sometime', and we could easily introduce 'For some l' as a semi-formal equivalent of 'somewhere', and 'For some m' as a semi-formal equivalent of 'somehow'. 'For some ϕ' can then be explained as standing in the same relation to 'is red-haired' as 'For some t' stands in to 'at Christmas', etc. Prior even contemplated coining a new set of colloquialisms 'somewhether', 'anywhether', etc., to correspond to 'For some p', 'For any p', etc.[10]

Again, as I remarked in section 9 of Chapter III, colloquial English already has a way of expressing what something like 'For some ϕ, Peter ϕ's' expresses. We can say 'Peter is something', or 'There is something which Peter is'. Variants of this are 'Peter does something' and 'Peter is or does something'. The 'something' which occurs in the phrase 'does something' is not an individual expression, nor is 'does' a transitive verb requiring a nominal expression as complement. 'Does' here is an auxiliary requiring a verbal expression as complement, and

---

[9] The difference between 'Something' and 'Somebody' or 'Someone' is not important here since they all belong to the category of individual expressions.
[10] Prior, *Objects of Thought*, p. 37.

'something' must here be regarded as a predicative variable, having verbs as its substitution instances: 'Peter does something, namely, play hockey, on Saturday afternoons.' The case is not so clear with the existing colloquial equivalent of 'For some p, James believes that p', which is 'James believes something'. Here the superficial grammar of 'believes' may be that of a transitive verb. If we say 'James believes something, namely, that grass is green', there is a possibility, as has earlier been mentioned, that the phrase 'that grass is green' should be thought of as standing for a Proposition. 'Something' here would in that case be an individual expression, and 'James believes something' would be, superficially at least, of the form $\Sigma x \phi x$ rather than $\Sigma p \delta p$. No doubt we should wish to say that the sentence thus understood, which would be tantamount to 'James believes some Proposition', should be reductively analysed as meaning 'For some p, James believes that p', just as 'Some property belongs to Peter' should be reductively analysed as meaning 'For some ϕ, Peter ϕ's'. But 'James believes something' could not be regarded without question as the colloquial equivalent of 'For some p, James believes that p'. Colloquial equivalents of propositions in which predicative variables are bound by quantifiers are, however, easy to find.

We may in any case be sure that by one or other, or several, of these means we can introduce expressions like 'For some ϕ' and 'For some p' into English. The English used by logicians and philosophers may be regarded as having already been enriched in this way, just as the English used by chemists or mathematicians or grammarians has been enriched by quasi-technical expressions. This being so, we shall have no difficulty in meeting the needs of those who construct formal systems and who require us to give a semantics, by way of necessary and sufficient conditions for truth, of formulae in their systems. We can produce definitions, understood in this way, of fully symbolic quantificational formulae. We may call these 'Prioresque' interpretations of quantification:

(P) $\Sigma x \phi x$ is true if, and only if, for some x, x ϕ's
(P') $\Sigma \phi \phi a$ is true if, and only if, for some ϕ, a ϕ's
(P'') $\Sigma p \delta p$ is true if, and only if, for some p, δp.

Here the expressions on the right of the biconditionals are to be regarded as expressions of an extended English language. It has already been explained how we can learn the meaning of these expressions. It would take sophisticated philosophical arguments to cause us to doubt the fact that we *do* know their meaning. The expressions on the left side of the biconditionals are to be regarded as uninterpreted expressions of the symbolism for which we are giving a semantics. It does not matter that their meaning, once they are given an interpretation, is the same as that of their *definientia*. This is regular form for definitions like this, which conform to Tarski's 'Convention T'.[11] Compare:

'Snow is white' is true if, and only if, snow is white.

The important fact, as has often been stressed, is that the expression said to be true is being *mentioned*, whilst the expression, which may on that account even be the same expression, which gives its truth-conditions, is being *used*.

4. *Prioresque quantification and Tarskian truth theory*

We have been considering the possibility of giving previously uninterpreted expressions like $\Sigma\phi\phi a$ and $\Sigma p\delta p$ an interpretation in a formal system. In recent years the task of providing such an interpretation—giving a 'semantics' for a system—has been held to be subject to very stringent requirements. Interpreting expressions like this has been regarded as part of the process of setting up a 'theory of truth' for the language in which they occur. There has been controversy over the question whether it is indeed possible to interpret formulae in which quantifiers bind predicative or propositional variables. It has been claimed that such attempts inevitably lead to paradox.[12] It has further been claimed that attempts to define truth for formulae of this sort fail to meet some of the requirements which have been made on adequate truth definitions. Saul Kripke has shown that none of these claims can be made good, at least for a substitutional interpretation of formulae like $\Sigma\phi\phi a$ and $\Sigma p\delta p$.[13]

But it may be asked whether the Prioresque interpretation we have just given similarly escapes these charges. The danger of paradox is one which requires more extended treatment

[11] A. Tarski, *Logic, Semantics, and Metamathematics*, 1956, pp. 187 f.
[12] Ibid., pp. 161 f.
[13] S. Kripke, 'Is there a Problem about Substitutional Quantification?' in *Truth and Meaning*, edd. G. Evans and J. McDowell, pp. 325-419.

than is possible here, but there is no reason to suppose that the ways of averting paradox that have been thought available for the substitutional interpretation should not equally be available for the Prioresque.[14] The charges that Wallace and others brought against the substitutionalist interpretation[15] might be thought to have more weight against the Prioresque: does the Prioresque interpretation of the quantifiers meet the requirements that have been thought necessary for an adequate theory of truth?

It is an essential feature of such a theory that the definition of truth that it provides should be recursive: that is to say, the truth of complex items should be defined in terms of the truth of the simpler items which are their components. The truth-conditions provided by the (S)'s possess this feature in the simplest way: the truth of propositions, e.g. of the form $\Sigma x \phi x$, is determined by the truth of propositions of the form ϕx. Those provided by the (O)'s are more complex: the truth of propositions of the form $\Sigma x \phi x$ is determined by what the predicate 'ϕ —' is *true of*. The relation *true of* is the converse of the relation *satisfies*: if 'ϕ —' is true of a, a satisfies 'ϕ —'. Because of the need for (O), or its variants, to employ the satisfaction requirement, Tarski, the originator of the idea of a truth-theory, found it necessary to define truth in terms of satisfaction and to provide as the required recursive definition a definition of satisfaction rather than truth. The Prioresque definitions, however, contain, after the words 'if, and only if,' no mention of either truth or satisfaction. They are neither in the simple nor in the complex way recursive. (P), the Prioresque interpretation of $\Sigma x \phi x$, is indeed equivalent to (O), which employs the notion *true of*, i.e. satisfaction. 'For some x, x ϕ's' was thought of as a modest extension of the ordinary-language 'Something ϕ's', which is equivalent to '"ϕ —" is true of something', i.e. 'Something satisfies "ϕ —"'. But (P') and (P''), the Prioresque interpretations of $\Sigma \phi \phi a$ and $\Sigma p \delta p$, cannot be defined in terms of satisfaction without blurring the

---

[14] Cf. R. Binkley, 'Quantifying, Quotation and a Paradox', *Noûs*, IV, 1970; G. Harman, 'Substitutional Quantification and Quotation', ibid., V, 1971; R. B. Marcus, 'Quantification and Ontology', ibid., VI, 1972.

[15] Cf. John Wallace, 'On the Frame of Reference' in D. Davidson and G. Harman (edd.), *The Semantics of Natural Language*, 1972; and see bibliography in Kripke, 'Substitutional Quantification'.

distinction between them and (O') and (O''), which the divorce between quantification and reference made so important. We do not have to understand the sentence 'There is something which roofs and sunsets are' as an abbreviation of 'Something satisfies the predicable "— is a property possessed by roofs and sunsets."'. To give a recursive definition of $\Sigma\phi\phi a$ in terms of truth would involve us in the unwelcome metalinguistic restrictions of the substitutionalist interpretation, and to give one in terms of satisfaction would involve us in an unwelcome objectualist commitment to properties. The Prioresque interpretation was designed to steer between just this Scylla and just this Charybdis; but the cost of the middle passage may be inability to provide a recursive truth-definition for the quantifier.

To persist in using the quantifier in a way which prevents a recursive truth-definition is to frustrate two distinct philosophical ambitions. One of these is Tarski's ambition to provide a paradox-free definition of *truth in a language*. Tarski believed it was necessary to provide such a definition because he supposed that a definition of 'true' involving quantifiers which bind propositional variables was unobtainable and, even if obtained, would lead to paradox. Since I believe that he was mistaken in this, I am not troubled by the frustration of a Tarskian attempt to give a recursive truth-definition of the quantifier in all its uses. Nor do I find it alarming that the second philosophical ambition is frustrated. This is Davidson's ambition of using recursive truth-definitions to provide an explanation not so much of truth as of meaning. In Davidson's view we cannot be confident of knowing the meaning of a linguistic item unless we have a theory which determines the contribution of that item to the truth-conditions of all the sentences in which it occurs. Such a theory derives the truth-, or satisfaction-, conditions of complex sentences from the truth-, or satisfaction-, conditions of atomic sentences. Quantified sentences are not atomic sentences. Unless we have definitions which define truth or satisfaction for quantified sentences in terms of truth or satisfaction for atomic sentences, we shall not have a theory of the kind Davidson demands. We shall not, in Davidson's view, be able to use the quantifier with a clear conscience. But again, my own belief is that Davidson's conscience is in this case unduly scrupulous. The suggestion that we do not know what is meant by 'For some ϕ, $a \phi$'s' and 'For some p, δp' is refuted by the account, in terms of an anological extension of the meaning of the ordinary-language quantifiers, given in the previous section of this chapter. The Prioresque interpretation of $\Sigma \phi \phi a$ and $\Sigma p \delta p$ is capable of giving them meaning, provided we accept this analogical account. Those who follow Davidson's puritanism in matters of meaning will be unconvinced, but I am not alone in finding the Davidsonian rigour unjustified.[16] $\Sigma \phi \phi a$ and $\Sigma p \delta p$ will have to be added to 'It is possible that p', 'John believes that p', and the vast number of other forms of complex propositions whose truth-conditions are not determined by whether or not their components are true or satisfied. Davidson's insistence on a recursive definition of truth or satisfaction is just another expression of the extensionalist dogma which cannot accommodate such forms. With Prior, I am content to say that 'I cannot see the slightest reason, other than stubbornness, for not drawing the moral that the law of extensionality is false.'[17]

5. *Are the quantifiers equivocal? The relation between the objectual and the substitutional interpretation*

It is time now to take stock of the labels that we have been using for these interpretations of quantification, 'substitutional', 'objectual', and 'Prioresque'. The first two were introduced originally by Quine, and it is sensible to let them keep the meanings Quine bestowed on them. The substitutional interpretation of existential quantification is given, with some allowance for our simplifications, by (S), (S'), and (S''). It is designed to give a meaning to existentially quantified formulae, regarded as previously uninterpreted, by a statement of necessary and sufficient conditions for their truth. The conditions are stated metalinguistically. If it is impossible to find names for all objects (or to specify all properties, or express every Proposition), the truth-conditions will differ from those provided by other interpretations of quantification. Since, for example, $\Sigma x \phi x$ will in this case come out as false on the substitutional interpretation for some substitutions for ϕ for

---

[16] Cf. Kripke, 'Substitutional Quantification' pp. 327, 412.
[17] Prior, *Objects of Thought*, p. 48.

which on other interpretations it comes out as true, the formula itself will on this supposition be equivocal.

The difference between objectual and substitutional quantification which we have so far been considering stems from the refusal of the latter to allow nameless objects to count for the purpose of verifying propositions of the form $\Sigma x \phi x$. This rigour with respect to nameless objects has been held to be balanced by leniency, on the part of substitutionalists, towards objectless names. No winged horse which lacked a name would count as lending support to the proposition '$\Sigma x(x$ is a winged horse)', substitutionally understood; but the alleged truth of 'Pegasus is a winged horse' is regarded as establishing the proposition, thus interpreted, notwithstanding the fact that 'Pegasus' fails to name any object. Again, objectual quantification into opaque contexts is thought by Quine to be illegitimate. Substitutional quantification, on the other hand, can, he holds, make perfectly good sense of sentences like 'For some x, Antony believed that x was his enemy'. Its substitutional truth-conditions ensure that it is true, because 'Antony believed that Octavian was his enemy' is true, despite Antony's lack of beliefs about Augustus. The topic of referential opacity is one that we shall turn to in Chapter IX. Following Prior, we shall there argue that there are no such things as referentially opaque contexts. It cannot therefore be a distinguishing feature of substitutional, as opposed to objectual, quantification that it permits quantification into such contexts. The topic of fictional or mythical proper names like 'Pegasus' is one that we shall discuss in Chapter X. The upshot of this discussion will be that, in the sense in which 'Pegasus is a winged horse' is true, 'Pegasus' does name an object, and in the sense in which 'Pegasus' does not name an object, it is not a proper name. There are in fact no proper names which fail to name objects. The possibility of objectless names, therefore, unlike that of nameless objects, cannot serve to distinguish substitutional from objectual quantification. They do not provide a further reason for regarding $\Sigma x \phi x$ as equivocal.

However, we still have the problem of nameless objects. Since we are regarding $\Sigma x \phi x$ as an uninterpreted formula, and since, given such objects satisfying a predicate 'ϕ —', the objectual and substitutional interpretations accord it different truth-values, the formula can only be regarded as equivocal. But nothing in that case can justify using the same symbolism for the two interpretations;[18] and if, following Kripke, we operate here with different symbols, it is misleading to call both symbols, thus interpreted, 'existential quantifiers'. Symbolic notation and logical terminology are supposed to be canonical, to be purified of the deficiencies of ordinary language such as ambiguity or equivocation. Not that the symbol Σ, as variously interpreted by the (O)'s and the (S)'s, could be supposed to be *purely* equivocal. It would have to be granted that, if used in these two senses, the expression would be used analogically, i.e. in senses which were partly different but partly the same.[19] The two senses of Σ would not be as unrelated as the two senses of 'prune'.

It is a point of controversy between philosophers whether the clauses which state the truth-conditions of substitutionally quantified propositions—clauses which the right-hand sides of the biconditionals (S) to (S″) are meant to represent—involve objectual quantification over objects other than expressions. But that such clauses involve objectual quantification over expressions is harder to dispute.[20] Thus the substitutional truth-condition of $\Sigma x \phi x$ says something about proper names, namely, that at least one of them yields a true proposition when substituted for x in ϕx. Can we avoid saying that this is what, on this interpretation, $\Sigma x \phi x$ *means*? In that case, we shall have made clear the analogy which exists between the two interpretations of $\Sigma x \phi x$: objectually interpreted the quantifier ranges over objects generally, substitutionally interpreted over those objects which are proper names. The two interpretations have in common the feature that they involve quantification; they differ in that the quantification involved is in one case unrestricted, in the other restricted. But exponents of substitutional quantification reject the view that the left-hand side of the biconditional *means* the same as the

---

[18] Cf. Kripke, 'Substitutional Quantification', pp. 328 f. Kripke uses '∃' with italicized variables for objectual and 'Σ' with roman variables for substitutional quantification.

[19] See above, Ch. I, pp. 12 f.

[20] Cf. Wallace 'On the Frame of Reference', and Kripke, 'Substitutional Quantification', p. 333 and *passim*. Kripke's remarks on pp. 341 f. make it not merely hard, but impossible, to dispute that the substitutional interpretation involves objectual quantification over expressions.

right-hand side.[21] The right-hand side states the necessary and sufficient conditions for the truth of the left-hand side; but not every sentence which states necessary and sufficient conditions means the same as the sentence whose truth-conditions it states. 'The number of Queens of England is its own square' gives necessary and sufficient conditions for the truth of 'There is only one Queen of England', but the two sentences do not mean the same. The meaning of the former depends on the meaning of the word 'square' which occurs in it, but the meaning of the latter has no dependence on the meaning of 'square'. The concept *square* is involved in the former, but not in the latter. Can we say that there are concepts involved in the right-hand side of (S) which are not involved in $\Sigma x \phi x$, interpreted substitutionally? The meaning of the right-hand side of (S) depends on the meaning of 'proper name'. Can we say that that of $\Sigma x \phi x$ does not?

The crucial difference between $\Sigma x \phi x$ substitutionally interpreted, and the same formula objectually interpreted, is that on the latter interpretation it can be verified by nameless objects. If 'ϕ —' represents '— is a pigeon in Tragalgar Square', on the substitutional interpretation $\Sigma x \phi x$ cannot be true unless some pigeon in Trafalgar Square has a name. Objectually interpreted, it can be true even if all pigeons in the square are nameless. How can the substitutional interpretation differ in this way from the objectual without depending in some way on the concept *name*? How could someone who lacked this concept recognize that '$\Sigma x(x$ is a pigeon in Trafalgar Square)', substitutionally interpreted, is falsified by the pigeons' namelessness? Despite protestations from the substitutionalists, it seems that $\Sigma x \phi x$ on their interpretation says something about expressions.[22] If we concede this point we have an explanation of the analogical use of Σ, or $\exists$, or of the term 'existential quantifier'. Given that $\Sigma x \phi x$ substitutionally interpreted means 'Something is a name which names an object which satisfies "ϕ —"', we can see that it is related to its objectual interpretation

---

[21] Cf. J. M. Dunn and N. D. Belnap, Jr., 'The Substitutional Interpretation of the Quantifier', *Noûs*, 2, 1968, p. 184; Barnes, *The Ontological Argument*, p. 59.

[22] Cf. Kripke, 'Substitutional Quantification', p. 349: 'Dunn and Belnap report (p. 184, point 5) that, independently of Wallace, many have regarded substitutional quantification as metalinguistic. Perhaps the result would show that these people were right.'

in exactly the same way as (A) 'This pig is healthy' is related to (B) 'This pig's urine is healthy'. Just as '— is healthy' in (B) has to be understood as shorthand for '— shows that the animal it comes from is healthy', where '— is healthy' has the same meaning as it has in the simpler (A), so $\Sigma x \phi x$ on the substitutional interpretation has to be understood as shorthand for 'Something is a name which, when substituted for x in ϕx, yields a true proposition'; and here 'Something —' has the same meaning as it has in the simpler 'Something satisfies "ϕ —"', which is the objectual interpretation of $\Sigma x \phi x$. The substitutional quantifier does not merely have its *truth-conditions* stated by means of the objectual quantifier; its *definition* has to be given with the help of the objectual quantifier. The objectual quantifier is here what medieval philosophers called 'the prime analogate'. 'Substitutionalists' who deny this owe us an explanation of the equivocation involved in the two interpretations of Σ.

6. *The relation between the objectual and the Prioresque interpretation*

If 'analogy' is the correct description of the relation between the substitutional and the objectual interpretation of quantification, what is the relation between the latter and the 'Prioresque' interpretation? The objectual interpretation is most often given by Quine in terms of ordinary language equivalents: $\Sigma x \phi x$ is true if, and only if, there exists an x such that $x \phi$'s. It is not metalinguistic, in that the colloquial quantifier which occurs in the *definiens* ranges, not over linguistic expressions of any sort, but over objects. Moreover, the only sort of quantification that is admitted as 'objectual' is that in which the variables bound by the quantifier are individual variables. If expressions like '$\Sigma \phi$(Peter ϕ's)' and 'Σp(James believes that p)' are given an objectual interpretation, their meaning is given as 'There is some property which belongs to Peter' or 'There is some Proposition which is believed by James'. Both, if understood in this way, are of the form $\Sigma x \phi a x$, and thus properly to be regarded as the result of binding with the quantifier, not a predicative or propositional, but an individual variable. The objectual interpretation allows no quantification except that which quantifies over objects.

The Prioresque interpretation occurs at two levels. It can be regarded in the same way as the other two interpretations as giving a sense to previously uninterpreted formulae. This is done by (P), (P'), and (P''). At this level it is in no way metalinguistic, and it interprets formulae like $\Sigma x \phi x$ by stating sufficient *and necessary* conditions of their truth. At the other level, the Prioresque concern is not to give a sense to formulae of a formal system, but to extend ordinary English by explaining how propositions like 'For some ϕ, Peter ϕ's' and 'For some p, James believes that p' are to be understood. They are to be understood by analogy with propositions like 'For some x, x is red-haired', which itself is introduced as equivalent to the colloquial 'Something is red-haired'. The analogy is powered by metalinguistic observations about the result of substituting appropriate linguistic expressions for x, ϕ, and p; but these observations concern only sufficient, not necessary and sufficient, conditions for the truth of the propositions to be explained.

There has been some confusion between the substitutional and the Prioresque interpretations. Quine treated the objectual and the substitutional interpretations as exhaustive of possible interpretations of quantification. In so far as the Prioresque account treats seriously formulae in which there is quantification of non-individual variables, it is certainly not an objectual account. It has therefore been assumed to be substitutional.[23] It certainly shares with the substitutional interpretation the willingness to quantify non-individual variables and the use of metalinguistic conditions for the truth of formulae. But it differs from the substitutionalist interpretation in using only sufficient, not necessary and sufficient, conditions for this purpose.

Where formulae which quantify individual variables are concerned, the Prioresque account does not differ from the objectual account. The truth values of quantified propositions are the same in each. Neither believes that a metalinguistic interpretation in terms of necessary and sufficient conditions for truth is possible. Each believes that the meaning of a sentence

---

[23] e.g. by L. J. Cohen in his review of *Objects of Thought*. R. D. Gallie, in controversy with Cohen in *Analysis*, 34, No. 3, 1974, and 35, No. 3, 1975 took, I believe rightly, the opposite view.

like 'Σx (x is red-haired)' can be given by ordinary-language locutions like 'Something is red-haired' or 'There exists a red-haired object'. There seems to be no reason to suppose that an expression of the form $\Sigma x \phi x$ is ambiguous as between the objectual and the Prioresque way of interpreting it. Where the two accounts differ is simply in the objectualist's refusal to attribute a sense to formulae which bind non-individual variables with quantifiers, unless these are interpreted as quantifying over properties or Propositions, regarded as objects, or are understood in the different, substitutional, sense. But by this refusal the objectualist cannot claim to have established a *sense* for Σ distinct from that given it by the Prioresque interpretation. There are not two meanings for Σ, one Prioresque and one objectual. The fact that the quantifiers can bind variables of different categories does not mean that by being attached to these different categories of variable they change their sense. The meaning of the quantifiers is intimately tied to the meaning of 'variable'; and x in $\Sigma x - x$ is a variable in the same sense of 'variable' as p is in $\Sigma p - p$. Similarly the symbol Σ has the same sense in $\Sigma x - x$ as it has in $\Sigma p - p$.[24] The objectualist should not be regarded as having identified a distinct sense in which the existential quantifier has been used. The substitutional interpretation attributes a distinct sense to the quantifier, but a derivative, analogical one. The prime analogate, the primary sense of the quantifier in terms of which the substitutional quantifier is defined, is the Prioresque one. This at bottom is the only one. All that distinguishes the objectualist is his stubborn refusal to allow that perfectly intelligible locutions like 'For some ϕ, Peter ϕ's' and 'For some p, James believes that p' have the sense they have. He has not distinguished a special sense of Σ.

7. *Objectualists misled by too much attention to ordinary language*

Nevertheless, the objectualist's refusal to countenance expressions of the form 'For some θ, — θ —' where the variable replacing θ is not an individual variable, is not *mere* stubborn-

[24] Because of this belief in the univocity of Σ, I find myself *pro tanto* in agreement with Scotus rather than Aquinas on the question whether *being* is univocal. For the tie between the meaning of the quantifier and the meaning of 'variable', see below, Ch. XI, particularly § 2.

ness. It is due in part to the connection between the existential quantifier and the ordinary language expressions 'There is —' and '— exists'. What fills the gap in these expressions is a singular noun or noun phrase with the indefinite article. Similarly the plural verb forms 'There are —' and '— exist' require completion with a plural noun or noun-phrase. These nouns and noun-phrases represent first-level predicables, that is to say, they represent expressions of the form '— is an A' in the more stylized readings of the quantified formulae which follow the pattern 'There is (exists) and x such that x is an A'.[25] Unlike the expression 'some', which can occur in 'somewhere' and 'somehow' as well as in 'someone' or 'something', and can thus be equivalent to quantifiers binding adverbial variables, the expressions 'there is —' and '— exists' are equivalent only to quantifiers binding individual variables.[26] When Quine said 'Existence is what the existential quantifier expresses' he meant originally to tie existence to the quantifier. It is to be feared that at times he and his followers have slipped into tying the quantifier to '— exists'. The ordinary-language expressions 'There is —' and '— exists' are second-level predicables. This is true also of the logical expression $\Sigma x - x$. But $\Sigma x - x$ should not be identified with the existential quantifier, which occurs also in $\Sigma \phi \phi$ — and $\Sigma p - p$, which are not second-level predicables. It seems that Quine has been led by the limitations of ordinary language to identify existential quantification as such, which is expressed by simple Σ, with the more complex $\Sigma x - x$, to which alone the English word 'exists' corresponds.

To this extent Quine has justification for his view that only objectual quantification has ontological commitments. If 'ontological' is construed, in accordance with its etymology, as qualifying those commitments which involve propositions of the form 'There *is* an A', it is true that the only quantificational formulae that do this are those of the form $\Sigma x - x$, i.e. those which 'quantify over objects'.[27] But this, contrary to

---

[25] See above, Ch. III, § 8.
[26] If we translate 'It's raining somewhere' from the 'some' idiom into the 'There is' idiom we import an artificial first-level predicable 'place': 'There is some place where it's raining'. (American-English 'It's raining someplace' obscures this point.)
[27] It is true that a formula like $\Sigma \phi K \phi a \phi b$ can be exemplified in ordinary English by 'There is something which George and Mary both are' (see above, Ch. III, pp.

the objectualist view, is a very superficial point. The meaning of Σ as it occurs in $\Sigma x - x$ has in no way to be distinguished from its meaning as it occurs in '$\Sigma\phi\phi$ —' and $\Sigma p - p$. $\Sigma x - x$ does not present us with a special variety of *quantification*. The differences between the variables take care of all the differences there are between $\Sigma x - x$, '$\Sigma\phi\phi$ —' and $\Sigma p - p$. The quantifier, Σ, is univocal throughout. If ordinary language has, in '— exists', a way of expressing what is otherwise expressed by $\Sigma x - x$, but lacks a way of expressing what is expressed by $\Sigma p - p$, this is a superficial deficiency of ordinary language.[28] The fact that only 'objectual' quantification is in this sense concerned with 'ontology' has no deep conceptual significance. Philosophers can dismiss it as unimportant.

8. *The philosophy of 'exist' and the philosophy of 'some'*

Opponents of 'objectualism' have sometimes represented themselves as driving a wedge between quantification and existence. They have given away too much to Quine, allowing him to use 'Existence is what the existential quantifier expresses' as an objectualist war-cry.[29] It is the main thesis of this book that every use of '— exist' has to be elucidated by the existential quantifier: in the simplest case 'Things which ϕ exist' is representable as $\Sigma x \phi x$. Existence is indeed what $\Sigma x - x$ expresses, but $\Sigma x - x$ is not the existential quantifier: it is the existential quantifier combined with an individual variable. The quantifier can be combined with other variables, but in being so combined does not cease to be existential. The point can be made without benefit of the symbols Σ or $\exists$, and without any of the logician's terms of art: Propositions which say that a so-and-so *exists* are equivalent to propositions which say that *something* is a so-and-so. Here the 'some' is the same

71 ff.). But the versatility of the expression 'There is something which —' is more a consequence of the occurrence of the word 'something' in it than of the phrase 'there is'. See the next section of this chapter for the greater power of 'some' than 'there is' to express precisely what the existential quantifier expresses.

[28] See my remarks about the genesis of the pseudo-predicate '— is true' in *What is Truth?*, pp. 46-8.

[29] Cf. Barnes, *The Ontological Argument*, p. 58: 'The existential quantifier should not be stipulatively tied to existence'; p. 59: 'On the substitutional view there is no general connection between existence and quantification'. Barnes, like other authors, assumes that the only alternative to the objectualist interpretation is the substitutionalist one.

'some' that is found in 'somewhere', 'somehow', etc., where it has nothing to do with *things*, i.e. objects. It is the 'thing' part of 'something' which is connected with objects, with proper names, with the issues that are debated under the heading of 'ontology'. But it is the 'some' part of 'something' which represents the concept of existence; the 'thing' part, after all, is there is 'nothing' and 'everything'. The ordinary-language expressions 'There is —' and '— exists' are, if you like, complex expressions, to be analysed in terms both of 'some' and of 'thing' (in terms both of Σ and of x). But the fact that in natural languages we do not take our existential concept neat, should not prevent the philosopher from identifying the important component. Perhaps it is an unfortunate historical, or geographical, accident that we find ourselves discussing the philosophy of *existence* rather than the philosophy of *someness*. Nevertheless it is an accident against whose consequences we can protect ourselves. 'Existence is what the existential quantifier expresses' should perhaps be rephrased: 'What is important in existence is what the existential quantifier expresses' would be more accurate. The objectualist is right in his determination to tie '— exists' to $\Sigma x — x$ and vice versa; where he goes wrong is in his failure to detect the fine structure of $\Sigma x —x$, to see it as a complex involving both Σ and x.

9. *Objectualists' hankering after a first-level concept of existence*

There is, however, a more sinister significance in the emphasis placed by the objectualist on the relation between $\Sigma x — x$ and '— exists'. As we have seen, he favours as a reading of $\Sigma x \phi x$ the form 'There exists an x such that ϕx'.[30] He finds accordingly that $\Sigma \phi \phi a$ and $\Sigma p \delta p$ require readings of the form 'There exists a ϕ such that ϕa' and 'There exists a p such that δp'. The expressions 'There exists a ϕ' and 'There exists a p' bother him, and he can only make sense of them by treating them as equivalent to 'There exists a property, ϕ', and 'There exists a Proposition, p'. But this seems to commit us to the *existence* of

---

[30] There are difficulties in construing the role of the variable x in this reading, as I remarked in *What is Truth?*, p. 13. Too much attention to these has led to the pursuit of false scents, e.g. by Wilfrid Sellars in 'Grammar and Existence: a Preface to Ontology', *Mind*, 69, 1960, 499-533, reprinted in Wilfrid Sellars, *Science, Perception and Reality*, 1963, pp. 247-81.

properties and Propositions. *Entities* of this sort will have to count as the values of our variables, and to be the value of a variable is to *be*. The values of our variables are objects, so to *be*, for Quine, is to be an object (just as to *be* in the primary sense, for Aristotle, is to be a substance). So the variables themselves, in objectual quantification, have to be of the same linguistic category as expressions which name objects, i.e. proper names. They must therefore be individual variables.

And here there is a sharp cleavage between those who, like Quine, define 'object' in terms of existence, and those who, in the manner of Wittgenstein, treat 'object' as a formal concept. To treat a concept as a formal concept is to treat it as the vehicle of a syntactic distinction. For those who treat 'object' in this way, the notion of object is to be explained in terms of the notion of proper name,[31] just as the notion of property has to be explained in terms of the notion of predicable. But, for Quine, proper names are an eliminable part of language; and quantification and its variables, which can do their work better than they can, are certainly not to be explained in terms of them. The objectualist's view of quantification could not, therefore, be described by the objectualist himself in terms of his refusal to quantify variables other than individual variables, themselves defined in terms of proper names. Objectual quantification is rather to be distinguished, in the objectualist's view, in terms of its ability to make clear to us our ontolgoical commitments. We are committed to the values of the variables of objectually interpreted quantification. These values are what *are*. It is the job of objectually interpreted quantification to tell us the answers to the question 'What is there?'. $\Sigma x \phi x$ has a special, and pre-eminently philosophical,[32] use, namely, to tell us what things *exist*. $\Sigma x - x$, which started life as a transparent way of expressing the fact that the concept of existence is a second-level concept, finishes, in Quine's system, by being explained in terms of 'exist' construed as a first-level predicable.[33] The objectualist has not iden-

[31] Cf. M. Dummett, *Frege: Philosophy of Language*, pp. 55-7.
[32] Cf. Quine, *Ontological Relativity*, p. 98: 'Here, then, prima facie, are two senses of the existence of rabbits, a common sense and a philosophical sense.' The philosophical sense is later identified with the sense expressible by objectual quantification.
[33] Cf. above, Ch. VI, § 4, and the discussion of Quine's use of sentences of the

tified a distinct interpretation of the existential quantifier. His view that he has done so shows him still to be the victim of a confusion over the meaning of 'exist', and it is precisely this confusion that the notion of existential quantification was designed to prevent.

form 'There exist all and only φ's' in Ch. VII, § 5. It is this inconsistency over the level of the concept of existence which led me to say in *What is Truth?* (p. 14, n. 3) that the objectual interpretation of quantification is 'incoherent'.

IX
Intentional Inexistence and Referential Opacity

1. *Opacity and Intentionality*

From the first, philosophers interested in what has become known as 'substitutional quantification' have seen in it a way of avoiding the difficulties which Quine raised in combining quantification with 'referential opacity'.[1] I have already indicated that I follow Prior in regarding these difficulties as unreal. But this point of view is likely to be regarded as eccentric, and some explanation is needed. Referential opacity is in any case closely connected with a phenomenon known as 'intentionality', which has relevance in its own right to the concept of existence. 'Intentionality' is an older name for the topic than 'referential opacity', and I shall first try to explain my position with regard to what Brentano called 'intentional inexistence' before going on to draw the consequences of this position for referential opacity and quantification.

2. *Three Examples of Intentionality*

I pointed out in an earlier chapter[2] that the car we need doesn't have to exist for the proposition.

(15) The car we need doesn't use much petrol

to be true. It seems that we can talk in this way about non-existent objects. There are many similar cases. It cannot be true that John is cleaning a car which does a hundred miles to the gallon unless there is a car which does a hundred miles to the gallon. But it can be true that John is looking for a car that does

---

[1] See above, Ch. VIII, § 5, and cf. Ruth B. Marcus, 'Modalities and Intensional Languages', *Synthese*, 13, 1961, 303-22.
[2] Ch. II, pp. 37 f.

a hundred miles to the gallon even though there is no such thing. I cannot clean what isn't there to be cleaned, but many a search is fruitless because the object searched for does not exist.

Again, if Matthew employs a wonderfully accurate typist we can sensibly ask who this wonderfully accurate typist is. But if

    (16) Matthew is hunting for a wonderfully accurate typist,

we cannot sensibly ask this: there may indeed by many typists whose accuracy is wonderful even to Matthew, without there being an answer to the question 'Who is the wonderfully accurate typist Matthew is hunting for?'. What I need and what I seek may not exist, but even if they do exist they seem to differ from the things I clean or the persons I employ in being unspecifiable and non-particular. There is no particular typist whom Matthew is hunting for; anyone with the wonderful accuracy required will do. And John's need of a car which does a hundred miles to the gallon will be satisfied by any old—or new—car, provided one with such absurdly low petrol consumption can be found.

Moreover if

    (17) Simon thinks that the typist Matthew employed last year is wonderfully accurate

is true, it does not follow that

    (18) Simon thinks that the typist John employed three years ago is wonderfully accurate,

even if the typist Matthew employed last year *is* the typist John employed three years ago. Let us assume, then, that Simon thinks what (17) says he does, but does not think what (18) says he does. We cannot suppose that Simon both thinks of a person that she is wonderfully accurate and does not think this of the same person. So it seems to be the case that what Simon thinks this of and what he does not think this of are different, that *qua* object of Simon's thought the typist Matthew employed last year is different from the typist John employed three years ago.

Objects of certain verbs such as 'need', 'search for', 'think so-and-so of' seem, then, to be quite different from objects of verbs such as 'clean' and 'employ'. They have been called 'intentional objects'. It has been held that intentional objects differ from ordinary objects by being different objects if described in one way from what they are if described in another, by being in some way non-particular or unspecific, and, most notoriously, by being capable of not existing. Since to say that such objects do not exist, if understood straightforwardly, would be to say that there are no such objects, it seems to become necessary to say that they have a peculiar sort of existence. Brentano followed the scholastics in using the phrase 'intentional inexistence' to describe the off-colour, low-key existence such objects might be thought to have.[3] If the attempt to distinguish a 'substitutional' from an 'objectual' notion of existence failed, perhaps this attempt to distinguish 'intentional inexistence' from existence of a more ordinary kind will fare better. Again, in arguing that existence is not a first-level concept, a concept under which objects fall, I imply that we have no need of such a concept. If, however, some objects do not exist (but possess only 'intentional inexistence') we shall have to have some way of distinguishing them from those which do. And how can this be done without the help of a first-level predicable '— exist' which can be truly predicated of some objects but not of others? This raises again the possibility of two senses of *existence* or *being*: one, which has just been sketched, in which those objects which have only intentional inexistence are said not to exist, and one wider sense in which they and everything else are allowed to possess existence, or at least being.

In fairness to Brentano it should be added that he sought to dissociate himself from those philosophers who made a distinction between existence and being. In the appendix added to the Second Edition of *Psychology from an Empirical Standpoint* he wrote:

I do not wish to bring this discussion of mental reference to a close without having given a word of consideration to the view that there is a distinction between 'being' and 'existing'. According to this view both are to be taken in a very peculiar sense. Namely, a person might be led to say that if someone is mentally referring to an object, the object really always has being just as much as he does, even if it does not always exist as he does ... I confess that I am unable to make any sense of this distinction between

---

[3] Franz Brentano, *Psychology from an Empirical Standpoint*, Eng. tr., ed. Linda L. McAlister, 1973, pp. 88 ff.

being and existence.... It is impossible to make use of that distinction ... for mental existence generally is already quite well enough proved by our earlier reference to those cases in which an object of presentation is at the same time an object of our correct denial.[4]

Brentano is trying to have it both ways. The phrase he translates *'intentionale Inexistenz'* is in Aquinas often given as *'esse intentionale'*. It is the same as that 'objective existence' which Descartes distinguishes from 'formal existence' in the Third Meditation. All these ways of talking commit one to the view that whatever we think of must 'exist' in some sense, even if in some other sense it does not exist. As had already been said,[5] phrases like 'imaginary', 'intra-mental', 'existing only in the mind', are systematically misleading. The very word 'object' is misleading, even if it is insisted that it means no more than 'what I am thinking of'. How it misleads is what I now wish to explain.

3. *Distinctions of scope sufficient to explain these examples*

The notion of intentional inexistence is unnecessary, since we can say all that we need to say without being committed to non-existent objects. By the same token we do not need to distinguish between different senses of 'exist' or to regard *existence* as a species of the wider genus *being*. The way to avoid all this is fundamentally that used by Russell in his Theory of Descriptions, but its application to the problems that concern us here has been more thoroughly carried out by Prior in the second part of *Objects of Thought* than by anyone else. What follows is largely repetition of points made by Prior.

I have already made use in Chapter IV of Russell's distinction between primary and secondary occurrence. It can be used again to get clear about the structure of proposition (15). This could mean

(15′) For some x, for every y, both x is the same car as y if, and only if, it is necessary for us that y be a car owned by us and x doesn't use much petrol;

but more likely it will mean

(15″) It is necessary for us that, for some x, for every y, both x be the same car as y if, and only if, y be a car owned by us and x not use much petrol.

[4] Ibid., pp. 274 f.   [5] See above, Ch. II, § 6, and below Ch. X, § 9.

If what is meant is (15′) then the truth of the proposition does require, roughly speaking, that the car we are talking about exists; but not so if it is (15″) that is meant. The pattern is not quite the same as that in which Russell distinguished primary and secondary occurrence of $(\imath x)(\phi x)$ in $\sim\psi(\imath x)(\phi x)$. It is complicated because of the hidden complexity of the concept of *need*. When we need something, we need, strictly speaking, to own it, or drink it, or read it, or the like. That is to say, it is necessary for us that it be owned, or drunk, or read, or the like, by us. 'I need a glass of beer' can therefore be spelled out as meaning 'It is necessary for me that I drink a glass of beer' which is of the form δp,[6] i.e. it is formed by attaching a sentential operator to a sentence. If I substitute a variable for 'a glass of beer' I get an open sentence of the form $\delta\phi x$. It is possible to add a quantifier to an expression of this form at two places, to produce either something of the form $\Sigma x\delta\phi x$ or something of the form $\delta\Sigma x\phi x$; so ambiguity is possible even at this level. 'I need to drink something' could be interpreted as being of either of these forms. However, the sentence which occurs in my analysis of (15), minus the necessity operator, like that which occurs in Russell's analysis of $\sim\psi(\imath x)(\phi x)$, minus the negation operator, is of the form $\Sigma x\Pi y KEIxy\phi y\psi x$. This is very much more complicated, and, accordingly, it permits insertion of an operator symbolizable by δ at seven different places. This produces the following combinatorial possibilities of analysis: $\delta\Sigma x\Pi y KEIxy\phi y\psi x$, $\Sigma x\delta\Pi y KEIxy\phi y\psi x$, $\Sigma x\Pi y\delta KEIxy\phi y\psi x$, $\Sigma x\Pi y K\delta EIxy\phi y\psi x$, $\Sigma x\Pi y KE\delta Ixy\phi y\psi x$, $\Sigma x\Pi y KEIxy\delta\phi y\psi x$, and $\Sigma x\Pi y KEIxy\phi y\delta\psi x$. Of these Russell rightly sees only the first and the last as providing semantically possible analyses of, e.g. 'The King of France is not bald'. I have claimed that the only two plausible analyses of (15) are of the first and sixth forms respectively. My (15′) is of the sixth, my (15″) of the first of these forms. But although the details of the analysis of (15) are different from those of Russell's analysis of 'The King of France is not bald', we can still distinguish analysis (15′), which is like the analysis in which Russell says that the definite description has primary occurrence, from analysis (15″), which is like that in which it is said to have secondary occurrence. With (15′), as in the case

[6] See above, Ch. III, p. 48.

of primary occurrence, existence of an object satisfying the first conjunct is implied: with (15″), as in the case of secondary occurrence, it is not.

Similarly, in order to obtain the necessary analyses of (16), we must break up 'Matthew is hunting for —' into something like 'Matthew is trying to bring it about that he has engaged —'. 'Matthew is hunting for Miss Marjoribanks', therefore, can be paraphrased as 'Matthew is trying to bring it about that he has engaged Miss Marjoribanks'.[7] This is of the form δp. 'Matthew is hunting for someone' will be ambiguous: it will either be of the form $\delta \Sigma x \phi x$, or of the form $\Sigma x \delta \phi x$. Similarly (16) may mean

(16′) For some x, both Matthew is trying to bring it about that x is engaged by him and x is a wonderfully accurate typist;

but more likely it will mean

(16″) Matthew is trying to bring it about that, for some x, both x is engaged by him and x is a wonderfully accurate typist.

Again, (17) may mean

(17′) For some x, both x alone is a typist employed by Matthew last year and Simon thinks that x is wonderfully accurate;

or, equally likely, it may mean

(17″) Simon thinks that, for some x, both x alone is a typist employed by Matthew last year and x is wonderfully accurate.

And if the typist Matthew employed last year actually is the typist John employed three years ago, it follows from this and (17′) that Simon thinks that the typist John employed three years ago is wonderfully accurate (=(18)), provided this is taken to mean

(18′) For some x, both x alone is a typist John employed three years ago and Simon thinks that x is wonderfully accurate

(this is a derivable from the logical law $C\Pi x C \phi x \psi x C \Sigma x K \phi x \chi x \text{-} \Sigma y K \psi y \chi y$); but not if it is taken to mean

---

[7] Cf. what was said about the need to unpack propositions with intentional verbs in Ch. V, § 4. I am, for present purposes, ignoring the occurrence of the indirect reflexive pronoun 'he' in this sentence.

(18″) Simon thinks that, for some x, both x alone is a typist John employed three years ago and x is wonderfully accurate.

We cannot deduce (18″) from the conjunction of the identity statement and either (17′) or (17″), nor can we deduce (18′) from the conjunction of the identity statement and (17″). All we can do is deduce (18′) from the conjunction of the identity statement and (17′).

Once these distinction have been made the claims made about intentional objects are seen to be unwarranted, and simultaneously one can see why philosophers have thought it necessary to make them. If (15) is understood as meaning the same as (15′), it does seem to be about a particular object. It will be true in this case only if there is just one car, George's car let us say, which we need to have. In a sense explained by Prior,[8] (15), thus interpreted, is 'indirectly about' George's car, which is of course a perfectly normal object and not in the least 'intentionally inexistent'. This sense of 'indirectly about' can be indicated precisely: a proposition p is indirectly about an object a if p is of the form $\Sigma x \Pi y KEIxy\phi y\psi x$ and a corresponding proposition of the form $\Pi y KEIay\phi y\psi a$ is true. It is the truth of $\Pi y KEIay\phi y\psi a$ in that case which makes it true that p: a's being the only ϕ'er and ψ'ing is what verifies p. So, in the case I have imagined, George's car's being the car we need and not using much petrol is what makes (15), understood as (15′), true. And if (15), thus understood, is true, it will have to be indirectly about something, some object, some perfectly ordinary object like George's car. But if (15) is understood as meaning the same as (15″), and is true, there is no existential proposition that has to be true, and so there does not have to be any proposition about (directly about) an ordinary object to make such an existential proposition true. Proposition (15″) is not an existential proposition: it does not say that there *is* such-and-such a thing, but that it is necessary for us that there be such-and-such a thing. It is not a quantifier, but a modal operator, which has widest scope in (15″). So (15″) is not even indirectly about any ordinary object like George's car (other than ourselves, for whom the possession of a car is necessary). The mistake made by the proponents of intentional inexistence

[8] *Objects of Thought*, p. 160.

is to conclude from this that what (15″) is about is an extraordinary object, an object that need not exist. They are perhaps victims of double vision brought on by the ambiguity of (15). Understanding (15) as (15′) they saw that there had to be some object for it to be indirectly about; understanding it as (15″) they saw that no such object need exist; conflating the two in a Hegelian synthesis they thought that there had to be such an object, but one which need not exist. What it had to do was something less than exist—*inexist*, perhaps, or *be*.

Just as (15), if understood as equivalent to (15′), seems to be about a particular car, so (16), if understood as equivalent to (16′), seems to be about a particular typist. It will only be true, if so understood, if there is just one typist, Miss Marjoribanks, let us say, for whom Matthew is hunting. (Perhaps he engaged her for a period six years ago, but has since lost her telephone number and is searching for it in old diaries and address books.) In Prior's sense, (16′) will be 'indirectly about' Miss Marjoribanks, who is of course a particular person with idiosyncrasies like the rest of us, who weighs exactly nine stone and wears gold-rimmed spectacles and owns a Pekinese. There is nothing non-particular or unspecific about Miss Marjoribanks, as there would be if she were an 'intentional object' of the kind described. But, when (16) is understood as meaning the same as (16″), it cannot, even if true, be verified simply by Miss Majoribanks or any fact whatsoever about Miss Marjoribanks, even the fact that Miss Marjoribanks is engaged by Matthew and is a wonderfully accurate typist. For (16″), unlike (16′), does not say that there *is* someone fitting a certain description, but that Matthew is trying to bring it about that there *be* someone fitting a certain description; and someone's actually fitting that description cannot make it true, but might even make it false, that Matthew is doing any such thing. (Can one try to bring about something which is already the case? Certainly not if one knows that it is; and Matthew presumably knows whom he has engaged.) So (16), understood as (16″), is not even indirectly about any particular typist, and so not about a typist who weighs exactly nine stone or anything else, nor about a typist who wears spectacles, nor about a typist who doesn't, nor . . ., etc. But it would be wrong to conclude from this that what (16), understood as (16″), is about is a typist who neither does nor does not wear spectacles, who is of no particular weight rather than any other, who is in fact entirely unspecific and non-particular. That people have thought so is again due to the ambiguity of (16). Seeing (16) as equivalent to (16′) the Friends of Intentional Objects have insisted that if Matthew is hunting for a typist there must be some object of his hunting. Seeing (16) as equivalent to (16″) they recognize that no particular typist, like Miss Marjoribanks with all her idiosyncrasies, could be such an object. With this unfocussed vision an unhappy combination of the two imposes itself on their minds, and they postulate an object lacking full determination, something akin to the triangle which so upset poor Berkeley, being neither scalene nor isosceles nor equilateral.

The application of the same argument to (17) and (18) is obvious. Interpreted as equivalent to (17′) and (18′), each is indirectly about a particular typist, and given that the typist employed by Matthew last year was the same as the typist employed by John three years ago they are both indirectly about the same typist. Let us call her Miss Sherborne. Miss Sherborne is an ordinary referent of a name, incapable of having contradictory predicables truly predicated of her viz. '— is thought by Simon to be wonderfully accurate' and '— is not thought by Simon to be wonderfully accurate'. She is not to be identified with what would normally be the sense rather than the referent of a name, as Frege thought,[9] nor with an individual concept, as Carnap and Church thought,[10] not yet with an intentional object. If, however, (17) and (18) are understood as meaning the same as (17″) and (18″), there is no typist, or object of any sort, that they are even indirectly about. Miss Sherborne may well have been employed by Matthew last year and by John three years ago and be thought by Simon to be a wonderfully accurate typist, but none of this will verify (17″) or (18″). These can be verified only by a fact about Simon. When (17) and (18) are understood in this way, the expressions 'the typist Matthew employed last year' and 'the typist John employed last year' are no more designations of some typist than the expression 'the number which is its square' is the

---

[9] See 'On Sense and Reference', *Philosophical Writings of Gottlob Frege*, edd. Geach and Black, 1952, p. 59.

[10] See Quine, *From a Logical Point of View*, pp. 152-4.

designation of a number in the proposition 'Every positive number except one is less than the number which is its square'. Here, however, we are not tempted to invent something for the expression to designate, because the proposition in question is unambiguous. Not so (17) and (18); and in their case, as in that of (15) and (16), it is the fact that the definite description can have either primary or secondary occurrence which has led philosophers to posit objects-which-are-not-objects in the attempt to do justice to the different possibilities they are dimly aware of, but fail clearly to distinguish.

4. *Proper names occurring in intentional contexts similarly explained*

The point I wanted to make with examples (17) and (18) essentially concerned identity. I needed to establish in what sense of (17), and in what sense of (18), (18) was derivable from (17) with the help of the identity statement 'The typist Matthew employed last year was the same as the typist John employed three years ago'. Two definite descriptions occurred in this identity statement, one of which occurred also in (17), and one also in (18). Following Russellian considerations, I hold, as indicated earlier,[11] that a statement of identity must always contain explicitly or implicitly at least one definite description. I cannot, therefore, use as a premiss a supposed proposition like 'Abyssinia is the same (country) as Ethiopia', where both names are assumed to be being used as proper names in the proposition. But, given the fact that one and the same country is called both 'Abyssinia' and 'Ethiopia',

(19) Geoffrey believes that Abyssinia is a Christian country

may seem to some people, if not to all, to entail

(20) Geoffrey believes that Ethiopia is a Christian country. Quine at one time[12] was among the people to whom (20) did not seem to be entailed in this way. Later[13] he joined the ranks of those who thought it both was and was not thus entailed, depending on how (19) and (20) were understood. The entailment holds good if, in Quine's terminology, the context

[11] See above Ch. I, p. 12; cf. Ch. XI below, pp. 287 f.
[12] When he wrote 'Reference and Modality': *From a Logical Point of View*, pp. 141 ff.
[13] When he wrote *Word and Object*: see p. 145.

'Geoffrey believes that —' is referentially transparent; not, if it is referentially opaque. To say that a context like 'Geoffrey believes that —' is referentially transparent is to say that a singular term occurring in a sentence embedded in that context can be exchanged for another having the same reference without change of truth-value. Proper names are included in the class of singular terms. What we had in the case of (17) and (18) was also a case of one singular term being exchanged for another, but in this case the singular terms involved were not proper names but definite descriptions. Definite descriptions can have either primary or secondary occurrence in a proposition, in a way that proper names cannot.[14] The reason for this is that definite descriptions are a sort of second-level predicable.[15] This comes out in (17') and (17''). Both have as a component the second-level predicable, 'for some x, both x alone is a typist employed by Matthew last year and — x'. They differ, however, in respect of the first-level predicable which the second-level predicable is 'wrapped around'.[16] In (17') this first-level predicable is 'Simon thinks that — is wonderfully accurate': in (17'') it is simply '— is wonderfully accurate'. The difference between (17') and (17'') and (18') and (18''), respectively, is a difference in the scopes of the second-level predicable and the sentential operator 'Simon thinks that —'. But in (19) and (20) there is, apparently, no second-level predicable, only the sentential operator 'Geoffrey believes that —'. There is no room for scope ambiguity. We have only the first-level predicable '— is a Christian country', which is wrapped around the proper names 'Abyssinia' and 'Ethiopia', and the sentential operator 'Geoffrey believes that —', which is wrapped round the propositions thus obtained. Both (19) and (20) are of the form symbolized by Prior as $\delta\phi N$,[17] and, as Prior maintains, where the expression subsituted for N is a proper name, $(\delta\phi)N$ is indistinguishable from $\delta(\phi N)$. The predicable '— is a Christian country' cannot in (19) and (20) be wrapped round anything but 'Abyssinia' or 'Ethiopia', and the sentential

---

[14] In Ch. IV I introduced an extended sense of 'primary' and 'secondary' occurrence in which this does apply to proper names, but it is only when the apparently embedded proposition is existential that this extended sense has application.

[15] See above, Ch. VI, § 2.

[16] See above, Ch. III, § 7, for an explanation of the phrase 'wrapped around'.

[17] *Objects of Thought*, p. 150; see above, Ch. III, pp. 48 ff.

operator 'Geoffrey believes that —' cannot be wrapped round anything but the propositions thus obtained. The difference between the two ways in which (17) and (18) could be understood, which were labelled by Quine 'referentially transparent' and 'referentially opaque', respectively, turned on differences of scope as brought out in (17′) and (18′), on the one hand, and (17″) and (18″), on the other. Because the definite descriptions, and thus the existential quantifier, had widest scope in (17′) and (18′), these were existential propositions. As such they were 'indirectly about' a particular typist—we agreed to call her Miss Sherborne. Given that Miss Sherborne and no one else was employed by John three years ago as well as by Matthew last year, (18′) was deducible from (17′). But neither (17″) nor (18″) was indirectly about anything, since they were not existential propositions, but propositions about what Simon thought. So no facts about Miss Sherborne could permit us to infer (18″) from (17″). But (19) and (20) are, not merely indirectly, but directly, about Abyssinia, otherwise known as Ethiopia. There seems no obstacle to our inferring (20) from (19), or vice versa. (The most that we might feel as a scruple is that (19) cannot entail (20), since (19) and (20) are in fact the same proposition, and the entailment relation is, arguably, irreflexive.) So what reason is there for calling 'Geoffrey believes that —' in (19) and (20) referentially opaque?

Quine once believed that sentences like (19) and (20) always involve referential opacity, and he has always believed that they sometimes involve referential opacity. Indeed it is not difficult for anyone to get the feeling that there is some sense of (20) in which it is not derivable from (19), despite the fact that Ethiopia and Abyssinia are identical. At least it does not follow from that fact, together with (19), that Geoffrey believes that the country called 'Ethiopia' is a Christian country —not if 'the country called "Ethiopia"' has secondary occurrence in 'Geoffrey believes that the country called "Ethiopia" is a Christian country'.[18] It seems then that sentences like (19) and (20) can be supposed to involve referential opacity only if one of them is taken as implying something of the form

---

[18] Of course, given (19) and the fact that Abyssinia is called 'Ethiopia', it follows that there is a country called 'Ethiopia' which Geoffrey believes to be a Christian country. See below, Ch. XI, pp. 287 f., for a related discussion of identity propositions.

$\delta\phi N$, where N is not a proper name, but a description of something as the thing called by a certain proper name. Definite descriptions require the existential quantifier for their explication. So we can say once again that propositions like (19) and (20) seem on occasion not to be about ordinary objects which obey Leibniz's Law, only because in understanding them we suppose them, like (17) and (18), covertly to involve existential quantifications. In the case we have imagined we do not interpret (20) as saying something about Ethiopia, i.e. Abyssinia, namely, that Geoffrey believes it to be a Christian country. Rather, we interpret it as saying something only about Geoffrey, namely, that he believes there is a country called 'Ethiopia' which is a Christian country. And this may well be false of Geoffrey, even if (19) is true. We need not therefore suppose that (20) is true of something other than Ethiopia, something which it is not legitimate to refer to by some other name that Ethiopia may have, because it is not an ordinary but an *intentional* object. If (20) is understood in a sense that involves referential opacity, it is not true of, i.e. about, directly or indirectly, any object other than Geoffrey; and so it is not about any 'intentional' object either. The case is the same as that of (17) and (18), and much the same as that of (15) and (16). An ambiguity involving scope has been overlooked or misconstrued; and as a result a monstrous object, called 'intentional', has been postulated, with incompatible properties designed to explain both the features the sentences have on one interpretation and the features they have on the other. What we have in fact in each case is not one proposition requiring for its interpretation the incoherent notion of an intentional object. We have, rather, one string of words capable of bearing now one sense, now another, and, according to the sense, requiring or not requiring a perfectly ordinary object to be, indirectly or directly, the object about which something is said.

5. *'Quasi-relations' or 'one-sided relations' an illusion*

If (20) is understood as being directly about Ethiopia, since it is in any case directly about Geoffrey, it posits a relation between Ethiopia and Geoffrey: Ethiopia is a country believed to be Christian by Geoffrey. This has been denied. J. N. Findlay has described Brentano as holding that intentionality 'is a relational property which is one-sided, which does not involve the being of a corresponding relation or related term'.[19] The term 'one-sided' does not occur in the passage from Brentano which Findlay cites here. Brentano says rather:

> In other relations both terms—both the fundament and the terminus—are real. . . . It is entirely different with mental reference. If someone thinks of something, the one who is thinking must certainly exist, but the object of his thinking need not exist at all. In fact, if he is denying something, the existence of the object is precisely what is excluded whenever his denial is correct. So the only thing which is required by mental reference is the person thinking. The terminus of the so-called relation does not need to exist in reality at all. For this reason, one could doubt whether we really are dealing with something relational here, and not, rather, with something somewhat similar to something relational in a certain respect, which might, therefore, be better called 'quasi-relational' (*etwas 'Relativisches'*).[20]

But although Findlay's term, 'one-sided', does not correspond exactly to anything in Brentano's text, it does fit the picture Brentano gives of some relations or quasi-relations. And it is a picture which has had a long and distinguished history. Its origins are in Aristotle. Aquinas uses it because it seems to him to provide a solution to certain problems that arise in talking about God. God, he holds, is absolutely simple. The distinction between the various predicables that truly apply to God, '— is wise', '— is powerful', '— is just', for example, is not mirrored by any corresponding distinction between attributes existing in God: what is referred to as 'God's wisdom' is the very same thing as what is referred to as 'God's power', and this thing is God himself. But, although '— created the world' is another predicable which truly applies to God, it is hardly possible that 'God's having created the world', like 'God's wisdom', is a phrase which refers only to God himself. It is obvious to the theist, if not to the pantheist, that the phrase refers as well to something other than God. Again, all that exists in God is necessary and eternal. His having created the world, however, is contingent, and since it has not always been true that there is something which God created, it cannot be eternal. The solution that Aquinas saw to these problems was to deny that there existed in God anything real corresponding to his having created

---

[19] J. N. Findlay, *Values and Intentions*, 1961, p. 35.
[20] Brentano, *Psychology from an Empirical Standpoint*, pp. 271 f.

the world, while affirming that there does exist in creatures something real corresponding to God's having created them. The relation of creature to creator, *qua* creator, and indeed every relation between a creature and its creator, was held to be a one-sided relation of the sort Findlay has in mind.

Aquinas indeed turned to what would now be called 'intentionality' to illustrate his theological claim. He drew on Aristotle's discussion of the relations between the measure and the thing measured, the knower and the thing known and the thinker and the thing thought.[21] Aristotle maintains that the second item in each of these pairs is said to be relative because something else is relative to it. So these cases are unlike the cases of the half and the double and the heater and the heated, which are relative because they are said to be what they are *of* something else. I have examined these claims, and the reasons Aristotle and Aquinas give for them, elsewhere,[22] and I shall not go into detail here. Suffice it to say that the only examples of the one-sided relationship which stand up to examination are those which involve intentionality—those, that is, that involve something thought of and its relation to a thinker.

Professor Geach used an illuminating example of a supposedly one-sided relation to assist our understanding of the Thomist doctrine on this matter.[23] Suppose that a girl called Edith envies a boy called Herbert. There is plausibility in the claim that Edith's envy of Herbert corresponds to something real in Edith, whilst Herbert's being envied by Edith does not so correspond to anything in Herbert. The reason may be thought to be that Herbert possibly knows nothing of Edith's envy, or if he does is completely unaffected by it.[24] He may even know nothing of Edith herself. But this will not do; for a man may be taller than another man, taller than Professor Findlay, for example, without knowing it and without being affected by it, and even without knowing of Professor Findlay's existence. But, according to Aquinas at least, a man's being

---

[21] *Metaphysics*, 1021^a26-$^b3$, 1056^b32-1057^a17 seem the main passages. *Categories*, 7^b15-8^a12 is less relevant than might have been expected.

[22] In 'Is God Really Related to his Creatures?—A Reply to Professor Geach', *Sophia*, 8, No. 3, October 1969.

[23] In the article to which my own was a reply, 'God's Relation to the World', *Sophia*, 8, No. 2, July 1969.

[24] Aquinas mentions this sort of thing as a reason in his commentary on the *Metaphysics* (No. 1027 in the Cathala edition, 1964).

taller than another man, *qua* relation of quantity, is a relation which really exists in him.[25] It could hardly be a one-sided relation, in any case. If my being taller than Professor Findlay corresponds to nothing real in me, Professor Findlay's being shorter than I am will hardly correspond to something real in him. More promising, and more in line with what Brentano and Findlay have said, is the explanation that in order to be the object of Edith's envy Herbert needs to be considered under some descriptions rather than others; and, most significantly, does not need actually to exist.

These considerations, however, might lead us to doubt, not merely whether Herbert is really related to Edith, but whether Edith herself is really related to him. Is it clear that what we have here is in fact a relation at all, even a 'one-sided' one? Could it be that what Edith's envy amounts to is that she thinks there is a person answering to such-and-such a description, and when she thinks of this she has such-and-such feelings. Herbert comes into it only as in fact answering to the descriptions in question; but this is a mere optional extra. Edith's envy could remain even if Herbert failed to answer to them, and even if no one answered to them.

Most philosophers would agree that when intentionality is involved in a proposition that proposition is in some way concerned with what someone thinks. To describe someone as envying another person is to ascribe some thought or other to the person who is envious: what that thought is, is not always clear. If Edith envies Herbert she must think of him in some way. Let us suppose that she thinks he is clever. As before in the case of (20), the point about intentionality can be presented in terms of alternatives between which we have to choose. On one way of understanding (20), we take it to be saying something about Ethiopia, namely, that Geoffrey believes it is a Christian country. Similarly we can understand

(21) Edith believes that Herbert is clever

as saying something about Herbert, namely, that he is believed by Edith to be clever. There could be no such fact about Herbert if there were no such person as Herbert for it to be about. Moreover, any definite description which truly applies to Herbert can be substituted *salva veritate* in (21) for the

[25] *Summa Theologiae*, Ia, q. 13, a.7.

name 'Herbert', provided such definite description has primary occurrence, Even if Edith is unaware that Herbert failed his O-level examinations, and would not think him clever if she knew, the sentence 'Edith thinks that the boy who failed his O-level examinations is clever' can still express a true proposition. In this case 'Edith thinks that x is clever' is no more an intentional construction than 'Edith is x's cousin'. If 'Herbert' is substituted for x in either case we have a proposition which quite straightforwardly asserts a relation between Edith and Herbert.

If we interpret (21) in this way as asserting a relation between Herbert and Edith, we attribute to Edith what is called 'a *de re* belief'. It is important to note that such an attribution is not made true entirely by the facts about Edith's mental state. For the truth of (21), understood thus, something has to be true of Herbert as well as of Edith. Herbert has to be connected in an appropriate way to Edith for us to be able to say that she has a belief about him. What this way is is much discussed. It may be a causal connection. It may be a matter of Herbert's corresponding with a certain description used of him by Edith. It may be some further sort of connection. This is not our present concern. The point which we are making is simply that when (21) is understood as attributing a *de re* belief to Edith, it is making a claim that goes beyond Edith, which could be discovered to be false in virtue of facts which have no reference to Edith's mental state.

If, on the other hand, we choose the alternative way of understanding (21), it would be possible that Edith should think that Herbert is clever even though there were no such person as Herbert; but it would not be possible for them to be cousins. What (21) means on this interpretation is that Edith thinks that there is someone who is called 'Herbert' and answers to one or two other descriptions, and who is clever. On this view (21) does not express a relational proposition, or even '*etwas Relativisches*'.[26] The first interpretation of (21) requires us to say that it relates Herbert to Edith just as much as it relates Edith to Herbert; the second interpretation allows us to deny that it relates Herbert to Edith, but only at the cost of denying that it relates Edith to Herbert or to anything at all. This distinction of interpretations shows us how Aquinas and others

[26] See above, p. 231.

were mistaken in believing that the phenomena of intentionality provided an analogy for the one-sided relation they wished to posit as existing between God and the world. But it also enables us to see how their mistake arose. If we look at (21) in the first way, it seems to say that Edith is related in the appropriate manner to Herbert. Looked at in the second way, it seems to be independent of Herbert, so that he is not thereby related to Edith. Superimposing the two views, one could be led to say that, while Edith is related to Herbert, Herbert is not related to her. But the two ways of looking at (21) are in fact incompatible, and superimposing the one view on the other can produce nothing but a blurred picture. Aquinas may have been right in saying that God was not really related to the world, but in that case he ought not to have said that the world was really related to God. One-sided relations are the product of an illusion.

6. *Intentionality and existence*

Two points emerge from this discussion of intentionality. One is that a possible reason for regarding existence as a property of objects is seen to fail. In order to make sense of the various ways in which sentences like (15) to (21) are used we do not, as some philosophers have thought, need to posit a sense of 'exist' in which some objects do and some do not exist. We have not, so to speak, 'got' Herbert *qua* object of Edith's envy, in such a way that it is an open question whether Herbert *exists*. If it is an open question whether there is such a person as Herbert, this can only be because (21) is interpreted as meaning 'Edith thinks that there is some person who is called "Herbert" and answers to such-and-such descriptions, and who is clever', and if this is all that is involved in Edith's envying Herbert, we have not 'got' Herbert *qua* object of Edith's envy, or *qua* anything else. Since there are not intentional objects of whom '— does not exist' can truly be predicated, we have one less reason for thinking that '— exist' can meaningfully be predicated of any object at all. Those who claim to have found a meaning for '— exist' as a first-level predicable have yet to make out their case.

As a second-level predicable, on the other hand, '— exist' or 'there is —' or 'something —' is invaluable for understanding the phenomena of intentionality. This is the second point to emerge from our discussion of the topic. The solution to all the problems we have discussed lay in determining, for each of the sentences whose sense was in doubt, what was the scope of the existential quantifier which was buried in their deep grammar. Ambiguities of scope, as has been argued,[27] cannot arise when the components of a proposition are a name, a first-level predicable, and a sentential operator. So long as (20) and (21) are thought of as built up out of proper names ('Ethiopia' and 'Herbert'), round which are wrapped first-level predicables ('— is a Christian country, and '— is clever') to produce complete propositions, round which are wrapped sentential operators ('Geoffrey believes that —' and 'Edith thinks that —')— so long as they are thought of in this way, there is nothing to provide leverage for the notion of an intentional object. Only when 'Ethiopia' is felt to be elliptical for 'a country called "Ethiopia"' and 'Herbert' to be elliptical for 'a person called "Herbert"' do we feel the need to talk about intentionality. And at this point we need the concept of existential quantification to help us understand what is going on. If we understand (20) and (21) in this way, we understand them as being of the form $\delta \Sigma x K \phi x \psi x$; and to understand the role of Σx — x — x in this formula is to understand the role '— exist' plays as a second-level predicate. Without Frege's discovery of the role such expressions play, the way in which the sentences discussed in this chapter work could never have been established. Ignorance of these points was precisely what engendered the confused cluster of notions which surround the notion of 'intentional inexistence'.

7. *Referential opacity and quantification*

Quine first introduced the notion of referential opacity with the help of examples similar to (17) and (18) above.[28] Such examples seem to illustrate 'failure of substitutivity'; failure, that is, of certain propositions to conform to the rule that if *a* and *b* designate the same thing, *b* may be substituted for *a* in any proposition without changing the truth value of the proposition. But substitutions for *a* and *b*,—'the typist Matthew

[27] See above, § 4, and Ch. III, § 3.
[28] Quine, 'Reference and Modality', *From a Logical Point of View*, pp. 141 ff.

employed last year' and 'the typist John employed three years ago', for instance—are what Quine calls 'singular terms'; and it is one of his principal doctrines that such terms have to be eliminated from a logically perspicuous language. My own examples of singular terms in (17) and (18) were overtly definite descriptions. The technique I adopted for explaining the phenomena of intentionality was to give Russellian analyses of propositions containing such definite descriptions, and to trace the misconceptions about intentionality to failure to observe Russell's distinction between primary and secondary occurrence. Quine too adopts a Russellian analysis of such propositions, and goes even further than Russell did in interpreting *all* proper names as 'truncated definite descriptions'.[29] Quine would treat 'Ethiopia' as a definite description, not only, as we have done, in intentional contexts like (20), but in contexts like 'Ethiopia is a Christian country' which do not even appear to make difficulties for the law of the substitutivity of identicals. Quine would replace 'Ethiopia is a Christian country' with 'Something Ethiopizes and is a Christian country'.[30] Why then does Quine still see contexts like (17), (18), (19), and (20) as problematic?

This point is well taken by Quine, and he believes that the notion of referential opacity can be explicated in terms only of quantification, without appeal to singular terms. His first attempt to do this makes use of an example we have already glanced at in section 1 of the last chapter. But

(22) For some x, x was so called because of his size

clearly fails, in default of some context capable of eking out its sense, to constitute a proposition. It fails simply because the backward-referring expression 'so called' lacks anything to refer to. But its failure does not tell us anything about 'objectual' quantification. It does not indicate a drawback possessed by the objectual quantifier which the substitutional quantifier might lack. It tells us, rather, that neither the proposition 'Giorgione was so called because of his size' nor any other proposition can be of the logical form 'x was so called because of his size': it is in fact of the logical form 'x was called N because of his size', with 'Giorgione' doing double duty as a

---

[29] Cf. Russell, *Logic and Knowledge*, p. 243.
[30] See above, Ch. VI, p. 163, n. 17.

substitute for both x and N. We cannot, therefore, regard (22) as true because some proper name substituted for x in 'x was so called because of his size' yields a true proposition, any more than we can regard it as true because '— was so called because of his size' is true of some object. The substitutional version of the truth conditions of quantification, (S), is no more able to legitimize (22) than the objectual version, (O). Only if we think of what is involved in substituting a proper name for x in some open sentence as a purely mechanical procedure, a matter merely of using the name to fill a physical gap produced by removing the variable from the open sentence, shall we be able to make (S) determine the truth value of (22) as true. A mechanical interpretation of this sort would, indeed, allow us to assign the value 'true' to another of Quine's examples,

(23)   For some x, 'x' contains six letters.

'"Cicero" contains six letters' is produced by filling the gap left by removing x from '"x" contains six letters' with a proper name. But the proper name thus substituted is not being used in this context as a proper name. A word which is not a proper name, like 'sneeze', could fill the gap in just the same way. 'Cicero' is being used here, not as a proper name, but as a word, considered orthographically. The variable x, on this mechanical interpretation, is in no way performing its function as a formal concept, as expressing a syntactic category.[31] If (22) and (23) are interpreted in this way, they are equivalent to the metalinguistic propositions,

(22')   Some word can be used to fill the gap in '— was so called because of his size' to produce a true proposition

and,

(23')   Some word can be used to fill the gap in '"—" contains six letters' to produce a true proposition.

But there is nothing mysterious about the use of quantification in these propositions. Quine could recognize it cheerfully as a use of objectual quantification—restricted, perhaps, but only in a way which he could remove by changing 'Some word can be used —' in each case to 'For some x, x is a word and x can be used —'.

[31] See above, Ch. VI, pp. 158 ff.; cf. Wittgenstein, *Tractatus*, 4.127–4.1272.

The examples Quine gives of quantification into referentially opaque contexts involving propositional attitudes rest heavily on the supposed difficulties of substituting singular terms. Where the singular terms in question are definite descriptions,[32] I believe that the analysis I gave in dealing with (17) and (18) above will remove all difficulties. Where the singular terms involved are proper names, the treatment needed is a little more complicated. Speaking of '$(\exists x)$(Philip is unaware that x denounced Catiline)', Quine says:

'What is this object, that denounced Catiline without Philip's having become aware of the fact? Tully, that is, Cicero? But to suppose this would conflict with the fact that (11) is false.'[33]

Quine's '(11)' is 'Philip is unaware that Cicero denounced Catiline'. But Quine later became aware that contexts like 'is unaware that' have a transparent as well as an opaque sense.[34] If it is understood transparently in these examples, and 'Philip is unaware that Cicero denounced Catiline' is false, so is 'Philip is unaware that Tully denounced Catiline'. So there can be no inference from it to '$(\exists x)$(Philip is unaware that x denounced Catiline)'. To understand 'Philip is unaware that Tully denounced Catiline' opaquely, as is necessary if it is to be accounted true in the circumstances Quine envisages, is in my view to regard it as equivalent to 'Philip is unaware that someone called "Tully" denounced Catiline'. This has already been argued in connection with my examples (19) and (20). But if 'Philip is unaware that Tully denounced Catiline' means 'Philip is unaware that $(\exists x)(x$ was called "Tully" and x denounced Catiline)' it does not imply '$(\exists x)$(Philip is unaware that x denounced Catiline)' at all. So this last proposition is not one that is likely to cause us trouble. If 'is unaware that' is understood transparently, the proposition which entails it just is not true; if it is understood opaquely the relevant proposition is true, but does not entail it. Quine's problem does not arise.

Quine admits[35] that his exposition of the difficulties of quantifying into an opaque context makes crucial use of the singular terms 'Tully' and 'Cicero', '9' and 'the number of the

---

[32] As in Quine's examples involving 'the man in the brown hat' and 'the man at the beach' in 'Quantifiers and Propositional Attitudes', *Reference and Modality*, ed. Linsky, 1971, p. 103. [33] Ibid., p. 24.
[34] Cf. ibid., p. 103, and *Word and Object*, § 30.
[35] *From a Logical Point of View*, p. 149.

planets', etc., which, in a canonical language, would be eliminated. He claims, however, that he can establish his point without this 'expository reversion'. But he attempts to do so only for the case of modal contexts, not for those involving propositional attitudes. He takes the example '$(\exists x)(x$ is necessarily greater than seven)'. This, he claims, is meaningless, because

necessary greaterness than 7 makes no sense as applied to a *number x*; necessity attaches only to the connection between '$x > 7$' and the particular method (32) ['$x=\sqrt{x}+\sqrt{x}+\sqrt{x}\neq\sqrt{x}$'], as opposed to (33) ['There are exactly x planets'], of specifying x.[36]

This is an appeal to the falsehood of essentialism. Not everyone is prepared to agree that essentialism is false. This is not the place to argue the point. And whatever consequences the falsehood of essentialism might have, if it were false, for quantification into modal contexts, it seems to have no consequences for quantification into contexts involving propositional attitudes. Quine has produced no argument, except for those which make use of singular terms, to show that such quantification is meaningless.

Our own arguments, however, are in a sense more radical than Quine's. They are designed to show, not that quantification into opaque contexts is meaningful, but that there are no such things as opaque contexts. This line of argument was originally put forward in Prior's essay 'Is the Concept of Referential Opacity Really Necessary?', and it undercuts Quine. Prior's claim is that the schema $CIxyC\phi x\phi y$, which may be taken as an expression of Leibniz's Law of the Indiscernibility of Identicals, has no violations which are not merely apparent. '"Cicero" contains six letters' and 'Giorgione was so called because of his size' are plainly not propositions formed by *using* the proper names 'Cicero' and 'Giorgione' and going on merely to predicate something of the persons thus named. They are not, therefore, substitution instances of ϕx. In the same way 'Philip is unaware that Tully denounced Catiline', in so far as it is not equivalent to 'Philip is unaware that Cicero denounced Catiline', is not the result of *using* the proper name 'Tully' to name someone, and going on to predicate of the person thus named that Philip is unaware that he denounced Catiline. It is

[36] Ibid.

not in this respect of the form ϕx, since 'Tully', on this interpretation of the proposition, which understands it as short for 'someone called "Tully"', is not used but mentioned. Propositions resembling this one, except that they have an explicit definite description in what Quine calls 'irreferential position', are still more obviously not of the form ϕx. What Quine regards as the transparent context is not, in this case, the context at all: the definite description is the context, and the distinction between 'transparent' and 'opaque' is more properly seen as the distinction between primary and secondary occurrence of the description. Here as elsewhere it is distinctions of scope which are necessary; and where these are clearly made, the concept of referential opacity turns out to be indeed not 'really necessary'. All this has been well argued by Prior and need not be repeated at greater length.

Just as the contrast between 'intentional inexistence' and real existence vanished as an illusion born out of confused awareness of scope distinctions, so the contrast between referentially transparent and referentially opaque contexts proves unnecessary if care is taken in distinguishing use from mention and primary from secondary occurrence. We are not forced by considerations of intentionality to distinguish between an austere and a generous sense of 'exist' or 'be'. Neither are we forced by considerations of referential opacity to distinguish two sorts of quantification: one 'objectual', which will not allow us to bind variables inside opaque contexts with a quantifier outside, the other 'substitutional', which is more permissive in such matters. If 'substitutional quantification' is a name for existential statements about what true propositions can be formed from the insertion of words in certain gaps in sentences, as in (22′) and (23′), its existence can be admitted. But it seems not to merit so much fuss. Once we have got rid of certain misapprehensions about fictional names, there will be nothing left to justify the excitement that has arisen about 'substitutionalism'. It is the task of the next chapter to destroy these misapprehensions.

X
Fictional Characters and Possible Worlds

1. *Substitutional quantification and fictional names*

One of the differences between objectual and substitutional quantification has been thought to lie in their relation to existential generalization. From 'Jane is married to a civil servant' I can cheerfully infer 'Someone is married to a civil servant' or 'For some x, x is married to a civil servant'. This is not disturbing, because 'For some x, x is married to a civil servant' is clearly true. Again 'Madame Giscard d'Estaing is a female President of France' entails 'For some x, x is a female President of France'. This last proposition is false, but this again is not disturbing, because the proposition of which it is an existential generalization is also false. But 'Pegasus is a winged horse' is apparently true, and yet it apparently entails 'For some x, x is a winged horse', which is apparently false. Which of these appearances is at odds with reality? The accepted answer is to say that 'Pegasus is a winged horse' is indeed true, but for the rest we must distinguish between the objectual and the substitutional interpretation of 'For some x, x is a winged horse'. If it is interpreted objectually it means that the predicate '— is a winged horse' is true of some object, and this is held to be false. Objectual quantification thus requires us to place restrictions on existential generalization, since the apparent entailment of 'For some x, x is a winged horse', objectually interpreted, by 'Pegasus is a winged horse' will turn out not to be justified. If, on the other hand, the existential proposition is interpreted substitutionally, it means that some proper name substituted for x in 'x is a winged horse' will yield a true proposition; and this, it is held, is true. There is no need in this case to place restrictions on existential generalization. The entailment is real, not merely apparent.

This is the conventional wisdom of the present day about the relation between a fictional or mythical name like 'Pegasus' and quantification. I have already mentioned, in Chapter VIII, section 5, some objections to this view. My task now is to examine more closely the connections between fictional characters and existence. In the course of doing so I shall show what is wrong with this further reason that has been given for distinguishing between a substitutional and an objectual interpretation of quantification. And I shall then consider ways in which philosophers have combined talk about existence with talk about possible worlds.

2. 'Most characters listed in the Classical Dictionary existed'

In the last chapter we looked at an alleged sense of 'exist' in which it is needed as a first-level predicable, i.e. as a possible predicate of objects, to pick out from the class of intentional objects those that possess not merely intentional inexistence but existence in the real world. Similarly philosophers have thought it necessary to employ a first-level concept of existence to distinguish real 'existents' from mere characters of fiction. Mr Powell exists, but Mr Polly does not. Pericles possessed existence in the real world, Perseus only in the world of mythology. G. E. Moore argued[1] that 'exist' was different from a predicable like 'growl' in that we could make sense of the sentence 'Most tame tigers growl', but not of the sentence 'Most tame tigers exist'. Strawson has countered with the argument[2] that we can make perfectly good sense of the sentence 'Most characters listed in the Classical Dictionary existed'. There are more entries in the Classical Dictionary informing us about characters like Pericles, who did exist, than there are about

[1] 'Is Existence a Predicate?', *Logic and Language* ed. A. G. N. Flew.
[2] 'Is Existence Never a Predicate?', *Freedom and Resentment*, p. 195. Jonathan Barnes, *The Ontological Argument*, p. 55, in effect repeats this argument of Strawson's (with acknowledgement). However, he includes in his list of recalcitrant examples, along with 'Very many of the heroes revered by the Greeks never existed' the proposition 'Only a few copies of the Shakespeare first folio exist'. *Nego paritatem*. 'Exist' in this last sentence can be replaced by 'There are': 'There are only a few copies of the first folio'. In Barnes's other examples and in Strawson's examples 'exist' cannot be thus replaced. Barnes has confused the locutions 'Only a few A's exist' and 'Only a few of the A's exist'. Only a proposition of the latter form would provide the sort of example his argument needs.

characters like Perseus, who didn't. In Chapters IV and V I discussed sentences like 'President Ford does not know that David Pears exists' and 'Arkle no longer exists' to which I attach a perfectly good sense, and in which prima facie 'exists' occurs as a first-level predicable. 'Most of the characters listed in the Classical Dictionary exist' belongs to the same class. In the cases already discussed I argued that appearances were misleading: the analysis of these propositions does not require that we find in them the employment of a first-level concept of existence. It remains to be seen whether Strawson's example can be defused in a similar manner.

3. *The reference of fictional names*

Philosophers who have concerned themselves with the problem of the existence of fictional or mythological characters have seen a connection between the notion of existence and the notion of reference. This will come as no surprise after what has been said of these notions in Chapter VI. Just as we want to say that Mr Powell exists but Mr Polly does not, so these philosophers have wanted to say that the name 'Mr Powell' has a reference while the name 'Mr Polly' does not. Are they entitled to this distinction? Can we not say that 'Mr Polly' refers to a middle-aged man of a nervous disposition who began some adventures by taking leave of his wife and walking off into the country, just as we say that 'Mr Powell' refers to a professor of Greek who took leave of scholarship to enter the army, and moving from there into politics became a controversial figure in the field of race relations? Use of 'Mr Powell' as a proper name commits us to existential statements, statements beginning 'There is' or 'There exists', where 'exists' is used harmlessly as a second-level predicate—'There exists a politician who was once a Conservative cabinet minister, and who is now an Ulster Unionist', for example. Use of 'Mr Polly' as a proper name commits us to existential statements like 'There was a nervous little man who once tried to commit arson and then got involved with the landlady of a riverside pub'. It has to be the case that some existential propositions like these are true, if propositions containing the corresponding proper names are true.[3] And it seems that we can discriminate between

[3] Cf. Barnes, *The Ontological Argument* p. 56: 'It seems that this inference

true and false propositions about Mr Polly. 'Mr Powell sits in the House of Commons' is true: 'Mr Powell sits in the House of Lords' is false. In the same way 'Mr Polly went on a bicycle round Surrey' is true, 'Mr Polly went on a flight in Concorde' is false. If we have true statements about Mr Powell and Mr Polly, there must be correspondingly true statements asserting the existence of the people referred to by the names 'Mr Powell' and 'Mr Polly'. These names accordingly have reference.

But are the statements about Mr Polly true? Are they not rather just sentences which occur in a novel by H. G. Wells? Or, perhaps, sentences which, if they expressed propositions, would express propositions entailed by other propositions which sentences that do occur in Wells's novel would express, if *they* expressed propositions? Such sentences have been held not to express anything which is either true or false. But this has usually been held for the very reason that expressions like 'Mr Polly', which occur in them, lack a reference. So to accept this would be to beg the question. Another view is that all, or most, of the propositions contained in works of fiction are false. (They cannot all be, because some novels, e.g. historical novels, contain singular propositions that are undoubtedly true, as that Charles I was beheaded in 1649; and all novels contain true general propositions, as 'It is a truth universally acknowledged that a single man in possession of a good fortune must be in want of a wife.') But if either of these positions, that fictional propositions lack truth-values, or that they are mostly false, is accepted, we shall be at a loss to explain the distinction we draw between 'Mr Polly went on a bicycle round Surrey' and 'Mr Polly went on a flight in Concorde'. Some have said that we are able to draw such distinctions because, when we say that it is true that Mr Polly went on a bicycle round Surrey, what we really mean to say is that H. G. Wells wrote in a book that someone called 'Mr Polly' went on a bicycle round Surrey. *That* is straightforwardly true, as it is straightforwardly false that H. G. Wells wrote in a book that someone called 'Mr Polly' went on a flight in Concorde. But not all such distinctions can be explained in this way. Many stories have no

(from Fa to $(\exists x)Fx$) will only be successful if the object designated by "*a*" *exists*: for if it does not, then the fact that it is an F will not guarantee that there *exists* an F.'

authors, or no known authors. It is true that the Prince's kiss wakened the Sleeping Beauty. It is false that the Sleeping Beauty died before the Prince succeeded in kissing her. But this distinction cannot be based on what is written in some particular book or what is enacted on some actual stage. If someone wrote in a book that the Sleeping Beauty died before the Prince reached her, we should say that he had got the story wrong. There *is* a story to be got right or wrong; and to say that is to say that we can discriminate between true and false statements about the Sleeping Beauty independently of what people write in books or perform in ballet.

Let us not face directly for the moment the question of what it is that we are doing when we discriminate between true and false propositions about, say, Mr Polly. The point to be emphasized first is that, granted we do say that certain propositions about Mr Polly are true, we have no right to deny that the expression 'Mr Polly' has reference or that there is such a person as Mr Polly. The same story in which we are told that Mr Polly went round Surrey on a bicycle may begin by telling us that *there was* a man who owned a small outfitter's shop in Fishbourne, who . . ., and who was called 'Mr Polly'. It is part of the story that *there is* such a man as Mr Polly and that the expression 'Mr Polly' has reference, just as much as it is part of the story that Mr Polly went round Surrey on a bicycle. We do not have to suppose that the expression 'there is' has a special meaning in the course of a fictional narrative, distinct from that which it has in factual discourse. If different senses of 'there is' were postulated in this way we should be hard put to account for what is going on in, say, historical novels, when historically accurate existential statements are set side by side with the author's inventions. For example, a historical novel about Evesham Abbey might contain the following passage: 'There was a small church dedicated to St. Lawrence in the Abbey grounds, used by pilgrims to Evesham. And there was an old monk, who had long been the Abbey's precentor, who was given charge of this church.' Does the first of these sentences, which states a historical fact, use 'there was' in a different sense from the second? We are not conscious of any equivocation in passing from the assertion of the small church's existence to that of the old monk. Would it not be as plausible to suggest that the word 'church' meant something different in the first sentence from what it meant in the second? Or do both of these uses of 'there was', since they are part of the story, differ from a similar use in a sentence identical with the first of our two sentences but occurring in a scholarly account of English monasteries in the fifteenth century? If the old monk is called 'Dan Thomas', and we are told in some later chapter of Dan Thomas's undue fondness for Malmsey wine, are we to suppose that the expression 'Evesham' has reference but the expression 'Dan Thomas' lacks reference? Can we say this and at the same time maintain that the proposition 'Dan Thomas laid by a cask of Malmsey for the celebration of Michaelmas' is true, whereas someone who claimed that it was sack he laid by would say something false, *qua* misremembering the novel?

If words had to acquire a new meaning each time we passed from an historical to a fictional context, we might be hard put to give an account of how we learned the fictional use. The intuitionists in mathematics may use a different logic from classical mathematicians, but we are not to suppose that the logic of Goldsmith is different from the logic of Gibbon. For 'there is' and 'exists', since what they express is expressible by the existential quantifier, rank as logical constants: and someone who claimed that in a certain context these expressions acquired a different meaning from their normal one would be asserting that a different logic was in force in that context. The logical constants, like *ta koina* of Plato's *Theaetetus*,[4] are supposed to be topic-neutral and to pervade all discourse. The language of fiction would be strangely segregated from the rest of our speech if a separate concept of existence were needed for it.

We need neither a separate concept of existence nor a separate concept of quantification In so far as 'Pegasus is a winged horse' is true, 'Something is a winged horse' is true, and 'For some x, x is a winged horse' is true. And this latter remains true even if it is interpreted, as the objectualists wish, as 'The predicate "— is a winged horse" is true of some object'. There is no need to introduce an alternative interpretation of quantification, as the substitutional interpretation purports to be, to

[4] *Theaetetus*, 184-5.

permit the entailment of the existential proposition from the singular one. What has to be investigated is what is meant by saying that 'Pegasus is a winged horse', or 'Mr Polly went on a bicycle round Surrey', is true. The answer to this will bring with it a proper understanding of quantification in this context. No special considerations about the logic of existence or the interpretation of the quantifiers are required.

4. *Fiction and pretending*

The true situation has been described accurately, if too concisely, by Michael Dummett.[5] All our words have meaning in virtue of conventions we adopt or follow for their use. If a word has more than one meaning there must be different conventions for its use which have to be followed in different contexts. If 'there is' did not have the same meaning in fiction which it has elsewhere—in historical narrative, for instance—some of the conventions which govern its use outside fiction would have to be suspended when we began to tell or hear stories. In fact, what happens when we enter the realm of storytelling is not that existing conventions are abandoned or curtailed in some way: rather, a new convention is superimposed on the existing ones. We use all the old words in the old ways, but what we are doing is subject to some extra constraint, is seen in a new context.

What is this new context? We need to be more precise, though precision is not easy in this area. Telling a story is like pretending: stories are pretend-histories. But, as Austin pointed out,[6] there are different sorts of pretence. Sometimes, when we pretend to do X, we are in fact doing X, sometimes not. Suppose we are children pretending to have a wedding breakfast. One of us pretends to be the bridegroom, another the bride— perhaps she puts a table-cloth over her head which she says is her wedding veil. We have an old loaf of bread which the 'bride' and 'bridegroom' cut, both hands on the same knife. We drink toasts to them in lemonade, which we pretend is champagne. In these circumstances, on the whole, what we pretend is the case is not the case. The 'bride' and 'bridegroom' pretend they are cutting a wedding cake, but they are

---

[5] *Frege: Philosophy of Language*, pp. 310 f.
[6] J. L. Austin, *Philosophical Papers*, 1970, pp. 253 ff.

not cutting a wedding cake. Everyone pretends he is drinking champagne, but in fact no one is drinking champagne.

Suppose now that I am a wealthy eccentric who likes to pretend he is a priest. I build a chapel in my house with a properly vested altar and the correct ornaments. I buy altar breads and wine from a firm which supplies Westminster Cathedral. I have a full set of vestments and retain the services of a small boy, whom I train to act as server. I then pretend to say Mass. The chance visitor who sees the ceremony will detect nothing to suggest that I am not a priest, expertly trained in the rubrics. Everything that a properly ordained priest does and says when he says Mass I do and say. I observe all the conventions; I follow all the rules. But I do not say Mass, I only pretend to. For me to have said Mass something else is necessary, something that might have been done twenty or forty years before, but was never done: I should have been ordained. In default of valid Orders, I can do and say what I like, use all the right instruments, follow all the conventions, but I cannot say Mass; I can only pretend to.

Consider now Austin's case of the thief who pretends to be cleaning windows. In fact what he is doing is 'casing the joint', having a good look through Her Ladyship's bedroom window in order to form some idea of where Her Ladyship keeps her pearls. He is not really a window-cleaner at all, but Bill Sykes, who has been sent down six times already for house-breaking and has a well-planned burglary set up for Easter, when Her Ladyship will be away. But although he is only pretending to clean windows, he is cleaning them. Maybe he is cleaning them better than they have ever been cleaned before, better indeed than the real window-cleaners did, who had the job before Bill took over. Nothing that a good window-cleaner does is left undone by Bill; and to clean windows one does not need valid Orders. Whether or not the windows are being cleaned depends entirely on what is going on *now*, not on what may or may not have happened twenty or forty years ago.

But now Bill Sykes is back home and telling his small son a bedtime story. It is told in the first person, an imaginary autobiography. Bill is pretending that when he left school he got a job as a cabin boy on a ship bound for Ceylon. He tells his son how they left Liverpool and sailed through Biscay, round Spain and into the Mediterranean. There is a lot of detail about the Barbary Apes on the Rock at Gibraltar, about porpoises playing round the ship in the Red Sea, Arab slavers sighted off Aden, and so on. Bill is only pretending: his real autobiography is exciting enough, but not the sort of thing he wants his son to know. He is pretending *that* he saw the Barbary apes and the porpoises in the Red Sea. He is *not* pretending to tell him the story of all these things, for that he is really doing; but he *is* pretending to tell him things that happened to himself. He is a good story-teller. No one watching the performance could be sure, without background information, that what was being said was not genuine autobiography—any more than the casual observer of the wealthy eccentric's 'Mass' could have told that what was being performed was a sacrilegious parody. Bill followed all the conventions for the correct use of the words he used, none the less correct for being the conventions of Cockney rather than the BBC, just as the eccentric followed every detail of each rubric in the Missal.

What sort of pretending is Bill engaged in with his small son? Is his pretending like that of the children's wedding breakfast or like that of the eccentric's 'Mass' or like that of Bill's own window-cleaning? Clearly it is not like the wedding breakfast, because we can tell by looking, or sniffing, that they are only pretending to drink champagne but are really drinking lemonade. We cannot tell simply by listening to what Bill says that he is only pretending that he went on a ship through the Red Sea. As we have imagined it, Bill's story cannot be recognized as fiction by anyone who does not know Bill. It is not a 'tall story'. If Bill had introduced mermaids and sirens, Circe and the Cyclops, into his tale of a Mediterranean cruise, we might have begun to suspect something. But not because Bill was using language in an idiosyncratic way. Homer obeys the conventions of Ionic as faithfully as Thucydides obeys the conventions of Attic Greek. If we beg leave to doubt the historicity of the more miraculous parts of the Odyssey it is because, with Hume, we take the reported violations of laws of nature as a counter-indication, not because we notice any infringement of the rules of syntax or semantics.

So far we have noted nothing that can distinguish Bill's story-telling either from the eccentric's 'Mass' or from his own window-cleaning. What the pseudo-window-cleaner pretends to do, he does. Does the story-teller do what he pretends to do? (Contrast: did the story-teller do what he pretends to have done?) He pretends to be telling his small boy an account of events in his own past life. Clearly he is not doing *that*. What he is telling him is not an account of events in his own past life. Whether or not the window-cleaner is cleaning windows is entirely determined by what he does now. The same is true of the question whether the children are drinking champagne. Not so the question whether the eccentric is saying Mass. That is determined partly by whether or not something took place in the past, namely, valid episcopal Ordination. Similarly the question whether Bill is giving his son an account of events in his past life is determined partly by what happened in the past, by whether or not the alleged events took place. It is not the words which make the difference here, it is the world. Indeed we have to establish what Bill is saying before we can establish whether what he says corresponds to the facts. So the meaning of his words must be discoverable independently of whether what he says is fact or fiction. It cannot be, therefore, that his words would mean something entirely different if what he said were fact, from what they mean when what he says is only fiction. If what the false priest was doing fell foul in some way of the rubrics, or at least of the more important conventions of saying Mass—if, for example, he used blackcurrant juice for wine—we should know that what he was pretending to do he was not in fact doing, without going into the question of his Orders. But to all appearances what the false priest is doing is entirely correct. Similarly, it is only because most of what Bill is doing is in accordance with the conventions of autobiographical narrative that we have to go behind what is now being done to find out whether what he is doing is, or is only pretended to be, the telling of his life-story.

5. *Pretending and proper names*

There is an important exception to what has been said. Bill introduces into his narrative a character named Ted Fenton, who he says was First Mate on this voyage. There is always the possibility that, although the voyage never took place, Ted Fenton really existed. Maybe he was a fellow-prisoner of Bill's down on the Moor some years back, a real merchant seaman who claimed at least to have had many of the experiences which Bill works into his story. That is a possibility. But it is not actually the case. Ted Fenton is a pure figment of Bill's imagination. No such person existed. When Bill said that he watched porpoises cavorting in the Red Sea he was pretending to tell his son something that had happened to him, but he was not pretending to use words having a certain meaning. The words he used really had the meaning he and his audience assumed they had. The conventions for the correct use of these words were current in Bill's society independently of him and his story, and he was using them in conformity with these conventions. But when he said that one day Ted dived overboard and swam in amongst the porpoises, the word 'Ted' was not one for whose use there was a complete convention existing in Bill's society independently of him and his story. In this it was unlike the name 'the Red Sea', whose accepted function for Bill's society, as for our own, was to name the stretch of water separating Africa from Arabia. To know the conventions for the use of 'the Red Sea' is to know what the expression names, and knowing this involves knowing that there is a stretch of water which separates Africa from Arabia. But, although 'Ted', or even 'Ted Fenton', is no doubt used according to conventions which have nothing to do with Bill and his story to name many men around the world, Bill was not using it in accordance with any of these conventions. (Which convention is in operation in any given conversation, e.g. which person is being named by a given use of 'Ted Fenton', is determined by context.) There was in fact no convention for using 'Ted' in the way Bill was using it: Bill was only pretending that there was. He was in fact pretending that there was a man who sailed on a certain ship as First Mate, etc., and that 'Ted Fenton' was the name of this man. Independently of this pretence 'Ted Fenton' had no use, or no relevant use. It was because there was, independently of Bill and his story, a convention by which 'the Red Sea' was understood as the name for a particular stretch of water that 'the Red Sea' was a genuine proper name, and genuinely used by Bill as such. In using 'Ted Fenton', on the other hand, Bill was merely pretending to use an expression as a proper name, pretending that there were conventions for its use in this way. When he said 'Ted dived overboard' we knew quite well what he meant by 'dived' and 'overboard' without having to know whether what he said was fact or fiction. So, in the case of the eccentric imitator of the Mass, the chance visitor knew that what he was doing was saying 'This is my body', although he did not know whether the man was actually consecrating a host. But we do not know what Bill meant by 'Ted', in the sense that, until we know whether there really was a man who sailed on a boat from Liverpool as First Mate, etc., we cannot say whether Bill was thereby using a genuine proper name or only pretending to do so.

It is sometimes objected against this view that the question of what syntactic category a word belongs to cannot depend on whether or not what is stated by means of the word is fact. If what the objection alleges is that we do not need to discover first whether what is said is fact or fiction before we can judge whether the given word belongs to one syntactic category rather than another, the allegation can readily be admitted. We do not have to find out whether Bill is or is not pretending in order to decide that 'Ted', as he is using it, is intended as a proper name rather than, say, a sentential connective. If 'Ted' has a genuine meaning at all, it is a proper name. We know, in Wittgenstein's phrase, at what post the word is stationed.[7] What is in question is its ability to perform the duties of its station. This can be ascertained only be establishing that it does in fact name somebody. Bill of course says, or at least implies, that it does. But if he is only pretending, part of what he is pretending is that 'Ted' is a proper name.

The situation could arise for words of other syntactic categories. Suppose that a famous dress-designer claims to have invented a new colour, which he calls 'Oregon violet'. Millions of pounds' worth of clothes advertised as being of this colour are produced by his establishment; and being in a position to dictate fashion he sells them to the young with little trouble. But at last someone begins to doubt whether Oregon violet is a new colour at all. (Could it be another case of 'the Emperor's clothes'?) Tests are carried out and it is found that cloth alleged to be of this colour is indistinguishable from cloth manufactured for centuries by traditional methods in Rome and worn

[7] Wittgenstein, *Philosophical Investigations*, Part I, § 257.

on ceremonial occasions by *monsignori*. The designer and his sales representatives continue to assert that they can discriminate between Oregon violet and *Monsignore* purple; but, since they decline to submit to independently conducted tests of their alleged powers of discrimination, no one believes them. Oregon violet is a fake. Otherwise stated, the dress-designer has only been pretending (not innocently, like Bill Sykes, but fraudulently, with an eye to money-making) that '— is Oregon violet', as the name of a new colour, is a genuine predicate. To know whether it was or not we had to establish a matter of fact: whether objective discriminations could be made between Oregon violet and *Monsignore* purple, since its alleged meaning required propositions of the form 'x is Oregon violet, not *Monsignore* purple' to be possibly true. Just so, it had to be established as a matter of fact that there was a man who sailed in a boat from Liverpool, etc., before 'Ted Fenton' could be accepted as a genuine proper name. Not that '— is Oregon violet' has aspirations to belong to any other syntactic category —say the category of quantifier—any more than 'Ted Fenton' is a candidate for recognition as a sentential connective. But whether or not there is a word having the meaning the speaker pretends it has, and thus really belonging to the syntactic category it is pretended to belong to, can in some cases be a question of fact.[8] And while this is rare with words of other syntactic categories, it is relatively common with words in the category of proper names.

If we hold that 'Ted Fenton' is not a genuine proper name, but only a word which Bill Sykes pretends is a proper name, the same will hold for 'Pegasus'. 'Pegasus', to be sure, is not part of just one person's pretence. It is part of a traditional story or myth. *In the world of Greek mythology* 'Pegasus' is a proper name. What stories are, and what is meant by a phrase like 'in the world of Greek mythology' is something which we shall investigate in the next section. But our present point is the negative one that 'Ted Fenton' and 'Pegasus' are not genuine proper names. This allows us to make the point that 'For some x, x is a winged horse' fares no better (and no worse) on the substitutional interpretation of the quantifier than on the

---

[8] It can also be a question of logic. Cf. Prior's pretence that a word 'tonk' is a new sentential connective in 'The Runabout Inference Ticket', *Analysis*, 21, 1960.

objectual. On the substitutional interpretation the quantified proposition is true if some proper name when substituted for x in 'x is a winged horse' yields a true proposition. This condition is not satisfied by 'Pegasus', because 'Pegasus' is not a genuine proper name. From time to time we pretend it is; but in just the same way and at the same time we pretend that something is a winged horse, that winged horses exist. *What we pretend is as well expressed by quantification objectually interpreted as by quantification substitutionally interpreted.* Indeed, it is hard to see any difference.

6. *Stories and fictional worlds*

We have been taking as the paradigm of fiction a bedtime story told by a father to his son. This made it plausible to talk of what was taking place as Bill's pretending that all these things had happened to him. But can we say that H. G. Wells *pretended* that the adventures he recounts happened to Mr Polly, or that we all *pretend* that the Prince wakened the Sleeping Beauty with a kiss? It would be far from natural to talk in these ways. But there are, surely, 'family resemblances' between bedtime stories and novels and classical ballets. The concept of *story* is not all that far removed from the concept of *game*, for whose elucidation Wittgenstein first brought in the notion of family resemblance. Stories, like games, are things we can enter into. It is quite possible for the same story to be developed by a series of different people—as in the game 'Consequences'. And well-known stories have their own conventions: that is why someone who said that the Sleeping Beauty died before the Prince reached her would have 'got it wrong'. When we talk about novels we find it natural to play along with the storyteller: 'What was the name of Dorothea Brooks's uncle? Wasn't it James?' Thus we can reject certain propositions as false: Agnes Wickfield did not marry Uriah Heep. And others as true: Young Jolyon did marry Irene. We are entering into a game of 'Let's pretend'. Not all pretending is done by a single person, as we saw from our example of the children pretending to have a wedding breakfast. Novels and novelists, plays and playwrights, ballets and their choreographers, films and their directors, are now of course taken very seriously. The family resemblance with 'let's pretend' has been attenuated. But it may well be that philosophical problems about fiction are more amenable to solution if we look at the simpler modes of this form of life rather than at the more august.

Talking of truth, existence, and reference in connection with fictional or mythical characters, we feel moved to say that 'Agnes Wickfield did not marry Uriah Heep' is true *in the world of Dickens's novel*, that 'Perseus slew the Gorgon' is true *in the world of Greek mythology*, and that *in Shakespeare's play* there was such a person as Ophelia and the name 'Polonius' had reference. Russell called this way of talking 'a most pitiful and paltry evasion'.[9] He says:

> To maintain that Hamlet, for example, exists in his own world, namely, in the world of Shakespeare's imagination, just as truly as (say) Napoleon existed in the ordinary world, is to say something deliberately confusing, or else confused to a degree which is scarcely credible.[10]

Russell does not say what the two things are which are being 'deliberately' confused; but I think that it can be said. It is true, as Russell here remarks that, 'it is of the essence of fiction that only the thoughts, feelings, etc., in Shakespeare and his readers[11] are real, and that there is not, in addition to them, an objective Hamlet.' So one thing that may be said is, for example, that Shakespeare imagined it to be the case that Hamlet was loved by Ophelia. That is a fact about Shakespeare. But it is also true that Ophelia loved Hamlet. That is a fact about Ophelia. So there was someone who had Polonius as a father and Laertes as a brother. So the name 'Ophelia' has a reference, is a proper name. It is not the case, as has sometimes been pretended, that in fiction propositions do not entail what they would entail elsewhere, that these entailments are in some way cut. 'Mr Darcy had an aunt' entails 'Mr Darcy's parents were not both only children' just as much as 'George V had an aunt' entails 'George V's parents were not both only children'.[12]

But in saying all these things about Hamlet and Ophelia and Mr Darcy, and indeed about the name 'Ophelia', what we are doing is joining in the appropriate game of 'Let's pretend'. Remembering *Pride and Prejudice* we say 'Let me see, Did Mr

[9] *Introduction to Mathematical Philosophy*, pp. 169 f.
[10] Ibid.
[11] It is interesting that Russell does not see fit to mention actors and audience.
[12] *Pace* J. M. Cameron, *The Night Battle*, 1966, pp. 13 ff. Cf. my critical comments in *Mind*, 78, 1969, p. 226.

Darcy have an aunt? Yes, of course, Lady Catherine de Bourgh.'
It is better to say that *we* have entered into the world of *Pride and Prejudice* than to say that Mr Darcy had an aunt in that world. To say *that* is to confuse two propositions:

(24) Jane Austen wrote or implied in *Pride and Prejudice* that someone called 'Mr Darcy' had an aunt,

and

(25) Mr Darcy had an aunt.

When (24) is said the topic under discussion is English literature: we are not pretending anything or, except in a Wittgensteinian sense, taking part in a game. But when (25) is said we are joining in the game that Jane Austen started, an excellent game called '*Pride and Prejudice*', in which we pretend together all sorts of delightful things, such as that 'Lady Catherine de Bourgh' is a proper name. To say 'Mr Darcy had an aunt in the world of *Pride and Prejudice*' is to get the two ways of talking exemplified by (24) and (25), not perhaps 'deliberately' confused, nor 'confused to a degree that is scarcely credible'—since it is a very natural confusion—but confused nevertheless.

David Lewis has recently provided analyses of propositions like 'In the world of *Pride and Prejudice* Mr Darcy had an aunt' which take more seriously than Russell was inclined to the notion of possible worlds.[13] The simplest of these analyses would render our proposition as follows: '"Mr Darcy had an aunt" is true at every world where the story of *Pride and Prejudice* is told as known fact rather than fiction'. Lewis's technique, here as elsewhere,[14] is to produce possible-worlds statements which are equivalent to counterfactuals. His more sophisticated analyses of propositions asserting truth in fictional worlds make use, as does his analysis of counterfactuals in general, of the notion of possible worlds differing more or less from the actual one. If any of these analyses are successful, translation should be possible from analysans to analysandum as well as vice versa. We should, therefore, be able to give a counterfactual-style rendering of '"Mr Darcy had an aunt" is true at every world where the story of *Pride and Prejudice* is told as known fact rather than fiction'. This indeed proves easy

---

[13] David Lewis, 'Truth in Fiction', *American Philosophical Quarterly*, 15, 1978, 37 ff.

[14] See Lewis, *Counterfactuals*, 1973.

enough: 'If what is said or implied in *Pride and Prejudice* were really true rather than just pretended, "Mr Darcy had an aunt" would be true.' But this counterfactual gives us no more information than the simple 'It is said or implied in *Pride and Prejudice* that "Mr Darcy had an aunt" is true', which is much the same as (24) above. So if the first of Lewis's analyses of fictional-world propositions were correct, it would make the sentence mean one of the two things which, in our view, those who utter it intend it to mean. In so far, however, as Lewis purports to be giving an *analysis* of the counterfactual, he induces in us the feeling that what can only properly be said, in the mood appropriate to counterfactuals, by '"Mr Darcy had an aunt" *would be* true', can in a qualified way be said in the indicative by '"Mr Darcy had an aunt" *is* true'. To say counterfactually, that if so-and-so *were* the case it *would be* true is to imply that it isn't: to say, indicatively, that *somewhere it is* true is to imply that it is. And this is to make the sentence mean the other of the things which, in our view, those who utter it intend it to mean, namely (25). So Lewis, it seems, is guilty of the confusion alleged by Russell.

Lewis's more sophisticated suggestions for the analysis of fictional-world propositions take account of some interesting points which it would be too much of a digression to enter into here. Nevertheless, they both involve forms of proposition equivalent, on his account, to counterfactuals, and this, taken together with his analysis of counterfactuals, makes them vulnerable to the same Russellian charge of confusion as is his first, simplest, analysis.

7. *Negative existential propositions containing fictional proper names*

If we say 'There *was* someone who was Mr Darcy's aunt; it was Lady Catherine de Bourgh' we are joining in Jane Austen's game of 'Let's pretend'. What then is going on when we say, with as great a 'robust sense of reality' as Russell could desire, 'There was no such person as Lady Catherine de Bourgh; Lady Catherine de Bourgh never existed'? We have certainly left the game of 'Let's pretend'. But part of what was pretended was that 'Lady Catherine de Bourgh' was a genuine proper name, and yet here we are using it as a proper name to make statements about 'the real world'. Or *are* we in fact *using* it as a proper name, or as anything at all? Are we not rather *mentioning* it? Not every mention of an expression requires inverted commas. 'Giorgione was so called because of his size' involves mention of the name 'Giorgione', although it has no inverted commas there. And it was argued in the last chapter that one way of understanding (20), 'Geoffrey believes that Ethiopia is a Christian country', requires us to take the name 'Ethiopia' as being mentioned rather than used in this sentence, although, again, (20) contains no inverted commas. To be sure, this involves understanding (20) as saying that Geoffrey believes that the country called 'Ethiopia' is a Christian country, just as we explicate the sentence about Giorgione by saying that it means 'Giorgione was called "Giorgione" because of his size'. But, in the same way, we can say what is meant by 'Lady Catherine de Bourgh never existed' is less misleadingly expressed by 'Jane Austen's use of "Lady Catherine de Bourgh" is only a pretence of using it as a proper name'. 'Lady Catherine de Bourgh never existed', like 'Giorgione was so called because of his size', is partly at least a statement about an expression. It is made from outside the 'Let's pretend' world of *Pride and Prejudice* about something which is used inside that world. Talk of 'worlds' here is not a pitiful evasion. All that is meant is that, when we say that Lady Catherine de Bourgh never existed, we are doing something which is not part of a 'Let's pretend' activity in which we sometimes take part (as when we ask whether Mr Darcy had an aunt), but is a comment on something we do when we are taking part in that activity, namely, use the expression 'Lady Catherine de Bourgh'. When we do this, the statement tells us, we are not genuinely using a proper name but pretending to do so. So far as I can remember, every use of an expression purporting to be a proper name in *Pride and Prejudice* is a pretended use. Not so in all novels. In *Henry Esmond* there is mention of the Old Pretender, James Francis Edward. In the 'Let's pretend' game of *Henry Esmond* we only pretend to use 'Henry Esmond' as a proper name, but we do not pretend to name the Old Pretender: we use 'James Francis Edward', or some other name for the same man, as a genuine proper name. That too is part of the game. Not everything that is done in a 'Let's pretend' game is a pretence. The children at the pretended wedding breakfast only pretend to drink champagne, but they really do drink.

'Lady Catherine de Bourgh never existed' is then, in part at least, a statement about an expression. It does not involve the use of 'exist' as a first-level predicate. A great part of this book has been taken up with discussing various prima-facie counter-examples to the thesis that 'exists' is never a first-level predicable. It is worth contrasting the different tactics I have used in rejecting these counter-examples. The way I dealt with the simplest case was peremptory. 'Aristides exists' was dismissed as an ill-formed string of words: it just is not a proposition. In some sense of 'grammatical' it is a grammatical sentence, whereas 'Something Aristides', which is similarly formed by juxtaposing a second-level predicable and a proper name, is not even grammatical. But it is no more a genuine proposition than, say, 'Aristides is numerous', which is in the same sense grammatical and is similarly ill-formed, in that it is the result of attaching a second-level predicable to a proper name. (See Ch. III, § 10.) More complicated was the analysis needed for the propositions 'President Ford does not know that David Pears exists', 'Socrates might not have existed', and 'Arkle no longer exists'. Here we have genuine propositions, and propositions in which genuine proper names are genuinely used. But the analysis of these propositions revealed that in their depth grammar they do not involve the attachment of 'exists' as a first-level predicable to the proper names they contain. 'David Pears exists', 'Socrates exists', and 'Arkle exists' do not occur in them, except at the level of superficial grammar, as embedded propositions. (See Chs. IV, V.) With 'Lady Catherine de Bourgh never existed', however, my tactic is different. I do not, as in the previous cases, admit that the purported proper name is actually being used as a proper name. Rather, it is being mentioned. We are not, properly speaking, saying of Lady Catherine de Bourgh that she never existed—for that way lies Plato's Beard. Rather, we are saying of 'Lady Catherine de Bourgh' that no one ever was both called by this name and truly describable by certain descriptions to be found in *Pride and Prejudice*. Even where the name occurring in the novel is a genuine proper name, as 'James Francis Edward' is, in saying that James Francis Edward did in fact exist we are talking, not about the Old Pretender, but about the expression 'James Francis Edward'. What we are saying about the name is not, of course, that *it* existed or never did exist. The expression 'Lady Catherine de Bourgh' certainly exists and existed, although Lady Catherine never did. On my analysis the proposition does ascribe a property to an object, and thus involves the use of a first-level predicable; but the object in question is a linguistic expression and the property is not the supposed property of existence.[15] I can thus claim that no counter-example has yet been found to the thesis that 'exists' is never a first-level predicable.

8. *Existence in possible worlds*

Not only have philosphers talked glibly about things existing 'in the world of literature' or 'in the world of Shakespeare's imagination', they have talked with equal nonchalance of things existing 'in different possible worlds'. What, if anything, do they mean? Charles II had no legitimate offspring. In a different possible world—one, perhaps, in which he married Nell Gwyn rather than Catherine of Braganza—he might have had children born in wedlock. Can we give names to such children? Can we say that there is a possible world in which King Charles married Nell Gwyn, and from this happy union had issue three children, Mary, Charles, and Elizabeth? Of course we can. I can, for a start, write a historical novel in which I pretend that King Charles has these children and similarly pretend that they have these names. If I say 'Mary, the eldest legitimate child of Charles II, existed in my novel' I am confusedly saying two things:

 (26) I wrote a novel in which Charles II was said to have legitimate children, the eldest of whom was called 'Mary',

and — something which is part of the 'Let's pretend' game that I began when I started to write the novel —

 (27) Charles II had legitimate children, the eldest of whom was called 'Mary'.

We know now how to deal with this.[16]

However, can we not say that, independently of anything

---

[15] Cf. Frege's remarks about the relation between the sentences 'There is at least one square root of 4' and 'The concept *square root of 4* is realized'. See above, Ch. III, p. 59.

[16] See above pp. 256 ff.

anyone might write or pretend, there is a possible world in which Mary, the eldest legitimate child of Charles II, existed? I have argued in Chapter III that a string of words like 'Mary exists', formed by attaching 'exists' to the proper name 'Mary', is ill formed. It is not made well formed by placing a definite description in apposition to 'Mary' and subjecting the whole to the complex operator 'There is a possible world in which it was the case that —'. We should not be deluded into thinking so by the fact that 'There is a possible world in which James, Duke of Monmouth, the illegitimate son of Charles II, did not exist' is true. I described in Chapter IV how to analyse such propositions. They use genuine proper names to state facts about the people named by those names. But, since Charles II had no legitimate children there cannot be a genuine name 'Mary' which names his eldest legitimate child. It was possible, of course, that he should have had such a child, and, if we like to express such a possibility in the bloated terminology of 'possible worlds', we can say:

(28) There is a possible world in which someone was the eldest legitimate child of Charles II and was called 'Mary'.

This, however, is ambiguous, in a way that is familiar to us from the last chapter. It could mean:

(28') For some x, there is a possible world in which both x was the eldest legitimate child of Charles II and x was called 'Mary'.

This could be true. If so, it would be 'indirectly about' someone. Perhaps there was an illegitimate child of Charles II called 'Jane Stuart'. It could not be true of anyone who was not the child of Charles II that he or she was the child of Charles II. We necessarily have the parents we have. But it could have been true of Jane Stuart that Charles II was legally married to her mother when she was born, and that Charles II had had no legitimate children before her, and that she had been called 'Mary'. But then it would be true of her only that these descriptions could have applied to her in some possible world, although not in the real one. It would not be true of her that she existed in that possible world, although not in the real one. For we are supposing in interpreting (28) as (28') that there was such a person 'in the real world'.

This, however, is not the only interpretation of (28). It could also mean:

>(28″) There is a possible world in which, for some x, both x was the eldest legitimate child of Charles II and x was called 'Mary'.

This too could be true. But if it were it would not be even indirectly about anyone. It is not therefore about anyone nameable by a proper name. It does not justify us in saying *of anyone* that in some possible world she was the eldest legitimate daughter of Charles II and was called 'Mary'. It certainly does not justify us in saying of anyone that in some possible world she existed. What makes (28′) true is that in some possible world a complex first-level predicable, not '— exists', truly applies to Jane Stuart. What (28″) says is that in some possible world a true proposition can be formed by attaching that complex first-level predicable to the second-level predicable 'for some x, — x'. The notion that there is a first-level predicable '— existed in some possible world' is the illegitimate offspring of an unholy confusion between propositions like (28′) and (28″), between, that is, different possible interpretations of propositions like (28). I can introduce a proper name by asserting an existential proposition like (28′) and saying 'Let "Jane Stuart" be the name of this person'. (28″) is not an existential proposition, so it cannot be used in this way to introduce a proper name. It is not an existential proposition, because a proposition is existential only if the operator having largest scope in the proposition is the existential quantifier. (If negative existential propositions do not come out as existential propositions on this definition, so much the better for our purposes.) The idea that we can introduce names for objects in possible worlds different from our own is due to the confusion between (28′) and (28″).

9. *Fictional characters and possible thalers*

Strawson, as we saw in section 2 of this chapter, countered Moore's claim that one could not meaningfully say anything of the form 'Most A's exist' by reminding us that we could meaningfully assert 'Most of the characters listed in the Classical Dictionary really existed'. Moore also claimed that we could not meaningfully say anything of the form 'Some A's do not exist'. It might be again objected that we could at least say 'Some possible legitimate children of English monarchs did not exist (except in possible worlds different from our own)'. Strawson's objection is now easily dealt with. 'Most characters listed in the Classical Dictionary (really) existed' is not a statement ascribing the property of (real) existence to most members of some class of persons. It is a statement ascribing the property of really naming persons, i.e. being genuine proper names, to most members of some class of linguistic expressions. It would have been less misleading to have said 'Most of the expressions which occur at the beginning of entries in the Classical Dictionary are proper names (The rest are simply expressions which people have pretended were proper names)'. To the objection involving possible but non-existent children of English monarchs we may reply in similar vein. The statement in question does not ascribe the property of non-existence (except in possible worlds different from our own) to some members of the class of possible legitimate children of English monarchs. It could do one of two other things. It could predicate of some actual children of English monarchs, e.g. Jane Stuart, that only in some possible world different from our own were they the legitimate children of those monarchs. Or it could predicate of some English monarchs that there was no one who was their legitimate child (though there are possible worlds in which there could have been someone). In neither case does it provide a genuine counter-example to Moore's claim.

'Most tame tigers exist' and 'Some tame tigers do not exist' are clearly ill-formed. This does not result from anything special about the concept *tame tiger*. Rather, it is due to the fact that attaching 'exist' to expressions of the form 'Most A's —' or 'Some A's do not —' produces ill-formed formulae. The counter-examples that have been alleged are not true counter-examples. This is because expressions like 'character listed in the Classical Dictionary' and 'possible legitimate child' are not appropriate substitutions for A in 'Most A's —' or 'Some A's do not —'. These purported substitutions are systematically misleading in the way that was hinted at earlier, when I was discussing Kant's 'hundred possible thalers' (Ch. II, § 6; cf. Ch. IX, § 3). Because they masquerade as general terms capable of replacing *A* in 'Most *A*'s —' and 'Some *A*'s do not —', they enable 'exist' to masquerade also as a first-level predicable capable of filling in the blanks. Why do I say that these expressions 'masquerade' as general terms? And what is it that is systematically misleading about phrases like 'a hundred possible thalers'.

If I say 'A hundred possible thalers contain no less than a hundred real thalers', I seem to be saying something which has the same form as 'A hundred Prussian thalers contain no less silver than a hundred Austrian thalers'; but in fact it is quite different. We should be sensitive by now to superficial similarities concealing deep syntactic differences. As Frege noticed,[17] we have the illusion that in 'four thoroughbred horses' the word 'four' modifies the concept 'thoroughbred horse' in just the same way as 'thoroughbred' modifies the concept 'horse'. There the illusion is dispelled by realizing that 'four' represents a second-level predicable which is wrapped round the first-level predicable 'thoroughbred horse which draws the King's carriage', not a further first-level predicable to be wrapped round what 'thoroughbred' and 'horse' are wrapped round. Here the illusion is to be dispelled by realizing that 'possible' represents, not a predicable at all, but a sentential operator which has to be wrapped round an open or closed sentence. To say that a hundred possible thalers contain no less than a hundred real thalers is to say that, if it were the case that I had a hundred thalers, I should have something which contained no less than the hundred thalers you have in the bank; or that, if it is possible that I should have a hundred thalers, then it is possible that I should have something which contains no less than the hundred thalers which you have (in fact). Here the possible hundred thalers reappear as a hundred thalers which *it is possible that* I might have, or my having them is *supposed* and consequences drawn. But what is possible or supposed is *that something is the case*.

The phase 'possible thaler' is misleading because it looks as though it had the same logical form as 'thoroughbred horse'. Whereas 'thoroughbred horse' can be understood as picking out from the class of horses the sub-class of those horses which are also thoroughbreds, there is no sub-class of thalers for the

[17] See above, Ch. II, p. 43.

phrase 'possible thaler' to pick out. A phrase 'possible thalers' will be understood only if the sentence in which it occurs is felt as equivalent to a sentence in which the word 'possible' appears as part of the sentential operator 'it is possible that'. Is the phrase 'character listed in the Classical Dictionary' misleading in the same way? In so far as it tempts us to form wrong ideas about classes, yes. Just as people can be misled into thinking that 'possible thaler' picks out a class—a sub-class of the class of thalers—so people can be misled into thinking that we can pick out a class by use of the word 'character'. Speaking of an imaginary conversation in which characters from Tolstoy's novels are being compared with real people, Strawson[18] talks of 'the class of *characters being talked about*'. And he goes on to say, 'the peculiarity of such a class is that it may be, and in the case under consideration actually is, radically heterogeneous; even, if you will permit the expression, ontologically or metaphysically heterogeneous'. The expression should certainly not be permitted. Nor should we allow Strawson to say that King Arthur and King Alfred are fellow members of a '*heterogeneous* class of kingly characters we talk about—a class which comprises both actual and legendary kings'. Strawson's willingness to regard 'exist' as a predicate which may be predicated of King Alfred, *qua* member of this 'heterogeneous' class, in such a way as to mark him out as a member of the sub-class of historical, as opposed to fictitious, kingly characters, is a sign of his being misled by the superficial grammar of the word 'character'. What he describes as a 'model' for interpreting sentences like 'Most of the characters listed in the Classical Dictionary existed' is a delineation of the deceptive superficial pattern of such sentences, rather than a contribution to their understanding.

Talk about 'people (characters) being talked about'[19] is not talk about people but talk about talk. Strawson shows a proper hesitation over saying that what are being talked about here are people: hence the parenthetical reference to 'characters'. Talk about Dickens's characters is not talk about any people other than Dickens. Talk about characters listed in the Classical Dictionary is talk about the expressions that constitute that

[18] *Freedom and Resentment*, p. 106.
[19] Ibid., p. 195.

list. To say that most of these characters existed is a misleading way of saying that most of these expressions are real names: the rest are just expressions which people at one time or another pretended, or mistakenly believed, to be names. Not that an author need pretend to use a name in a story in order to be said to have created a character. The Fool in *King Lear* is no less a character for having only an office, not a name. But to say of him that unlike some of the characters in Shakespeare's plays he never really existed, is to say that Shakespeare only pretended that there was such a person. *King Lear* is a story, not a history; and if we say that the Fool is a fictitious, whereas Hotspur in *Henry IV* is a historical, character, we are not assigning to different sub-classes members of a metaphysically heterogeneous class of actual-or-imaginary figures from the past. We are distinguishing two sorts of activities that Shakespeare and those who perform his plays carry out: on the one hand, enacting events which really happened by representing on the stage people now dead, and, on the other hand, pretending to do this. This is not just one possible model for understanding what is meant when people say 'Most of Shakespeare's characters never existed': it is the only way of understanding such sentences.

The word 'character' and the words 'real', 'existent', 'actual', 'historical', and, on the other side, 'imaginary', 'fictitious', 'legendary', 'non-existent', live by taking in each other's washing. It is only because 'character' has the false appearance of picking out a class that 'existent', 'non-existent', etc., have the false appearance of picking out sub-classes of that class. It is only because 'character' masquerades as a general term that 'exists' can masquerade as a first-level predicate. This misleading appearance of both terms must be recognized simultaneously, if we are to see the fallacy in Strawson's attempt to show that existence is sometimes a predicate.

We should not allow ourselves so easily to be dislodged from the position Moore secured for us. 'Most tame tigers exist' and 'Some tame tigers do not exist' are vicious in virtue of their form. It is not just these strings of words which are ill-formed: an unlimited number of substitutions for 'tame tigers' in these strings would leave them in the same unhappy state. There are obviously *forms* of expression, 'Most *A*'s —' and 'Some *A*'s do not —', which do not permit 'exist' to fill the blank in them.

The truth to which Moore drew our attention is a truth of very wide generality. It cannot be upset by a handful of dubious exceptions using misleading notions like *character* and *possible child*. Before such exceptions are allowed to disprove the rule, the deep grammar of the sentences containing them must be thoroughly examined. This chapter has been devoted to this task. It has shown that the exceptions can be disallowed. Moore's insight, like Frege's, resists challenge. The case for a sense of 'exist' in which it is a first-level predicable has still to be made.

10. *Existence of possible worlds*

Possible-world theorists have been troubled about the sort of existence possessed by objects existing only in a possible world. But they have been equally concerned over the question 'What sort of existence is possessed by a possible world itself?' The proposition (28) above began with the words 'There is a possible world in which —'; and the technique of possible-world theorists is, in general, to substitute the expression 'There is a possible world in which —' for the simple modal operator 'Possibly —' and the expression ' In every possible world —' for the modal operator 'Necessarily —'. Quantification over possible worlds thus replaces modality, and the ordinary predicate calculus can be used to prove truths of modal logic which would otherwise be provable only in an independent modal system. But this very talk of 'quantification *over* possible worlds' seems to introduce 'ontological commitment' to suspect 'entities', namely, these possible worlds themselves. Where 'Possibly, Charles II had a legitimate child called "Mary"' commits us only to Charles II, 'There is a possible world in which Charles II had a legitimate child called "Mary"' seems to commit us, as well as to Charles II, to a whole range of things called 'possible worlds'. To say '*There is* a possible world in which —' seems to commit us, over and above our commitment to the actual world in which we live, to a world which *exists*, despite being not actual but merely possible. The reality or existence of possible worlds thus becomes a matter of controversy for the theorists who talk so much about them.

We should by now be immunized against infection from phrases like 'possible thaler' or 'possible world'. If I say that there is a possible world in which Charles II had legitimate children, I am talking in a way which no one would have thought misleading, were it not for the fact that philosophers have been so misled. I am saying, in effect, that amongst the many possible histories there might have been of the world there is one which describes children born in wedlock to Charles II. Histories of the world, idealized, are collections of propositions which between them state everything which has ever happened in the world. The actual history of the world would be given by a conjunction of all the true propositions which state what has happened; and we could define such a proposition as that proposition, p, which, being itself true, for any true proposition q, strictly implies that q. (Since logical falsehoods strictly imply everything, we need to stipulate that p itself is true.) This already includes more than would normally be included even in an idealized history of the world, which we should expect to tell us only what *has* happened, since among the true propositions strictly implied by our proposition would be found, not only true propositions stating what is happening and is going to happen in the world, but all 'timeless' truths such as laws of nature and truths of mathematics and logic. No matter: we are interested in the notion of a *history* only in so far as it helps to elucidate the notion of a *world*. To say that there is such a history of the world is, then, to say that for some p, both p and, for every q, if q, then the fact that p strictly implies that q ($\Sigma p K p \Pi q C q L C p q$). A total history, if correct, is one which includes everything that is the case.

So much for the actual history of the world. What about possible histories? As well as correct histories there are incorrect ones, and histories, which we might prefer to call 'stories', or even 'tall stories', which do not so much as aim to given an account of what actually happened, but only of what might have happened. Such stories, if total, will state, for every q, whether or not q. Their totality consists in their having an answer, Yes or No, to every question. That is to say, a story of this kind can be defined as a proposition, p, such that both it is possible that p, and for every proposition q, either p strictly implies that q or p strictly implies that not-q. Such a story gives the account of a possible world. To say that *there is* a possible world in which Charles II fathered legitimate offspring is to say that some story of this kind contains the statement that Charles II fathered legitimate offspring. Let us abbreviate this proposition about Charles II to r. Then 'There is a possible world in which Charles II fathered legitimate offspring' is equivalent to $\Sigma pKKMp\Pi qALCpqLCpNqLCpr$. Let us further abbreviate $KMp\Pi qALCpqLCpNq$, which says that p is a possible world proposition, to Qp.[20] Then 'There is a possible world in which it is the case that r' comes out as $\Sigma pKQpLCpr$ and 'It is the case in every possible world that r' as $\Pi pCQpLCpr$. Such formulae are susceptible to manipulation in the predicate calculus in the way possible-world theorists wish. We can also introduce formulae like $\Sigma aTar$, which abbreviate 'There is a possible world, a, in which it is the case that r', and which are translatable into formulae like $\Sigma pKQpLCpr$. To do so we need only suppose that $a,b,c, \ldots$ take as substitution instances substitutions for p which satisfy Qp, and regard 'Tar (In a it is the case that r)' as equivalent to '$LCar$ (a strictly implies r)'.

What of the ontological commitment of formulae like $\Sigma pKQpLCpr$ and $\Sigma aTar$? Over what do the bound variables p and a range? We know from the arguments of Chapter VIII that such questions embody misunderstandings. The bound variables p and a are propositional variables. They do not have a range of values in Quine's sense. Their substitution instances, being propositions, are not names which refer to anything, and so have no bearing on the question of what individual expressions we need in our language. That question, as we have seen, is the only question which people can properly be taken to mean when they talk, improperly, about 'ontological' questions. We know how to understand sentences of the form $\Sigma pKQpLCpr$ and $\Sigma aTar$ in precisely the same way as we know how to understand sentences like 'For some p, James believes that p'. This way has been sufficiently explained.[21] Since 'There is a possible world in which Charles II had legitimate children' has been explained as meaning just what $\Sigma pKQpLCpr$ and $\Sigma aTar$ mean, there is no further problem about the existence of possible worlds. In saying 'For some p, James believes that p' we commit ourselves to no entities over and above

[20] The symbolism used in the following pages is that used by Prior in *Worlds, Times and Selves* (by A. N. Prior and Kit Fine, 1977), pp. 42 ff.
[21] See above, Ch. VIII, pp. 200 ff.

EXISTENCE OF POSSIBLE WORLDS

James: in saying 'There is a possible world in which Charles II had legitimate children' we commit ourselves to no entities over and above Charles II.

Possible worlds thus give rise to two problems in connection with existence: what is meant by existence *in* possible worlds, and what is meant by existence *of* possible worlds. A proposition like (28) has been thought to refer to, to be about, undesirable entities of two sorts: possible, though not actual, persons, and possible, though not actual, worlds. Both ideas are confused, though for different reasons.

Propositions like (28), as has been explained, are not directly about anything at all, other than any actual objects, such as Charles II, that they may mention. But interpreted as (28'), (28) is indirectly about a person who was a child of Charles II: only such a person could provide a 'verification' of (28'). If (28) is so interpreted, however, it is indirectly about, not a merely possible, but an actual person – indeed in this case about one of Charles II's many illegitimate children, whose possibility was actualized on a large scale. If (28) is interpreted as equivalent to (28") it is not even indirectly about anything, so not about non-actual persons any more than actual. So interpreted the operator having widest scope in the proposition is not a quantifier binding individual variables (and thus is not about any objects named by names substitutable for the individual variable it contains). The operator which has widest scope is instead the quantifier implicit in the phrase 'There is a possible world in which — ', but this, as we have seen, must be regarded as binding not an individual but a propositional variable. Such propositions are not indirectly about anything at all, although they may be directly about some object, in this case Charles II, mentioned in the matrix of the proposition. The confusion which gives rise to the idea that (28) refers to non-actual persons is a confusion of scope of a kind which has been sufficiently examined in the preceding chapter.

The confusion which gives rise to the idea that (28) refers to entities called 'possible worlds', on the other hand, is a confusion that is removable by reductive analysis. Possible worlds are eliminated in the same way as events or causes. 'The event which Alcibiades reported caused his respect for Socrates to increase' seems to make something which is referred to as an 'event' one of the subjects of each of the two-place predicates '— reported....' and '— caused....'. When the proposition has been paraphrased by 'For some p, Alcibiades reported that p, and, because p, Alcibiades' respect for Socrates increased' these two-place predicates disappear in favour of the relator[22] '— reported that ....' and the sentential connective 'Because —, ...', which do not require individual expressions to fill all their argument-places. Similarly, 'There is a possible world in which Charles II had legitimate children' seems to say that something called a 'world' is subject to a relator 'T—, ... (In — it is the case that ....)' whose second argument-place is filled by a proposition. But when we see that this apparent relator means no more than 'LC —, ... (Necessarily if —, then ....)', and that the whole proposition can be analysed as meaning $\Sigma p K Q p L C p r$, we no longer see it as referring, even indirectly, to mysterious entities called 'possible worlds'. Possible worlds, like events and Propositions, are suitable stubble for Ockham's razor. Existence *in* possible worlds has to be understood by getting the scope of our quantifiers right. Existence *of* possible worlds has to be understood by getting the categories of our variables right.

11. *Realism about possible worlds and '— exist' as a first-level predicable*

Neither the existence of, nor existence in, possible worlds would imperil the good health of philosophy, if philosophers were immune from the tendency to link existence with reference and to treat '— exist' as a first-level predicable. In another possible world *there were* legitimate children fathered by Charles II. *There is* a possible world in which Charles II had legitimate offspring. So far there is nothing amiss. The trouble begins when one moves from these claims to the assertion that such children *had existence* in that world, or that the world in which they had it *exists*. These uses of 'exist' are no longer representable by the quantifier. Plantinga, for instance, believes that Socrates exists in some but not all possible worlds.[23] As we have seen (Ch. IV, § 1; Ch. V, § 7), he construes the proposition that Socrates might not have existed as affirming the

---

[22] For the notion of 'relator', see my *What is Truth?*, p. 56.
[23] See *The Nature of Necessity*, pp. 46–7.

possibility that the proposition 'Socrates existed' might have been false. Part of the conclusion of Chapter IV, above, was that this way of understanding 'Socrates might not have existed' is mistaken: we can recognize the fact that Socrates' existence is contingent without being forced to admit that a genuine proposition is formed by attaching '— exist' as a first-level predicate to the proper name 'Socrates'. But Plantinga, who thinks that we *are* forced to admit this, will construe 'There are possible worlds in which Socrates existed', as well as 'There are possible worlds in which it is false that Socrates existed', as involving the predication of existence of Socrates. Now Socrates of course existed. And Plantinga, at least, does not think that we can predicate of an object which never existed that in some possible world *it* existed. There are no non-existent objects; and nothing, not even existence in some possible world, can be predicated of what does not exist. Plantinga's realism does not at this point outstrip his 'robust sense of reality'. Lewis, on the other hand, is committed to non-existent objects. He regards himself as a 'realist', and informs us that 'Realism about unactualized possibles is exactly the thesis that there are more things than actually exist'.[24] This is another way of saying that there exist things which do not actually exist. Lewis defends this doctrine against the charge of self-contradiction by insisting that we distinguish two 'idioms of quantification', one unrestricted, one restricted 'to our own world and things in it'. He advocates using 'there are —' for unrestricted and 'there actually exist —' for restricted quantification. Unfortunately, no quantifier, however restricted, will serve to play the role which the second 'exist' in 'There exist things which do not actually exist' is designed to play. This sentence, in so far as it can be understood at all, must be taken to be of the form $\Sigma x N \phi x$. The expression substituted for ϕ must be a first-level predicable: a quantifier in this position, even if carefully distinguished typographically as $\exists a - a$ from the unrestricted quantifier symbolized by $\Sigma x - x$, would produce the ill-formed formula $\Sigma x N \exists a a x$.[25] The only way to make even superficial sense of 'There exist things which do

---
[24] Lewis, *Counterfactuals*, p. 86.
[25] Lewis would use the formula $\Sigma x N \exists a I a x$, which bears out my claim, since '$\exists a I a -$' is a first-level predicable. Moreover he would define $\exists a I a a$ as $\Sigma x K I x x \phi x$ where ϕx represents '*x* is actual'. It is thus abundantly obvious that the 'restricted'

not actually exist' is to construe the second 'exist', or 'actually exist', as a first-level predicable; and the same is true for 'actually exist' in 'There are more things than actually exist'.

Lewis's realism about unactualized possibles can only begin to be understood if 'exist' is construed as a first-level predicable, and the same may be said about Plantinga's realism about possible worlds. 'There are any number of possible worlds; each of them exists—exists in the actual world—although none is actual'.[26] To say that each possible world exists is to say something of the form $\Pi x \phi x$—again there is no possibility of construing it as being of the form $\Pi x \exists a a x$—and if 'exists' or 'exists in the actual world' is to be substituted for ϕ it must be regarded as a first-level predicable. We have already seen how Quine surreptitiously introduces *being* as a property of objects by using the unfortunate mode of speech 'What there are — are all and only —'.[27] Any sentence introduced by 'All and only —' or 'Each of them —' will require completion by a first-level predicable. Plantinga clearly regards possible worlds as objects, in Frege's sense, and existence as a property of these objects.

What Plantinga says explicitly about each possible world, Lewis says implicitly about 'our actual world'. He assures his reader that he, the reader, believes in our actual world already, and merely asks him to believe in more things of the same kind.[28] To believe in fairies is to believe that fairies exist. To believe in 'our actual world' is, presumably, to believe that our actual world exists. It is, for Lewis, a pleonasm to call a world 'ours' as well as 'actual'; for 'we call it alone actual ... because it is the world we inhabit'.[29] To believe in it is, then, to believe that the world we inhabit exists. Lewis cannot intend us to interpret this along the lines that Russell interpreted 'The King of France exists'. This would make it a matter simply of believing that just one world is inhabited by us. If we answered Lewis's call to 'believe in more things of the same kind' we should then believe merely that some worlds are not inhabited

quantifier is able to do the job required of it only in virtue of its dependence on a first-level concept of actuality or existence.

[26] *The Nature of Necessity*, p. 48.
[27] See above, Ch. VII, pp. 178 ff.
[28] *Counterfactuals*, p. 87.
[29] Ibid., p. 85.

by us, i.e. are not actual. But this would not make us realists about possible worlds. Propositions like 'Some worlds are not inhabited by us and in them Napoleon won the Battle of Waterloo' are open to interpretations like Prior's; and assenting to them does not make us realists on this issue. Belief in the actual world and in more things of the same kind must have more content, must require greater credulity, than this. This 'more' can only, I suggest, be indicated by requiring that 'exist' in 'The world we inhabit—like all the other worlds—exists' be taken as a first-level predicate. What we are supposed to extend from our actual world to more things of the same kind is our belief that it *exists*. Those who can find no sense in the idea of existence as a property of objects will find it difficult, not so much to extend this belief, as to identify it. This variety of realism is not false but unintelligible.

Those who take fright at such an excess of realism have tended to turn, in true nominalist fashion, to words, or to those collections of words called sentences: to say that there is a possible world in which Charles II had legitimate children is to say that there is a consistent sentence which affirms that Charles II had legitimate children. But these counsels of desperation are unnecessary. Talk about possible worlds can be interpreted without quantification over 'world-entities', or sentence-types, or token utterances or inscriptions. We need quantification, but not quantification *over* anything. Existence, as we have seen in Chapter VI, has nothing to do with reference, and 'exist' is never a first-level predicable. Neither existence *in* nor existence *of* possible worlds need involve us in the snares of ontology. Most tame tigers may be presumed to growl; but we have no need to say, misleadingly, that most of Shakespeare's characters and most possible objects do not exist, let alone that every possible world does exist. Russell remarked that 'an almost unbelievable amount of false philosophy has arisen through not realizing what "existence" means'.[30] The correct account of what it means is his own, and Frege's—the thesis, namely, that existence cannot be a property of objects, of individuals. The sad truth is that sixty years after Russell wrote these words, and nearly a hundred years after Frege made his great discovery about existence, philosophers

[30] *Logic and Knowledge*, p. 234.

continue to make the same mistakes. Russell wrote, optimistically, in the perfect tense of false philosophy *having* arisen. His hopes for human progress might have been dashed if he could have foreseen how much false philosophy, for the same reason, was still to arise.

XI
Existence, Validity, and Instantiation

1. *The relation between the existential and the universal quantifier*

'Existence is what the existential quantifier expresses.'[1] This echo of Quine summarizes the claim that has so far been made in this book. But what *does* the existential quantifier express? Can the explanation be pushed any further back? If this could be done, it might be possible to give a characterization of the 'existential' sense of 'be' which is independent of the verb 'exist' or the phrase 'there is'. We should then be in a better position to complete the task left unfinished in Chapter I, namely, to give some comprehensive account of the various senses of 'be'. But is it possible to define existential quantification in terms of anything else, of anything more simple?

The answer to the last question is well known. It *is* possible to define the existential quantifier in terms of something else, but not in terms of anything that is in any obvious way more simple. The existential quantifier can be defined in terms of the universal quantifier and negation: $\Sigma x \phi x = N \Pi x N \phi x$. And generally speaking, for any variable, θ, of any syntactical category, $\Sigma \theta = N \Pi \theta N$. But then the universal quantifier can equally well be defined in terms of the existential quantifier and negation: $\Pi x \phi x = N \Sigma x N \phi x$. And generally speaking, for any variable, θ, of any syntactical category, $\Pi \theta = N \Sigma \theta N$. Π and Σ are interdefinable. Frege in the *Grundgesetze* takes the universal quantifier as primitive; Quine in *Philosophy of Logic* takes existential quantification as primitive.[2] On this basis it

---
[1] Quine, 'Existence and Quantification', p. 97.
[2] *Philosophy of Logic*, p. 22.

is possible to object to Kant's Table of Categories[3] in which Plurality (representing 'Some'), Universality (representing 'All'), Negation, and Existence figure as separate and independent basic concepts. In fact two of them could have done the work of four. If existence is what the existential quantifier expresses, the second category which Kant lists under the heading of 'Modality', namely, Existence, is the same as the second category listed under the heading of 'Quantity', namely, Plurality.[4] And if 'Some' can be defined in terms of 'All' and 'Not', or alternatively 'All' in terms of 'Some' and 'Not', one or other of the categories of Universality and Plurality should be taken as primitive, but not both.

A concept which can be constructed out of another concept with the help of negation is not properly speaking *another* concept: *eadem est scientia oppositorum*.[5] This remains true even if negation has to figure twice in the definition. $\Sigma x \phi x$ and $\Pi x \phi x$ are not contradictories, but $\Sigma x \phi x$ and $\Pi x N \phi x$ are. $N \phi x$, moreover, is a permissible substitution for ϕx in $\Pi x \phi x$: $\Pi x N \phi x$ is itself of the form $\Pi x \phi x$. And this form is equivalent to the negation of an existentially quantified proposition. We can say, therefore, that there is just one concept of quantification: existential and universal quantifiers no more express distinct concepts than do 'odd' and 'even'.

2. *The relation between quantification and the notion of valid inference*

Can anything more be said about this concept of quantification? Must we accept it as primitive and indefinable, one of Locke's simple ideas (though not entering the mind through either of the inlets of sensation and reflection)?

I believe that something more can be said, but in order to say it we have to follow a roundabout route. Prior was not the first to bind propositional variables with quantifiers, to write formulae according to the pattern $\Pi p \delta p$. The Polish school of logicians of the early part of this century used regularly to attach quantifiers binding propositional variables to formulae

[3] *Critique of Pure Reason*, A. 80, B. 106.
[4] See above, Ch. VII, p. 175 n. 6. The passage to which the note just cited is a footnote gives the explanation of Kant's inclusion of existence under the heading of modality.
[5] See above, Ch. II, p. 40.

QUANTIFICATION AND NOTION OF VALID INFERENCE

belonging to the Calculus of Propositions. Where Russell would have written $(p \supset q) \equiv (\sim q \supset \sim p)$ the Polish logicians would have written $\Pi p \Pi q E C p q C N q N p$. The Russellian formula is a schema. It is not itself true, although any consistent substitution of propositions for p and q in the formula will produce a true proposition. The Polish formula is itself a proposition, and a true one. Logic was conceived by the Polish school as a body of knowledge, a systematically developed collection of true propositions. The axioms and theorems of any part of logic were just as much truths as the axioms and theorems of arithmetic or geometry. They were not mere schemata, formal patterns waiting to be fleshed out with genuine propositional content. That part of logic which we are accustomed to calling 'The Calculus of Propositions' was part of what the Polish logicians called 'Protothetic'. This includes amongst its theses every formula which results from prefixing to a tautological truth-functional schema universal quantifiers binding each of its variables. A formula is an axiom or theorem of Protothetic if it is, in Quinian terms, the closure of an axiom-schema or theorem-schema of the Propositional Calculus.

Note, however, that the only quantifiers which are needed for that part of Protothetic which corresponds to the Propositional Calculus are universal quantifiers. Theses of the Propositional Calculus are interpreted as holding good for *all* uniform substitutions of propositions for propositional variables. The Propositional Calculus is not concerned to tell us when we have a formula which will come out as true for *some* substitutions of propositions for its variables. This means that propositions of the form $\Sigma p \Sigma q N E C p q C q p$, though true, do not occur as theses of the calculus. Existentially quantified propositions of this sort are, of course, equivalent to the negations of universally quantified propositions: $\Sigma p \Sigma q N E C p q C q p = N \Pi p \Pi q E C p q C q p$. But just as asserting a universally quantified proposition of this sort is tantamount to treating the corresponding unquantified tautological formula as a thesis, so asserting its negation is tantamount to rejecting it as a thesis. Logicians have toyed with the idea of using a reversed 'turnstile' (⊣) as a symbol of thesis rejection, just as the 'turnstile' itself (⊢) is used as a symbol of thesis acceptance. But the Propositional Calculus has no need of a separate symbol for thesis rejection, and similarly Protothetic, in so far as it corresponds to the Propositional Calculus, has no need of negated universally quantified propositions or of the existentially quantified propositions that are their equivalents.

If theses of the propositional calculus are presented as quantified propositions, like $\Pi p \Pi q ECpqCNqNp$, they are easily thought of as logical truths, even as very general and fundamental facts about the world. If on the other hand they are thought of as schemata, like $\vdash ECpqCNqNp$ they can more easily be thought of as rules of inference: From any proposition of the form Cpq it is legitimate to infer a corresponding proposition of the form $CNqNp$, and vice versa. Contraposition, after all, began life as a recognized form of valid 'immediate' inference. To every rule of inference there corresponds a universally quantified proposition. Logicians regard it as their business primarily to pick out valid forms of inference and only secondarily to reject invalid ones. It is no wonder that the Propositional Calculus can do without the reversed turnstile and the corresponding part of Protothetic without the existential quantifier.

Nevertheless, other branches of logic, less basic than the logic of truth-functions, do make use of the existential quantifier, even when that quantifier binds propositional variables. Thus certain interpretations of modal and tense logic interpret 'possibly' and 'sometimes' by formulae which begin with Σp.[6] But it is when the internal logic of propositions is investigated, in the predicate calculus, that the existential quantifier comes into its own. Indeed, the start of the predicate calculus has usually been thought of as synonymous with the introduction of the quantifiers into logic. That, as was shown in Chapter VI, is a mistake. All logic deals with valid inference and, as we have just seen, any valid inference, even in truth-functional logic, can be represented by a universally quantified proposition. The universal quantifier is implicitly present in every branch of logic. This is shown by the presence of variables. The use of variables begins with Aristotle, that is to say it begins with logic itself. Quine may be anxious[7] to distinguish variables from schematic letters, but it is a distinction without a difference.

[6] Cf. Prior and Fine, *Worlds, Times and Selves, passim.*
[7] See above, Ch. VI, § 4.

Part of the use of schematic letters is to register that any uniform substitution of appropriate expressions for them in a formula containing them will result in a truth. But that is also implied by a formula in which a variable is bound by the universal quantifier. Indeed, Russell's distinction between 'real' and 'apparent' variables, mirrored by Quine's distinction between 'free' and 'bound' variables, is equally dispensable when we look at their function in asserted formulae: x in $C\phi xp$ is properly regarded as free so long as $C\phi xp$ is regarded as a mere matrix or open sentence; but if it is asserted, if we write $\vdash C\phi xp$, it is just as if Πx had been prefixed to the C. The variable, in some of its uses at least, expresses the very same concept as the universal quantifier.

This concept, of which one aspect is universality, is, as I have already argued, the very same concept as that whose other aspect is existence, just as 'odd' and 'even' are two sides of one concept. Are we then to say that existence is no more than an aspect of the concept whose other manifestations are the use of variables and the notion of valid inference? That is indeed the theory I wish to maintain. But I have so far applied the theory only to the case of propositions in which the quantifier binds propositional variables: it is not difficult to be persuaded that the assertion of $\Sigma p \Sigma q NECpqCqp$ is much the same as saying that Affirming the Consequent is a fallacy, i.e. as denying that a certain inference form is valid. It is less easy to see that the person who asserts that there are aristocratic Australians is doing nothing more than denying the validity of an inference. And yet it is arguable. Instead of saying 'Aristocratic Australians exist' I might say 'It doesn't follow that because someone is Australian he is plebeian'. And 'There is an even prime number' might be thought to assert the same as 'The inference schema "n is prime/n is odd" is not valid'.

One philosopher who has visited this territory before us is Gilbert Ryle, although he affirmed the connection between inference and universality without drawing out its implications for existence. Ryle's manner of expressing the point was to say that a general statement was an 'inference ticket'.[8] The general statements he had in mind were universal generalizations. But just as the assertion of a universal generalization can be

[8] Ryle, *The Concept of Mind*, 1950, p. 121.

regarded as the issuing of an inference ticket, so the assertion of an existential generalization (equivalent to the denial of a universal generalization) can be regarded as the refusal of an inference ticket.

Universal generalizations can, of course, be hypothesized as well as asserted. They and their negations can occur as disjuncts in disjunctive propositions. We can wish that what they would assert if they were asserted were the case. But the Rylean analysis can take care of this. If the assertion that every prime greater than 2 is odd is the issuing of a ticket licensing the inference from propositions of the form 'n is a prime greater than 2' to propositions of the form 'n is odd', supposing that every prime greater than 2 is odd is supposing that inferences of this form are valid. 'Either aristocratic Australians exist or Michael is no Australian' is equivalent to 'Either the inference from propositions of the form "x is an Australian" to propositions of the form "x is plebeian" is invalid, or Michael is no Australian'. 'Would that kindly bank managers existed!' comes out as 'Would that the inference from "x is a bank manager" to "x is unkind" were invalid!' Clumsy, but possible.

These considerations serve to distinguish the analysis I am suggesting—which I have called 'Rylean'—from the view put forward by Ramsey some twenty years before Ryle.[9] Otherwise it would have been more proper to call the analysis 'Ramseian' than 'Rylean'. But Ramsey made a point of denying that what he called 'variable hypotheticals', expressible by formulae like $\Pi x C \phi x \psi x$, were propositions. He made no allowance for their negation, let alone their occurrence as the antecedents of conditionals or as disjuncts of disjunctive propositions. And if they do not admit of negation, they are clearly of no use for the analysis of the concept of existence. For Ramsey, a variable hypothetical is not something which can be true or false. Believing that all men are mortal is not a matter of assenting to a truth: it is merely having the habit of passing from judgements of the form 'x is a man' to judgements of the form 'x is mortal'. Clearly one could have this habit without possessing the concept of validity at all. But it is this concept which we are suggesting is at bottom the same as that of universality or existence. To possess oneself the habit of passing

[9] F. P. Ramsey, *The Foundations of Mathematics*, 1965, pp. 237-55.

QUANTIFICATION AND NOTION OF VALID INFERENCE 283

from judgements of the one sort to judgements of the other would not require such a concept, though to ascribe such a habit to another would require it. Even if a universal belief involves no such concept, the concept of a universal belief does. For the sake of argument, we may grant Ramsey that John's belief that all men are mortal does not constitute any attitude on John's part towards a proposition. It remains true that, when I believe that John believes that, for every x, if x is a man x is mortal, my belief constitutes an attitude on my part to a proposition about John; and this proposition can only be expressed by means of the notion of generality, or validity, or quantification—or existence. Ramsey's view was that variable hypotheticals were not propositions, but were describable in terms of inferential tendencies. My view is that they are propositions, but the same propositions as those which ascribe validity. I do not propose to substitute the concept of validity for that of universality, but to identify the two.

No one will want to question the correlation between the proposition ΠpΠ$qECpqCNqNp$ and the rule that the inferences from Cpq to $CNqNp$ and vice versa are valid. But where the quantified proposition is an empirical, or even an accidental, truth the correlation may seem less obvious. 'Every boy in the Fourth Form has measles' can surely be true without our having to allow that inferences of the form 'x is a boy in the Fourth Form/x has measles' are valid. The inference that John has measles from the fact that John is a boy in the Fourth Form is a paradigm case of a logically invalid inference. Not all valid inferences, however, are *logically* valid. The pompous headmaster may say to a parent, 'Ah, if John is in the Fourth Form, you may properly conclude that he has measles'. The propriety of such an inference just is what is conveyed by 'Every boy in the Fourth Form has measles'. If the chosen mode of expressing this proposition were 'If x is in the Fourth Form, x has measles' where x is a 'free' or 'real' variable, the connection would be obvious. It is an invitation to infer the truth of any proposition obtained by substituting a name for x in the consequent from a true proposition in which the same name replaces x in the antecedent.[10]

[10] This claim is not unlike that made by Quine in *Roots of Reference*, §§ 17-18. 'A dog is an animal' is assented to because it is realized that 'animal' deserves assent whenever 'dog' does.

3. *Quantified propositions with simple matrices, to which no inference corresponds*

For a universally quantified proposition to be interpretable in this way it must have as its matrix a conditional or biconditional; that is to say it must express what Russell called a formal implication or formal equivalence.[11] But not all universally quantified formulae are of the form $\Pi x C \phi x \psi x$ or $\Pi x E \phi x \psi x$, even if these forms do correspond, as is sometimes held, to the ordinary-language forms 'Every A is a B' and 'All and only A's are B's'. The syntactic rules for universally quantified propositions do not rule out propositions of the simpler form $\Pi x \phi x$, where there is nothing conditional in the substitutions for ϕx.

How would a proposition of this sort look? 'Everything is a lion', 'Everything swims' or 'Everything is yellow' are instances of the form $\Pi x \phi x$ without being instances of the form $\Pi x C \phi x \psi x$ or $\Pi x E \phi x \psi x$. What can we make of them? Syntactically they seem to be faultless, but semantically they present a difficulty. If everything were a lion how would we be able to learn, or to teach people, what it was to be a lion? Recognizing lions as such is a matter of discriminating between lions and things which are not lions. Someone who possesses the concept *lion* must also possess the concept *non-lion*. Indeed, as has been said often enough already, there are not two concepts at work here, but one: *eadem est scientia oppositorum*. A concept is a sort of boundary, but there can be no boundary where nothing is on the other side of it. If everything, including bees, Old Uncle Jim, and the washing machine could truly be said to swim, what occasion would there be for remarking the fact? And if everything were yellow, how could the meaning of 'yellow' ever be taught—particularly if everything was shiny as well? Without things that are yellow but not shiny or shiny but not yellow, the meanings of 'yellow' and 'shiny' would be indistinguishable.

We have here an application of what has been called the 'Contrast Theory of Meaning'.[12] Given an expression whose

---

[11] A. N. Whitehead and Bertrand Russell, *Principia Mathematica to *56*, 1962, pp. 20 ff.

[12] This title was used by Ernest Gellner (*Words and Things*, 1959, pp. 40 ff.) as

meaning is in question, the 'Analytic' philosopher tends to ask, 'What would it be like for the expression to be *in*applicable to something?' When something is said to be 'abstract' or 'real' or 'socially conditioned', it may well serve to clear up confusion about what is meant if we ask 'As opposed to what?' This requirement of opposition has played a conspicuous part in 'analytic' philosophy. Strawson's famous doctrine of Persons pivots on the claim that in order for me to ascribe predicates of a certain sort to myself I must be able to ascribe them also to others.[13] He uses the Contrast Theory of Meaning again in a later book to produce a version of Kant's 'Transcendental Deduction': if sense is to be made of the notion of how things seem to be (are experienced as being) this can only be by contrast with a notion of how things *are*, objectively.[14] These two uses of the Contrast Theory are to be distinguished, as Strawson makes clear (pp. 102 ff., 108). The first establishes 'owners' of experiences who are distinguishable from each other and each of which is identifiable with what Kant would call an empirical unity of apperception. The second establishes only the contrast between things as they are and things as 'experienced', and thus fails to yield any real notion of an owner of experience: an 'I think' which accompanies all my representations, the transcendental unity of apperception, is not to be thought of as an identifiable substance. This second application of the Contrast Theory is parallel with the simpler thesis that 'yellow' could not have the meaning it does if there was no contrast between things that are yellow and things that are not yellow. The contrast between things *being experienced* as thus and so and things *being* thus and so is a binary contrast, as is that between any description and its negation. 'It seems to be the case that p', like 'It is known to be the case that p' or 'It ought to be the case that p',[15] contrasts with simple p, in the same way as does 'It is not the case that p'. But the first of the applications we mentioned as being made by Strawson is not a binary contrast but one which admits of an indefinite number

---

a vehicle of abuse, but there is no reason why it should not be used without any pejorative sense, since the abuse was unjustified.

[13] Strawson, *Individuals*, Ch. III, § 4.
[14] Strawson, *The Bounds of Sense*, 1966, p. 107.
[15] See above, Ch. VII, § 2.

of variations: 'I am in pain' contrasts, not only with 'You are in pain', but with 'She is in pain', 'Eric is in pain', 'The parrot is in pain', and so on, for as many creatures as we are prepared to regard as sentient. But whether it is binary contrast or many-valued contrast that is in operation, the point remains that it is only as contrasting elements that linguistic expressions can have a function. This is a principle which operates at every level at which language can be analysed, not only semantic and syntactic, but phonological.[16] Strawson's use of the principle is one of the most striking to occur in philosophy since Frege directed philosophers' attention to the relevance to their subject of language, and the ways in which language works.

If the Contrast Theory of Meaning has the importance that has been ascribed to it, a sentence like 'Everything is yellow' has the paradoxical feature that if what it states were true one of the words it contains could not have the meaning it in fact has. If there was nothing which was not yellow, the contrast on which the meaning of 'yellow' depends would not obtain and no one could learn what 'yellow' means. The situation is not so simple with regard to 'Everything is a lion'. Perhaps, though this is disputed,[17] 'lion' is a term which is capable of definition: a lion is a mammal with a tawny coat, carnivorous, weighing when fully grown so many pounds, etc. If so, we could understand 'lion' provided we understood all the terms which enter into its definition. But, at least in so far as those terms occur as conjuncts in a conjunctive description serving as the *definiens*, our problem will recur for each of these terms. If a lion is a mammal which is tawny and carnivorous, etc., then if everything is a lion everything is tawny. We shall then have for 'tawny' precisely the same problem we envisaged for 'yellow'. 'Everything swims' may be thought liable to the same difficulty. 'Swims' is perhaps definable as 'moves by propelling itself in water', but then if everything swims everything moves, and there will be no contrast between motion and rest on which to base our understanding of the word 'moves'.

Russell, wanting to find a definition for the Universal Class,

[16] Cf. J. Lyons, *Introduction to Theoretical Linguistics*, p. 67: 'the principle of *contrast* (or opposition) is fundamental in modern linguistic theory.'

[17] e.g. by Kripke, in 'Naming and Necessity' 316 ff. If Kripke is to be followed, 'lion' is the name of a race, and we shall have the paradox of a race of which *everything* is a member.

QUANTIFIED PROPOSITIONS WITH SIMPLE MATRICES

pitched on self-identity as the only property everything possessed. Speaking of the Universal Class, he wrote:

Its definition is as follows:
  *24.01 $V = \hat{x}(x=x)\ Df$

Any other property possessed by everything would do as well as '$x=x$', but this is the only such property that we have hitherto studied.[18]

Other such properties have been studied by logicians since Russell wrote this passage, but they have been properties like *being square if it is square* or *being either hot or not hot*. Predicates which signify such properties will all be of the form $C\phi x\phi x$, or be reducible to this form. Propositions asserting that such properties are possessed by everthing will be of the form $\Pi x C\phi x\phi x$, and therefore representable as assertions of the validity of inferences of the form $\phi x/\phi x$. They do not constitute counter-examples to our claim that universally quantified propositions can be regarded as asserting the validity of inferences. Russell's $\Pi x I x x$ however, if allowed, will constitute such a counter-example. But should we allow it? Should we, that is to say, allow that the formula $\Pi x I x x$ properly represents a (true) proposition which asserts that everything is identical with itself?

I think not. A proposition like 'Abyssinia is the same (country) as Ethiopia' is not, in my view, a proposition in which something is predicated of the country Abyssinia, nor by the same token one in which something is predicated of the country Ethiopia.[19] It is rather a proposition about the expressions 'Abyssinia' and 'Ethiopia', saying of them that there is something (some country) which they both name. It is of the form $\Sigma x K \phi x a \phi x b$. It is not a reflexive proposition like 'Robert

[18] Whitehead and Russell, *Principia Mathematica,* p. 216.

[19] It would be possible to regard this proposition as one in which something is predicated of Abyssinia, namely, that it is called 'Ethiopia', or as one in which something is predicated of Ethiopia, namely, that it is called 'Abyssinia'. That is, it can be regarded either as asserting a relation between two names, as in the text, or as asserting, in one or other of the ways just outlined, a relation between a name and a country: what it cannot be regarded as asserting is a relation between a country and itself (or, if false, between two countries). If 'Abyssinia is the same country as Abyssinia' is interpreted as asserting a relation between a country and a name, as saying that Abyssinia is called 'Abyssinia', it is in no way reflexive; i.e. it is of the form ϕxy, not of the form ϕxx. It is also contingent, and what it predicates of Abyssinia, so far from being true of everything, is true of nothing but Abyssinia. So $\Pi x I x x$ could not symbolize its universal generalization, nor, if it could, would it be the truism it is intended to be.

shaves Robert' which asserts that someone or something stands in a certain relation to himself, and it is not therefore a proposition of the form ϕxx and cannot be symbolized by Ixx or '$x=x$'. So much for the more obvious examples of identity propositions. It would be possible to find a proposition of the same form $\Sigma x K\phi xa\phi xb$, and where b was replaced by a second occurrence of a: in this case, if 'Abyssinia is the same country as Ethiopia' means 'Some country is called both "Abyssinia" and "Ethiopia"', 'Abyssinia is the same country as Abyssinia' means 'Some country is called both "Abyssinia" and "Abyssinia"'. Such a proposition would be of the form ϕxx (being of the form $\Sigma y K\phi yx\phi yx$) and could properly be symbolized by Ixx. The universal generalization of this proposition, which $\Pi x Ixx$ would now be taken to represent, would obviously be untrue. (It would be of no use to Russell for defining the Universal Class.) Since it is of the form $\Pi x \Sigma y K\phi yx\phi yx$ it entails a corresponding proposition of the form $\Pi x \Sigma y \phi yx$, i.e. 'Everything names something', which is again manifestly untrue. It could only be made true by limiting the range of the universally quantified variable, x, to names, but this would have the effect of making it equivalent to the proposition 'Every name names something'. This proposition, which is of the same form as 'Every father is the father of someone', is again of the form $\Pi x C\phi x\phi x$, and I have already shown that such propositions do not constitute counter-examples to my thesis.[20]

4. *Existential propositions with indefinable predicables*

That thesis, that universally quantified propositions can be regarded as asserting the validity of inferences, depended on my claim that no true proposition could be found of the form

[20] The argument of this paragraph depends on the assumption that at least one of the terms of an identity proposition must be understood as representing a definite description. 'Ethiopia' is being taken as standing for 'the country called "Ethiopia"'. It was found necessary to take it in the same way in the proposition 'Geoffrey believes that Ethiopia is a Christian country' discussed in Ch. IX, § 4. The need to take at least one term of an identity proposition as a definite description has been argued for by Roger White, in 'Wittgenstein on Identity', *Proc. Arist. Soc.* 1977-8, 172-4. White in this article says many interesting things in support of Wittgenstein's remarks in the 5.5s of the *Tractatus*, remarks which include the claim that $(x)(x = x)$ is nonsense. I have developed these Wittgensteinian views about identity further in 'Is Identity a Relation?', in *Proc. Arist. Soc.* 1979-80, 81-100.

$\Pi x \phi x$ which was not also of the form $\Pi C \phi x \psi x$. $\Pi x \phi x$ is equivalent to $N\Sigma x N \phi x$ and $\Pi x C \phi x \psi x$ to $N\Sigma x K \phi x N \psi x$. I am therefore committed also to the claim that no negative existential proposition is true which does not have as its matrix a conjunctive open sentence. The only sort of predicable which is not, or is not reducible to, a conjunctive predicable capable of forming a conjunctive open sentence of this sort is an indefinable expression. If we suppose 'is yellow' to be indefinable, we are committed to saying that 'Nothing is yellow' cannot be a true proposition. This has sometimes to be taken to imply that the truth of an affirmative existential proposition, e.g. 'Yellow things exist' follows from the indefinability of the first-level predicable involved in it.[21] But from the fact that 'Nothing is yellow' cannot be a true proposition it does not follow that 'Yellow things exist' must be. It is possible that neither of these strings of words amounts to a proposition at all. If universally quantified propositions can all be regarded as asserting the validity of inferences, 'Nothing is yellow' cannot be regarded as a universally quantified proposition (and there is no other sort of proposition it can be). 'No raven is yellow' can be regarded as licensing the inference of any proposition of the form 'x is not yellow' from the corresponding proposition of the form 'x is a raven'. 'Nothing is yellow' might possibly be regarded as licensing the inference of a proposition of the form 'x is not yellow' from any proposition whatsoever; but it is not clear that a rule that allows us to assert a proposition of a certain form, given the truth of any proposition whatsoever, is properly called a rule of inference. Nor is it clear that we have any need for strings of words like 'Nothing is yellow' or 'Yellow things exist' to serve as propositions. It is preferable to regard them as the result of illegitimate extrapolation from propositions of the form $\Pi x C \phi x \psi x$ or $\Sigma x K \phi x \psi x$. Propositions of this latter form are equivalent to propositions employing, not unrestricted quantifiers like 'Nothing' and 'Something', but restricted ones like 'No one' (i.e. 'No person') or 'Some raven'. The connection between quantification and inference for which I have been arguing suggests that we have a use only

---

[21] Cf. Arthur Pap, 'Indubitable Existential Statements', *Mind*, 55, 1946. Pap's argument had affinities with a type of argument which became famous a few years later under the title 'Paradigm-Case Argument'.

for restricted quantification, and that Frege was mistaken in taking the notion of unrestricted quantification as primitive. This is a large question, which I have examined elsewhere.[22] The theme of the present work is too distant from it for a more detailed discussion to be embarked upon at this point. Enough has been said to show the very close connections between existence and universality and between universality and valid inference.

5. *Confirmation of this view from Kahn's study of the uses of* 'einai'

It may at least be remarked, however, that this doubt about the ability of sentences which exemplify the form $\Sigma x \phi x$, but not the form $\Sigma K \phi x \psi x$, to express genuine propositions finds support in Kahn's account of the uses of 'einai' in Ancient Greek.[23] As my fuller account of this in Appendix A makes clear, Kahn's 'Type VI' of the 'existential' uses of '*einai*' covers sentences in which an appropriate part of the verb is attached to a common noun in either the singular or the plural, or, in one case quoted by him, to a proper name. This last case, where Aristophanes (*Clouds*, 367) makes Socrates say 'There is no Zeus' or, perhaps, 'Zeus does not even exist' (*Oud' esti Zeus*), is to be dealt with in the way that propositions about fictional characters were dealt with in Chapter X. To say that 'Zeus does not exist' or 'Lady Catherine de Bourgh never existed' is, as we saw in section 7 of Chapter X, to say something about an expression. It is to say that a particular use of 'Zeus' or 'Lady Catherine de Bourgh' is not a genuine use of an expression as a proper name, but only a pretended use. In so far as the pretended use of 'Zeus' as a name carries with it certain descriptions we may say that 'Zeus does not exist' is tantamount to 'There is no one who is called "Zeus" and who lives on Olympus and who . . .'. What we have here is certainly not a clear example of a proposition which exemplifies the form $\Sigma x \phi x$ without exemplifying the form $\Sigma x K \phi x \psi x$.

What about those of Kahn's examples of Type VI uses which combine some part of '*einai*' with a singular or plural common

[22] In an unpublished D. Phil. thesis accepted by Oxford University in 1965, entitled 'Existence and Definability'.
[23] *The Verb 'Be' in Ancient Greek*.

noun rather than with a proper name? Almost all these examples concern the question whether there is a god, or whether there are gods. The sentence *'Eisi theoi* (Gods are)' does not appear in Greek, according to Kahn, before the middle of the fifth century BC. It appears, that is to say, only with the onset of philosophical scepticism about religious belief. And the only other examples of the Type VI use of *'einai'* have a similar philosophical background. Aristotle's 'whether or not there is such a thing as a god or a centaur'[24] interestingly couples the word 'god' with the name of a mythological beast. 'Centaur', 'hippogryph', 'dragon', etc. stand to 'horse', 'hippopotamus', 'dragon-fly', etc., as 'Perseus' stands to 'Pericles'. The former are names for mythological species as the latter is the name of a mythological person. It may thus be argued that 'Centaurs do not exist' is a remark about a particular use of the word 'centaur' in exactly the same way as 'Zeus does not exist' is a remark about a particular use of the word 'Zeus'.[25] In neither case do we have a sentence exemplifying the form $\Sigma x \phi x$ without exemplifying the form $\Sigma x K \phi x \psi x$. And 'Gods do not exist' will most likely be regarded, by those who assert it, as parallel to 'Centaurs do not exist'. Those who deny the gods typically believe that the word 'god', like the word 'centaur', has a use only in myth. So propositions formed simply by coupling a common noun with some part of the verb 'be' will normally involve the mention rather than the use of the noun in question.

Fifth-century sophists or twentieth-century positivists more often than not intended their claim 'There is no god' to be in this way a comment on the language used by believers. But atheism is not condemned to be metalinguistic in this way. It can be regarded as the denial of a genuine existential claim which is in no way concerned with language. What the believer

[24] See below, Appendix A, p. 332.
[25] See my article 'Baier on the Equivocal Character of "Exist"', *Mind*, 78, 1969, 223 ff. The point that is made in this article assimilates names of mythological species to names of mythological persons. By implication it assimilates genuine names of natural kinds to genuine proper names. Just as 'dragon' is not to be regarded as an abbreviation of 'fire-breathing outsize lizard', so 'lion' is not to be regarded as an abbreviation of 'mammal with a tawny coat, carnivorous, weighing when fully grown . . ., etc.' It is thus in line with the remarks about common nouns made by Kripke in 'Naming and Necessity', pp. 316 ff, which a number of recent authors have echoed and developed (see *Naming, Necessity, and Natural Kinds*, ed. Stephen P. Schwartz, 1977).

asserts the disbeliever can deny; but this will typically be something which at least allows of explication, of being unfolded into something more complex than the brief 'There is a god'. What is at stake will be whether there is an almighty father, creator of heaven and earth, or whether there is a being than which no greater can be conceived. It is not obvious that these propositions are of the form $\Sigma x \phi x$ without being of the form $\Sigma x K \phi x \psi x$.

Kahn tells us[26] that the construction which he labels 'Type VI' is often taken by philologists as representing the fundamental and original use of '*es', the Indo-European root of most of the verbs which are synonyms in Indo-European languages of the English verb 'be'. These philologists understand such sentences in a way which would make them exemplify the form $\Sigma x \phi x$ without exemplifying the form $\Sigma x K \phi x \psi x$. Kahn regards this view of what is fundamental amongst the uses of '*es' as a mistake. Instead, of the uses he lists under the heading 'existential', he takes as basic those which are exemplified by 'There is a cave, broad and deep down in the gloom of water, lying midway between Tenedos and Imbros'[27] and by 'There should be some companion who could carry the message quickly to Peleus' son'.[28] The first of these Kahn calls 'Locative-Existential'. The second can obviously be symbolized by $\Sigma x K \phi x \psi x$. We shall see, in the next chapter, the importance of these two forms for the explanation of the different senses of 'is'. But neither has the apparent simplicity of $\Sigma x \phi x$ or Kahn's Type VI propositions. Neither is formed simply by wrapping a second-level predicable round a single non-complex first-level predicable. In each 'There is' is attached, not simply to a common noun, but to a common noun followed by something else, in the one case by a locative expression, in the other by a relative clause. The latter form, at least, is amenable to my analysis of existential propositions in terms of denial of the validity of an inference, of refusal of an inference-ticket; and the former is analogous to this in a way we shall explore later. If I say 'There is a priest who will avert the plague for us' I am refusing to license the inference from propositions of the form

[26] *The Verb 'Be'*, p. 297.
[27] Ibid., p. 247, Example 31, from *Iliad*, 13.32.
[28] Ibid., p. 278, Example 87, from *Iliad*, 17.640.

'x is a priest' to propositions of the form 'x will not avert the plague for us'. And if I say 'There is a lion behind the bush' I am refusing to license the inference of propositions of the form 'x is not behind that bush' from propositions of the form 'x is a lion'. It would be difficult to construe 'There is a centaur' in this way.

6. *Validity, variables, instantiation, and existence*

These considerations, then, allow me to persist in my claim that the concept of existence is at base the same as the concept of valid inference. Validity is always a matter of form. If p is inferable from q it is because p is of a form and q is of a form such that propositions of the latter form imply corresponding propositions of the former. For instance, a proposition of the form 'n is a prime number greater than 2' implies the corresponding proposition of the form 'n is odd'. Existentially quantified propositions, we are saying, amount to denials of the validity of inferences of a certain kind. Thus 'For some n, n is an even prime number' is equivalent to the denial that the inference from a proposition of the form 'n is a prime number' to the corresponding proposition of the form 'n is odd' is valid. 'For some n, n —' is, as has been argued, a second-level predicable. But the connection between quantification and validity extends to quantifiers which bind variables other than individual variables, to expressions like 'For some ϕ, ϕ —' and 'For some p, — p', for example, which are not second-level predicables but expressions of different syntactical categories. 'Paul said something true' may be analysed as 'For some p, both Paul said that p and p': this too involves existential quantification. Accordingly the person who says this can be described as denying the validity of the inference from propositions of the form 'Paul said that p' to corresponding propositions of the form 'It is not the case that p'. For instance, if Paul said that sodium was a metal, we cannot infer that sodium is not a metal. Just so the existence of an even prime number prevents us from inferring from the mere fact that 53 is a prime number the proposition that 53 is odd. It is the notion of instantiation that is important here. It goes hand in hand with the possibility of using variables, and whatever can be expressed with the help of quantifiers can be expressed also with the help of variables.

It is the variable which allows us to display the form of a proposition, and, as has been emphasized, validity has to do with form. If we are to understand the words 'a proposition of the form "*n* is odd"' or 'a proposition of the form "Paul said that *p*"' we must understand what would count as instances of these forms. Just so, if we are to understand 'There is an even prime number' or 'Paul said something' we must understand what it would be for something to instantiate these propositions, that they would be instantiated, for instance, by 'Five is an even prime number' and 'Paul said that sodium was a metal'. As will be seen from this suggestion for the instantiation of 'There is an even prime number', there is no need in this context for the instantiating proposition to be true. What we are looking for is a necessary condition, not of an existential proposition's being true, but of its being understood. We have recognized that there may be true existential propositions which cannot be instantiated by any true proposition.[29] But we can still say that 'There is an unnamed pigeon in Trafalgar Square' is understood only if it is recognized that something like 'Joey is an unnamed pigeon in Trafalgar Square' would count as an instantiation of it, although clearly no such proposition is true. Indeed, the recognition of an existential proposition as one which no true singular proposition would instantiate requires that we have some idea of what sort of proposition, true or false, would instantiate it. So my requirement that it be intelligible to ask for an instantiation of any proposition classifiable as existential does not commit me to a substitutionalist account of quantification.

7. *The existential sense of 'be' not definable in terms of 'exist' or 'there is', but in terms of instantiation*

At the end of the discussion in Chapter I of the distinction between the copulative and the existential senses of 'be' I drew attention to the need for a clarification of the meaning of 'existential' in this context. Since then I have nailed my colours to the mast of Quine's dictum 'Existence is what the existential quantifier expresses'. This means that a use of the verb 'be'

---

[29] See above, Ch. VIII, § 2. It may be objected that in its normal use what is meant by 'instantiation' is a truth-preserving operation. If this is right, my use of 'instantiation' is abnormal; but I hope that it is nevertheless clear how it is intended to be understood.

will count as existential only if the proposition in which it occurs can be paraphrased by using instead the existential quantifier. The possibility of paraphrase by 'exist' is thus rejected as a criterion for 'be' being used in an existential sense. 'The natives are in a miserable condition' can be paraphrased by 'The natives exist in a miserable condition', but this does not make the use of 'are' here existential. 'Arkle still exists' is not, in my sense, an existential proposition, although I have argued that quantifiers are required at more than one point in its analysis.[30] The reason why neither 'The natives exist in a miserable condition' nor 'Arkle still exists' is an existential proposition in my sense is that it does not make sense to ask for an instantiation of either of them. If someone has said that there is a priest who will avert the plague, it is intelligible to ask 'Who is it?'; and if someone has said that there is something Paul said which is true, it is intelligible to ask 'What did he say?' But 'Arkle still exists' and 'The natives exist in a miserable condition' do not give rise to 'Who?' or 'What?' questions of this sort. The use of interrogative pronouns is analogous to that of variables,[31] and it is the variable, connected as it is with valid inference, which captures the essence of quantification. A proposition which can be instantiated is one which gives rise to the question 'Who?' or 'What?' So the connection between existence, on the one hand, and quantification and its variables, on the other, is maintained when it is insisted that it is the possibility of instantiation which must serve as the criterion for a proposition's being existential. And it is this criterion too which gives us the only clear way of attaching sense to the notion of an existential sense or use of the verb 'be' and its synonyms.

A proposition is not existential, by this criterion, merely because it contains the word 'exist'. Nor does our criterion for regarding a use of the verb 'be' as existential coincide with its inclusion in the phrases 'There is', 'There are', 'There will be', etc. The fact that a part of the verb 'be' occurs in a proposition as a component of one of this group of phrases is neither a necessary nor a sufficient condition for that proposition's being existential, or for 'be' here having its existential sense.

That it is not a necessary condition is clear from much that

---

[30] See above, Ch. V, p. 142.
[31] Cf. Ryle, 'Categories', *Collected Papers*, 2, 170 ff.

has been earlier in this book. 'Something is an even prime number' is an alternative way of expressing what is also expressible by 'There is an even prime number'; and since the structure of the proposition expressed—second-level predicate wrapped round first-level predicable—is more clearly visible in 'Something is an even prime number' than it is in 'There is an even prime number', we may regard the former as nearer a 'canonical' form of an existential proposition than the latter.[32] But the word 'some' and compounds formed from it are no more necessary to the expression of an existential proposition than 'There is' or 'There are'. 'Some man was seen by Peggy walking through the garden' differs only in emphasis from 'Peggy saw a man walking through the garden', and 'Apostles are depicted on one side of the throne' is as much an existential proposition as 'Some apostles are (There are apostles) depicted on one side of the throne'. All these forms admit of instantiation 'Peggy saw Francis walking through the garden' is the instantiation of, and a sufficient condition for, both 'Peggy saw a man walking through the garden' and 'Some man was seen by Peggy walking through the garden'; and 'James and John are depicted on one side of the throne' instantiates 'Some apostles are (There are apostles) depicted on one side of the throne' as well as the more economical 'Apostles are depicted on one side of the throne'. The important point is that 'a man' and 'Apostles' occur here as expressions for first-level concepts, as *Begriffswörte*, in Frege's terminology. A noun is a word for a concept, not the name of an object, if it occurs in the plural or prefixed by the indefinite article. Where we have a concept-word of this sort, there we have, as Frege would put it,[33] a proposition in which a property is ascribed, not to an object, but to a concept. These are propositions in which the number nought is denied of the concepts *man seen by Peggy walking through the garden* and *apostle depicted on one side of the throne*. They are thus existential propositions, although they do not contain 'There is' or any inflected form of this expression.

The occurrence in it of 'there is' cannot, therefore, be

---

[32] See above, Ch. III, § 8.
[33] I have discussed the misleading character of this way of putting it, and prescribed means to avoid being misled by it, in Ch. III, §§ 6, 7.

regarded as providing us with a necessary condition for a proposition's being existential. Nor can it provide us with a sufficient condition for identifying a form of words as an existential proposition. J. L. Mackie has produced an illustration of this.[34] Mackie is looking for 'exceptions to the rule that "there is" calls for a general term', i.e. the rule that 'There is' is a second-level predicable which requires a first-level predicable, not a proper name, for its completion into a proposition. He produces two apparent exceptions to the rule. Asked whether there are any good pubs in London, I may reply 'There's the Mermaid'. Again, if the topic has shifted to the competence of women in posts of high responsibility I may say 'There are women Prime Ministers; there is Mrs Gandhi'. When you ask me whether there are any good pubs in London I may reply, equivalently, 'The Mermaid is one' or 'There's the Mermaid'; and in support of the proposition that there is at least one woman Prime Minister I may say 'Mrs Gandhi is a woman Prime Minister' or, more economically, 'There is Mrs Gandhi'. As Mackie points out, this use of 'There is' occurs only to specify an individual which instantiates a concept in a context where the main topic is whether this concept is instantiated. That is to say, it occurs only when our interest is in some question of the form 'Is it true that there are A's?' where A represents a first-level predicable and 'there are' functions as a second-level predicate. Nevertheless, in 'There's the Mermaid' or 'There is Mrs Gandhi' the expression 'There is —', like the expression '— is one', functions rather as a stand-in for a first-level predicable. Words like 'she' in 'Mrs Gandhi lost the election and she was replaced as Prime Minister' have been called by Geach[35] 'pronouns of laziness'. Expressions like '— is one' or 'There is —' in the sort of context I have been considering may be counted as 'pro-verbs (or pro-predicates) of laziness'. 'There's Mrs Ganhi', like 'Mrs Gandhi is one', is simply a shorter, lazier, way of saying 'Mrs Gandhi is a woman Prime Minister', and '— is a woman Prime Minister' is a first-level predicable. The pro-verb which does the same work as this verb-phrase must be supposed to belong to the same syntactic category as it. I find therefore that neither 'There's the Mermaid' nor 'There is Mrs Gandhi' deserves to rank as an existential

[34] 'The Riddle of Existence', p. 251.   [35] *Reference and Generality*, § 76.

proposition, and by the criterion given above we do not have in these cases existential uses of the verb 'be'.

8. Purpose of this chapter

At the beginning of this chapter I recalled two tasks which I left unfinished at the end of Chapter I. The main task was to find some explanation of the double use of 'be', as copula and as verb of existence. Mill's view that this was a case of accidental equivocation seemed incredible. Surely 'be' in this respect is not purely equivocal, but analogical. If so, however, some connection must be discoverable between the copulative and the existential use. And this has not so far been done.

The second task was subsidiary to the first. It was to get clear what was meant by an 'existential' sense of the verb 'be'. Linguists have gone astray on this matter for lack of a thorough examination of the logical features of the concept of existence. It is hoped that the present enquiry will at least have avoided this danger. This chapter has attempted to bring out the consequences of the logic of existence for establishing a clear sense of 'existential'. The crucial matter has been seen to be instantiation. A proposition can be regarded as existential, only if some other proposition can be regarded as an instantiation of it. Otherwise expressed, a proposition is existential, only if it can be seen as an existential generalization of some other proposition. This is what the idiom of quantification expresses so clearly: $\Sigma x \phi x$ is obviously, blatantly, the existential generalization of ϕa. The verb 'be' is used in an existential sense if, and only if, the sense it contributes to a sentence is the sense of the quantifier. 'There is' is existential when it is expandable to 'There is something which is'. 'Is' is existential when it does the work of 'some'.

In pressing this argument I have been led to make claims about the connection between existence and validity. These claims, it must be admitted, are more dubious than the claim about the connection between existence and instantiation. It should not be supposed that someone who finds reason to object to the thesis that existence, univerality, and validity are all at bottom the same concept has thereby shaken the doctrine that existence is intrinsically connected with instantiation. It is the establishment of this latter doctrine which constitutes the performance of my subsidiary task. Armed with this understanding of what it is for 'be' to be used in an existential sense, I go on in the next chapter to the main task of this concluding part of the book, the discovery of some connection between this sense of 'be' and the copulative sense.

XII
Being and Existence

1. *The use of 'There is' in feature-placing propositions*

How to explain the fact that 'be' can occur both in sentences like 'Roger is a great Talker' and in sentences like 'There are sound arguments for verificationism'? The point we reached at the end of the last chapter is a good one for starting to solve this problem. We had just seen the uselessness of 'There is' as a criterion for a sentence's being an existential proposition. But there is something superficial about Mackie's example, 'There's Mrs Gandhi'. The trouble is that this sentence is not only not an existential proposition: it is not a proposition at all. It can only be understood as saying something true or false if helped out by our knowledge of the context of its utterance. Uttered in isolation it makes no move in the language game. However, it is possible to pick out a whole class of propositions, genuine propositions, containing the words 'There is' which fail just as clearly to pass the instantiability test for being an existential proposition. This class of propositions turns out to be crucial for explaining the connection between the existential and the copulative senses of 'be'.

Consider the proposition 'There's gold in them there hills'. It is ridiculous to suppose that it requires support from a statement of the form 'N is gold in them there hills', where N is a proper name. We can form propositions by attaching a mass-noun like 'gold' to the phrase 'There is' and completing the sentence with a designation of place. But we cannot make sense of the notion of an existential instantiation of such propositions. Propositions like this, e.g. 'There is coal in the Mendip Hills', are more akin to 'It's raining over the Pennines' than to

'There is a Prime Minister who is a woman'. Such propositions have been called by Strawson 'feature-placing statements'.[1] Impersonal constructions like 'It's raining —', 'It's cold —', or 'It's foggy —', when followed by a locative expression, belong to this class. These impersonal constructions can often be replaced, without change of sense, by constructions formed by attaching 'There is' to a mass noun: 'There is rain —', 'There's cold —', or 'There's fog —'. In neither form do they admit of instantiation. I can respond to the claim 'There's a book on the table by the fireplace' by asking 'Which book?'—a request for instantiation. But I cannot respond to the claim 'There is corn in Egypt' by asking 'Which corn?' (unless I mean 'What sort of corn?', a request for specification, not instantiation). I might as well try to follow up the remark that it's raining in London by asking 'What is?' We cannot find an impersonal verb paraphrase of every feature-placing statement introduced by 'There is'; but this is not important. It seems to be a mere linguistic accident that we have the form 'It's foggy' as well as the form 'There's fog', but lack the form 'It's coaly' as an alternative to 'There's coal'.

Coal, and even fog, can be regarded as a sort of stuff. Rain and snow can also be regarded as stuff, but the nouns here have close connections with happenings described by the homophonous verbs 'rain' and 'snow'. Rain and snow typically do something, namely fall, but there is nothing that coal and fog typically do in the same way. 'There's rain over the Pennines' does not so much tell us about the location of a certain quantity of stuff as tell us about the occurrence in a given place of a certain sort of event, or the existence there of a certain sort of state of affairs. This allows us to see how there is a progression from propositions like 'There's coal in the Mendips' via 'It's raining (There's rain) over the Pennines' to 'It's smelly (There's a smell) in the Dining Room'. While it is just possible to think of rain as a sort of stuff—less concentrated and static perhaps than coal, but still a sort of stuff—it is hardly possible to think of a smell as a sort of stuff. And certainly 'There's a smell in the Dining Room' is not an existential proposition requiring, or even admitting, instantiation. We cannot respond to the allegation about our Dining Room by asking 'Which

[1] Strawson, *Individuals*, Ch. VI, § 6.

smell?', unless this is again understood as meaning 'What sort of smell?'. As before, the demand in that case is for specification not instantiation. If the complaint is already specific, e.g. 'There's a smell of cabbage in the Dining Room', the response 'Which smell?' is even more clearly out of place. There is nothing which could count as the existential instantiation of 'There is a smell of cabbage in the Dining Room'. So this proposition cannot, on my criterion, be regarded as an existential proposition, nor can the word 'is' which occurs in it be regarded as occurring in an existential sense.

2. 'There is' as a verbalizer: connection with the copula

From smells to sounds is no great leap. The example 'There is a smell of cabbage in the Dining Room' recalls a Homeric example given by Kahn: 'And around him (there) was a clamour of the dead.'[2] Kahn draws our attention to an important class of uses of *'einai'* in which its grammatical subject is an abstract, usually verbal, noun. He labels this class 'Type V Existential'. He postulates a deep structure for such sentences in which a sentence with a corresponding verb 'Around him the dead cry out' is nominalized to form a phrase 'A clamour (crying out) of the dead around him' which is then reconverted into sentence form by the addition of a finite part of the verb *'einai'*. In English we have a wide range of verbs to choose from if we want a verb to attach to a nominalized expression like 'A clamour (crying out) of the dead'. Rather than using 'There was' we find it more natural to place 'arose' at the end, or 'There arose' at the beginning, of a sentence containing a nominalization of this sort. 'Occur', 'take place', 'happen', are further possibilities in similar contexts. But 'There was a crying out of the dead' is perfectly possible. We can regard the verb 'be' here as an operator which takes a noun phrase obtained from the nominalization of a sentence and converts it back into a sentence. The finite verb necessary for sentencehood, lost when 'cry out' is transformed into 'a crying out', is restored by the addition of the all-purpose verb '(There) was'.

The function of 'be' here is strikingly similar to its function as copula. That function, as I argued in section 4 of Chapter I, is simply the conversion of nouns and adjectives into verbs. I

[2] See below, Appendix A, p. 331.

imagined an extension of the use of the suffix '—ize' which would enable me to transform any noun or adjective into a verb by adding '—ize': thus from 'mammal' we could get 'mammalize' and from 'just' we could get 'justize'. The function of 'be' as copula would be no different from the function of this suffix. Where adjectives are concerned, there are languages, Chinese and Japanese being notable examples,[3] where there is neither the necessity nor the possibility of adding a verbal expression to a string of words comprising a proper name and an adjective in order to produce a complete sentence. If English were such a language, 'Aristides just', would be sufficient, and there would be no need to convert 'just' into 'justizes' or 'is just'. Where this is the case linguists debate whether the word thus attached to a proper name is to be classified as an adjective or as a verb, or whether indeed there is any rationale in such languages for a distinction between adjective and verb.[4] This is reinforcement for the view that the function of 'is' as copula can be described as purely syntactic terms. It has no 'semantic' force. It is nothing but a 'verbalizer'.

What applies to finite parts of 'be' when added in this way to a string composed of a proper name and a common noun or adjective applies equally to finite parts of 'be' added to nominalized forms like 'a crying out of the dead'. In both cases we have something which completes a string of words so that they form a sentence. Forms like 'a crying out of the dead' are themselves transformations of underlying sentences, and the force of the final 'There was a crying out of the dead' is no different from that of the original 'The dead cried out'. The joint effect of the two operations of nominalization and addition of 'There was' is here to cancel each other out. In the same way first nominalizing 'Toby sighed' by the addition of 'That —', and then adding '— is true' to the result to produce 'That Toby sighed is true', have together the effect of leaving everything as it was in the beginning. Nominalization *plus* 'There is (was)' is as redundant as 'It is true that —'. Those who like to attribute to the present writer a 'Redundancy Theory of Truth'[5] may find in these remarks a parallel 'Redundancy Theory of

[3] See A. C. Graham, '"Being" in Classical Chinese', in Verhaar, Part 1, pp. 3, 12; Seiichi Makino, 'Japanese "Be"', in Verhaar, Part 3, p. 13.
[4] See Lyons, *Theoretical Linguistics* pp. 323 ff.
[5] See my comments in *What is Truth?*, pp. 43 ff., on the view put forward by

Being'. But just as '— is true' is redundant only when attached to a designation of a Proposition which already contains the expression of that Proposition, so 'There is —' is redundant only when the expression to which it is attached as 'verbalizer' is already the nominalization of a sentence containing a finite verb. This 'redundant' use of the verb 'be' and its synonyms certainly does occur (though it is probably more common in Greek than in English), just as the redundant use of 'true' occurs, but the explanation of the meaning of 'be', like that of 'true', is to be sought elsewhere.

The parallel between 'true' and 'be' goes further than the possibility of constructing redundancy theories for each of them. Another point made by Kahn—and it had earlier been made by Aristotle—is that in Greek the verb *'einai'* has a use which makes *'esti'*, the synonym of 'is', in some contexts equivalent to 'is the case' or 'is true'. Kahn calls this 'the veridical construction'.[6] Thus a Homeric sentence whose literal translation is 'This word of yours could be' would have to be rendered in idiomatic English as 'This word of yours could be true' or 'What you have now said could be the case'. I have argued elsewhere[7] that propositions like 'What you have now said is the case (is true)' are to be analysed as equivalent to 'For some p, both you have now said just that p and p'. Isomorphic propositions like 'What you have now bought is expensive' are to be analysed as equivalent to 'For some x, both you have now bought just x and x is expensive'. Here 'What you have now bought' is represented by 'For some x, both you have now bought just x and x', and 'is expensive' remains unchanged. But in the case of 'What you have now said is true' the analysans has 'For some p, both you have now said just that p and p' to represent 'What you have now said', while 'is true' has evaporated in the course of the analysis. The underlying structure which represents 'What you have now said' in the deep grammar of 'What you have now said is true' has no need of completion by a predicate. But 'What you have now said' in the

Kneale in *The Development of Logic*, 1960, pp. 584-6; and the review of *What is Truth?* by T. R. Baldwin in *Philosophy*, 51, 1976, 482 f.

[6] See below, Appendix A, pp. 327 f. Cf. Aristotle, *Metaphysics*, 1017ª 31 ff.

[7] *What is Truth?*, pp. 38 ff. Certain qualifications are made to the analysis given here in chapter IV of *What is Truth?*

surface grammar of the sentence demands a predicate for its completion. Just so 'You have now bought just one thing and it', which uses a pronoun to do the work done by the second bound variable in 'For some x, both you have now bought just x and x' demands completion by a predicate; and so does 'You have now said just one thing and it', in which a pronoun does the work of the second bound variable in 'For some p, both you have now said just that p and p'. But the bound variable in this latter case is more properly thought of as a prosentence than a pronoun. English has no natural prosentences. The pronoun 'it' has to do the job done by p as well as that done by x. But the word 'it' cannot by itself stand after 'and' as a conjunct of a conjunctive open sentence. It has to be eked out by a predicative expression, and this is what 'is true' does in English, and the simple 'is' (or its synonym) in Greek.[8] This function of 'is true' in English and '*esti*' in Greek is a purely syntactic one: it is to convert the word 'it' from a pronoun into a prosentence. This is how it appears in 'You have now said just one thing and it is (is true)' which represents 'What you have now said is (is true)' at a deeper level. Nearer the surface it is possible to say that 'is (is true)' converts the noun-phrase 'What you have now said' into a complete proposition. We have here a close parallel with the 'There was' which converts the noun-phrase 'a crying out of the dead' into a complete proposition.

The word 'is' (or the suffix '—ize') has the effect of converting the adjective 'just' into a one-place predicable. The word 'is' is similarly attached to an adjective in the sentences 'It is foggy' or 'It is cold'. But here, since the introductory 'It' is a mere dummy serving to preserve the rule that a finite verb is not placed first in a declarative English sentence, 'is foggy' and 'is cold' are not one-place predicates, but complete propositions. What traditional grammarians call 'impersonal verbs' are complete in themselves, requiring nothing which the logician can recognize as a subject-term to enable them to express something true or false.[9] The existence of these expressions gives us good reason to adopt the convention, suggested by

[8] Professor John Lyons has pointed out to me that even in English there are idioms in which 'be' can be used in this way without needing to be supplemented (or complemented) by 'true' or 'the case', e.g. 'Martin said that John was angry and it could well *be*', 'It may *be* that Labour is going to win the election.'

[9] See Barry Miller, 'Logically Simple Propositions', *Analysis*, 34, No. 4, 1973,

Peirce,[10] of regarding complete propositions as nought-place predicables. 'Aristides is more just than Themistocles' can be regarded as formed by wrapping the two-place predicable '— is more just than —' round 'Aristides' and 'Themistocles', *or* as formed by wrapping either the one-place predicable '— is more just than Themistocles' round 'Aristides', or the one-place predicable 'Aristides is more just than —' round 'Themistocles', *or* as standing by itself as a nought-place predicable. 'Aristides is just' can be regarded as formed by wrapping the one-place predicable '— is just' round 'Aristides', *or* as standing by itself as a nought-place predicable. 'It is foggy' can only be regarded as a nought-place predicable. It is the fact that we cannot regard 'It is foggy' as an n-place predicable for any n other than nought that forces us to acknowledge the possibility of regarding 'Aristides is more just than Themistocles' or 'Aristides is just' as nought-place predicables. We can accordingly say that '(It) is' has the effect of converting the adjective 'foggy' or 'cold' into a nought-place predicable. In the same way the English 'is true' and the Greek '*esti*' have the effect of converting the noun-phrase 'What you have now said' and its Greek equivalent into nought-place predicables or propositions. The same function can be discerned in the use of 'There was' in 'There was a crying out of the dead'. We called the function of 'is' in constructing 'is just' out of the adjective 'just' the function of verbalization: one-place predicables like '— is just' are, in an extended (or restored[11]) sense of the word, verbs—more specifically, one-place verbs. In so far as '(It) is', 'is true', or 'There was', in 'It is foggy', 'What you have now said is true', and 'There was a crying out of the dead', convert adjectives or noun-phrases into propositions, which are nought-place predicables or nought-place verbs, we can say that the function of these expressions is still that of verbalization. We begin to find in the function of verbalization a continuous thread running through the various uses of 'be' and its synonyms.

'There was a crying out of the dead' attaches the verbalizing expression 'There was' to the nominalization of the sentence

---

123-8, and the reference there to 'Miklosich on Subjectless Sentences' in F. Brentano, *The Origin of our Knowledge of Right and Wrong*, ed. R. Chisholm.

[10] See Prior, *Objects of Thought*, p. 33; and cf. my *What is Truth?*, pp. 9-10.

[11] See Plato's use of '*rhema*', *Sophist*, 262a ff.

'The dead cry out'. 'There is rain over the Pennines' could perhaps be regarded as formed by attaching the same verbalizer to the nominalization of 'It is raining over the Pennines'. The noun 'rain' could, I argued, be regarded as the name for a sort of stuff. But it is perhaps more plausible to regard it, as I have just done, as derived from the verb—a verbal noun. Not so 'coal'. This is indubitably the name of a certain sort of stuff. There is no verb 'to coal' from which one could plausibly suppose the noun 'coal' to be derived. 'There was a crying out of the dead' (and perhaps 'There is rain over the Pennines') involves a redundant use of 'There was (is)', just as 'It is true that Toby sighed' involves a redundant use of 'is true'. But in 'There is coal in the Mendips' the use of 'There is' is as essential as the use of 'is true' in 'This word of yours is true'. The noun 'coal', having no verbal correlate, just *has* to be verbalized if we are to get a proposition. Perhaps there are languages which treat the synonym of 'coal' as a verb, just as there are languages which treat the synonym of 'just' as a verb; but English is not one of them. English needs a verbalizer for the feature-placing statements which are formed from mass nouns, and 'be' fulfils this function. It is not alone in having this need, nor in having it satisfied.

Kahn lists the use of 'be' in sentences like 'There was a clamour of the dead' under the heading of 'Existential Uses'.[12] In this he seems to be mistaken, at least if one accepts the criterion set out in the last chapter for what is to count as an existential use of 'be'. We should be hard put to find an existential instantiation of the proposition 'There was a clamour of the dead'. To follow up someone's assertion of this proposition with the question 'Which clamour?' would be unintelligible. If existence is what the existential quantifier expresses, this use of 'There was' has nothing to do with existence. The point about instantiation that I made earlier with regard to 'There is' in 'There is coal in the Mendips', 'There's rain over the Pennines', and 'There's a smell of cabbage in the Dining Room' applies equally to Kahn's Type V of the 'existential' uses of *'einai'*.

[12] It is included in Kahn's chapter 'The Verb of Existence' in *The Verb 'Be'*, as Type V of the existential uses of *'einai'*. See below, Appendix A, pp. 330 f.

3. *Feature-placing statements not internally negatable*

The criterion of instantiability has been used to show that certain propositions introduced by 'There is', notably feature-placing propositions, are not, in my sense of the word, existential. In Chapter III I drew attention to another feature of genuinely existential propositions, which distinguishes them from singular propositions: in an existential proposition there will be a distinction between external and internal negation. 'Some men are just', or 'There are just men', is not contradicted by 'Some men are unjust', or 'There are unjust men'. 'No men are just', or 'There are no just men', is the true contradictory, the external negation, of this proposition. Negating the first-level predicable '— are just' produces only an internal negation. But in the case of singular propositions like 'Aristides is just' there is no such distinction between internal and external negation.[13] It will be interesting to see whether this criterion for a proposition's being existential can be used to confirm the result of the instantiability criterion as applied to the feature-placing propositions.

It seems that it can. The external/internal negation contrast can get no purchase on propositions like 'There is a smell of cabbage in the Dining Room'. The only sentence that can at all plausibly be said to give us its negation is 'There is no smell of cabbage in the Dining Room', but this is clearly equivalent to 'It is not the case that there is a smell of cabbage in the Dining Room'. If the external/internal contrast is applicable here at all, this is the external negation. How could the proposition be negated internally? What could such negation latch on to? We might try 'There is a smell of something other than cabbage in the Dining Room' or 'There is a smell of cabbage elsewhere than in the Dining Room', but these are no more negations of 'There is a smell of cabbage in the Dining Room' than 'Someone other than Aristides is just' is a negation of 'Aristides is just'. Indeed, 'There is a smell of cabbage in the Dining Room' is closer to 'Aristides is just' than to 'There is a Prime Minister who is a woman', as can be seen from the fact that it can be paraphrased by 'The Dining Room smells of cabbage'.[14] Here

[13] See above, Ch. III, pp. 45 ff.
[14] Lyons regards a paraphrase of this kind as indicating the deep structure of

'The Dining Room' can no more be negated than 'Aristides' can. The only way of negating the paraphrase is to say 'It doesn't', just as the only way of negating the proposition which it paraphrases, namely, 'There is a smell of cabbage in the Dining Room', is to say 'There isn't'.

So 'There is a smell of cabbage in the Dining Room' fails to pass the negation test for a proposition's being existential, just as it failed to pass the instantiation test. The same will hold for Kahn's Type V 'existential' propositions and for my meteorological examples. This is what we should expect. 'There was a crying out of the dead' was said to be equivalent to 'The dead cried out', and this is susceptible of only one form of negation. 'There is rain over the Pennines' cannot have two sorts of negation unless 'It's raining over the Pennines' can. Propositions formed by attaching a mass noun to 'There is' and appending a locative expression seem to follow the same pattern. 'There's coal in the Mendip Hills' is negated by 'There's no coal in the Mendip Hills'. There seems to be no other negation for this proposition.

Or does there? 'There's coal in the Mendip Hills' seems to mean the same as 'There's somewhere in the Mendip Hills where there's coal' and this has two negations. Its external negation is 'There's nowhere in the Mendip Hills where there's coal' and its internal negation is 'There's somewhere in the Mendip Hills where there's no coal'. This draws our attention to a respect in which 'There's coal in the Mendips' is more like 'There's a doctor in the house' than it is like 'There's rain over Manchester'. 'There's a doctor in the house' has, not only 'There's no doctor in the house' as its external negation, but 'There's someone in the house who's not a doctor' as its internal negation. There's room 'in the house', presumably, for people who are not doctors as well as for people who are, just as there's room in the Mendip Hills for a good deal of carboniferous limestone as well as for the coal it bears.

This feature, however, is determined more by the contrast

all feature-placing propositions. Thus the deep structure of 'It's cold in London' is given by 'London is cold'. This requires indications of place to be categorized as names in the deep structure, which seems mistaken. However, in this view, the function of 'There is' or 'It is' will still be that of verbalization, though it will be one-place, not nought-place, verbs which are so formed. (See Lyons, *Semantics*, 1977, 2, Ch. XII, § 3.)

between 'in the Mendip Hills' and 'over Manchester' than by any contrast between 'There's coal' and 'There's rain'. Implicit in the phrase 'in the Mendip Hills' is a quantifier which makes the proposition existential independently of 'There is'. Instead of 'There's coal in the Mendips' I might just as well have said 'There's coal *somewhere in the Mendips*'. This proposition, of course, can have an existential instantiation (as well as an internal negation). Let us instantiate it: 'There's coal at the point in the Mendips marked by Normal National Grid Reference ST 669530, four hundred feet below the surface'. Here we have reference to a particular point, at which there is coal. We need not be too fussy about extensionless points. From the point of view of the weather forecast 'over Manchester' is a sufficiently accurate specification of the place of current precipitation. 'There's rain over Manchester' tells us the *place at which* it's now raining, whereas 'There's coal in the Mendip Hills' tells us of the *area within which* we can find coal. The locative phrases that we need to make our point about 'There is' clearly must be phrases which specify a *place at which*, not an *area within which*. Phrases of the latter sort introduce an irrelevant element of quantification which confuses the issue. Since 'There's coal in the Mendips' = 'There's coal somewhere in the Mendips' = 'There's somewhere in the Mendips where there's coal', the use of 'There is' that we are looking for is the one that occurs as the penultimate word in the last of these paraphrases. The 'where' that occurs in this sentence is a relative 'pro-adverb' corresponding to a bound variable whose substitution instances would be phrases specifying a *place at which*, rather than an *area within which*.

4. *The transition from mass-nouns to count-nouns*

Let us stick then to phrases specifying the *place at which*. Let us use τ to represent such phrases. The sort of propositions we are interested in are those which have the form 'There is ϕ at τ'. The replacement for ϕ here may be a noun like 'coal', a noun with the indefinite article like 'an explosion' or a noun-phrase like 'a crying out of the dead'. Since substitutions for ϕ can be nouns with the indefinite article, there is nothing so far to stop us substituting a count-noun with the indefinite article, a phrase like 'a girl'. Let us suppose that 'in Father's chair' is a phrase specifying a *place at which*, discounting the possibility of two people at the same time being in Father's chair. Is the proposition 'There's a girl in Father's chair' an instance of our schema 'There is ϕ at τ'? It seems not to suffer from the defects of 'There's a doctor in the house'—there is no quantification implicit in the locative phrase.

It is not difficult, however, to find an instantiation for 'There's a girl in Father's chair'. 'Who is she?' we may ask, and be told 'Barbara'. Barbara, then, is a girl, and she is in Father's chair; from which facts, by existential generalization, we may obtain our original proposition. This proposition could accordingly be formalized so as to read 'For some x, x is a girl and x is in Father's chair'. Nor is there any difficulty about obtaining an internal negation of this proposition: 'For some x, x is a girl and x is not in Father's chair' will do. By both of our criteria, therefore, 'There's a girl in Father's chair' comes out as an existential proposition, and 'There is' here will embody an existential use of 'be'.

The problem we were left with at the end of Chapter I was what, if anything, the two uses of 'be', copulative and existential, had in common. We have now seen that the 'is' which serves as copula in a sentence like 'Aristides is just' and the 'is' which occurs in 'There is coal at Normal National Grid Reference ST 669530, four hundred feet below the surface' have a great deal in common: both are verbalizers. The phrase 'is just' is tantamount to a possible verb, 'justizes', and the phrase 'There is coal' to a possible impersonal verb construction, 'It coalizes'. We have, not just a similar, but the same use of 'is' in both cases. But this use is sharply distinguishable from the existential use, marked by the possibility of instantiation and internal negation. And so our problem has become highlighted as the problem of what, if any, community of meaning can be found between the two uses of 'There is' in 'There is coal at Normal National Grid Reference ST 669530, four hundred feet below the surface' and 'There is a girl in Father's chair'.

Quine has a description of the way in which a child comes to learn the use of general terms of the kind called 'count-nouns', which postulates a primitive stage in which a word later to rank as a count-noun is used by the child as a mass-noun.

We in our maturity have come to look upon the child's mother as an integral body who, in an irregular closed orbit, revisits the child from time to time; and to look upon red in a radically different way, viz., as scattered about. Water, for us, is rather like red, but not quite; things are red, stuff alone is water. But the mother, red, and water are for the infant all of a type; each is just a history of sporadic encounter, a scattered portion of what goes on. His first learning of the three words is uniformly a matter of learning how much of what goes on about him counts as the mother, or as red, or as water. It is not for the child to say in the first case 'Hello! mama again', in the second case 'Hello! another red thing', and in the third case 'Hello! more water'. They are all on a par: Hello! more mama, more red, more water.[15]

It is not difficult to imagine a child's use of 'girl' developing in the way imagined by Quine. The most primitive stage of this development would probably be the use of this single word 'girl' as what Quine calls an 'occasion sentence': confronted with a girl the child utters the word 'girl'. But before reaching the stage where the child can count girls, can say that this is the same girl as the one who came into the room ten minutes ago, or can describe someone as 'the girl I played with yesterday', he may learn to *place* girlhood, i.e. to say, with appropriate gestures, 'Girl here', 'Girl there', 'No girl over there'. No doubt 'Girl in Father's chair' is too complicated a sentence for him to have mastered in default of an ability to 'divide the reference', as Quine puts it, of 'chair', If his concept of 'chair' has divided reference, why not his concept of 'girl'? The mastery of general terms that divide their reference is a necessary condition for making such complex references to particular places as 'in Father's chair', let alone 'at Normal National Grid Reference ST 669530, four hundred feet below the surface'. Nevertheless, it remains a conceptual possibility that the use of 'Girl' as an occasion sentence, which we imagined extended to a feature-placing statement expressed by 'Girl here' or 'Girl there', could be further extended to 'Girl in Father's chair' or 'There is a girl (It girlizes) in Father's chair', where 'Girl' or 'There is a girl' or 'It girlizes' has the same status as 'There is coal' or 'It coalizes' in 'There is coal (It coalizes) at Normal National Grid reference ST 669530, four hundred feet below the surface'. Now the truth conditions of 'Girl in Father's chair', understood in this sense, are for all practical purposes the same as those of 'Some girl is in Father's chair'. If Barbara is in Father's chair, or Susan, 'Girl in Father's chair' or 'It girlizes

[15] Quine, *Word and Object*, § 19, p. 92. Cf. Aristotle, *Physics* 184^b 3–5.

in Father's chair' will be true, as will be 'Some girl is in Father's chair'.

Can this be generalized? Can we say that, for any proposition of the form 'Some A is at τ', where A is a count-noun, there will be a sentence 'There is an A at τ' which can be understood either as the same proposition as 'Some A is at τ' or as a feature-placing proposition, expressible also by 'It A-izes at τ', with A interpreted as a mass term? And will the truth-conditions for the two interpretations of 'There is an A at τ' be the same? It looks at first sight as though the answer is 'No'. Take the word 'lamb'. The proposition 'Some lamb is in the boot of the car' could certainly be taken as asserting that the car has a young animal in its boot, with 'lamb' interpreted as a count-noun. The same sentence, however, with 'lamb' interpreted as a mass term, would appear to have quite different truth-conditions. (We are all familiar with the schoolboy joke: 'Mary had a little lamb—Oh! Did she have mint sauce with it?') But to regard this as a valid objection to what we are saying is to misunderstand Quine. Quine would postulate that a child growing up on a farm would learn 'lamb' in the first place as an occasion sentence, in the same way as he learns 'Mama' or 'water'. Learning the word 'lamb', on this account, is 'a matter of learning how much of what goes on about him counts as' a lamb. But this would be a completely different exercise from learning how much of what he eats, or sees his mother cooking, counts as lamb. So far as the child's early learning of 'lamb' as an occasion sentence is concerned, the word is purely equivocal. The 'stimulus meaning' which it has when correlated with young animals gambolling in the fields is completely different from that which it has when connected with a certain sort of food. And it is stimulus meaning which is in question, since we are talking about the meaning the word has for the child before he has learnt to 'divide the reference'. The word 'lamb' which, on Quine's account, is going to graduate from being a mass term to being a count-noun will not in the process change the truth-conditions for its application in contexts of the form 'There is a lamb at τ'. Unlike 'lamb' in its sense as a name of food, it is never going to be applicable to *detached* lamb-parts. That is why Quine's doctrine of the inscrutability of reference allowed only for the possibility that what might be meant by one person as 'There is a lamb at τ' might be what another would mean by 'There is an *undetached* lamb-part at τ'. The sense in which Quine's child, before dividing the reference, would understand 'There is a lamb at τ' would not be the same as that in which we adults here and now understand 'There is lamb at τ'. The presence of a leg of lamb in the boot of the car would not be a sufficient condition for 'There's a lamb in the boot of the car', even where what this expresses is equally expressible by 'It lambizes in the boot of the car'. Stimulus meaning determines the truth-conditions for sentences like 'There is a lamb in the boot of the car'. Quine's whole point is that differences of reference for 'lamb', or even its having reference, will not show up at the level of stimulus meaning. Such differences therefore cannot affect the truth-conditions for the sentence.[16]

The obvious objections to generalizing my account of 'There is a girl in Father's chair' can thus be seen to fail. It seems that the stimulus meaning of a mass term which is capable, in the way Quine describes, of acquiring later the status of a count-noun would have to be such that the truth-conditions of 'There is an A at τ', where A is such a mass term, would be the same as those of 'Some A is at τ' where A is a count-noun. But, in any case, I do not need to prove the generalization. I am interested in showing how we can make sense of the fact that an expression of the form 'There is an A at τ' could be interpretable as equivalent either to 'It A-izes at τ' or to 'For some x, x is an A and x is at τ', and thus explain the actual use of 'There is' both as a verbalizer and as an expression of the concept of existence. And for this I do not need to show that every existing count-noun could have a use as a mass term in this way, but only that many could. Nor do I need to show that the truth-conditions of 'There is a girl in Father's chair', understood as equivalent to 'It girlizes in Father's chair', are exactly the same as those of the same sentence, understood as equivalent to 'Some girl or other is in Father's chair', in all possible imaginable circumstances. All I need to show is that, in the vast majority of likely contexts for the utterance of such a sentence, the truth-

[16] For Quine's account of 'stimulus meaning' and 'the inscrutability of reference', see *Word and Object*, §§ 8, 12; and *Ontological Relativity*, Index, under 'inscrutability of reference'.

conditions for 'There is a girl in Father's chair' understood in the one way would coincide with the truth-conditions for the same sentence understood in the other way. A large degree of overlap in a wide variety of cases is enough to provide an explanation of how 'is', the verbalizer, comes to have an existential sense. And that is what I am seeking to explain.

5. *Locative phrases as adverbial and as predicative*

This analogical use of 'There is' can be explained in another way. The difference in the two interpretations of sentences of the form 'There is an A at τ' will lie, as we have just seen, partly in the fact that A on one interpretation represents a count-noun and on the other interpretation a mass term. But the difference will also lie partly in another important difference of which we must take cognizance: 'at τ' on one interpretation represents an adverbial phrase and on the other a predicative expression. If the sentence 'There is a girl in Father's chair' is understood as equivalent to 'Some girl is in Father's chair' the phrase 'in Father's chair' must be understood as something which can be predicated of Susan, Barbara, or the like. If the sentence is understood as equivalent to a postulated 'It girlizes in Father's chair', the phrase 'in Father's chair' must be understood as equivalent to an adverb.

The distinction between a predicative expression and an adverbial phrase looks at first sight as though it were hard and fast. An adverbial phrase is what linguists call an 'adjunct'.[17] That is to say, its omission from a sentence in which it occurs leaves the sentence syntactically complete. It is an optional extra, peripheral to the main sense of the sentence. Thus in 'Margaret is singing in the kitchen' we could omit 'in the kitchen' and still have a proposition. But in 'John is at the wheel' we cannot similarly omit the phrase 'at the wheel'. It is here a predicative expression, or is convertible into one by the verbalizing activity of the copula.

However, even in their predicative use the expressions symbolized by 'at τ' do not behave in all respects like adjectives. Corresponding to 'John is busy' we have 'John seems busy' or 'John became busy', but we do not similarly have 'John seems at the wheel' or 'John became at the wheel'. Again, 'in

---
[17] See Lyons, *Semantics*, 2, 235.

Manchester' can be omitted from 'It's raining in Manchester' *salva congruitate* (though not, as 'in the kitchen' can be omitted from 'Margaret is singing in the kitchen', *salva veritate*). But 'at Normal National Grid reference ST 669530, four hundred feet below the surface' cannot similarly be omitted from the feature-placing statement about coal. Something has to be added to the bare 'There is coal', even if it is the vaguer *area within which* designation, 'in the Mendips'. In this context the locative phrase seems no longer to be an adjunct.[18] The ambivalence of such an expression as 'in Father's chair' with respect to its status as an adverbial or predicative expression is not, therefore, confined to our two interpretations of 'There is a girl in Father's chair'.

Whatever its ambivalence, one can hardly deny that 'in Father's chair' has a predicative role in 'There is a girl in Father's chair' when this is understood as equivalent to 'Some girl is in Father's chair'. It must have the same role here as it has in a proposition which instantiates it, e.g. 'Barbara is in Father's chair'. Confirmation of this view can be found by noticing that 'There is a girl in Father's chair', in this sense, can be transformed into 'There is a girl *who is* in Father's chair'. No such transformation is possible for 'It's raining (There is rain) over Manchester'. This possibility constitutes a similarity between 'There is a girl in Father's chair' and 'There is a girl singing hymns', which can similarly be transformed into 'There is a girl who is singing hymns'. Kahn has noted sentences of this type in his list of existential uses of *'einai'* in Greek.[19] He labels such uses 'Type IV', and he already remarks that these approximate most closely to formulae constructed with the existential quantifier. Relative pronouns like 'who', as well as anaphoric pronouns like 'it', play in ordinary language the role played in quantificational logic by bound variables.[20] Clauses like 'who is singing hymns' or 'who is in Father's chair', therefore, function in the same way as open sentences whose variable is bound by a quantifier, 'x is singing hymns', 'x is in Father's chair'. 'There is a girl who is in Father's chair' is easily transformed into 'There is a girl, x, such that x is in Father's chair'.

[18] For further discussion of locative phrases, see below, Appendix A, pp. 328 f.
[19] *The Verb 'Be'*. See below Appendix A, pp. 330 f.
[20] Cf. Geach, *Reference and Generality*, Ch. V, and see above Ch. VI, § 2.

6. 'Dividing the reference', locative phrases, and the ambiguity of 'be'

The problem of explaining the ambiguity of the word 'be' narrows itself down to the problem of explaining the relation between the two ways in which sentences of the form 'There is an A at τ' can be understood. The explanation turns on two considerations. First, there is the phenomenon which Quine called 'dividing the reference'. A concept may start life as expressible by a mass-noun, an occasion sentence or an impersonal verb: 'Girl' or 'It girlizes'. It may then develop into a general term, provided those who possess it become capable of individuating or identifying particular instances—capable, that is, of using such expressions as 'this girl', 'the same girl', 'Susan', 'Barbara'. Once this has happened a relation is discernible between what was stated by the sentence in its original interpretation and what is stated when we substitute one of the 'singular terms' thus derived for the verbalized mass-noun in a sentence of the form 'There is an A at τ'. This relation is precisely that of existential instantiation: to substitute 'This girl is' for 'There is a girl' in 'There is a girl in Father's chair' is to produce an existential instantiation of the latter. 'This girl is in Father's chair' is related in just the same way to 'It girlizes in Father's chair'. The existential interpretation of 'There is a girl in Father's chair' is what we get when we make explicit the role of the sentence as expressing the existential generalization of its particular instances. To say that 'There is a girl in Father's chair', or, for that matter, 'It girlizes in Father's chair', means the same as 'For some girl x, x is in Father's chair' is to say that 'This girl is in Father's chair', 'That girl is in Father's chair', etc., *already* constitute sufficient conditions for its truth.[21] Dividing the reference makes possible such singular propositions; and once they are possible, we can, and indeed must, look on 'It girlizes in Father's chair' as their existential generalization. It is this consequence of dividing the reference which is the principal element in our explanation of the relation between the existential and the verbalizing sense of 'There is'.

[21] In the same way 'What Percy says is true' can be seen, *as it stands*, as an existential generalization of 'Both Percy says just that Mabel has measles and Mabel has measles', etc. Analysing it as 'For some p, both Percy says just that p and p' is simply recognizing this already existing relation.

The second phenomenon which our explanation refers to is the ambivalence of the expressions symbolized by 'at τ'. Where 'There is a girl' functions simply as a verbalization of 'girl', as equivalent to 'It girlizes', the locative phrase which accompanies it has to be understood adverbially. Where 'There is a girl' has a properly existential sense, the locative phrase has to be understood adjectivally, i.e. predicatively. It is only locative phrases which have this ambivalence. 'Singing hymns' can be substituted for 'in the kitchen' in 'There is a girl in the kitchen' as in 'Susan is in the kitchen' but it cannot be so substituted in 'It girlizes in the kitchen'. 'It girlizes singing hymns'. makes no more sense than 'It is foggy singing hymns'. The ability of locative phrases to play the role of adverbs as well as that of adjectives is essential to the possibility of 'There is' having the double role as verbalizer and quantifier. Given the possibility of interpreting sentences of the form 'There is an A at τ' in such a way that 'at τ' plays the role of an adjectival phrase, the way is open to constructing existential propositions with other, non-locative, adjectival phrases in this position. We thus obtain the possibility of saying things like 'There is a girl singing hymns'. This can be transformed into 'There is a girl who is singing hymns', which gives us a model for propositions like 'There is a prime number which is even', and 'There is an even prime number', into which this in turn can be transformed. The capacity of locative phrases to function as adjectival phrases thus makes possible the whole range of existential propositions whose logic can be made explicit with the help of the existential quantifier.

7. *Location and existence*

The connection between the concepts of place and existence has been long recognized, but as long misunderstood. Aristotle prepared the way for Empiricist dogmatism by remarking 'For all men assume that things which are (*ta onta*) are somewhere (for that which is not (*to mē on*) is assumed to be nowhere—for where is a goat-stag or sphinx?)'[22] And Hume's only attempt to make sense of negative existential propositions, which as we have seen provide an *experimentum crucis* for his theory

[22] Aristotle, *Physics*, the second sentence of Book Δ, 208ᵃ 29-31.

of existence,[23] is expressed in the following remarks:

> But let us consider that no two ideas are in themselves contrary, except those of existence and non-existence, which are plainly resembling, as implying both of them an idea of the object; though the latter excludes the object from all times and places, in which it is supposed not to exist.[24]

Hume's attempt here to analyse the notion of non-existence is of course viciously circular: it is no use seeking to explain what is meant by 'There is no such thing as a goat-stag' by paraphrasing it as 'There is no time and no place at which there is a goat-stag.' And if Aristotle's rhetorical question about the sphinx is supposed to demonstrate its non-existence, how would he avoid the conclusion that there is no even prime number? Where, after all, is it to be found? Such considerations have led philosophers to the lame reply that mathematical existential propositions make no claim about 'real' existence. Russell's phrase 'a most pitiful and paltry evasion' is apt as a description of such moves.[25]

We should not, however, write off these ideas completely. That there is some connection between the concepts of location and existence seems to be confirmed by the linguistic evidence supplied by empirical study of very diverse languages. We have already noticed the possibility, which exists in many languages, of forming a complete sentence by simply juxtaposing an adjective to a name.[26] In some of these languages, such as Chinese, Japanese, and the West African language, Twi, it is not similarly possible to form a complete sentence by juxtaposing a common noun to a name: the translations in such languages of 'Robert is a teacher' would contain a word corresponding to 'is'. So these languages do not lack altogether a synonym of 'is' in its use as copula. But this form of the copula would not be appropriate for translating 'is' in such sentences as 'The University of Illinois is in Illinois' or 'The school is at Kumasi',[27] where

---

[23] See above, Ch. II, pp. 20 f.

[24] Hume, *A Treatise of Human Nature*, Book I, Part 1, § 5. We may also cite the more recent view of Lyons, *Theoretical Linguistics*, p. 390: 'The assertion that something exists, or existed, requires "complementation" with a locative (or temporal) expression before it can be interpreted.'

[25] See above, Ch. X, p. 256; and my criticisms of Baier in *Mind*, 78, 1969, 212-21.

[26] See above, p. 303.

[27] See Makino, 'Japanese "Be"', in Verhaar, Part 3, pp. 1-3; Jeffrey Ellis and Lawrence Boadi, '"To be" in Twi', in Verhaar, Part 4, p. 27.

mere juxtaposition is again inadequate. These languages have a separate word for the locative copula. Now in the case of Japanese and Twi the same word serves both as the locative copula in renderings of sentences like those just given, and as the equivalent of 'There is' in translations of existential sentences like 'There is a book on the desk' or 'There is a school in Kumasi'. Japanese would use the form *'ar-ru'* for both these purposes. Many languages have a word like this which performs both the function of locative copula and that of locative existential verb. Chinese, on the other hand, while making a distinction between the nominal and the locative copula, differentiates between the latter, *'Tsai'* or *'zai'*, and the word needed to translate 'There are' in, for example, 'There are fat horses in the stables' which would be *'yu'*. Thus 'There are fat horses in the stables' is *'Chi yu fei ma'*, whereas 'He is outside' is *'Ta zai waimian'*.[28] But *'tsai'*, without an adverb or adverbial phrase of location, can also translate 'is alive', thus corresponding to Type I of Kahn's 'existential' uses of *'einai'*:[29] *'fu tsai'* is a rendering of 'His father is alive'. Commenting on this, Professor Graham writes:

Modern translators have compounded *tsai* with *ts'un* 'survive, persist' to coin the word *ts'un-tsai*, 'exist', writing 'X *ts'un-tsai*' for '*yu* X'. This enables them to translate Western arguments which assume that existence is a predicate, arguments unstatable in terms of *yu*.[30]

This detailed linguistic information, culled from various monographs in Verhaar's collection *The Verb 'Be' and its Synonyms*, is not, of course, enough to give substance to a philosophical theory. Followers of Aristotle, who maintain that to exist is to exist somewhere, should not rush too quickly to Verhaar for ammunition for their cause. There does, however, seem to be a tendency in a wide variety of languages to use as a word for existence (in some sense or other of 'exist') a word which also functions as copula in connection with locative phrases. It would be a mistake to look around for some locative phrase to complement 'exists' in 'There exists a rational square root of 81'. (Are we to 'locate' it between 8 and 10 or between

---

[28] Graham, '"Being" in Classical Chinese', p. 6; Anne Yue Hashimoto, 'The Verb "To Be" in Modern Chinese', in Verhaar, Part 4, p. 73.
[29] See above, Ch. I, n. 26, and below, Appendix A, p. 330.
[30] Graham, '"Being" in Classical Chinese', in Verhaar, Part 1, p. 14.

− 8 and − 10?). Nevertheless, propositions which do involve locative phrases, like 'There is a book on the table', are important for understanding how 'is' comes to have the meaning it has in propositions like 'There is a rational square root of 81'. This last proposition is existential but not locative. A proposition like 'There is a mess on the table' is locative but not existential (we cannot sensibly ask 'Which mess?'). 'There is a book on the table' is both; and the fact that it can be regarded either as being of the form 'It ϕ's at τ' or as being of the form 'Some A ψ's' is, as we have maintained, a crucial factor in the explanation of 'be' having its existential sense. It is the ambivalence of phrases like 'on the table' or 'in Manchester', which can function either as adverbial or as adjectival phrases, which facilitates this extension of the role of the verb 'be'. A locative copula, appropriate for rendering 'is' in 'Aristotle's *Physics* is on the table', is naturally used to express 'There is a book on the table', and eventually finds a use in the totally non-locative 'There is a rational square root of 81'. But this is a syntactic, not a semantic, feature of these phrases. It is the versatility of 'in Manchester', which allows it to occur both in 'It's raining in Manchester' and in 'Susan is in Manchester', which explains how 'be' comes to have an existential sense. We should not look for some conceptual link between existence and place such as Aristotle asserts when he claims that things which are are somewhere. Existence is as topic-neutral as disjunction or negation. Even the concept of location, Aristotle's category of place, is too specific to be tied semantically to the concept of being. Being transcends the categories. Nothing but syntax has the generality required for an understanding of the role of the verb 'be'.

8. *Summary of the argument of this chapter*
In this chapter I have attempted to answer the question left unanswered by my first chapter: are the copulative and existential senses of the verb 'be' totally unconnected, or do they have something in common? Otherwise stated, is the verb 'be' in these uses purely equivocal or is it used analogically? In order to attach a clear sense to the question I needed to define the notion of an 'existential' use of the verb 'be'. This I was able to do in Chapter XI, in the light of the sustained examination

to which the concept of existence was subjected in the central chapters of the book. Existence, it seems, is what the existential quantifier expresses. But, in a certain sense, the existential quantifier and the universal quantifier are expressions of a single concept, which is also expressed by the use of variables, and which is at base the same as the concept of valid inference. It is, therefore, essential to the notion of an existential proposition that it is expressible by a formula which contains a variable, and that the idea of a substitution instance of this variable should be intelligible. Existential propositions are propositions which must be capable of meaningful, though not necessarily true, instantiation.

Armed with this criterion of 'instantiability', I showed that the occurrence of the expression 'exist' or 'there is' in a proposition was neither a necessary nor a sufficient condition of the proposition's being existential. In particular, feature-placing propositions, like 'There is rain over Manchester', since they are not instantiable, are not in my sense existential. Such propositions have the same logical form as subjectless propositions like 'It is foggy in Manchester', in which 'is', which as copula regularly converts an adjective into a one-place predicable, has the function of converting 'foggy' into a nought-place predicable. What 'it is' does for adjectives, 'there is' does for nouns. 'There is rain' is a nought-place predicable, and 'There is', in this context, has exactly the same role as the copula, namely the role of a verbalizer.

The question of the connection between the existential and the copulative uses of 'be' can now be narrowed to the question of the connection between the role of 'There is' in propositions like 'There is rain over Manchester' and its role in propositions like 'There is a girl in Father's chair'. Its role in the first is the same as the copulative role: in the second it is existential in my sense of the word, since 'There is a girl in Father's chair' is clearly instantiable. Here I invoked Quine's notion of 'dividing the reference'. It is possible to conceive of a use of 'girl' as a mass term, according to which 'There is a girl in Father's chair' is no more instantiable than 'It girlizes in Father's chair'. This use, however, could be developed into the use of 'girl' as a count-noun, with intelligible uses being found for expressions like 'this girl', 'that girl', and 'the same girl again'. With the appearance of divided reference 'This girl is in Father's chair' or 'Barbara is in Father's chair' can be seen as instantiations of 'There is a girl in Father's chair', which in turn can be seen as their existential generalization. But the logical relation between the singular proposition and its existential generalization is already present between the singular proposition and the feature-placing statement 'It girlizes in Father's chair'. The acquisition of existential import (in *my* sense of 'existential') by 'There is a girl in Father's chair' is a simple consequence of 'girl' acquiring divided reference. 'There is', which begins by verbalizing a mass-noun, finishes by producing a proposition capable of instantiation, in virtue of the conversion of the mass-noun into a count-noun. The relation of the existential proposition to its instantiation is what the quantifier with its variable visibly expresses. And once the apparatus of quantification and variables is available, it is applicable to syntactic categories other than the proper names introduced with the development of count-nouns. 'There is a girl in Father's chair' has passed from meaning 'It girlizes in Father's chair' to 'Some girl is in Father's chair'. From 'Some girl' we can advance to 'Somewhere' and 'Somehow', and eventually to 'For some ϕ' and 'For some p'.

The transition from 'It girlizes in Father's chair' to 'For some x, x is a girl and x is in Father's chair' is eased by the syntactical ambivalence of locative expressions like 'in Father's chair'. In 'It is foggy in Manchester' the locative expression is adverbial; it is what grammarians call an 'adjunct'; that is to say, its removal from the sentence leaves a complete sentence. In 'Barbara is in Manchester' the locative expression is adjectival or predicative: its removal from the sentence does not leave a complete sentence. 'Barbara is', unlike 'It is foggy', is a mere fragment of a sentence with a yawning gap in it. So long as 'girl' in 'There is a girl in Father's chair' has undivided reference, 'in Father's chair' is a mere adverbial adjunct. As soon as 'girl' becomes a count-noun and 'There is a girl in Father's chair' instantiable, the locative expression becomes predicative. The proposition becomes interpretable as being of the form $\Sigma x K \phi x \psi x$, with ψx representing 'x is in Father's chair'. The ambivalence of the locative expression therefore joins with the division of reference in facilitating the passage from 'There is' as verbalizer to 'There is' as quantifier. The connection between the copulative (verbalizing) sense of 'be' and the existential (quantificational) sense has become clear. The verb 'be' is in this respect analogical, not purely equivocal. J. S. Mill's belief that the double use of 'is' as a 'mere sign of predication' and as 'signifying existence' is a case of equivocation, definitively identified by his father, is an oversimplification.[31] The use of the same word in different senses is not, after all, as Russell thought, 'a disgrace to the human race',[32] but a phenomenon which we can understand as easily as the use of 'healthy' in different senses. The Analogy of Being is not a mere accident of Indo-European speech.

9. *Syntax, semantics, and formal concepts*

In Chapter I, after identifying the role of 'be' when it occurs as copula in a verbalizing role, and thus as purely syntactic, I asked whether there are other uses of 'be' which, by contrast, demand a semantic account.[33] The alleged 'identity' use turned out to be a mirage, indistinguishable from the copula. The existential use proved a harder nut to crack. There are languages enough which do without a verbalizer, which simply say '*Justus Dominus*' when we say 'The Lord is just'. But it is hard to imagine a language which has nothing corresponding to 'There is' in 'There is an even prime number'. The existential role of 'be' is the role also performed by 'some', and this seems to demand a semantic account. When the syntactical role of 'be' as copula, i.e. as verbalizer, is known, there seems no question about its meaning left unanswered. But the role of 'some', so long as we restrict ourselves to the point of view of syntax, is no different from that of 'every'. We must look to semantics for an account of the difference between them. What is necessary for 'some' must surely be necessary also for the existential sense of 'be'.

And yet this existential sense of 'be', as that which both quantifiers express, has seemed to us explicable in terms of the notion of *variable*. Valid inferences, which seem always to correspond with generalization, are expressible by variable-

---

[31] See above, Ch. I, § 6, where I have quoted from his *A System of Logic*.
[32] Ibid., p. 10; although Russell was not referring to *these* senses.
[33] See above, p. 10.

containing schemata. $Cpq \vdash CNqNp$ expresses what $\Pi p \Pi q CC$-$pqCNqNp$ expresses, and both depend on the use of variable letters. But to know the syntactical role of a variable is to know all there is to know about it.

Again, the role of 'There is' in 'There is a smell of cabbage in the Dining Room' is that of the verbalizer, one of which a syntactic account is sufficient. Such an account suffices too for 'There is a girl in Father's chair' if this is taken as a feature-placing proposition, as equivalent to 'It girlizes in Father's chair'. But what permits us to pass from this use to a fully existential use, equivalent to 'Some girl is in Father's chair', is the possibility of dividing the reference of 'girl' and the ambivalence of the locative expression 'in Father's chair'. And both these phenomena are syntactic phenomena. The distinction between mass-noun and count-noun and the distinction between adverbial phrase and adjectival phrase are both syntactic distinctions. But it is on these that the distinction between the existential senses of 'be' has been shown to pivot. Syntax has again proved adequate to our needs. It is with 'being' as it is with 'truth'. We need the word 'true' to supply a deficiency of ordinary language, namely, its lack of prosentences: 'is true' is needed to transform the pronoun 'it' into the prosentence 'it is true'. The distinction between pronoun and prosentence is a syntactic distinction; and nothing else is needed for an understanding of the concept of truth.[34] What Aristotle calls 'being as truth' is thus syntactically explained.

Logic, whose heart is the understanding of syntactic distinctions and relations, thus becomes the true heir of metaphysics, at least of that part of metaphysics which studies Being *qua* Being. *Esse* is not *percipi*, nor *percipere*. Nor is it to be identified with activity, or the occupancy of space or time. It is understood by understanding such notions as *proposition*, *predicable*, and *variable*. Wittgenstein spoke of 'the confusion between formal concepts and concepts proper, which prevades the whole of traditional logic'.[35] *Existence* and *being* are not formal concepts in exactly Wittgenstein's sense. But the confusion of which he spoke, the confusion which is involved in

---

[34] See *What is Truth?*, pp. 46-8; also D. L. Grover, J. L. Camp, Jr., and N. D. Belnap, Jr., 'A Prosentential Theory of Truth', *Philosophical Studies*, 27, 1975.
[35] *Tractatus*, 4.126.

mistaking syntactic distinctions for something else, is at work here too. It is a confusion which is almost inescapable, and thus produces an illusion similar to those Kant spoke of as the illusions of transcendent metaphysics. It pervades, not only the whole of traditional logic, but almost everything that has ever been said under the heading 'Philosophy of Being' or in answer to the question 'What is existence?' What is hoped of this book is that it will do something to keep this illusion at bay.

Appendix A

Kahn's Survey of the Uses of *'Einai'*

Professor Kahn, in *The Verb 'Be' in Ancient Greek*, has carried out a thorough examination of the uses of the Greek synonym for 'be', *'einai'*, in early, that is to say chiefly Homeric, Greek. It is worthwhile to summarize some of the points he makes at somewhat greater length than would be supportable in the main text. I shall not, however, attempt to give even a summary account of all the distinctions he draws in the course of an extremely long book.

Kahn, of course, uses the major categories 'copulative' and 'existential' to distinguish the most conspicuous senses of the verb *'einai'*. But he also lists two senses which, in his view, are different from both of these. He calls them the 'potential construction' and the 'veridical construction'. As an example of the first he gives[1] *'All' ouk esti Dii Kronioni machesthai'* from *Iliad* 21. 193. Literally translated, this is 'But *is not* to fight Zeus son of Kronos'. Something like 'it is not possible' is needed to render *'ouk esti* (is not)' into intelligible English. This use of *'esti'* to mean 'it is possible' is a feature of the Greek verb which finds no parallel in English. Again, some of Kahn's examples of the 'veridical construction' resist literal translation into English.[2] For instance, *'Eiē ken kai touto teon epos'*, from *Iliad* 24.56,[3] would be rendered literally as 'This word of yours could be', but 'be true' rather than simple 'be' is needed to make sense in English. Plato's puzzles about 'judging the thing

---

[1] p. 294, Example 115.

[2] Some of what Kahn regards as examples of the veridical construction probably ought to be classified differently. Thus Example 2 on p. 336, translated literally enough as 'These things are just as you say, Socrates', is more likely to be an instance of what he calls the 'Adverbial Copula', discussed by him in Ch. IV §§ 21-2.

[3] p. 346, Example 14. See above, Ch. XII, pp. 304 ff.

which is not', where he trades on an ambiguity between 'judging what is not the case' and 'not judging anything at all' are well known to philosophers. They depend on there being a sense of *'esti'* where it means not just 'is', but 'is true' or 'is the case', which lacks an exact parallel in English.

As well as listing these independent senses of *'einai'* Kahn subdivides the copulative use (p. 82). Not all of these subdivisions call for comment here, but we may notice that he distinguishes what he calls the 'nominal' from the 'adverbial copula'. The 'nominal copula' covers those cases where some form of *'einai'* is followed by a noun, adjective, pronoun, or participle in the same case as the subject of the sentence, usually, of course, the nominative. These are cases which exactly fit a syntactic account of what is meant by calling *'einai'* the copula. The 'adverbial copula' requires subdivision. Where a form of *'einai'* is followed by a simple adverb, we seem often enough merely to be encountering a superficial idomatic phenomenon, though it is one which occurs in English as well as in Greek. The sense of the word 'is' does not seem to be significantly different in 'Albert is well' from what it is in 'Albert is sick', despite the fact that 'well' is an adverb and 'sick' an adjective. As in English, so in Greek not all adverbs can be used in this way as complement for the copula: the use seems to be a feature of particular adverbs like 'well' in English or *'akēn* (silently)' in Greek, rather than to involve a special sense of the verbs 'be' or *'einai'*. It would be nearer the mark to say that we have here a special adjectival use of 'well', *'akēn'*, etc., rather than a special adverbial variety of the copula construction.

More interesting are the cases, far more numerous than those we have just mentioned, both in Greek and in English, where the copula is followed, not by an adverb, but by what seems to be an adverbial phrase expressing location. Examples are 'Margaret is in the kitchen', 'John is at the wheel'. A few sentences containing simple adverbs belong to this class rather than to the class represented by 'Albert is well'. A sentence like 'Sidney is near' is, as Kahn has argued (p. 157 f.), elliptical: Sidney is being said to be near the speaker or the hearer or some person or object whose mention is supplied from the context. Similarly 'Violet is here' may be regarded as equivalent to 'Violet is in this place'. It is arguable whether or not the word 'is', as it occurs in a sentence of this type, is to be regarded as copula. On the one hand, the possibility or necessity of omitting the word's equivalent in, for example, the Latin, Hebrew, or Russian translations of such sentences seems to range it with sentences like 'The Lord is righteous', where the equivalent of 'is' can similarly be omitted. This seems to suggest that we have in 'Margaret is in the kitchen' just another instance of the '*S* is *P*' form. On the other hand, where the substitution instance for *P* is an adjective, or, with qualifications, a noun-phrase,[4] 'is' can be replaced *salva congruitate* by a number of other verbs: thus 'John is angry' can be transformed into 'John looks angry', 'John became angry', or 'John was made angry'. But 'Margaret is in the kitchen' cannot similarly be transformed into 'Margaret looks in the kitchen', 'Margaret became in the kitchen' or 'Margaret was made in the kitchen'. Contrariwise, many verbs *can* replace 'is' in 'Margaret is in the kitchen' which cannot so replace it in 'John is angry'—many more, in fact. Thus, 'Margaret stayed in the kitchen', 'Margaret washed up in the kitchen', 'Margaret used to sing in the kitchen', etc., are all in order. These similarities make 'is' in 'Margaret is in the kitchen' look more like an intransitive verb than a copula requiring a complement. Greek is no different from English in its use of '*einai*' in this way with locative phrases.

Another type of Greek sentence using forms of '*einai*' does not have an English equivalent with 'be', although here English is very much the odd man out. This is what Kahn calls the 'possessive construction' with '*einai*'. He gives as an example (p. 267, Example 62) '*Oude moi esti patēr kai potnia mētēr*' from *Iliad* 6.413. The literal translation of this is 'Nor to me is father and lady mother', but it is impossible not to use 'have' in putting it into simple intelligible English: 'I have no father, no lady mother'. One of the most widespread uses of synonyms of 'be' is that of equivalents of 'is to me (you, John, etc.)' to mean 'I (you, John, etc.) have'. Homeric Greek is here at one with Zuni, Japanese, and Telugu, amongst innumerable other languages. It is not only when hesitating between '*être*' and '*avoir*' that we have to think whether the word we want is the word normally translated 'is' or the word normally translated

---

[4] 'John became a general' and 'John was made a general' are acceptable, but not 'John seems a general'.

'has'. Linguists talk of the relation of 'have' to 'be' as that of active to passive.

Sentences of this form 'Noun (in the nominative) + is + noun (in the dative)', are not significantly different from the sentences like 'Margaret is in the kitchen' which we have just been considering. Many languages like English use a preposition with a noun to represent what in Greek is represented by a noun in the dative case; and, although English does not use the verb 'be' with 'to' and a noun to represent possession, there are plenty of languages which do. In such languages the locative construction and the possessive construction are visibly parallel: thus we could easily find Hebrew sentences literally translatable 'The throne [is] in Jerusalem' and 'The throne [is] to David' where location and possession are syntactically indiscernible.

Kahn discusses the 'possessive construction' in the course of his chapter entitled 'The Verb of Existence', and the same chapter has a section on what he calls 'the locative-existential'. There is overlap here, as he admits, with 'the locative copula', which he treats of in the chapter headed 'Description of the Copula Uses'. The question whether 'be' and *einai* are purely equivocal or analogical has, as we have seen, to take special note of these borderline cases. But we must look briefly at the cases Kahn presents as unambiguously 'existential'.

'Type I' of his existential uses covers cases to which I myself have devoted much attention in Chapter V. These are the cases where the verb 'be' receives, not a locative, but a temporal qualification. In these contexts, where the subject is animate, the verb 'be' is synonymous with 'live': *vivere viventibus est esse*. Kahn accordingly talks of this as 'The Vital Use'. Examples of this use almost all contain a Greek adverb, translated 'still', or the negation of this, translated 'no longer': 'Your parents are (living) still', 'Though Hector is (lives) no longer'. A frequent Homeric example is the phrase '*Theoi aien eontes*', 'The gods who always are (live forever)'. There is no temptation here to treat 'still' or 'always' as complement of the copula.

Kahn's second and third types of existential use do not stand out so clearly as distinct species, and we shall pass quickly to his Type IV, which he claims conforms most closely to the existential quantifier of logicians. Sentences of this type employ an idiom which is very common in Greek. It consists of some form of the verb *'einai'* followed by a clause introduced by the relative pronoun: *'estin hos* —'. We should naturally translate this as 'There is someone who —' or 'There is something which —'. But it is so frequent a formula that it is often better rendered by the simple 'Someone —' or 'Something —'. Very often it occurs in negated form: *'Nun d'ouk esth' hos tis thanaton phygēi* (Now is not who shall escape death)'. We have the choice, when rendering this into good English, of expanding 'is not who' to 'there is not anyone who', or of contracting it to 'no one'. Either way we have something which could well be symbolized by $N\Sigma x\phi x$.

The distinguishing feature of Kahn's Type V of the existential use of 'einai' is that the verb takes as its subject an abstract, usually a verbal, noun. Examples are *'Amphi de min klangē nekyōn ēn* (And around him a clamour of the dead was)' from *Odyssey* 11.605, and *'Ek gar Orestao tisis essetai* (For from Orestes vengeance shall be)' from *Odyssey* 1.40.[5] Where the Greek has *'ēn* (was)' and *'essetai* (shall be)', idiomatic English would require the use of some verb other than 'be': we should more naturally say that a clamour of the dead *arose*, or that vengeance *will come* from Orestes. Generally, when the Greek uses a part of *'einai'* with an abstract noun as subject, English looks for some synonym of 'occur'. Kahn therefore describes this use of *'einai'* as its use as a verb of occurrence. His own account is that the deep structure of the sentence is given by an underlying sentence ('The dead cry out'), and this is then nominalized ('A crying out of the dead') and made to stand as subject to a form of *'einai'*, which thus has the sense 'took place'. It is interesting that a similar use of the Japanese verb *'ar-ru'*, when its subject is an event, calls for the translation 'will be held', as in *'Olympics-ga Mexico-de ar-ru* (The Olympics will be held in Mexico)', whereas the same verb, when its subject is other than an event, can be translated 'is', as in *'Illinois daigaku-wa Illinois syuu-ni ar-ru* (The University of Illinois is in the State of Illinois)'.[6]

The last of Kahn's types of existential use of *'einai'*, Type

---

[5] pp. 283 f., Examples 9 and 99. See also the discussion of the first of these examples in Ch. XII, above, § 2.

[6] Makino, 'Japanese "Be"', Verhaar, Part 3, p. 3; see also XII above, p. 320.

VI, is one which he cannot find in the Homeric literature, but only in texts of the fifth century and later, which are either philosophical or influenced by philosophical usage. He cites passages from Aristophanes' *Clouds*, Protagoras, Hippocrates, Melissus, and Aristotle. The last, from the *Posterior Analytics* II, Ch. 1 (89^{b}32): '*Ei estin ē mē esti kentauros ē theos* (Whether is or is not a centaur or a god)' requires 'there is or is not such a thing as' to be substituted for 'is or is not' if the literal translation is to be rendered idiomatic. Alternatively, it could be translated 'Whether or not centaurs or gods exist'. Most of Kahn's examples of this type of use consist of a common noun followed by a part of the verb 'be'. Noun and verb can be singular or plural. One example couples '*esti*', or rather its negation '*ouk esti*', with a proper name. These are the cases where the synonym of 'be' approximates most closely to those uses of 'exist' whose syntactical category is hardest to distinguish at the superficial level from that of straightforward predicates like 'growl'. The question is, do they occur, as a Wittgensteinian would say, 'outside philosophy'?[7]

[7] These cases are discussed in Ch. XI above, § 5.

Appendix B

Kant's Criticisms of the Ontological Argument

In Chapter II I briefly discussed Kant's arguments in *The Critique of Pure Reason* against the view that existence is a real predicate. These are, of course, part of a wider enterprise, which involves establishing that every existential proposition is synthetic, and whose main purpose is to disprove the possibility of an ontological proof of the existence of God. The arguments of the section are difficult, and any more detailed discussion of them than was given in Chapter II would have been too great a distraction to the reader. I gave there a fairly thorough examination of Kant's argument from B 626 to the end, but there remain some arguments from the first part of the section, B 620-6, which deserve attention, and I wish to look more closely at them in this appendix.

The passage starts with an examination of the concept of an absolutely necessary being. Kant holds that there is a pressing question about the intelligibility of this concept. Its meaning, he says, has been supposed to have been exhibited in a number of examples; but he only gives one of these, the absolute necessity of the proposition that a triangle has three angles, although this proposition is treated as a representative of any geometrical proposition you care to produce. Kant's objection to this way of illustrating the notion of absolute necessity is that it ignores the difference between the absolute necessity of judgements and that of 'things and their existence'. We must probe into this. First, why has he switched from talking of the *proposition* that a triangle has three angles to talking of *judgements*, with the example in mind of the judgement that a triangle has three angles? What is absolutely necessary, of course, is the judgement, not in the sense of an act of judging, but in the sense of what is judged; and this is, if anything, the same as the proposition. We need to emphasize this to be on our guard in case Kant is attributing necessity to some psychological occurrence. Secondly, he contrasts judgements with 'things and their existence', apparently regarding things and the existence of things as equivalent. But the necessity of the existence of something, say, of a house that Robert owns, is the same thing as its being necessary that there be a house that Robert owns, i.e. as the necessity of the proposition that there is a house which Robert owns. And that, in the appropriate sense of 'judgement', is the same as the necessity of the judgement that there is a house that Robert owns. Where then is the contrast between the judgement and the thing? Nothing else can be meant by the absolute necessity of a thing, e.g. a house which Robert owns, except the absolute necessity of the proposition that there is such a thing, that there is a house which Robert owns. Necessity in each case is expressed by an operator on propositions, 'It is necessary that —'. How else could it be expressed, since necessity can be defined in terms of possibility and negation? 'It is necessary that —' is equivalent to 'It is not the case that it is possible that it is not the case that —', and 'It is not the case that —' is incontrovertibly an operator on propositions, not a predicate of things.

By 'necessity of things' Kant means, and confesses that he means, 'necessity of the existence of things', i.e. 'necessity that things exist'. What then has he in mind when he goes on to say 'the absolute necessity of the judgement is only a conditional necessity of the thing, or of the predicate in the judgement'? Let us look at his own example. The absolute necessity of the judgement that a triangle has three angles should be the same thing as the conditioned necessity of the predicate in the judgement, i.e. of the existence of the predicate in the judgement. But what could this phrase mean? 'The exstence of "— has three angles"' seems to be a nonsense. What Kant could mean is, perhaps, 'the existence of something of which the predicate in the judgement is truly predicable', i.e. 'the existence of something having three angles'. The conditional necessity of this would presumably be asserted by the proposition 'If there is a triangle, then it is necessary that there is something having three angles'. Such propositions, however, are notoriously ambiguous. This one could mean, 'If there is a triangle then the existence of something having three angles is a necessary truth', expressible symbolically by $C\Sigma x\phi x L\Sigma y\psi y$. But this is not even entailed by, let alone equivalent to, the proposition 'It is necessary that a triangle has three angles $(L\Pi x C\phi x\psi x)$'. What this latter proposition does entail is the proposition 'If there is a triangle, then it is necessary that there is something having three angles' in its other sense, as equivalent to 'It is necessary that, if there is a triangle, there is something having three angles $(LC\Sigma x\phi x\Sigma y\psi y)$'.

Kant, however, does not seem to use 'the necessity of the predicate in the judgement' to signify its being necessary that there is something having three angles, but rather the necessity of three angles. These, he says, are not declared by the above proposition to be absolutely necessary; so we might take him to mean that from the necessary truth that a triangle has three angles it follows, not that it is necessary that there are three angles, but that, necessarily, if there is a triangle, there are three angles. And this is true enough. Unfortunately, when Kant comes to spell out the proposition that is entailed by the necessary truth that a triangle has three angles, he expresses it thus: 'Under the condition that there is a triangle (that is, that a triangle is given), three angles will necessarily be found *in it*'. The words which I have italicized are in fact bracketed in the original German, and Kant might well be slightly sheepish about them. 'Necessarily, if there is a triangle, there are three angles' is of the same form as 'Necessarily, if there is a triangle, there is something which has three angles $(LC\Sigma x\phi x\Sigma y\psi y)$', if we overlook the difference between the simple existential quantifier and the numerical quantifier 'there are three'. But with the addition of the words 'in it' the proposition is in danger of being taken as being of the form $LC\Sigma x\phi x\Sigma y K\psi y\chi yx$, where χyx can be read 'y is in x', and where the last x is the equivalent of a 'dangling pronoun'. The 'it' in fact must refer back to the triangle of the antecedent, but this cannot be achieved by the x of our formula, since the scope of the quantifier which binds the first occurrence of x is limited to the antecedent of the conditional. The repetition of x in the consequent, as an unbound variable, thus makes the expression a mere open sentence. In order to bind it, as is required, by the same quantifier as binds the other occurrence of x, we must include the conditional as a whole in the scope of the quantifier which binds it. It will be easily seen that the quantifier needed for this purpose is the universal quantifier. 'Necessarily, if there is a triangle, there are three angles in it' will thus be of the form $L\Pi x C\phi x \Sigma y K\psi y\chi y x$. But since $\Sigma y K\psi y\chi y x$ is a substitution instance of ψx, the proposition is also of the form $L\Pi x C\phi x \psi x$, which was the form of the original proposition, 'Necessarily a triangle has three angles'. 'There are three angles in x' is, after all, only a stylistic variant of 'x has three angles'. The proposition that 'Under the condition that there is a triangle (that is, that a triangle is given), three angles will necessarily be found in it' is, therefore, nothing but a clumsily extended variant of the original 'Necessarily a triangle has three angles'. Kant's 'absolute necessity of the judgement' and 'conditional necessity of the thing' turn out to be identical.

Well, wasn't that what Kant said? Not quite. The absolute necessity of the judgement does not involve existence, whereas the conditioned necessity of the thing is precisely the conditioned necessity of the existence of the thing. 'A triangle has three angles' is indeed of the form $\Pi x C\phi x \psi x$, which contains no existential quantifier: 'Under the condition that there is a triangle three angles will be found in it' is of the same form, but also of the form $\Pi x C\phi x \Sigma y K\psi y\chi y x$, which does contain an existential quantifier. It is, perhaps, an accident of the example Kant has chosen that the predicate of the original proposition, '— has three angles', is repesentable by a form which explicitly involves existential quantification '$\Sigma y K\psi y\chi y$—' ("There are (three) angles in —'). Another example, 'A vixen is female', might have been chosen which was not representable by a formula containing an existential quantifier. The only way existence could be brought in here would be by observing that 'A vixen is female' implies 'If something is a vixen then something is female'. It is not, however, equivalent to it, and Kant says that the absolute necessity of the judgement *is* the conditioned necessity of the thing.

To summarize we may say that, although Kant shows some confusion in the detail of his argumentation, he does wish to maintain that no necessary proposition is existential, in the sense that the existential quantifier is the operator having widest scope in its formalization. However, he allows that there can be necessary propositions containing the existential quantifier, but where this quantifier is included within the scope of some other operator. 'Necessarily, if anything is a triangle, there are three angles in it' is of this form. So are 'Necessarily, if anything is a number, there is some number which is its successor' and 'Necessarily, if anything is in motion, there is something which causes it to move'. Propositions of this form are certainly of great importance for Natural Theology, but not in the context of the Ontological Argument.

In a long and obscure sentence which immediately follows his discussion of the example of the triangle (B 623) Kant appears to say that the necessary existence of God can be affirmed only by analogy with that of the three angles of the triangle. It is difficult to be sure what he has in mind, but presumably it is this: 'Necessarily, if anything is a God, it exists'. From this we can derive 'Necessarily, if there is a God, then there is something which both is a God and exists'. And to assert this is to assert only the conditioned necessity of God and his existence, and that only by 'arbitrarily assuming' a concept in which existence has been included.

In the next paragraph (B 622-3) Kant examines the connection between necessity and contradiction. 'If, in an identical proposition, I reject the predicate and retain the subject, contradiction results.' What does he mean by 'reject' and 'retain' here? The example he has in mind is the contradiction of 'A triangle has three angles', which is 'There is a triangle in which there are not three angles'. To reject is to deny, and to retain to affirm, the existence of something (cf. 'the not-being or rejection of its object' (B 624)). 'There is a triangle in which there are not three angles' is of the form $\Sigma x K \phi x N \Sigma y K \psi y \chi y x$; but since, as we have seen, $\Sigma x K \psi y \chi y x$ is a substitution instance of ψx, this is also of the more general form $\Sigma x K \phi x N \psi x$. Since Kant's model of an 'identical', or analytic, proposition is a proposition of the form $\Pi x C \phi x \psi x$, and since $\Sigma x K \phi x N \psi x = N \Pi x C \phi x \psi x$, this is exactly right. Kant is saying that contradictions—i.e. the negations of analytic propositions—are all of the form $\Sigma x K \phi x N \psi x$, i.e. that they are all affirmative existential propositions. He continues: 'But if we reject subject and predicate alike, there is no contradiction, for nothing is then left that can be contradicted.' To reject is to deny existence, so Kant could have in mind a proposition of the form $KN\Sigma x\phi x N\Sigma y\psi y$; but I suspect that what he actually has in mind is something of the form $N\Sigma x K\phi x\psi x$—'There is nothing which both is a triangle and has three angles'. This would fit the description 'rejecting the triangle together with its three angles', generalized as 'rejecting the thing with all its predicates', or 'rejecting the predicate of a judgement together with the subject'. If so we have a proposition which is entailed by a simple proposition of the form $N\Sigma x\phi x$. If the entailed proposition is self-contradictory, so must the entailing proposition be. But how could a proposition of the form $N\Sigma x\phi x$ be self-contradictory?

Such a proposition is equivalent to one of the form $\Pi x N\phi x$. It might be argued that a universally quantified proposition is self-contradictory if a self-contradictory proposition is obtained by replacing the variables in its matrix by proper names. Consider, in this case, certain substitution instances of $\Pi x N\phi x$, for example, $\Pi x NIxx$ and $\Pi x NC\phi x\phi x$. If the variable in the matrices of these formulae is replaced at each occurrence by a proper name, say a, we obtain $NIaa$ and $NC\phi a\phi a$, which is equivalent to $K\phi aN\phi a$, i.e. 'a is not identical to itself' and 'a both ϕ's and does not ϕ'. All such propositions are self-contradictory. It looks then as though self-contradictory instances of the form $\Pi x N\phi x$ can easily be found.

However, $\Pi x NIxx$ is equivalent to $N\Sigma xIxx$. If this is self-contradictory, its contradictory, namely $\Sigma xIxx$, must be analytic. This appears to state that there is something which is identical with itself. Russell was much distressed to find that this proposition had to be accepted as true in the system of *Principia Mathematica*, although it seemed to him plainly a contingent, synthetic. *a posteriori* truth.[1] Such truths, on his view, had no business to appear in the ranks of the intuitively or demonstrably *logical* truths of which alone he desired that system to consist. Russell took $\Sigma xIxx$ to be tantamount to the proposition 'There is something'. $\Sigma xC\phi x\phi x$ has been understood in the same way. It is equivalent to $\Sigma xAN\phi x\phi x$; and thus to $A\Sigma xN\phi x\Sigma x\phi x$, which might be regarded as false if there

[1] See Russell, *Introduction to Mathematical Philosophy*, p. 203, n.

were in fact nothing. So if these propositions are indeed contingent, synthetic, and *a posteriori*, their contradictories, which are of the form $N\Sigma x\phi x$, are not after all self-contradictory.

The argument of the last two paragraphs is an argument *a fortiori*. It is designed to show that no proposition of the form $N\Sigma x\phi x$ can be self-contradictory. Propositions of this form are equivalent to corresponding propositions of the form $\Pi x N\phi x$. If any propositions of this form can be self-contradictory, surely these propositions, $\Pi x N I x x$ and $\Pi x N C \phi x \phi x$ (for any substitution for ϕ whatsoever), will be. But these propositions, it was urged, amount to the denial that there *is* anything; and that *there is something* is a contingent truth. So not even these propositions are self-contradictory. *A fortiori*, no propositions of the form $N\Sigma x\phi x$ are self-contradictory.

Much that has been said already in this book casts doubt on the soundness of this argument. What are we to make of the claim that it is a contingent truth that *there is something*? At first sight it seems that this would have to be interpreted as asserting that something exists, where '— exists' is a first-level predicable. But the main thrust of my argument is to deny that any more sense can be made of '— exist' than of '— are numerous' as a first-level predicable. Existence is what the existential quantifier expresses. But 'something' is also identifiable as what the existential quantifier expresses. How then can 'Something exists' or 'There is something' be construed? How could the quantifier to double duty by symbolizing 'There is' as well as 'something' in this proposition? $\Sigma x \Sigma y x y$ is not well formed.[2] Introducing the identity predicable is one way of regularizing this: $\Sigma x \Sigma y I x y$ is well formed and just means, if it means anything, $\Sigma x I x x$. But I am persuaded by Wittgenstein that no more sense can be made of '— is the same as —' as a two-place predicable of first level than can be made of '— exist' as a one-place predicable of first level.[3] Another way of amending $\Sigma x \Sigma y x y$ in order to make it well formed would be to change the second variable to a predicative variable. This would give us $\Sigma x \Sigma \phi \phi x$, Leśniewski's interpretation of 'Something exists'.[4] But this too would give us a logically

[2] See my remarks in Ch. X, p. 273, about Lewis's attempts to make sense of 'There are things which do not actually exist'.
[3] See above, Ch. III, p. 77, n. 34; Ch. V, p. 139, n. 31; Ch. XI, pp. 286 ff.
[4] See above, Ch. V, p. 139.

true proposition. The same may be said of $\Sigma x C\phi x\phi x$. Whatever we may think of the meaningfulness of $\Sigma x I x x$, $\Sigma x C\phi x\phi x$ is meaningful and indeed true for any interpretation of ϕ as a first-level predicable. And since $C\phi a\phi a$ is an instantiation of $\Sigma \phi\phi a$, $\Sigma x C\phi x\phi x$ entails $\Sigma\phi\Sigma x\phi x$, which is equivalent to $\Sigma x\Sigma\phi\phi x$. Any proposition of this form is well formed, but it is a tautology. We do not seem able to produce a logically acceptable expression of what we want 'There is something' to mean which keeps this as a contingent truth.

And yet there seems to be something intuitively acceptable about the statement that no proposition of the form $\Sigma x\phi x$ can be logically true. What guarantee have we that there are values for the variable x in, say, 'For some x, x is square-if-it-is-square'? Given that we can find a name to substitute for x in 'x is square-if-it-is-square', we shall inevitably produce a true proposition by making the substitution. And this can be generalized existentially. But could it not be that there *are* no genuine proper names—no names, that is, that name genuine objects? Strawson holds the view that 'the introduction of particulars into discourse' requires the knowledge of some empirical fact. His final view is that the empirical fact in question will be of the kind stated by feature-placing statements, like 'There is coal in the Mendip Hills'.[5] Such statements will not themselves be logically true. In so far as proper names have the function of introducing into discourse what Strawson calls 'particulars', it seems then that it is a contingent truth that any proper names are available to us at all. But is the introduction of particulars the only function of proper names? Frege, for one, thought that some proper names had the function of referring to objects whose existence was in no sense an empirical or contingent matter—numbers, for instance. *Qua* proper name, for Frege, there is nothing to choose between 'Sixteen' and 'Louis the Sixteenth'. Not only is it logically necessary that any proposition formed by attaching the predicable '— is square-if-it-is-square' to a proper name for the number sixteen is true, but it is logically necessary that there should be something for the name 'Sixteen' to name. If Frege is right in counting numbers among objects, i.e. among what proper names name, our scruples about

---

[5] Strawson, *Individuals* Ch. 6, §§ 1, 6. For 'feature-placing statements' see above, Ch. XII, § 1.

APPENDIX B 341

admitting 'For some x, x is square-if-it-is-square' as a logically necessary truth are ill founded. But Frege's use of a single-sorted first-level quantification, of variables which range over all objects, abstract as well as concrete, is highly controversial. Wittgenstein, for instance, regards 'number' as a formal concept distinct from 'object', and would use a distinct style of variable—m and n, perhaps, as distinct from x and y—to range over numbers as opposed to objects.[6] There is plenty of room for dispute over the character of the variables of first-level quantification, and over the proper names which are the constants substitutable for them. The important point is that this is a dispute, not about quantification as such, but about individual expressions and proper names. If basic proper names are those which refer to particulars, and the individual variables of propositions of the form $\Sigma x \phi x$ occupy positions only otherwise occupiable by such proper names, there is a case for saying that no proposition of this form can be logically true, no proposition of the form $N\Sigma x \phi x$ self-contradictory. And this may be what lies behind Kant's claim to this effect. But if it is, it is the consequence of a doctrine about proper names, not a consequence of a doctrine about the concept of existence.

If existence is what the existential quantifier expresses, and if the existential quantifier is capable of binding variables of categories other than the category of individuals, we have a short way to refute the claim that no existential proposition can be a logically necessary truth. Take any logically necessary proposition whatever: say, 'If grass is green, grass is green'. Substitute a propositional variable for this proposition and bind it with the existential quantifier. The result is an existential generalization of the original logically necessary proposition. Since 'If grass is green, grass is green' is logically necessary, any proposition which is entailed by it is logically necessary. But Σpp is its existential generalization, and is therefore entailed by it. Σpp is thus a logically necessary proposition, and must be so, if any proposition at all is logically necessary. There can be no incompatibility between being logically necessary and being an existential proposition, if by this we mean a proposition which has the existential quantifier as an operator which has wider scope in the proposition than any other

[6] See *Tractatus* 4.127.

operator. And if Σpp is logically necessary, $N\Sigma pp$ is self-contradictory. Kant's view that only an affirmative existential proposition can be self-contradictory will not hold water. Rejecting by itself *can* lead to contradiction: there does not have to be some positing combined with the rejecting.

When Kant turns, as he does in the next paragraph (B 623-4), to the possibility that 'there are subjects which cannot be removed', i.e. rejected, he is in effect enquiring whether there is a form of impossibility which is distinct from self-contradiction. The first attempt to do this, which occupies the succeeding paragraph (B 624-5), is difficult but can perhaps be interpreted thus: Any expression which does not signify something impossible can be used to define a concept. Nothing impossible is signified by the expression 'being which possesses all reality'. Since 'all reality' includes existence, if we defined 'God' as 'the being which possesses all reality', 'God exists' would be true in virtue of this definition. If we deny the existence of God, this can only mean that we deny the possibility of such a being, deny, that is, that we *can* introduce the word 'God' by means of the definition 'being which possesses all reality'. But that is contradictory, since it contradicts the premise that nothing impossible is signified by this phrase (not '*self*-contradictory' as Kemp Smith misleadingly translates '*widersprechend*' here).

Kant's answer is that a contradiction *is* involved in introducing a term by the definition 'being which possesses all reality', which involves existence. He uses the difficult phrase 'a thing which we profess to be thinking solely in reference to its possibility'. What I think he means by this is: If you ask me to allow you to define a predicate P_1 by stipulating that it means the same as the (complex) predicate P_2, I must accede to your request, provided that there is no internal inconsistency in P_2. The introduction of P_1 into our discourse in this way cannot, therefore, involve any claim that goes beyond mere possibility. To use the definition to infer an existential proposition, a proposition about what actually exists, is thus to go back on the claim that all that was being requested was agreement to a definition.

Kant attempts to reinforce this argument by a dilemma (B 625-6). The proposition 'This or that thing exists' is either

APPENDIX B 343

analytic or synthetic. If analytic, the predicate is contained in the subject. He interprets this possibility in two ways. The first regards it as tantamount to saying that 'The thought, which is in us, is the thing itself'. This is somewhat baffling, but must presumably be taken to mean that we replace the quasi-variable subject-expression 'This or that thing' with an expression referring to our own thought. In this way the subject which replaces the words 'This or that thing' is self-referring and thus guarantees its own existence. But a proposition construed in this way has no bearing on the question of God's existence.

The second way of interpreting the possibility that 'This or that thing exists' is analytic is equally baffling.[7] Perhaps Kant means that the only other way in which we could suppose such a proposition to be analytic would be if the concept of existence had already been included in the concept of the subject term substituted for 'This or that thing'. This would be the case in the proposition 'A being possessing all reality exists'. This proposition would be taken by Kant as equivalent to 'If anything possesses all reality, it exists'[8] and the antecedent of a hypothetical like this is thought of as being concerned with 'the realm of the possible'. If we hypothesize a thing possessing all reality, we are making existence belong to this realm. In the consequent of the proposition we infer existence from this hypothesized possibility. (We should note the confusion between the assertion of a hypothetical and the inference of the proposition which is its consequent from the proposition which is its antecedent.) We may agree that this is a miserable tautology. Kant explains that it is no less a tautology because the crucial word that occurs in the antecedent is 'reality' and that in the consequent 'exists': to posit something is to assert its existence, and this is to call it real. So in a proposition of the form 'If x is real, x exists' the predicate merely repeats what was assumed in the subject. So if a proposition is analytic in this sense it again can have no bearing on the question of God's existence.

Kant however believes, with 'every reasonable person', that all existential propositions are synthetic. (He must have in mind

---

[7] I am grateful to Miss Katherine Minister and Mr Chalon Mullins for suggestions about possible ways of understanding this dilemma.

[8] See above, pp. 334 ff., on 'A triangle has three angles'.

only true affirmative propositions.) So it is the second horn of the dilemma on which he would choose to sit. But a synthetic proposition, by definition, can be denied without contradiction. It cannot therefore be absolutely necessary, nor can the thing whose existence it affirms.

This brings us to the parts of the argument examined above, in Chapter II, sections 4-6.

Bibliography

Ackrill, J. L. 'Plato and the Copula: *Sophist* 251-259', in Vlastos.
Anscombe, G. E. M., and Geach, P. T. *Three Philosophers*, Oxford: Basil Blackwell, 1961.
Aquinas, St. Thomas, *Summa Theologiae*, ed. P. Caramello, Turin: Marietti, 1950.
—— *In XII Libros Metaphysicorum Aristotelis expositio*, ed. M. R. Cathala, Turin: Marietti, 1964.
Aristotle, *Prior and Posterior Analytics*, ed. W. D. Ross, Oxford: Clarendon Press, 1949.
—— *Categories and De Interpretatione*, Engl. tr. with notes by J. L. Ackrill, Oxford: Clarendon Press, 1963.
—— *De Anima*, Books II and III, Eng. tr. with notes by D. W. Hamlyn, Oxford: Clarendon Press, 1968.
—— *Physics*, Books I and II, Eng. tr. with notes by W. Charlton, Oxford: Clarendon Press, 1970.
—— *Metaphysics*, Books Γ, Δ, E, Eng. tr. with notes by Christopher Kirwan, Oxford: Clarendon Press, 1971.
—— *Posterior Analytics*, Eng. tr. with notes by Jonathan Barnes, Oxford: Clarendon Press 1975.
Austin, J. L. *Philosophical Papers*, Oxford: Oxford University Press Paperback, 1970.
Baldwin, T. R. Review of C. J. F. Williams, *What is Truth?*, *Philosophy*, Vol. 51, 1976.
Bambrough, R. (ed.) *New Essays on Plato and Aristotle*, London: Routledge and Kegan Paul, 1965.
Barnes, J. *The Ontological Argument*, London: Macmillan, 1972.
Bednarowski, W. *see under* Mackie, J. L.
Belnap, N. D., Jr. *see under* Dunn, J. M., and Grover, Dorothy L.
Binkley, R. 'Quantifying, Quotation and a Paradox', *Noûs*, Vol. 4, 1970.
Brentano, F. *Psychology from an Empirical Standpoint*, Eng. tr. ed. Linda L. McAlister, New York: Humanities Press, 1973.
Butler, R. J. (ed.) *Analytical Philosophy* (1st Series), Oxford: Basil Blackwell, 1962.
Cameron, J. M. *The Night Battle*, London: Macmillan, 1966.
Camp, Joseph L., Jr. *see under* Grover, Dorothy L.

Castañeda, H. -N. 'On the Phenomeno-Logic of the I', *Proceedings of the XIVth International Congress of Philosophy*, Vienna, 1968.
Cohen, L. J. Review of Prior's *Objects of Thought*, *Mind*, Vol. 82, 1973.
Davidson, D., and Harman, G. (edd.) *The Semantics of Natural Language*, Dordrecht: Reidel, 1972.
Dummett, M. *Frege: Philosophy of Language*, London: Duckworth, 1973.
Dunn, J. M., and Belnap, N. D., Jr. 'The Substitutional Interpretation of the Quantifier', *Noûs*, Vol. 2, 1968.
Ellis, Jeffrey, and Boadi, Lawrence, '"To Be" in Twi', in Verhaar, Part 4.
Evans, G., and McDowell, J. (edd.), *Truth and Meaning: Essays in Semantics*, Oxford: Clarendon Press, 1976.
Findlay, J. N. *Values and Intentions*, London: George Allen and Unwin, 1961.
Fine, Kit, *see under* Prior, A. N.
Flew, A. G. N. (ed.), *Logic and Language* (2nd Series), Oxford: Basil Blackwell, 1961.
Frege, G. *Die Grundlagen der Arithmetik*, published with Eng. tr. by J. L. Austin *en face* as *The Foundations of Arithmetic*, Oxford: Basil Blackwell, 1952.
— *Translations from the Philosophical Writings of Gottlob Frege*, edd. Peter Geach and Max Black, Oxford: Basil Blackwell, 1952.
Gallie, R. D. 'A. N. Prior and Substitutional Quantification', *Analysis*, Vol. 34, 1974.
— 'Substitutionalism and Substitutional Quantification', *Analysis*, Vol. 35, 1975.
Geach, P. T. 'Subject and Predicate', *Mind*, Vol 59, 1950.
— 'On What There Is' (a symposium with W. V. Quine), *Proceedings of the Aristotelian Society*, Supp. Vol. 25, 1951.
— *see under* Anscombe, G. E. M.
— *Reference and Generality*, Ithaca: Cornell University Press, 1962.
— *God and the Soul*, London: Routledge and Kegan Paul, 1969.
— 'God's Relation to the World', *Sophia*, Vol. 8, No. 2, July 1969.
— *Logic Matters*, Oxford: Basil Blackwell, 1972.
— Review of Strawson's *Subject and Predicate* in *The Times Literary Supplement*, 28 February 1975.
— 'Names and Identity' in Guttenplan.
Gellner, E. *Words and Things*, London: Victor Gollancz, 1959.
Godfrey-Smith, W. 'Prior and Particulars', *Philosophy*, Vol. 53, 1978.
Graham, A. C. '"Being" in Linguistics and Philosophy', *Foundations of Language*, Vol. l, 1965, reprinted in Verhaar, Part 5, pp. 225-33.
— '"Being" in Classical Chinese', in Verhaar, Part I.
Grover, Dorothy L., Camp, Jospeh L., Jr., and Belnap, Nuel D., Jr. 'A Prosentential Theory of Truth', *Philosophical Studies*, Vol. 27, 1975.
Guttenplan, S. (ed.) *Mind and Language*, Oxford: Clarendon Press, 1975.
Harman, G. 'Substitutional Quantification and Quotation', *Noûs*, Vol. 5, 1971.
— *see under* Davidson, D.

Hashimoto, Anne Yue 'The Verb "To Be" in Modern Chinese', in Verhaar, Part 4.
Hobbes, T. *Leviathan*, Oxford: Clarendon Press, 1909.
Hume, D. *A Treatise of Human Nature*, ed. L. A. Selby-Bigge, Oxford: Clarendon Press, 1951.
Jones, O. R. 'Truth and Predication', *Analysis*, Vol. 32, 1972.
Kahn, Charles H. *The Verb 'Be' in Ancient Greek*, Dordrecht: D. Reidel, 1973 (Part 6 of Verhaar).
Kant, I. *Critique of Pure Reason*, Eng. tr. by N. Kemp Smith, London, Macmillan, 1963.
Kenny, A. J. P. 'Practical Reason', *Analysis*, Vol. 26, 1966.
— *The Five Ways*, London: Routledge and Kegan Paul, 1968.
Kneale, W. and M. *The Development of Logic*, Oxford: Clarendon Press, 1960.
Körner, S. *Kant*, Harmondsworth: Penguin Books, 1955.
— (ed.) *Philosophy of Logic*, Oxford: Basil Blackwell, 1976.
Kripke, S. 'Naming and Necessity', in Davidson and Harman.
— 'Is There a Problem about Substitutional Quantification?', in Evans and McDowell.
Leibniz, G. W. *Die Philosophischen Schriften*, ed. C. I. Gerhardt, Hildesheim: Georg Olms, 1960.
Lewis, David. *Counterfactuals*, Oxford: Basil Blackwell, 1973.
— 'Truth in Fiction', *American Philosophical Quarterly*, Vol, 15, 1978.
Linsky, L. (ed.) *Reference and Modality*, Oxford: Oxford University Press, 1971.
— *Names and Descriptions*, Chicago and London: University of Chicago Press, 1977.
Locke, J. *An Essay Concerning Human Understanding*, ed. A. C. Fraser, New York: Dover Publications, 1959.
Lyons, J. *Introduction to Theoretical Linguistics*, Cambridge: At the University Press, 1971.
— *Semantics*, Cambridge: At the University Press, 1977.
McDowell, J. *see under* Evans, G.
McGinn, C. 'The Necessities of Origin', *Journal of Philosophy*, Vol. 73, 1976, No. 5.
Mackie, J. L. *Problems from Locke*, Oxford: Clarendon Press, 1976.
— and Bednarowski, W. 'The Riddle of Existence', *Proceedings of the Aristotelian Society*, Supp. Vol. 50, 1976.
Makino, Seiichi, 'Japanese "Be"', in Verhaar, Part 3.
Marcus, Ruth B. 'Modalities and Intensional Languages', *Synthese*, Vol. 13, 1961.
— 'Quantification and Ontology', *Noûs*, Vol. 6, 1972.
Mill, J. S. *A System of Logic*, London: Longmans, Green, Reader and Dyer, 1872.
Miller, B. 'Logically Simple Propositions', *Analysis*, Vol. 34, No. 4, 1973.
— 'In Defence of the Predicate "Exists"', *Mind*, Vol. 84, 1975.
Moore, G. E. 'Is Existence a Predicate?', in Flew.

BIBLIOGRAPHY

—— *The Commonplace Book of G. E. Moore*, ed. Casimir Lewy, London: George Allen and Unwin, 1962.
—— *Lectures on Philosophy*, London: George Allen and Unwin, 1966.
Munitz, Milton K. *Existence and Logic*, New York: At the University Press, 1974.
—— and Unger, Peter K. (edd.), *Semantics and Philosophy*, New York: At the University Press, 1974.
Owen, G. E. L. 'Aristotle on the Snares of Ontology', in Bambrough.
Pap, Arthur, 'Indubitable Existential Statements', *Mind*, Vol. 55, 1946.
Passmore, J. *Hume's Intentions*, Cambridge: At the University Press, 1952.
Plantinga, A. *God and Other Minds*, Ithaca: Cornell University Press, 1967.
—— *The Nature of Necessity*, Oxford: Clarendon Press, 1974.
Plato, *Sophist*, in *Platonis Opera*, Vol. 1, ed. J. Burnet, Oxford, Clarendon Press, 1953.
—— *Theaetetus*, Eng. tr. with notes by J. McDowell, Oxford: Clarendon Press, 1973.
Prior, A. N. *Formal Logic*, Oxford: Clarendon Press, 1955.
—— 'The Runabout Inference Ticket', *Analysis*, Vol. 21, 1960.
—— 'Nonetities', in Butler; reprinted in *Essays in Logic and Ethics*, by A. N. Prior, London: Duckworth, 1976.
—— 'Is the Concept of Referential Opacity Really Necessary?' *Acta Philosophica Fennica*, Vol. 16, 1963.
—— *Past, Present and Future*, Oxford: Clarendon Press, 1967.
—— *Papers on Time and Tense*, Oxford: Clarendon Press, 1968.
—— *Objects of Thought*, edd. P. T. Geach and A. J. P. Kenny, Oxford: Clarendon Press, 1971.
—— *Essays in Logic and Ethics*, London: Duckworth, 1976.
—— and Fine, Kit, *Worlds, Times and Selves*, London: Duckworth, 1977.
Quine, W. V. *Mathematical Logic*, New York: Harper and Row, 1962.
—— 'On What There Is', in *From a Logical Point of View*, 2nd Ed., New York and Evanston: Harper and Row, 1963.
—— 'Reference and Modality', in *From a Logical Point of View*, 2nd Ed., New York and Evanston: Harper and Row, 1963, and in Linsky *Reference and Modality*.
—— 'On What There Is' (a symposium with P. T. Geach), *Proceedings of the Aristotelian Society*, Supp. Vol. 25, 1951.
—— 'Quantifiers and Propositional Attitudes', in *The Ways of Paradox*, New York: Random House, 1966, and in Linsky *Reference and Modality*.
—— *Word and Object*, Cambridge, Mass.: The M. I. T. Press, 1960.
—— *From a Logical Point of View*, 2nd Ed., New York and Evanston: Harper and Row, 1963.
—— *The Ways of Paradox*, New York: Random House, 1966.
—— 'Variables Explained Away', *Selected Logic Papers*, New York: Random House, 1966.
—— 'Existence and Quantification', in *Ontological Relativity and Other Essays*, New York and London: Columbia University Press, 1969.

BIBLIOGRAPHY

— *Ontological Relativity and Other Essays*, New York and London: Columbia University Press, 1969.
— *Philosophy of Logic*, Englewood Cliffs: Prentice Hall, 1970.
— *The Roots of Reference*, La Salle, Illinois: Open Court, 1973.
Ramsey, F. P. *The Foundations of Mathematics*, Totowa, New Jersey: Littlefield, Adams and Co., 1965.
Russell, Bertrand, *A Critical Exposition of the Philosophy of Leibniz*, London: George Allen and Unwin, 1958.
— *see under* Whitehead.
— *Introduction to Mathematical Philosophy*, London: George Allen and Unwin, 1919.
— 'Lectures on the Philosophy of Logical Atomism', *Logic and Knowledge*, ed. R. C. Marsh, London: George Allen and Unwin, 1966.
— 'On Denoting', also in *Logic and Knowledge*.
Ryle, G. 'Categories' *Proceedings of the Aristotelian Society*, Vol. 38, 1938, and in *Collected Papers*, London: Hutchinson, 1971, Vol. 2.
— 'Plato's "Parmenides" ' in *Mind*, Vol. 48, 1939, reprinted in *Collected Papers*, Vol. 1.
— *The Concept of Mind*, London: Hutchinson's University Library, 1950.
— *Collected Papers*, London: Hutchinson, 1971.
Schwartz, Stephen (ed.) *Naming, Necessity and Natural Kinds*, Ithaca and London: Cornell University Press, 1977.
Sellars, Wilfrid, 'Grammar and Existence: a Preface to Ontology', *Mind*, Vol. 69, 1960, reprinted in Wilfrid Sellars, *Science, Perception and Reality*, London: Routledge and Kegan Paul, 1963.
Stevenson, Leslie, 'Frege's Two Definitions of Quantification', *The Philosophical Quarterly*, Vol. 23, 1973.
Strawson, P. F. *Individuals: an Essay in Descriptive Metaphysics*, London: Methuen, 1959.
— 'Is Existence Never a Predicate?', in *Freedom and Resentment*.
— *Freedom and Resentment*, London: Methuen, 1965.
— *The Bounds of Sense*, London: Methuen, 1966.
— 'Positions for Quantifiers', in Munitz and Unger.
— *Subject and Predicate in Logic and Grammar*, London: Methuen, 1974.
Tarski, A. *Logic, Semantics, and Metamathematics*, Oxford: Clarendon Press, 1956.
Unger, Peter K. *see under* Munitz, Milton K.
Verhaar, John W. M., (ed.) *The Verb 'Be' and its Synonyms*, Philosophical and Grammatical Studies, in *Foundations of Language*, Supplementary Series, Dordrecht: D. Reidel, 1967 onwards.
Vlastos, Gregory, (ed.) *Plato, A Collection of Critical Essays*, London: Macmillan, 1972, Vol. 1.
Wallace, John, 'On the Frame of Reference', in Davidson and Harman.
White, Roger, 'Wittgenstein on Identity', *Proceedings of the Aristotelian Society*, Vol. 78, 1977-8.
Whitehead, A. N., and Russell, B. *Principia Mathematica to *56*, Cambridge: At the University Press, 1962.

Williams, C. J. F. 'Existence and Definability', an unpublished D. Phil. thesis accepted by Oxford University in 1965.
—— 'Baier on the Equivocal Character of "Exist"', *Mind*, Vol. 78, 1969.
—— 'On Dying', *Philosophy*, Vol. 44, 1969.
—— 'Is God Really Related to His Creatures?—A Reply to Professor Geach', *Sophia*, Vol. 8, 1969.
—— 'Prior and Ontology', *Ratio*, Vol. 15, 1973.
—— *What is Truth?*, Cambridge: At the University Press, 1976.
—— 'Is Identity a Relation?', *Proceedings of the Aristotelian Society*, Vol. 80, 1979-80.
Wittgenstein, L. *Tractatus Logico-Philosophicus*, Eng. tr. by D. F. Pears and B. F. McGuinness, London: Routledge and Kegan Paul, 1966.
—— *Philosophical Investigations*, Oxford: Basil Blackwell, 1953.
Woods, M. 'Existence and Tense', in Evans and McDowell.

Formulae and Expressions given Labels in the Text

Page
69   (A) 1. Aristocratic Australians are rude
        2. Aristides is an aristocratic Australian
        3. *Ergo* Aristides is rude
69   (B) 1. Aristocratic Australians are numerous
        2. Aristides is an aristocratic Australian
        3. *Ergo* Aristides is numerous.
69   (C) 1. Aristocratic Australians drink gin
        2. Aristides is an aristocratic Australian
        3. *Ergo* Aristides drinks gin.
69   (D) 1. Aristocratic Australians exist
        2. Aristides is an aristocratic Australian
        3. *Ergo* Aristides exists.
84   (1) President Ford does not know that David Pears exists.
87   (2) Hardly anyone knows that the sheltered bay we found yesterday exists.
92   (3) For some ϕ, both David Pears ϕ's and President Ford does not know that, for some x, ϕx.
93   (4) For some ϕ, both David Pears alone ϕ's and President Ford does not know that, for just one x, ϕx.
94   (5) It is not the case that, for some ϕ, both David Pears alone ϕ's and President Ford knows that, for just one x, ϕx.
95   (6) For most x, is is not the case that, for some ϕ, both the sheltered bay we found yesterday alone ϕ's and x knows that, for just one y, ϕy.

FORMULAE AND EXPRESSIONS

101 (7)   For some ϕ, both I alone ϕ and it might not have been the case that, for just one x, ϕx.

119 (8)   It could have been the case that, for some ϕ, both Socrates alone ϕ's and it is not the case that, for just one x, ϕx.

135 (W) $\Pi x \mathrm{E}\,(x \text{ exists at } t)(\Sigma f(fx \text{ at } t))$

139 (9)   For some τ, for some n, both it was the case n time units ago that Arkle occupied τ, and (now) it is not the case that, for some x, x has reached the place where it now is by a continuous route over n units of time from τ, and x is an animal.

141 (10) $\Pi x \Pi y L C P n \phi x C \psi y I^A xy$

141 (11) $\Sigma \phi \Sigma \psi \Sigma n K (\Pi x \Pi y L C P n \phi x C \psi y I^A xy) K P n \phi a N$-$\Sigma z \psi z$

141 (11A) $\Sigma \phi \Sigma \psi \Sigma n K P n \phi a N \Sigma x \psi x$

142 (12) $\Pi \phi \Pi \psi \Pi n C (\Pi x \Pi y L C P n \phi x C \psi y I^A xy) C P n \phi a \Sigma z$-$\psi z$

142 (12A) $\Pi \phi \Pi \psi \Pi n C P n \phi a \Sigma x \psi x$

142 (13) $\Sigma n N \Sigma \phi \Sigma \psi K (\Pi x \Pi y L C P n \phi x C \psi y I^A xy) K P n \Sigma z$-$z \psi a$

142 (13A) $\Sigma n N \Sigma \phi \Sigma \psi K P n \Sigma x \phi x \psi a$

143 (10^{Orde}) $\Pi x \Pi y L C P n \phi x C \Pi w \Pi m C P m \phi w I^A wy I^A xy$

148 (14) $N \Sigma m K \chi m P m \Pi \phi \Pi \psi \Pi n C (\Pi x \Pi y L C P n \phi x C \psi y I^B$-$xy) C P n \phi b \Sigma z \psi z$

148 (14A) $N \Sigma m K \chi m P m \Pi \phi \Pi \psi \Pi n C P n \phi b \Sigma x \psi x$

189 (O) $\Sigma x \phi x$ is true if, and only if, 'ϕ —' is true of some object.

190 (S) $\Sigma x \phi x$ is true if, and only if, some proper name substituted for x in ϕx yields a true proposition.

195 (S') $\Sigma \phi \phi a$ is true if, and only if, some predicable substituted for ϕ in ϕa yields a true proposition.

195 (S'') $\Sigma p \delta p$ is true if, and only if, some proposition substituted for p in δp yields a true proposition.

195 (O') $\Sigma \phi \phi a$ is true if, and only if, some property belongs to a.

FORMULAE AND EXPRESSIONS 353

195 (O'') $\Sigma p \delta p$ is true if, and only if, 'δ' —' is true of some Proposition.

202 (P) $\Sigma x \phi x$ is true if, and only if, for some x, x ϕ's.

202 (P') $\Sigma \phi \phi a$ is true if, and only if, for some ϕ, a ϕ's.

202 (P'') $\Sigma p \delta p$ is true if, and only if, for some p, δp.

218 (15) The car we need doesn't use much petrol.

219 (16) Matthew is hunting for a wonderfully accurate typist.

219 (17) Simon thinks that the typist Matthew employed last year is wonderfully accurate.

219 (18) Simon thinks that the typist John employed three years ago is wonderfully accurate.

221 (15') For some x, for every y, both x is the same car as y if, and only if, it is necessary for us that y be a car owned by us and x doesn't use much petrol.

221 (15'') It is necessary for us that, for some x, for every y, both x be the same car as y if, and only if, y be owned by us and x not use much petrol.

223 (16') For some x, both Matthew is trying to bring it about that x is engaged by him and x is a wonderfully accurate typist.

223 (16'') Matthew is trying to bring it about that, for some x, both x is engaged by him and x is a wonderfully accurate typist.

223 (17') For some x, both x alone is a typist employed by Matthew last year and Simon thinks that x is wonderfully accurate.

223 (17'') Simon thinks that, for some x, both x alone is a typist employed by Matthew last year and x is wonderfully accurate.

223 (18') For some x, both x alone is a typist John employed three years ago and Simon thinks that x is wonderfully accurate.

224 (18'') Simon thinks that, for some x, both x alone is a typist John employed three years ago and x is wonderfully accurate.

227 (19) Geoffrey believes that Abyssinia is a Christian country.

227 (20) Geoffrey believes that Ethiopia is a Christian country.

233 (21) Edith believes that Herbert is clever.

237 (22) For some x, x was so called because of his size.

238 (23) For some x, 'x' contains six letters.

238 (22') Some word can be used to fill the gap in '— was so called because of his size' to produce a true proposition.

238 (23') Some word can be used to fill the gap in '"—" contains six letters' to produce a true proposition.

257 (24) Jane Austen wrote or implied in *Pride and Prejudice* that someone called 'Mr Darcy' had an aunt.

257 (25) Mr Darcy had an aunt.

261 (26) I wrote a novel in which Charles II was said to have legitimate children, the eldest of whom was called 'Mary'.

261 (27) Charles II had legitimate children, the eldest of whom was called 'Mary'.

262 (28) There is a possible world in which someone was the eldest legitimate child of Charles II and was called 'Mary'.

262 (28') For some x, there is a possible world in which both x was the eldest legitimate child of Charles II and x was called 'Mary'.

263 (28") There is a possible world in which, for some x, both x was the eldest legitimate child of Charles II and x was called 'Mary'.

Index

Ackrill, J. L. 10n
actual world 175-7, 257, 262, 268, 271, 274-5
actualité 173-4
adverbial phrases 201, 315-16, 318, 320-1, 325, 328
analogy 12-14, 16, 70-2, 80, 206, 208-12, 298, 321, 324
analysis, reductive 188, 196, 202, 271
analytic *versus* synthetic: *see* synthetic *versus* analytic
Anscombe, G. E. M. 28, 29n
Anselm 18, 35
anti-realists 183-5
Aquinas, St. Thomas viii, xi, 123, 212n, 221, 231, 232, 234
area-within-which 310, 316
Aristotle viii-ix, 4, 6, 13, 20, 28n, 44, 45, 123, 134, 138, 140n, 153, 164n, 184, 186, 216, 231, 232, 280, 291, 312n, 318-321, 325
'Arkle never existed' 117-22
Austin, J. L. 248-9

Baldwin, T. R. 304n
Barnes, J. 38n, 214n, 243n, 244n
'be' viii-x, 2-16, 172-3, 177-8, 188, 292, 306-7, 317-18, 321, *see also einai*; copulative sense of 4-16, 31, 147-8, 173, 177-8, 294, 298-300, 302-3, 311, 319, 321-2, 324, 327-30; existential sense of viii-ix, 2-16, 31, 147-148, 173, 178, 188, 277, 294-5, 298-300, 302, 307, 311, 315, 321, 322, 324, 327, 330-1; identity sense of 10-12, 324; possessive construction of 329-30; potential construction of 327; veridical construction of 304, 327; 'vital use' of 15n, 330

Bednarowski, W. 58
Begriffswort 65, 66, 68, 78, 296
being *qua* being viii, 188, 325
Belnap, N. D., Jr. 209n, 325n
Berkeley, G. viii
Binkley, R. 204n
Boadi, Lawrence 319n
brackets 48-52
Brentano, F. 218, 220, 221, 230, 231, 233

Cameron, J. M. 256n
Camp, Joseph L., Jr. 325n
Carnap, R. 226
Castaneda, H.-N. 101n, 120n
categories: logical 185-7; ontological 185-7; syntactical *see* syntactical categories
ceasing to exist 123, 128, 129, 133, 134-9, 141, 145, 148
characters 242-4, 263-4, 266-8
Church, A. 226
Cohen, L. J. 198n, 211n
colloquial language 199-202, *see also* ordinary language
coming to exist 102, 108, 123, 128-9, 133, 134-9, 144-5
concept-word: *see Begriffswort*
concepts: first-level 56, 63, 166, 220, 296; formal 74, 187, 216, 238, 324, 325, 341; second-level 56, 63, 166
Contrast Theory of Meaning 284-6
conventions for the use of words 248, 252
correspondence 32, 36
corruption 143-4
counterfactuals 103-5, 257-8
cross-referencing 158, 161

Davidson, D. 205-6

de re belief 234
definability 277, 286, 294, *see also* indefinability
definition 51, 189-97, 199, 202-6, 210, 212, 216, 277-8, 342; analytic 191, 199; recursive 192, 204-6; stipulative 191
Descartes, R. viii, 18, 75, 221
Dummett, M. 70-2, 80, 146-7, 149-52, 165n, 216n, 248
Dunn, J. M. 209n

einai ix, 3, 4, 12, 15, 17n, 173, 184, 290-3, 302, 304, 307, 316, 320, 327-32
elimination of singular terms 237
Ellis, Jeffrey 319n
empirical 176-7, 340
entity 157-8, 161-2, 164-5, 182, 185, 216, 268, 270-1
epistemology 173-8
equivocation 12-14, 16, 31, 70, 71, 72, 80, 206-8, 210, 246, 298, 321, 324
essentialism 102, 104, 106, 134-5, 138, 143n, 240
evaluative 173, 175-7
exist: *see* 'Arkle never existed'; ceasing to exist; coming to exist; 'I exist'; knowledge of *x*'s existence; 'Lady Catherine de Bourgh never existed'; modal contexts; no longer existing
existence: idea of ix, 18-23; *in* possible worlds 261-3, 268, 271-3, 275; *of* possible worlds 268-72, 274-5; temporal and atemporal *see* temporal and atemporal existence
existential generalization 72-3, 163, 183, 242-3, 282, 298, 311, 317, 323, 340-1
existential instantiation 159, 317
extensionalism 206

factual 175-7
falsehood 126-9
fictional world 255-8
Findlay, J. N. 173-4, 230-3
Frege, G. ix, xi, 4, 7n, 10, 16, 17, 29, 30, 41, 42-80, 82, 106-7, 153, 154, 155n, 158, 164, 165-6, 179, 186, 187, 226, 236, 261n, 265, 267, 274, 275, 277, 286, 290, 296, 340-1

Gallie, R. D. 211n
games 255-8, 261
Geach, P. T. xi, 6, 12n, 15, 24, 28n, 29n, 44-6, 48n, 63, 64n, 70-2, 80, 117-19, 120n, 146, 151-2, 155n, 157-8, 162, 170, 178n, 232, 316n
Gellner, E. 284n
generation 143-4
Graham, A. C. ixn, 303n, 320
Grover, Dorothy L. 325n

Harman, G. 204n
Hashimoto, Anne Yue 320n
Heidegger, M. vii
histories 267, 269
Hobbes, T. 7n, 14
Hume, D. viii, 17, 18-23, 25, 30, 183, 318-19

'I exist' 82, 85, 101, 104, 129-30
identity 10-12, 77, 99, 102, 136-7, 139n, 224, 227, 287-8, 339; criterion of 29, 141, 143n
impersonal verb 301, 305, 311, 317
indefinability 278, 288-90
individuating facts 102-5
inexistence 218, 220-1, 224-5, 236, 241
inference 278-84, 287-90, 292-3, 295, 322, 324
'inference tickets' 281-2, 292
instantiability 300, 308, 322-3
instantiation 55-60, 63, 72, 76-7, 159, 277, 293-8, 301-2, 307, 309-11, 316-17, 322-3, 340
intentional object 219-21, 224-7, 230, 235-6
intentional verb 111-12, 218-30 *passim*
intentionality 111-13, 116, 218-41
interrogative pronouns 295

Jones, O. R. 145n
judgements 282-3, 333-4

Kahn, Charles H. 2n, 11n, 15n, 290-3, 302, 304, 307, 309, 316, 320, 327-32
Kant, I. viii-ix, 17-18, 19, 23-37, 40, 75, 96, 123, 175, 278, 285, 326, 333-44
Kenny, A. J. P. 8, 134
Kneale, W. and M. 304n

knowledge of x's existence 79, 81, 84–101, 106, 260
Körner, S. 26n
Kripke, Saul 102n, 116, 203, 204n, 206n, 208, 209n, 286n, 291n
'Lady Catherine de Bourgh never existed' 79, 258–61, 290
Leibniz, G. W. 26–9
Lejewski, C. 17n
Leśniewski, S. 139, 339
Lewis, David 257–8, 273–4, 339n
Linsky, L. 77n
location 301, 318–21, 328
locative copula 15, 320–1, 330
locative phrases 15, 310–11, 315–18, 320–1, 329
Locke, J. 28, 102, 191n, 278
logical categories: see categories
Łukasiewicz, J. x, xix, 49, 51
Lyons, J. 148n, 286n, 303n, 305n, 308n, 309n, 315n, 319n

McGinn, Colin 102n
Mackie, J. L. 58n, 79n, 82, 83–4, 87, 88n, 90, 93n, 95n, 102, 105–6, 297, 300
Makino, Seiichi 303n, 319n, 331n
Marcus, Ruth B. 204n, 218n
Mayberry, John 161n
mention versus use: see use versus mention
metaphysically heterogeneous classes 266–7
metaphysics viii–ix, 325
Mill, James 14
Mill, John Stuart 13–14, 16, 24, 298, 324
Miller, B. 123–4, 128–9, 131, 305n
modal contexts 81–5, 101–6, 118–22, 128–31, 240, 260, 268, 272–73
Moore, G. E. 57, 81–3, 101, 105–6, 119–20, 129, 243, 263, 267–8
'most' 243–4, 263–7
Munitz, Milton K. 58n, 135n, 172n

names 45–6, 49, 76, 96, 118, 125, 142, 157, 165, 186, 209, 287–8, see also proper names; fictional 207, 241–8, 258–61; objectless 110, 207
necessary versus sufficient conditions 198–200, 202, 206, 209, 211
necessities of origin 102–4

necessity 333–7, 341–2, 344
negation 20–1, 45–8, 93–5, 124–7, 278, 282, 308–9; internal 48, 93–5, 124–7, 168–9, 308–11
no longer existing 71n, 79, 108, 110–12, 114, 116, 117, 122–4, 128, 134–6, 138–41, 143–52, 260
nominalists 196, 275
nominalization 302–3, 306–7, 331
non-particular 219–20, 225–6
nought 43–4, 54–5, 75, 296
nouns 157, 165–7, 296; count- 134, 310–15, 322–3, 325; mass- 300, 307, 309–17 passim, 323, 325
number-statement 42–4, 54–5, 96
numbers, formally indefinable 161n
'numerous' 67–81 passim, 260, 339

objects: nameless 193, 197, 207; non-existent 44, 56, 219–20, 273
Ockham's Razor 182–4, 272
one 43, 75, 76
one-sided relations 230–5
Ontological Argument 17, 18, 54, 337
ontological: categories see categories; commitment x, 36n, 153, 161–4, 170–1, 183, 185, 189, 195–7, 213, 216, 268, 270
ontology 162–3, 171–89, 214–15, 275
Orde, Simon 143n
ordinary language 78–9, 212–14, 325, see also colloquial language
ousia viii, 184–5
Owen, G. E. L. 134

Pap, Arthur 289n
Parmenides viii, xi, 37, 188
Passmore, J. 19n
Paul, St. vii
'Pegasus' 207, 242–3, 247–8, 254–5
Peirce, C. S. 306
place-at-which 310
Plantinga, A. 38n, 82–3, 85, 101, 105–6, 123–6, 128, 131, 175, 272–4
Plato viii, 4, 6, 8, 10, 13, 20, 37, 44, 74, 103, 306n, 327
Plato's Beard 18, 37, 40, 43, 56, 58, 74, 108–10, 117–18, 135, 137, 145, 151, 154, 164, 260; qualified version of 109–11, 117, 123, 135, 141–5
Polish notation x, xix, 49–52, 62, 129
positing 26, 28, 30–3, 36–7, 342–3
possible thalers 32–5, 263–8

possible worlds 83, 120, 175-7, 242-3, 257, 261-4, 268-75
predicables 24, 44-8, 61, 64-78 *passim*, 126, 325; *n-A*-reidentifying 141-2, 143n, 148; nought-place 306, 309n, 322; third-level 71-2, 106-7, 154
predicate 24, 44-8, 127; 'a merely logical —' 23-6, 40
predicate calculus 268, 270, 280
predication 53, 60-4; direct and indirect 113-15; ultimate subject of 28, 182, 184
pretending 248-62, 264, 267, 290
primary and secondary occurrence 48, 88-94, 100, 119-20, 122, 221-3, 227-8, 237, 241
Prior, A. N. x, xix, 44-9, 50, 53-4, 61-4, 82, 117-18, 120-2, 123, 125, 129-34, 139n, 155, 169-70, 173-5, 198-201, 206, 207, 218, 221, 224, 228, 240-1, 254n, 270n, 275, 278, 280n, 306n, *see also* quantification, Prioresque
pronouns 36, 157-8, 165, 167, 177-8, 305; of laziness 178, 297
proper names 48, 49, 56-7, 73, 76, 78-9, 87, 96, 118, 120-1, 142, 154-5, 157, 161, 165, 167-71, 190, 192, 194-5, 207-9, 216, 227-30, 237-8, 251-64, 290, 291n, 340-1; causal theory of 100, 116
properties: of concepts 43-5, 54-9, 63, 76, 179-80; of objects 42-4, 54, 75, 105, 151, 179-81, 235, 274-5; of reidentification 141-5, 148, 150; spatial and temporal 147, *see also* temporal and atemporal properties; universal 19, 287
Propositional Calculus 279-80
propositional function 57-8, 74
propositions: causal 114-17; embedded 81-8, 105-8, 119, 122, 130, 168, 228, 260; feature-placing 300-1, 307-9, 312, 313, 316, 322-3, 325, 340; metalinguistic 192-9 *passim*, 205-6; necessary existential 39, 120, 333-44 *passim*; negative existential 20, 27-8, 30, 39-40, 56, 83, 108, 118, 124, 258-61, 263, 289, 318; possible world 175, 257, 270; and Propositions 120-1, 125-33, 195; singular 26, 29, 44-5, 59, 81, 84, 105, 118, 125-6, 135, 146, 151-2, 154, 170, 308; temporal and atemporal *see* temporal and atemporal propositions
proponouns 157, 165-7, 170
Protothetic 279, 280
pro-verb 178, 297

quantification: higher-order 106-7; objectual 154, 167, 169, 189-98 *passim*, 206-17, 237-8, 242-3, 255; Prioresque xix, 198, 202-6, 210-12; referential 154, 167, 170, 189; restricted 208, 273, 289-90; substitutional 189-98 *passim*, 204-12, 214n, 218, 237-8, 241-3, 247, 254-5, 294
quantifiers: adverbial 201; interdefinability of 277
'quantifying over' 161-2, 268, 275
quasi-relations 230-1
Quine, W. V. vii, ix-x, 28, 37, 98, 139n, 143n, 152, 153-4, 156-8, 161-71, 172, 178-81, 185-6, 189-94, 197, 198, 201, 206-7, 210, 213, 214, 216, 218, 226n, 227, 229, 236-41, 270, 274, 277, 280-1, 283n, 294, 311-14, 317, 322

Ramsey, F. P. 174, 282-3
real and possible 32-7 *passim*, 264, 265
realism about possible worlds 272-5
realists 183, 185, 196, 273-5
reductive analysis: *see* analysis, reductive
Redundancy Theory 303-4
reference 153-8, 161-2, 165-71, 185, 189, 244-7, 256, 272, 275; divided 312-14, 317, 322-3, 325; of fictional names 244-8
referential opacity 53n, 97-9, 190, 207, 218, 228-30, 236-7, 239-41
referential transparency 98, 99, 228, 229, 239, 241
Russell, Bertrand 10-11, 27, 38, 41, 48, 57-8, 69n, 73-4, 75n, 82, 87-93, 96, 111, 126n, 154-7, 164, 165, 168, 170, 221-2, 237, 256-8, 274-6, 279, 281, 284, 286-8, 319, 324, 338
Ryle, G. 74, 75n, 161n, 187n, 281-2, 295n

Sartre, J.-P. vii-viii
schemata 279-80, 325
schematic letters 166-7, 280-1

scope x, 49–51, 89, 91, 121, 125, 131–2, 221, 228–30, 236, 241, 271, 335, 337, 341
self-identity 77, 287–8, 338
Sellars, Wilfrid 215n
semantics x, 5, 10, 199, 202–3, 284, 303, 321, 324
sentences: nominal 8; occasion 168, 312–13, 317; standing 168–9
'some' 213–15, 263–5, 267, 278, 296, 298, 323–4
'somehow' 201, 213, 215, 323
'someplace' 213n
'something' 55, 60, 64, 67–8, 73, 154–7, 163–5, 199, 201–2, 210, 213–15, 247, 260, 331
'sometime' 201
'somewhere' 201, 310, 318, 320–1, 323
Stevenson, Leslie 193n
stories 245–55 *passim*, 269–70
Strawson, P. F. 58n, 134, 185–8, 243–4, 263–4, 266–7, 285–6, 301, 340
subject 29, 31, 40, 108–9, 186, 305, 343; logical 29
substance viii, 28–9, 123, 134, 138, 143n, 184–7, 216
substantial change 136
substitution 51, 94–7, 100–1, 104–6; instance 59, 90, 138–40, 160–2, 166–7, 170, 196, 201–2, 270, 322, 336–8
sufficient *versus* necessary conditions: *see* necessary *versus* sufficient conditions
syntactical categories 10, 24–5, 36, 45–6, 72, 121, 187, 238, 253–4, 277, 293, 297, 323, 332
syntax x, 5, 10, 51, 216, 284, 303, 305, 321, 324–6
synthetic *versus* analytic 34, 333, 338–9, 343–4

Tarski, A. 203–5
temporal and atemporal: existence 38, 147; properties 145–7, 149–52; propositions 150
tense 8–9, 108, 110, 115–17, 129–52 *passim*, 173–6

'there is' 2, 3, 15, 32, 42–3, 59, 65–6, 68, 107, 164, 178–9, 213, 243n, 244, 246–8, 258, 268, 270, 273, 277, 292, 295–325 *passim*
'there is Mrs Gandhi' 297, 300
'there is something' 72, 73, 201, 214, 331, 338–40
transmigration of souls 103
truth 1, 174, 177, 188, 203–5, 303–7, 317n, 325
truth-condition 189–211 *passim*
truth-value of fictional propositions 245–6, 255–8

universal generalization 281–2, 287n, 288
universal instantiation 159
unspecific 219, 220, 225, 226
use *versus* mention 85n, 109n, 127, 128, 130, 133, 190, 203, 240, 241, 259, 260, 291

vacuity 173–4, 177
validity 277–98 *passim*
value theory 177
values 161–2, 164–7, 170, 179
variables, bound 153–8, 161–5, 170, 270, 281, 305, 310, 316
verbalization 6–11, 302–4, 306–9, 311, 314–18, 322–4
Verhaar, John W. M. ixn, 2n, 4n, 15n, 319n, 320, 331n
vincula 158, 160, 161

Wallace, John 204, 208n
White, Roger 288n
Whitehead, A. N. 284n, 287n
Williams, C. J. F. 32n, 38n, 48n, 118n, 127n, 139n, 145n, 155n, 156n, 214n, 215n, 217n, 232n, 256n, 272n, 288n, 290n, 291n, 303n, 304n, 319n, 325n
Wittgenstein, L. ix, 25n, 41, 51, 52n, 67, 77n, 109n, 187n, 216, 238n, 253n, 255, 288n, 325, 339, 341
Woods, M. 73n, 74–5, 134–5, 137–8
'world of *Pride and Prejudice*' 256–60
'wrapped around' 53, 60–5, 76, 228–9